WHERE THERE IS BREATH,
THERE IS LIFE

Where There is Breath, There is Life

A memoir

by

SUSAN M. DAVIS

Adelaide Books
New York/Lisbon
2018

WHERE THERE IS BREATH THERE IS LIFE
A memoir
By Susan M. Davis

Published by Adelaide Books, New York / Lisbon
adelaidebooks.org
Editor-in-Chief
Stevan V. Nikolic

For any information, please address Adelaide Books
at info@adelaidebooks.org
or write to:
Adelaide Books
244 Fifth Ave. Suite D27
New York, NY, 10001

ISBN-10: 1-949180-16-6

ISBN-13: 978-1-949180-16-9

Printed in the United States of America

To Karen Kozawa, by partner, wife, best friend and soul mate. Life with you is filled with love and incredible moments. We create happiness in our home with one another and with our doggies: Benson, Joshua, Madi and Miles. May everyone create a blessed home life like ours. Love you my Bear.

Content

Foreword

**by Mary Kay Bader RN MSN CCNS FNCS
FAHA Neuro/Critical Care CNS, Mission Hospital**

Karen and Susan's story are a testament to the strength, commitment and love that defines their relationship. The "sudden event" of a ruptured brain aneurysm took them on a harrowing journey into hospitals, rehabilitation units, and care facilities. The title, "Where There is Breath, There is Life", defines the journey from the perspective of simply the act of breathing and the hope that life is still present. The word, **'BREATH'**, represents key concepts for the reader.

B defines "BIG Crisis": Aneurysmal Subarachnoid Hemorrhage (SAH) is a type of hemorrhagic stroke that is usually caused by a ruptured brain aneurysm. Twenty percent of individuals who sustain SAH from this cause perish within hours of the event. The survivors are faced with countless potential complications and crisis that are known to commonly occur after SAH and threaten their lives. In Susan's book, the natural course of the disease was evident as Karen's body was affected in every organ system. Her brain suffered from increased pressure and the risk of rebleeding of the aneurysm while her heart and lungs experienced a shock similar to a heart attack. Once the aneurysm was sealed, the left-over blood in her brain produced irritation causing the 2-3-week period of vasospasm which can cause more strokes in the brain. Treating the vasospasm to avoid those strokes involve high risk procedures and require a highly advanced team of doctors, nurses, and technicians. This "BIG Crisis" had Karen fighting for her life, the hospital team using every treatment option and skill to keep her from dying, and Susan watching from the bedside as all of this unfolded. Susan's reflections of the days in the ICU describe the perilous and stressful minutes, days and weeks that patients loved one's experience while patients are fighting for their lives! How do all involved function and provide the best environment to survive?

R defines RELATIONSHIPS: When an individual (patient) enters the hospital, a relationship is established with the health care team. The patient's loved ones become part of the team. Personal connections between staff, patients and families/loved ones are key to establishing trust between all involved. Nurses spend the most time with patients and their loved ones at the bedside and when patients remain in the hospital for a long period of time, relationships continue to develop and mature. It is not uncommon for families of ICU patients to become "part of the unit family" when the caring relationships mature over time. The goal for all involved is to optimize the outcome of the patient. Sometimes the eventual outcome is not what all hoped for and staff feel the loss as greatly as the families. The transition to another level of care often results in a frightful time for the patient and loved ones. As Susan describes it is like leaving the "womb". The relationships help ease that transition.

E defines EMOTIONS: Loved ones of the patient may experience highs and lows in an hour or in a day. The critical care unit cares for individuals who are critically ill and often unstable. When talking with the patient's loved ones, the team will describe a roller coaster to define the various emotions that are experienced. Staff are present to support the patient and family. It is ok to be scared. Staff keep in the backs of their minds how frightened families can be of the known and the unknown. Listening and providing reassurance and communicating information honestly and as often as necessary are essential to help ease the ups/downs.

A defines ADVOCATE: Susan's perseverance and dedication to Karen are evident throughout the journey. Susan is Karen's advocate and will move "heaven and earth" to ensure Karen receives the best care. Advocacy is essential and every patient must have an advocate! The ADVOCATE questions and reviews what is best for their loved one. In today's health care system, an advocate is important to maximize the outcome for their loved one.

T defines TEAMWORK: Often most individuals refer to the health care team as the ones that possess teamwork. While that is true, true teamwork is when healthcare teams, patients, and their support team (families/loved ones/friends) come together to implement the treatments needed for the patient to survive. A simple example is when a physical therapist (PT) provides range of motion (ROM) for the unconscious patient in the bed to promote mobility. The PT can teach the family and loved ones to do the same ROM as they are sitting at the bedside for hours. Susan, her mother/brother, and close friends/family comprised TEAM KAREN as their presence on a daily basis created the larger team of practitioners caring for Karen.

H defines HOPE: There are two mottos on the wall in the SICU. The first is, "Where there is life-There is Hope"! The second is, "NEVER GIVE UP…NEVER SURRENDER". The TEAM works tirelessly 24/7 to provide the best care possible and are driven by hope that the patient will survive and have an optimal outcome. Families and loved ones pray and believe in hope. Without hope, a hospital would be a very dim place. It keeps us going in the direst of circumstances. Physicians use their incredible skills and talents to save lives. Sometimes, they deliver grave news when complications occur, such as Karen's cardiac arrest. The physicians also provide an outline or path of treatment that hopefully will result in an improved outcome. The team of nurses and therapists believe and maintain hope that the outcome will be successful. Karen's support team maintains hope throughout the entire journey. Hope she would survive! Hope she would return home! Hope that Karen would be Karen once again! Hopes do come true especially when someone has BREATH and Life!

Chapter 1—Day One

I needed to stay calm. I failed to call 911. Staying calm was the key. Haven't we all been trained to dial 911 in an emergency? If I knew the symptoms, why didn't I pick up the phone and call the paramedics?

On July 28ᵗʰ, 2008, in our perfectly planned community of Irvine, California, I woke up to the sound of vomiting coming from the bathroom on the second floor of our lavender-walled, wainscoted condominium. Wainscoting suits me well because I like neat and orderly things; I suffer from Obsessive Compulsive Disorder (OCD). Symmetry is my life. When things are aligned, I'm in order.

The noise was harrowing. Jolted from sleep, I heard loud vomiting. I ran down a flight of stairs to find my partner Karen hugging the toilet. She stood up.

"Bear, what's wrong?" I asked.

"I don't know, Boo. I have this horrendous headache, and I can't stop vomiting. My arms are tingling too."

Years ago, Karen and I met on Match.com. It seemed like an easier way to meet a new partner. I had been in seven other relationships, including a sixteen-year relationship where the woman brought me out at twenty years old. She was thirteen years older than I and married to a man with whom she had two daughters. It was a wild introduction to the gay world, and I remained her mistress until her husband found out we were together nine years later. She was a professional bowler. I wanted to become one too and asked her to coach me. Little did I know that I would be coached in more than bowling.

One evening I visited Match.com, and there she was--a gorgeous Japanese-American woman dressed in a black suit with thick black hair and a sassy short haircut. Her eyes gleamed at me through the screen. I was mesmerized. With a click of a button, a wink was sent to Tranquil Garden.

Signing back on to Match.com later, I found Tranquil Garden had winked back. I wrote to her that evening, and she wrote back. Our first date was P.F. Chang's in Irvine, California. The second date was with a U-Haul. Lesbians do that. We meet and then move in.

Seeing Karen's terrible condition that morning didn't allow me to connect the dots, but the tingling in her arms was signal enough to get her to an emergency room. We had been together for four years, and Karen had never before complained about an illness except when she was diagnosed with Rhumatoid Arthritus in 2005.

I didn't dial 911, too afraid of the idea of an ambulance coming to our home.

Instead, I ran back upstairs to brush my teeth. *Never leave home without brushing your teeth.* My parents' voices still echoed in my head at the age of 50. In heading back downstairs, I failed to notice our cell phones charging.

On the bathroom floor, Karen's small face was pressed against the tile. She was wearing her soft blue and green flannel pajamas. She was always cold--fragile like a bird--and wore flannel pajamas even in the summer. Her face was white, but that was all I noticed.

"Bear," I said, "can you stand up? I have to get you to the hospital."

Before she could answer, I grabbed cookies from the kitchen for our three cocker spaniels. Any time we leave home, the puppies each get a cookie. They lined up on the green carpet for their treats.

Running back to the bathroom afterward, I didn't see Karen. She'd managed to get herself up off the floor to walk down the 15 stairs to the garage. I told the pups we loved them, locked their gate, and ran to the garage. Karen had grabbed a plastic bag. "I don't want to throw up in your car," she said.

She was always meticulous. At that moment, she seemed normal enough-- walking, talking, and considerate as always.

"I'm going to lie right here in your backseat, Boo," she said.

She seemed in control of her movements, which I took as a good sign. I closed her door, got in, backed out of the garage, and drove to the automatic gates. I had never noticed before how long they took to open. With no cars around, I ran a red light at the corner and sped to the freeway less than two minutes away. The lush green trees lining the road swayed as we raced past them.

There were three hospitals nearby. The first had a bad reputation and so wasn't an option. Karen's aunt had been there just two months earlier, and the nursing staff wasn't great. The new hospital across the street was an HMO, and we weren't sure about the quality of care there either. The third hospital was down the freeway a bit. Then came Mission Hospital, where my brother worked as a computer tech. I felt I would need him with me as soon as we got there. He was a man of strength.

"Bear, we're going to Mission. Michael's working today."

"Good choice, Boo. I don't think I can make it to Hoag."

Hoag, another well-known hospital in Orange County, was far

on the other side of town. It was amazing that Karen, even in the midst of a health crisis, could remember a hospital I hadn't considered.

Running my second red light of the day, I merged onto the 405 freeway. It was Monday morning at 7:15 a.m. No traffic. God must have cleared the path for us.

My heart began racing, guilt raging inside of me because I didn't call the paramedics. I was deathly afraid of ambulances and especially the stretchers inside of them--a huge phobia since childhood--I couldn't handle dealing with the paramedics.

"Boo, how's the traffic?" Karen asked in a normal tone.

"There isn't any."

"We're fortunate. I bet all the traffic is going north this morning."

"Bear, grab my arm."

She grabbed my wrist and squeezed. Her grip was firm.

"Love you, Bear."

"Love you too, Boo."

After exiting the freeway, I turned left and ran another red light. At Mission Hospital, I took a sharp left into the parking lot at the large red sign: "Emergency."

I sighed loudly. "Bear, we're here."

There was no answer from the backseat. The thought of Karen dying in the backseat of our car was not even an option. We had come so far together.

"Hurry, go get someone, Boo. I can't walk."

I ran across the parking lot to the ER, huffing and puffing. At least Karen was still talking.

The double doors opened, hitting me with a gust of cold air, and I yelled at the receptionist, "My partner's having a stroke. We need a wheelchair."

A young man with a wheelchair materialized, and I pointed toward the car. "Over there--the burgundy BMW,

Karen's in the backseat. She's been vomiting and has a horrific headache."

Frozen on the edge of the curb, I began to sob, warm tears wetting my cheeks. Though my vision was blurred, I spotted a sheriff exiting the ER to get on his motorcycle. I realized I needed to call my brother, whose office was just across the parking lot from where we were. I searched my purse and frantically patted my pockets. Then I realized that our cell phones were charging back at home.

I hurried over to the sheriff. "Sir, I forgot my cell phone. I have to call my brother. My partner is in that BMW having a stroke."

"What's his number, Miss?" he asked in a stern, deep voice. After I gave it to him, he dialed it quickly and handed me his phone. I was shaking and crying and nearly dropped it.

"Michael, we're at the ER. Something happened to Karen. I need you."

"Susie, slow down. What's wrong?"

Always a fast talker, I forced my tongue to explain. "Something happened to Karen. We're at the hospital now."

"I'll be right over."

"Thank you," I said to the sheriff, hanging up. Karen was being pushed toward me in a wheelchair. The attendant shouted as he pushed her across the parking lot.

He yelled, "Head up! Keep your head up. You'll aspirate."

Aspirate? What's 'aspirate?' Stop yelling at her. I caught up with them at the double doors, which opened at once, sucking us in.

The attendant wheeled Karen over to the fish tank in the middle of the ER walkway. He stopped on the left side of the tank, which showcased blue and purple fish swimming calmly among green plants and colorful coral.

I ran to the admission desk. The receptionist slapped a clipboard on the desk. "Fill this out," she said.

I wrote Karen's first name on the pink top document and glanced at her. She was vomiting again. All of a sudden, she screamed, "My head! My head hurts."

Her features contorted in pain, the color draining from her face. She scrunched up her features like someone who had just eaten a lemon. When I saw her dilated pupils, I thought, *this is looking bad.*

I threw the clipboard up in the air and shouted in my loudest, sharpest teacher's voice, "Help us! Can't someone help us?"

A woman from the waiting room ran over and grabbed my arm, "Honey, you need to calm down--not only for you, but for her, too." I turned and saw a glimpse of her brown hair. "You can go back with her, but you need to calm down." I wanted to smack her, whoever she was. This was my partner, and I was going to scream as loud as I could to get her help. Karen was the love of my life. She was my soul mate.

The door to the trauma unit flew open. The same male attendant came out and pushed Karen inside. Medical staff started running toward us.

"What's your name?" one of the nurses asked Karen.

"Her name is Karen!" I yelled.

"What's your name?" a nurse asked again, having received no response from Karen.

"Her name is Karen!" I repeated anxiously.

Her tiny head dropped to her left shoulder. She had fainted-- limp, helpless. I smelled that sterilized aroma that only hospitals have. People were rushing over and surrounding Karen in her wheelchair. I stood behind her, perplexed. She was no longer able to talk, I knew, but I didn't fully understand what unconsciousness meant. My own breathing was fast and deep. I think I was breathing for both of us.

The team hustled Karen into a trauma room on the right.

In that moment, I realized they were asking Karen what her name was, to see if she could respond.

I stood still for a second, watching the commotion in front of me. Suddenly, I felt a sturdy hand rest on my shoulder. It was my brother Michael, dressed in khakis and a white shirt--his work attire. His was a protective hand, and I was instantly calmed by his quiet presence. Michael was my older brother by two years and the quiet winter to my loud summer. I trusted him.

I followed the nurses. People were yelling all around us, but thankfully, I couldn't understand a word.

"Where do you think you're going?" My brother grabbed my arm and pulled me back.

"I'm going in there with Karen."

"No, you're not. You let those doctors and nurses do their jobs."

"I'm going in there."

He turned me around with a firm hand and guided me through the thick steel double doors. "We're waiting out here," he said.

A nurse led us back into the hallway, where she set a chair next to an empty room. She prompted me to sit down.

"What did Karen have for breakfast? What medications did she take? When did the vomiting and headache begin?"

I couldn't think straight but was surprisingly able to name all the medications Karen took for rheumatoid arthritis except one. I had no idea if Karen had eaten breakfast. I remembered giving the dogs their cookies, locking the gate, and deciding not to call the paramedics. OCD was beginning to kick in; it allowed me to remember details that most other people forget.

Stress crawled up my spine. *Why didn't I call 911?* I knew why. Though I was fifty years old, ambulances still scared me to death. There was no way I would have called the paramedics even in a time of danger.

As I gave the nurse the information she asked for, Karen was pushed right in front of me. Medical personnel surrounded her gurney, and a blue bag covered her nose and mouth. They whisked her away.

I muttered, "Love you, Bear," but this time, Bear couldn't respond.

I sat motionless on the chair with Michael by my side. The trauma had begun at 7:15 a.m. It was just 7:45 a.m.

Within minutes, a doctor came out in scrubs and black-rimmed glasses.

"Kozawa?" he asked.

"Right here," I responded. "I'm her registered domestic partner, and this is my brother."

"I'm Dr. Kim, the neurosurgeon. Follow me to the computer and I'll show you what's going on with Ms. Kozawa. We performed a cranial CT scan and found that she has suffered a brain aneurysm."

My brother and I stared at the images of Karen's brain that Dr. Kim showed on the screen, noticing gray, black, and white areas. "The aneurysm," said Dr. Kim, "is located on the left anterior communicating artery." *What is that?* I knew what a brain aneurysm was, but I had no concept of where the left anterior communicating artery was, nor of the real devastation that had just taken place in Karen's brain.

Dr. Kim looked at us pointedly. "It doesn't look good. Only thirty percent of the population survives a brain aneurysm of this magnitude. That means there's a seventy percent chance Karen could die. We're going to take her into surgery immediately. I need you to sign the consent papers."

Brain surgery? Seventy percent of the population dies from this. I couldn't think straight. I knew I had to sign the consent papers immediately. Karen had to survive; she was my partner, the love of my life, and a brilliant woman who had traveled to Hong Kong and Egypt and was the overseas manager of a clothing company. We loved to travel together and had stayed at the best hotels in Hawaii. When Karen got her first glance at the ocean on our trip there, she gazed speechlessly out at the water --a moment I'll never forget. It was the breezeway that intrigued her.

I remember when we traveled to Big Sur, our heaven on earth, and stayed at Post Ranch Inn. We clambered up the steps of our tree house and played like kids in the surrounding wilderness. We treasured these moments for years. I think our traveling connected us to one another and the earth.

I didn't read all the fine print about the risks and benefits of the surgery. The biggest risk was death; I knew that. I looked at my brother.

"Sign it," he said assertively.

Dr. Kim took the paper and left. We wouldn't see him again for several hours.

Michael had to make a quick trip to his office. After he left, an older woman came over to me and introduced herself as a hospital volunteer. She was there to escort me to the waiting room in the Surgical Intensive Care Unit. Though I felt only urgency, she pointed out gardens on the way--places where Karen and I could sit outside and talk. Did this woman understand that Karen had just sustained a ruptured brain aneurysm? Spinning with anxiety, I couldn't have cared less about any damn garden.

When I arrived in the SICU waiting room, Michael had returned from his office and was waiting for me.

"Susie, give me your car keys. I need to move your car to the back of the hospital." Michael always knew what to do. He had taken charge when our father passed away twenty-three years ago, becoming the patriarch of our small family and taking care of Mom and me. We were close, too; he had often stuck up for me when I was in trouble. Michael is calm and reserved, whereas I'm loud and anxiety-prone.

People filled the waiting room, their eyes on me, the newest member of this room of endless waiting. I wondered how long everyone had been here. The volunteer explained that the doctors would come out to talk to me after Karen's surgery was over.

How long would I have to wait?

"Thank you," I said, and she left. Perhaps she was off to escort some other family member whose loved one was in grave danger.

A middle-aged woman with dark brown hair stood up, walked over to me, and gave me a tight hug. "My son was involved in an auto accident and has a brain injury. He's recovering, but he's blind now."

Nearly everyone in the waiting room had a loved one in the SICU with a brain injury.

What is *a brain injury, exactly? Does it mean that if Karen lives, she'll be disabled?* She was only fifty-five. We had many things we still wanted to do. *Will she be able to talk?* My mind went wild; yet waiting was all I could do. I didn't have kids, and in my personal life, I hadn't ever been in charge of anyone but myself. Karen and I definitely had our differences, but they were minimal compared to those of other people we knew. We loved sharing our home and loved our dogs. We had fabulous restaurant experiences that were always important to us, had great conversations about our work, and even loved the same television shows. Karen made our lunches every night. She wrote "Ms. Davis" on my brown bag. Would everything change?

The woman who had approached me said, "Don't worry, the doctors and nurses will take great care of her. We're all in here together. We laugh and cry together."

Laugh? I couldn't imagine myself laughing anytime soon. "Thank you," was all I could muster.

I sat and waited. The smell of Purell, which everyone had to use before and after seeing a patient, permeated the waiting room. Doctors in scrubs and white coats came and left. Weeping could be seen and heard throughout the room. As I looked around, I noticed a small television on the front wall. I couldn't tell what was on it, and I didn't try to watch, too distracted by my thoughts.

Michael returned and handed me the keys. "Your car is parked right outside the double doors in the back," he said.

"Thanks."

The room was loud, everyone talking and doctors walking in to update families about the outcome of their loved ones. All I could do was sit with my brother and wait.

"Michael, we have to call Karen's work to tell everyone what happened." I had her direct line, which went to her voicemail. Michael managed to find the main phone number for her office, and he finally got through to Karen's boss, Jim. Everyone from Karen's work started coming to the hospital shortly after. It was only 9:30.

Does every part of this hospital have automatic double doors that suck patients inside? Does Michael know something that I don't know? Does a brain injury take a long time to recover from?

"Do you want Mom here?" Michael asked.

"Yes."

Someone would have to bring Mom to the hospital; she didn't drive freeways.

For the next hour, phone calls needed to be made—some easy, some difficult. Karen's sister would be the most difficult call, but I wasn't about to be the one to call her. She and Karen were fighting about a house Karen and I had bought together four years earlier. The fight had something to do with inherited family money.

I called our dear friends Sue and Peter Mordin. Sue sprang into action right away and rushed to the hospital to keep me company. Peter came right after work.

Mom came, and I cried as I fell into her warm embrace. Mandie, my niece, also came, bringing her two-year-old daughter, Becca. We waited together in the back row of the waiting room.

Within two hours, Karen's cousin Brian had brought his mom and Karen's other aunt. I liked both of them, as both had accepted me into the family. Karen and I had gone out to dinner several times with them.

We waited.

It was now noon--five hours after I sped to bring Karen to the hospital. Dr. Kim returned with two ominous-looking men who wore white coats and stern expressions.

Dr. Kim introduced them, saying, "This is Dr. Lempert, the interventional neuro-radiologist, and this is Dr. Nwagwu, a cerebral vascular neurosurgeon. We've been working on Karen in the vascular lab. She suffered a massive subarachnoid bleed from an aneurysm; in other words, a blood vessel in her brain ruptured. Hers was on the left anterior communicating artery. It's a small blood vessel that bridges the two larger anterior cerebral arteries." I would later find out that this is one of the most common brain aneurysm sites.

"We went in to coil her aneurysm, and the wall of the artery collapsed. We took an intricate piece of coil and placed it in her groin, advancing it through her body. We maneuvered it around her heart and lungs until it reached the aneurysm. Then the sidewall of the aneurysm ruptured. Blood splattered everywhere in Karen's brain. We took the coil out, re-threaded it, and threaded it again through Karen's groin. We successfully sealed off the ruptured aneurysm, but the damage had already been done."

"Damage? What kind of damage?" I asked.

"We won't know for some time," replied Dr. Kim. "We put Karen in a medically induced coma. She will be in this state for a month." *A month?* I thought. *How could Karen be asleep for a month?* "Karen's in grave danger, and we're taking her back to the OR, where we will scan her brain again. She's been placed in a hypothermic state, which means we're cooling her body down. Slowly lowering Karen's body temperature will help stabilize her brain. We'll soon take her to a room in the SICU. We warn you— this will be a marathon, Susan, not a sprint. The only reason Karen's alive right now is that you brought her to Mission. She would have died at any other hospital. We have state-of-the-art machines, technology, and staff trained to handle brain traumas of this magnitude."

I felt like I was in a sinkhole, falling deeper and deeper into an unknown abyss where no sun shines and no air circulates. My OCD kicked in, and my mind raced in relentless circles. *Hypothermia, coma,* and *aspirate*--words I had not heard before that were sure to become part of my daily vocabulary.

Karen was the first of three patients with a brain aneurysm rupture that morning. July isn't exactly brain aneurysm month--not that there is one--but it sure seemed like it that day.

I went out to the hallway and just stood there, trying to calm down. The hallway was beautiful, with a shiny floor and black-and-white diamond motif painted on the linoleum. My OCD appreciated this pattern; I could count tiles if I needed to, and the diagonals were drawn with precision. I wanted to get on my knees and touch them. This pattern radiated clarity and, I felt, eliminated some of my feelings of danger. Perhaps I saw this as a beacon of light in the darkness I was mired in.

I eventually went back to the waiting room, where Dr. Kim returned an hour later.

"Karen's taken a turn for the worse. Her heart has taken a hit. A cardiologist has been called; he will come and talk to you when he arrives."

I felt my body begin to shake from the inside out. I needed to go out to the hallway and count tiles. I had to use rituals to relieve the stress that felt like it was eating away at my soul. How much more could happen?

Karen's boss, Jim, arrived, and after I updated him, he asked if we were hungry. None of us had eaten or had any coffee. I couldn't even think of eating, but I was definitely thirsty. Jim went to the hospital's cafeteria, bringing back chips, fruit, and soda. Jim loved Karen, and I could imagine he was distraught too. They had worked together for over twenty years.

It was one o'clock. In six hours, Karen had gone from a horrific headache and vomiting to the precipice of death.

A while later another man walked toward me, neatly groomed and, of course, wearing a pristine white coat.

"Susan, I'm the cardiologist. Karen's heart has an irregular rhythm. It's called Tako Tsubo syndrome." *Another medical term I need to learn.*

"We gave her medication to help her heart pump more effectively. It takes about three days for the heart to return to a normal rhythm. Karen's very sick, Susan. We'll keep you informed about any changes."

Karen had only been in a hospital once--the day she was born. I was the one who'd had several surgeries, and Karen had always taken care of me. In the aftermath of two knee surgeries and the ablation of my uterine wall, she was at my side.

While I brought newcomers up to speed, I saw Dr. Kim coming toward me once again. He was a man of few words-- brilliant, direct, and blunt. "Karen has taken another turn for the worse. We're doing everything possible for her." He turned and breezed down the lit hallway, leaving as quickly as he had come. All my family and friends heard the news.

Jim spoke first. "Susan, we've heard the worst. We need to believe that everything that can be done for Karen is being done. It's now up to God to watch over her and heal her."

Karen didn't believe in God. She believed in Buddha. Who was praying to him? Karen certainly couldn't.

We returned to our seats. At this point, we each had a specific seat. We stared at one another, fearful of anything that might jinx Karen.

Time was certainly dealing us one blow after another.

Another man in a white coat entered the waiting room. It seemed I could no sooner sit down than another doctor would beckon me into the hallway to announce more bad news.

"Hi, Susan. I'm Dr. Marquez, Karen's pulmonary doctor. Her lungs endured trauma because of the intensity of her vomiting. Things are not looking good for her right now. I will keep you updated as we continue to assess her."

Dr. Marquez left. I began to wonder how many blows it took before you were eliminated.

A woman entered the waiting room, introduced herself to me, and told me her story. She smiled as she explained she'd had a ruptured brain aneurysm a year before. She was the worst patient Mission Hospital SICU had ever seen until I brought Karen in. Lisa seemed to have recovered well. According to what she told me, she was able to drive and could even ski. I listened intently to see if she was slurring her speech; she wasn't. I tried to smile, and hope filled my heart. She handed me a photo album and I saw an image of her lying in a large bed, a blue covering on her head and tubes sticking out of her skull.

She looked horrible.

"Is this what Karen is going to look like?"

She nodded.

"How bad was your aneurysm?" I asked.

"I can tell you it was so bad that my family was preparing to donate my organs. I had a grand mal seizure too. I lived and have recovered well. I even went to my daughter's wedding a few months after my rehabilitation phase."

People stood around me, poring over the album that chronicled Lisa's recovery.

Why would someone even want to capture these horrific memories, let alone keep them in an album? It wasn't until I reached the end of the album that I saw the point; the final picture was a blurred image of a slick skier standing tall on the white, snowcapped slopes of Big Bear. There, in all its glory, was the hope at the end of the tunnel--or at least a glimpse of it. It was what I needed more than anything else on the most horrific morning of my life.

I wasn't a runner, but every neuron inside me knew this was the biggest race of my life. *Will I be able to stay with Karen?* Fueled by my OCD, questions raced through my mind. *What if Karen is paralyzed? How is it that I signed up for this on Match. com? Was the initial wink four years ago my signature on a form obligating me to care for someone incapacitated? Do I have the guts to endure this change?*

I was never stuck at home; I was always on the go and loved being free. However, everything had just changed. It had been less than eight hours since Karen's brain aneurysm had ruptured, yet I had met more doctors than I had known in my entire lifetime. Karen was going to spend her first night in a hospital, and praying was all I could do.

Another man in a white coat came into the waiting room, heading toward me. My heart raced. I begged God, *Please let him be for another family.* I couldn't take much more.

"Good morning, Susan. I'm Dr. Guu, and I'll be Karen's internist. I'm known as the quarterback of the medical team.

The team gives me input; then I gather all the information and make decisions."

Dr. Guu was an Asian man with beautiful thick black hair that reminded me of Karen's hair.

Mom, seated next to me, was listening intently.

"Karen's very sick, Susan. She's in grave condition. We're doing everything possible to keep her alive. I was told she sees someone at UCLA for her rheumatoid arthritis. What medications does she take?"

"She takes an Enbrel shot once a week, and she also takes methotrexate. She took that last night."

"Do you have the number for her rheumatologist at UCLA? I'll need to call. I'll update you as things happen."

As things happen? What did he mean?

"Expect the worse and hope for the best; that is the motto we use here."

Dr. Guu quietly walked away.

Expect the worst? Hadn't the worst already happened?

As time went on, the waiting room started to feel smothering. People went in and out as doctors talked to other families; some were crying, while others were elated. There was too much emotion to handle. I couldn't fathom how people could be smiling and even laughing. There was nothing joyful I could think of at this point.

All of Karen's family arrived except for her sister, Carol, who lived in Florida. She would fly out three days later. I told Karen's family what had happened, amazed that I could remember and verbalize every detail.

"Susan, why didn't you call 911? How come you drove Karen here instead of having the paramedics bring her?" Karen's auntie questioned me.

Because I'm damn afraid of them, ok? I wanted to blurt out, but didn't.

The pot had been stirred. After being praised for my quick thinking by three prominent neurosurgeons, I was being questioned by one of Karen's aunts.

I didn't say a word. I didn't have to; Mom spoke up.

"Karen's here where she needs to be, because of Susie's fast thinking. Everyone should be thankful for that. The doctors told us that Karen would have died at any of the other hospitals that Susie passed on the way here."

Mom--with her precious white hair, red manicured nails, and blue outfit matching her purse--was there to defend her daughter. If anyone challenged me, they would experience Mom's wrath.

At 6:00 pm, I was told Karen was being set up in SICU room 12. She was being hooked up to all her monitors, and the nurses were getting her settled. In just a while, I would get to see my Bear.

At last, at 6:45 pm a redheaded nurse walked through the double doors and came over to me. "Hi, Susan. I'm Lynda, one of Karen's nurses. She will have two nurses for quite some time. Her other nurse, Christine, is with her now. Karen's settled in her room, and we're ready to take you back to see her."

Lynda stood and looked me in the eye so she could be sure I had her full attention. "There are rules: Karen can only be touched very lightly. Anything more than this could agitate her, and she is barely hanging on to life as it is, so we have to be rule-followers. We've found that when patients come out of their coma, they say that rubbing sensations were annoying to them. You may gently touch her arm or hands, but that is all. She's extremely fragile. Also, you must talk quietly, and ten minutes is the maximum time anyone can stay in the room. Two of you may come with me. Follow me," she said, gesturing.

I chose Auntie June to come with me. My brother had security access to the entire hospital, so he walked beside me. Lynda stopped him.

"Michael, two at a time. You can't come through here right now."

"Lynda, I have access to the entire hospital."

"I know, but this is different, Michael. This is family."

"My sister might not be able to handle seeing Karen."

Though reluctant, Lynda allowed Michael to go with me.

I walked over to Auntie June to take her hand. She was in her seventies, with hands that were beautifully manicured and a face as smooth looking as that of a porcelain doll. I had a good rapport with June, and I wanted her to be one of the first to see Karen.

We followed Lynda through more double doors and down a short hallway. In the center of the room was a station where a secretary sat. More monitors than I had ever seen rested on the desks. People dressed in scrubs raced everywhere, and the rooms were full of staff and patients' families. Loud noises reverberated off each wall.

We turned right and arrived at Karen's room. Lynda stopped us before we entered, saying, "I will warn you that Karen is hooked up to a lot of machines. She has tubes in her skull and several parts of her body. It will be a shock when you see her. However, this is where she needs to be. All these machines are keeping her alive."

Room 12. Karen's new home. I stepped inside with June and Michael, and there she was. My Bear. There were tubes and machines everywhere--some beeping, some with lights. Karen was hooked up to a heart monitor, and I noticed several IV bags hanging from poles around her.

Karen's head had been shaved on the right side, her beautiful black hair painfully absent. I made note of a tube in her mouth, a tube in her nose, and a stick with tape poking out of her skull, and a blue bandage wrapped around her head. Across her forehead was tape securing a device that constantly monitored her brain waves. She wore a boot on one foot, I learned, to prevent atrophy. There were blue cooling pads on her stomach and legs, forming the cooling system that kept her in a hypothermic state. A respirator breathed for my Karen, who weighed a mere 97 pounds. It was hard to believe she needed all this.

I kept saying aloud, "She looks good, she looks good!"

I'm not sure what I expected to see, but I convinced myself that Karen looked good. Michael and Auntie agreed. What else could we say when our loved one was a mass of machines, tubes, and bandages?

Standing within inches of Karen, I glanced around at all the machines and lights that lit up the entire room like a Christmas tree. The mood in the room hardly made me think about Christmas, though. The only gift I wanted was for Karen to live.

Our ten minutes were soon up, and others were anxious to see Karen. Everyone had waited all day. They went into room 12 two at a time, returning to the waiting room with tears and long faces afterward. The tubes and machines were too much for some.

When everyone had taken a turn, I went back in. I needed to see Karen one more time.

At 7:00 pm, the nurses changed shifts. Lynda and Christine stayed a bit longer to bring the new nurses up to speed.

I didn't understand how Lynda and Christine could go home. Didn't they realize that Karen almost died? How could they leave and turn my Bear over to two other nurses who knew nothing about her? I shakily listened to Lynda tell me they were going home, unable to really process what she was saying. I knew I had to do something to keep them with Karen.

I thought about Christine sitting outside Karen's room for hours, typing away. She had been recording every detail about Karen's condition. I so badly wanted Christine and Lynda, with her take-charge personality and flaming red hair, to stay with Karen forever.

"Susan, I'll be on vacation beginning tomorrow."

Vacation? What about Karen? Who will take care of her?

My begging began. "Lynda, I'll buy you a round-trip ticket to Hawaii if you stay and don't go on vacation."

I knew nothing about hospitals--at this level of care, anyway--and certainly didn't realize that other nurses were educated enough to take care of Karen. I couldn't stop. "Lynda, please stay," I exclaimed, breathless. "Karen is alive because of you and Christine. You have to stay."

Highly trained and educated people worked here every day and handled crises like Karen's regularly, but I was afraid. *My Bear was on the verge of death; how could she be handed over to others?*

"The other nurses are as knowledgeable as we are. Please believe me. Nurses who deal with brain aneurysms and head trauma all the time will take care of Karen. Your job is to go home and get a good night's sleep. You have a marathon in front of you."

I had never before begged for anything as an adult, but I had just pleaded and offered round-trip tickets to paradise in the same breath. It was no good, though; Lynda and Christine left, their shift over. At least I could still beg to God.

Because of our dogs, I couldn't stay through the night like many other patients' family members. Each seat in the waiting room became a bed for others, but I had Joshua, Benson, and Madi needing to be fed and walked. They were waiting for me.

Mom, the Mordins, and I drove to a Japanese restaurant near home--a place Karen and I frequented. It was in one of our favorite areas, which we called "The Center," and we knew many people from the several establishments there. It felt almost impossible for me to tell anyone what had happened to Karen, but I told some of the workers at the restaurant, and they were flabbergasted. They had just talked to her the night before.

I ordered sushi and tempura, but nothing tasted good. I didn't want to eat without Karen. We ate at this restaurant at least twice a week, and now she wasn't sitting across from me--surreal. I was done. I needed to go to a place where I could feel her--our home with our dogs.

It was a tranquil, balmy evening that belied the day we had just experienced. There was a full moon, one that Karen would have loved to see. She adored a big moon--any moon, really. She often gazed at the sky and would point out stars, telling me what they were.

I was grateful that Mom offered to stay with me overnight in case I couldn't handle being alone. As I drove us to my condominium, I trembled with fear, terrified about Karen dying.

I pulled into the garage where Karen had climbed into my car fourteen hours before. As I got out of the car, I grabbed the yellow Mission Hospital bag I was given that was filled with her clothes, her black-rim glasses resting on top. "Mom, should I throw these clothes out? Karen vomited all over them. I can't even look at these pajamas."

Mom had no idea what my battle with OCD was like. I couldn't look at the vomit on the pajamas, unwilling to touch the clothes or the flip-flops because I felt death was written all over them. Petrified of death and anything affiliated with it, my anxiety rose to such a level that I felt I might explode. The anxiety coursed up and down my spine.

"I think so, Susie," said Mom, her steady voice calming me. "You don't need a tangible reminder of this morning."

I turned the yellow bag upside down into the large green garbage can in our garage, releasing its contents piece by piece. Gone were the pajamas Karen had worn and loved--and the blue flip-flops she loved as well. The washing machine was only two steps away from where I was standing, but I knew that if she didn't make it, I didn't want a reminder of the clothes she had worn that morning.

I stopped at her eyeglasses, which I had removed from the top of the bag. I wanted to throw them out too, as they were another reminder of this fateful day. The image of Karen's distressed face was etched into my mind; I saw her wearing her glasses while she held the small pink bucket she vomited into. Why did hospitals return these items to the family? How could I possibly want the pink vomit bucket?

"What about her glasses?" I asked Mom.

"No, honey. Karen will need those when she wakes up."

I hadn't even thought that far along. Everything in that yellow bag was a reminder of the day. I wanted no reminders. Despite this, I kept the glasses, putting them in Karen's purse. I set the purse on our bench by the door and never touched them again.

I opened the door to the house, reaching in and turning off the house alarm that I barely remembered having set. I went up the fifteen stairs with hunter green carpet that my feet luxuriated in, Mom following me. Behind the wrought iron gate at the top of the stairs, Joshua, Benson, and Madi barked and wagged their stubby tails so fast they looked as if they would fall off. When I unlocked the gate, they jumped all over me at once.

I hugged the dogs and went into the kitchen to get them each a treat. Then I peeked into the bathroom where Karen's brain aneurysm had ruptured. Besides the vomit on the toilet, everything was in order. The room looked surprisingly normal.

"'I'll go in there, honey. Let me clean it up," Mom said over my shoulder.

Amazingly, Mom still looked like she had ten hours ago--neatly pressed clothes, makeup still perfectly placed on the contours of her face, and her hair neatly coiffed. Having Mom with me meant so much.

When she finished cleaning, we went up another flight of stairs to the master bedroom. "Mom, if the phone rings, will you answer it? I can't," I said, exhausted.

Mom sat on the bed as I walked over to my computer and turned it on. Within minutes, the phone rang. I looked at Mom and then at the phone. I was closest to the phone, so I answered it, trembling with fear. It was my niece, who wanted to know how I was doing. I told her, "Please don't call again tonight. My nerves are shot."

I didn't want to think or feel anymore that evening. I was a bedraggled mess because I hadn't showered in the morning. I had gone the whole day with no make-up and no lipstick, and everyone who knows me recognizes I am a lipstick lesbian; I carry at least ten tubes of lipstick in my purse at all times.

I Googled "brain aneurysms" as Mom sat next to me, looking on. Mission Hospital had given me a white notebook about head trauma, but I didn't want to read it. I didn't know then what degree of severity Karen's aneurysm rupture was, what the long-term damage would be, or what type of recovery we were looking at. I knew one thing for sure there were no guarantees. Every doctor had said emphatically that "Karen was a very sick woman" and that I had "started the marathon."

The dogs gathered on our bed, and Mom went downstairs to sleep on the sofa. Karen, with all her tubes and machines, was all I could think of. That night, I prayed harder than I'd ever prayed before, begging God to let Karen live through the night.

When I was young, I was baptized in a Lutheran church. Mom sang in the choir, and Dad was the treasurer of the church. Michael and I went to church every Sunday with our parents until we were about five and seven years old, respectively. I wasn't sure that I had a close relationship with God at that age, but my parents always made us go to church with them. As we got older, my parents stopped going to church, and I wasn't reacquainted with church going again until I was in my twenties, which is when it became an important part of my life again. I went every Sunday morning and every Sunday evening for years, as I was gay and needed to know that God would approve of me. The feeling that God was there was vital.

Chapter 2—Day Two

The next morning, I woke at 6:00 am and got ready for day two. Mom was already up as well. We had received no calls that night, so I knew Karen was still alive. I fed the dogs and, when we were about to leave, gave them their usual treats as they lined up on the stairs. The dogs would be spending another twelve hours at home, but I could get my niece to walk them and feed them dinner.

We drove to Coffee Bean near our home, at which point my OCD began to percolate. This had been my routine for over eight years, and I wasn't ready to make changes, superstitious and unwilling to jinx anything that could hurt Karen's chance of survival.

We got our coffee and Danish to go and drove to the hospital. I had hoped I could eat, but instead I felt sick to my stomach. I didn't go eighty-five miles an hour on the freeway this time. I was afraid.

Three weeks before Karen's aneurysm ruptured, I had been flirting with the idea of leaving Karen. I had gone to Coffee Bean and talked with Lisa and Sue, two of my favorite coffee friends. I cried and said that perhaps Karen and I were meant to be best friends. I loved Karen and knew she loved me, but I missed having a sexual relationship with her. Lisa and Sue were disappointed but understood my dilemma.

At the age of fifty, I had to make a decision about whether sex was more important than having a loving, stable life with someone who had become my best friend. The bottom line was that we loved one another and appreciated living together with our dogs. The only time we really argued was when the house needed vacuuming, as, ironically, we both loved to vacuum.

A few days after that, Karen and I went to dinner and talked. We had tried separating once before, but it hadn't worked. We enjoyed living with one another. Did we have to say we were lovers? Could we live together, come, and go as we pleased? What level of commitment would this entail?

After many such conversations, we decided no labels were needed and that we wanted to continue to live together. I had had so many relationships in the past and really didn't want to go look for another one if I left Karen. Prior to being with me, Karen had lived on her own for twenty-five years and had dated both men and women. She was tired of living alone and wanted to live with me forever. We had once made a decision to live together until the end, but at the time, I didn't know death was looming so perilously close.

On the car ride to the hospital that day, I again turned to God, telling him I would be by Karen's side and was completely committed to her if she lived. *God, please give me another chance to say, 'I love you, Bear.'* I wanted to hug her and show her how great life could be. If God granted me this opportunity, I would prove my commitment to Karen--and to him.

The drive to the hospital was quiet. Perhaps Mom and I were thinking the same things. *Is Karen alive? If so, who will her nurses be today?* One nurse would be with Karen and the other would be sitting outside her room, typing everything into the computer.

I turned left into the parking lot and took a ticket from the parking machine, noticing again that I was driving slower than usual. We went to the back of the hospital to park directly across from the sliding doors that I had walked out of less than twelve hours before. I pulled into an open parking spot that became my permanent parking space for the next three months. Everyone would come to know my car by its special license plate: ITEEECH.

As Mom and I went through the hospital doors, an eerie feeling washed over me. My heart raced, my palms sweaty. Karen was alive, but how bad would her condition be this morning? Given the pace of all that had happened the day before, I wondered what had taken place during the night.

There was a phone on the right side of the wall in the brightly lit hallway. I punched in the code to speak to someone in the SICU. It would be the first of many times I would pick up that phone and dial in to gain entrance.

Someone picked up the intercom.

"I'm Susan Davis, Karen Kozawa's partner." Mom and I were admitted.

Before we stepped into the SICU, a woman emerged from a little room on the left side, saying, "Hi, I'm Marjorie. I'm in charge of the SICU, and I'm here to help answer any questions you may have." I didn't know at the time that Marjorie was like a mother to all--families, nurses, and patients alike. She played an essential role in the SICU.

The doors to the unit slid open, and the unit secretary greeted us, saying "Hi, I'm Tracy."

"Hi, Tracy. This is my mom, Joyce. How's Karen?"

"The nurses are with her. You can go in." My eyes filled with tears as I entered room 12.

Though the two new nurses looked professional, I already missed Lynda and Christine, whose sincerity had given me hope. I realized that they had to change shifts as part of their job, but I felt sad about them not being with Karen.

OCD is such a strange disorder. At times, I never know when it will take over my thinking, making it completely irrational. At this point, the change in nurses made me nervous, exacerbating my need for rituals. I began counting the machines in the room and the tiles on the floor, making sure I stood on what I felt was the correct side of Karen's bed. I had to have order, and my OCD rituals gave me order. If everything were in order, then nothing would happen to Karen. I truly believed that.

One of the nurses sat outside her room typing; the other nurse was at Karen's bedside. The overhead lights were bright. *Don't the lights hurt Karen's eyes? How can she deal with nonstop light?* Then I remembered her eyes were taped shut and she was in a coma. I imagined she could see only darkness.

She looked tiny in the large, burgundy hospital bed. There were bumpers inside the bed rails. *Do they really think that she can fall out of bed while in a coma?* The number of machines in the room was even more astounding than the night before. They were everywhere: on the floor, at the foot of the bed, on the left of her, and on the right of her; of course, there were also tubes in every orifice of her body. A urine bag hung on the outside of her bed. Perhaps I had been in shock the day before, but the piteous reality of what I was seeing on the second day demanded a huge chunk of my heart and soul. Was I ready to give it? It wasn't too late to turn around and walk out.

I introduced myself to the nurse by her bed. "I'm Karen's partner, Susan. How is she?"

"She had a good night," the nurse replied.

Really? A good night? How was that possible when every machine known to mankind was controlling her?

My mind was flooded with questions. *What am I supposed to do now? Sit and wait? How long can I stay in her room? Is there still a ten-minute time limit? How often can I visit?* I took her small, delicate hand and gently placed it on my arm. *Can she feel me? Does she know it's me?*

"Bear, it's Boo," I said softly. "The puppies and I love you, and we missed you at home last night. Can you hear me, Bear?"

Of course, there was no answer. She was in a medically induced coma that kept her nestled deep in her own abyss.

What would I do without her at home? She made our lunches in the morning. She helped feed the dogs, and we walked them nightly. She was the tech authority, fixing the computers in our home.

When ten minutes was up, no one told us to leave, but Mom and I turned around and walked out the double doors, heading over to the SICU waiting room. It was filled with people. When we entered, everyone began to stand, forming a circle. *Is this a daily ritual?* I wondered. Though my OCD thrived on rituals, I felt nervous. I didn't want to stand with everyone or talk to anyone. I didn't have anything to say. *Do I have to join? Will I automatically become an outcast if I sit outside the circle?*

A handsome young man approached, saying, "Susan, would you and your mom like to join us?" He had apparently heard my name the day before. "My wife, Melisa, is having eye surgery this morning. She fell asleep and crashed her car into a tree two weeks ago. She wasn't expected to live, but she did. Today Dr. Nwagwu is doing surgery to find out the scope of damage to her eyes. She had severe head trauma, and there's a chance she might have lost her eyesight. We're saying a prayer for her."

Mom and I joined in, unsure if social pressure carried us into the circle or if the need to pray to the same god these people were praying to had sucked us in. Praying took on new meaning when you were in the SICU waiting room. I didn't mind praying for Melisa, but I wanted to make sure that God didn't take this prayer in place of my prayers for Karen. What if he only heard one prayer a day and I was using mine for this other woman? What would that mean for Karen? Your mind plays tricks on you when you are saving all you have for your loved one lying on her deathbed.

All of a sudden, there was a loud boom, and the windows rattled. My brother yelled, "Go outside! Everyone go outside!" We scattered quickly and ran out the double doors. An earthquake registering around 4.0 had just hit. Mom, who was terrified of earthquakes, went over to the far side of the parking lot and stood by Mr. Tran, the husband of another brain aneurysm patient. She lit a cigarette.

Mom had stopped smoking at one point in her life, but when the Northridge earthquake happened in 1994, Mom was so shaken that she began smoking again. That day frightened Mom beyond words.

What about Karen and the other patients? They couldn't run outside.

I stood in silence. Michael came over to me as tears slid down my cheeks. He handed me a Kleenex.

"It's ok, Susie. They know what to do in the SICU. Karen will be safe."

We all stood outside on the patio waiting for the rolling to stop. It was a hot summer day, so the sun beat down on us uncomfortably.

I had plenty of time for my mind to wander while we waited. Karen and I had been through a few earthquakes together. They didn't really shake us up. We used to walk to a doorway and stand there until the shaking stopped.

Thankfully, about ten minutes later, we were allowed to go back inside.

Chapter 3—Counting the Days

In the SICU, everyone talked in terms of days. "What day is your loved one on?" was a common question. When I heard someone say they were on day 30, I held my breath. I couldn't imagine enduring the level of anxiety I was experiencing for that long. For Karen, the days were extremely important, representing the vasospasm time frame; days 3 through 10 were most important. It had only been 26 hours and already I was mentally exhausted.

Dr. Kim had warned us about vasospasms the day before. He'd written the time frame on a tiny piece of lined yellow paper: "days 3-10: vasospasms." Within this period, the arteries in Karen's brain could close up and set her up for another stroke. I wanted to skip days 3 through 362 so all of this, hopefully, could be behind us.

I welcomed every visitor who came to see Karen. I talked about her condition with anyone who entered her room. Her boss Jim came daily with his wife, Diane, whose warm personality gave me a chance to smile. A well-groomed woman with soft brown hair, Diane had eyes that spoke volumes about how much she loved Karen. She talked softly, was encouraging, and always prayed for Karen.

Others from Karen's work joined us on day two. They cried upon seeing her. She had been a big presence where she worked; she oversaw a department that made clothing in other countries, making sure products were manufactured and sent back to the United States in a timely manner. Many people counted on her to keep the business running.

That day, Jim sat next to me with his Blackberry in hand. "I don't know how I can work without Karen."

She had been integral in her company, but now she was a huge part of the SICU.

Visitors continued to come and go that day.

While sitting in the waiting room, I was summoned out to the hallway. I was asked the big question unexpectedly. Dawn asked, "Susan, do you have power of attorney for Karen?"

I told her we were registered domestic partners in the state of California. "Would you like me to bring a copy of the certificate?"

"Yes," she said. "That's all we need. That paper will allow you to make all her medical decisions--and there will be many to make." I smiled weakly.

Only two weeks before Karen's aneurysm ruptured, I had cleaned out our file cabinet and put our partnership document on top. Though coincidental, I think it was a random occurrence--just like the brain aneurysm.

This crucial, precious certificate would cause a fight when Karen's sister, Carol, flew in the next day. Karen and Carol had not talked for a while because of a long-standing argument; when Karen and I first got together, we both sold our homes and bought a new house together, which infuriated Carol. She knew that their parents had paid for Karen's home twenty-five years prior.

As our home was being built in 2004, Carol called Karen and screamed at her, saying, "You are spending family money and buying a house with your girlfriend! That is our money! She is going to move in with you and then take your money!" I had met Carol the month after we made the decision to purchase our home. At the time, she was friendly and seemed happy that Karen had finally found someone to share her life with. Four weeks later, however, she had obviously changed her ways and become vicious with her words. I had taken the phone from Karen to see if I could calm her down, saying, "Carol, this is Susan."

"I don't give a damn who you are. You're a gold digger, and my sister is an embezzler stealing family money. I will give Karen ten thousand dollars not to buy the house with you."

After five minutes of her ranting, I handed the phone back to Karen. She hung up on Carol, marking the beginning of an ongoing feud. I'm not quite sure how I became a gold digger, but Carol went on to call everyone in the family to tell them I would be calling them and asking for money. Karen and I went through with our plans regardless, and until the aneurysm incident, Karen hadn't heard from her sister.

One of Karen's aunts called Carol, who flew in on day three. The SICU waiting room was again filled with people wanting to support Karen. My mom and niece, Mandie, were among those with me that day.

Carol sauntered into the SICU waiting room and up to the front desk without once looking at us. Her flowery dress swished back and forth, her open-toed pumps clacking on the shiny linoleum floor. She was fifty-seven years old, with shoulder-length black hair. She didn't look like Karen at all.

Her twenty-year-old son, Bob, was with her. He wore a blue derby cap pulled slightly over his eyes and kept his head down so as not to look at any of us. Bob and Karen had once been extremely close. However, when his mother decided I was a horrible person because Karen and I bought a home together, Bob never called Auntie Karen again.

Carol barked orders at the receptionist. Every set of eyes turned, but she never once looked around.

I'd had enough. I stood up and went over to her. "Hi, Carol. They're working on Karen right now, and no one is allowed in the room," I said in a sweet yet firm tone.

I gave her a hug--she resisted--then hugged Bob, mostly for show. Mandie later told me that Carol had rolled her eyes when I hugged her. I went back to my seat, and Mom said to Carol, "Hi, I'm Susan's mom."

"I know who you are," Carol spat.

They had never met before. Carol didn't know half the people in the waiting room, and those she knew—like Jim and some of Karen's other co-workers--she didn't acknowledge. No one dared speak, aware that Carol was ready to attack. I believed she only wanted money; she didn't care about her sister, whom she hadn't spoken to in over four years.

The nurse came out to say that they'd completed their procedure and that I could go in to see Karen.

I glared at Carol. *The twister has hit—she'll whirl around as fast as she can.* I wasn't prepared for any drama this early in the game. Her whirlwind attitude from years before was still ingrained in my mind.

"You can go back for ten minutes," I told Carol. I said this with trepidation because I was fearful of what she might say to Karen. I knew that Karen would not want her sister's face staring at her.

I didn't fear Karen waking from her coma while Carol was there. Everything was about time--waiting and waiting some more. *Aren't we all just prisoners of time?*

After a long while, Mom said, "Susie, it's been over thirty minutes and she hasn't come out. Go tell her that her time is up."

"The nurses will tell her. I want to say something, but I'm not ready for that battle today."

Forty-five minutes went by. I was furious. People were walking around the waiting room chatting to one another. Someone was on the computer in the back corner updating *Caring Bridge;* the online journal where many of us left notes about our loved ones' progress. I sat down next to my mom, who was talking to other visitors about rules and looking frustrated. We had followed the rules the first three days; why didn't they apply to Carol?

Tracy buzzed me in, and I walked gingerly into the SICU and peeked around the corner into Karen's room. Carol's mere presence was enough to warrant caution.

I felt the tension build as I watched Carol through the window of Karen's room. We had put pictures on the window so that Karen could see them the minute she woke up. My anxiety crawled beneath my skin, my heart racing. My palms were wet with sweat. *What if Carol sees me? Karen was in the hands of the enemy.*

I couldn't make out Carol's body language, but she was standing on the right side of the bed, her head next to Karen's. I knew she was talking to her, but what was she saying? They had not spoken in four years, and I knew Karen did not want her sister near her. No matter how much Carol tried to weasel information out of Karen, she wouldn't find out about the certificate I had given to the hospital, as Karen couldn't talk. Bob stood at the foot of the bed, his gaze on the floor. He looked powerless. Bob seemed shy, and I often wondered if he was immobilized given the dominance of his mother.

I knew that Carol and Bob would have to leave soon. Someone would surely tell them they had exceeded their allotted time. I turned and walked away, not wanting Carol to know I had been watching her through the window. She would have screamed at me.

I heard her raucous voice in my mind; this woman was capable of spitting venom at anyone who stepped in her path. She didn't know, though, that I had the ace in the hole--the certificate I had given to the hospital that would rock her world.

Mom came up behind me and said, "What in the world is going on in there?" "They're with Karen. I can't say anything. Do you think I should go in and kick them out? I'll talk to the nurses as soon as Carol leaves."

"It's not fair we're all out here waiting to go in and see Karen." *Gosh, I love my mom. She loves her kids unconditionally, and when we need her, she is always at our side.*

"I have to be careful. The nurses say Karen might be able to hear us. I want to believe that too, so I don't want to have a fight with Carol in there."

Carol and Bob finally came out, and soon after, a nurse exclaimed, "Susan, oh my God--come over here!"

Three nurses were assembled outside Karen's room as I ran over.

"Karen's sister just ripped me a new asshole," one of Karen's nurses, Dawn, said, her hand on her hip and a look of shock on her face. The two other nurses frowned. "She's rude. Believe me, I've come across hundreds of rude family members in here, but she's something else. She told us all at least ten times that she was from Florida. Who cares? Is that supposed to mean something?"

"I'm sorry you guys had to deal with her," I said.

I was pissed off. We had focused on Karen for two days, so I was annoyed that I had to watch over my shoulder to make sure Carol wasn't doing anything that could harm her. I've never been to Florida, so I wasn't sure what her pleasure was in repeating her hometown to the nurses, but making a scene and acting like she was in control of everything was typical of Carol. Well, the nurses, doctors, and I wouldn't be manipulated.

"We're used to bad family members, but she's really horrible." Dawn lowered her voice, whispering, "Here's the worst part: she told us to unplug all the machines because she knew Karen wouldn't want to be on any machines."

Though stunned, I wasn't actually surprised by her actions. She wanted money. Karen owned another property that was being rented out. Karen also had life insurance worth two hundred thousand dollars.

Then the impact of what she said hit me. "She basically told you to take Karen off all the machines that were keeping her alive?" All three of the nurses looked at me, and each one nodded, and then gave me a hug. The bonding had begun.

"Those were her exact words," said Dawn. "All the doctors heard her, too. One of the doctors told her to get back on the plane and go home so the doctors and nurses could do their job with Karen."

"I told her that you were the one making all the decisions for Karen," she said.

This was the time to let her know I was in charge, not her.

I thanked the nurses and went into Karen's room. The machines beeped repeatedly. The beeps were soft high notes just loud enough to alert the nurses to the fact that they were working. The respirator made low whooshing sounds. I knew that as long as the lights continued to blink, Karen was alive.

I whispered in her ear, "Bear, it's Boo. I'm here. Please don't think your sister is the only one with you. She has no control over your treatment. I'm doing everything I can to help you survive this huge ordeal. I love you so much. Please continue to fight and come home to the doggies and me."

When my 10 minutes were up and I walked into the waiting room, Carol and Bob went to the patio.

I gathered my mother, nieces, and Karen's coworkers around me, telling them, "Carol wanted to have all the plugs pulled. She told the doctors and nurses that Karen wouldn't want to be on the machines."

The nurses said they'd told Carol we were registered domestic partners, and one of Karen's cousins said Carol had questioned them about it. She wanted to know when Karen and I had registered. No one knew. It was no one's business but ours.

Carol didn't have the power to take her sister off the machines, and she didn't know that Karen's only beneficiary was me.

Carol and Bob eventually left later that afternoon for the home of one of Karen's aunties. I had an afternoon and evening of reprieve.

On day five--August 1, 2008--Mary Kay Bader, the neurological SICU specialist, convened a meeting that would allow the medical team to talk openly and honestly with Karen's family. I was allowed to choose who could attend the conference. Carol was not on my list, but the nurses advised me to include her. They told me that if I didn't allow her in, she would probably cause trouble.

I agreed, thinking an invitation might change her icy demeanor. Michael, our dear friends Peter and Sue Mordin, one of Karen's nurses, Alison, the chaplain, and Carol attended. Mom stayed in the waiting room with the others.

We first met in the SICU, gathering around a computer. Mary Kay pulled up images of Karen's brain. We looked first at an image from day one. "On the scan, you'll see white, which is bone. The gray is the brain tissue, and the gray-white areas are pools of blood. As you know, Karen suffered a massive subarachnoid bleed in her left anterior communicating artery." Mary Kay pointed to this area on the screen. "The ruptured aneurysm caused the pools of blood to form in the brain cavity; blood also went down her spine.

"The aneurysm was treated with an electronically detachable coil embolization. A small piece of coil was threaded through her groin and into her brain aneurysm. During this procedure, the wall of the aneurysm ruptured. The interventional radiologist was able to close off the aneurysm site so it wouldn't bleed again, but there was an increase in pressure when the aneurysm bled the second time." Mary Kay straightened her back and looked at me. "We don't know the extent of the brain damage, and we won't know for quite some time."

Brain damage? Karen might have brain damage?

"We began to cool her body quickly to get her temperature to 91 degrees. We are now working to slowly return her temperature to normal; if we do it too quickly, brain damage is more likely to result. Karen's brain pressure is being closely monitored, and we'll be watching for vasospasms. She'll have a daily ultrasound taken through the thinnest part of her skull using an instrument called a Transcranial-Doppler. If the speed of blood is higher than it should be, there will be vasospasms. This is one of the most crucial times for Karen."

The images of Karen's brain screamed loudly that her condition was dangerously grave. I remembered the ripped piece of yellow paper on which Dr. Kim had mapped out days three through ten. I stared at the pictures on the computer screen, lost in thought. I didn't understand what I was seeing. *What's a Transcranial Doppler? Vasospasms? Isn't EVERYTHING crucial for Karen? How can it get worse than it already is?* While Mary Kay explained everything to us, I kept an eye on Carol, who looked distraught. I tried to focus on what I was seeing and hearing, but I didn't trust Carol and wanted to keep her in my line of sight.

After viewing the slides of Karen's brain, we were escorted into a large conference room with white walls and big whiteboards covering two of the walls. I shivered in the cold air conditioning that signified danger and finality.

Michael sat next to me, his strength sure to keep me safe. The Mordins sat across from us, Sue taking notes for me. Mary Kay sat at the middle of the table. Carol was on the other side of the chaplain, and this time I was glad I couldn't see her face. When Mom and I had met the chaplain on day one, I was so in shock that I had tuned him out. I didn't want to see a chaplain at all that day, and besides, Karen was Buddhist. When I saw the chaplain at this meeting, however, I found myself inwardly begging to his God.

I asked few questions and listened intently, but it was difficult to focus.

Carol asked Mary Kay, "What's the prognosis for my sister? Does she have brain damage? What are the machines really doing for her?"

Sue Mordin, trying to be helpful as always, said, "Carol, have you talked with Lisa Foto? She's a recovered brain aneurysm patient who was treated at Mission Hospital." Sue knew about our family dynamics, and I truly think she was trying to protect not only Karen, but also me.

Carol raised her voice. "Why would I want to talk to her? She has nothing to tell me about my sister!"

After twenty minutes of listening to Carol unsuccessfully trying to run the show, I had had enough. I stood up. "Thanks for this conference, Mary Kay, but I think we need to end it here. I know you and your staff are working hard trying to save Karen's life."

My brother put his arm around me as we walked out. I also saw Carol leave, and I had no idea where she went, nor did I care. Fireworks would have erupted if I saw her again that day. My patience had been severed, and the Irish in me was starting to rise to the surface.

I said goodbye to my brother and went to see Karen. Her eyes were taped shut; she didn't seem to want to keep them closed. It was hard to look at them. Since I knew her beautiful brown eyes well, it was hard to recognize her.

Karen had a blood clot in her left arm, so an inferior vena cava filter had been inserted below her renal veins to prevent the clot from traveling to her heart, lungs, or brain. As I thought about the conference, I remembered that Carol wanted to unplug her sister from every one of the machines that were keeping her alive.

Karen's boss Jim took on the job of being our scribe. He would manage Karen's page on *Caring Bridge* so everyone could get updates about her condition. On this day, he wrote:

> *We were informed that almost all hospitals in Orange County would have given up on Karen if she had been brought in, but miraculously, Susan took her to the best hospital. If she had been taken elsewhere, they would not have tried as hard to save Karen, as they wouldn't have had the staff, equipment, and doctors who could handle such a severe brain aneurysm.*
>
> *As I write this, my eyes are full of tears. My sweet friend has gone through so much. Everyone is surrounding her with love and prayers, which has helped keep her alive. Karen has always been a happy person who has accepted each one of us as we are. Miracles happen, and they will continue to happen for Karen. She has had another good day because nothing has changed. In a world where we are all so caught up in things changing, what an incredible thing it is to know that someone so dear has had her life extended because of love.*

Chapter 4—Week One

On day one, my mom had asked me if I had called Dr. Kaplan, my therapist. I hadn't because I didn't want to bother her while she was on the vacation she'd just begun.

I was referred to Dr. Susan Kaplan twenty-four years ago because I was having difficulty trying to leave my first lesbian relationship of 16 years. I was with a woman thirteen years my senior who was married with two children. She had made me comfortable expressing my sexuality, and she had kept me as her mistress for nine years. Eventually her husband found out about our affair and they divorced; we remained together for seven years, but she still lived a lie with many people, and I never felt fully comfortable. It was Dr. Kaplan who had helped me to leave the relationship. Without her expertise, I wouldn't have managed everything as well as I had. Dr. Kaplan offered me a place of refuge in her beautiful office with purple sofas, soft lighting, and her erudite self. I was blessed to have her in my life.

As the first week closed in on me, I decided to call her that Friday afternoon. She answered right away, and I heard the devastation in her voice when I told her what had happened. Her voice was soft yet assertive, commanding my attention. I knew she would have the right words to help me make it through another day. She said she was coming home the next day, and she promised to call to set up a meeting with me.

On Saturday afternoon, Dr. Kaplan called. She was on the tarmac at John Wayne airport in Orange County, California. I will never forget the moment she called me; she had not even deplaned and yet was already on the phone with me. She had always supported me during the previous 16 years and was with me through every relationship that had ended in disarray. She was the rock that I continued to hold onto. A few years after Karen's aneurysm ruptured, I even had her name tattooed on my right arm. I know she was shocked about it, but I think that ultimately she was honored.

With Dr. Kaplan's help, I developed a routine for the summer while school was out. I arrived at the hospital between 8:00 and 8:30 each morning and stayed until early evening. In the waiting room, I'd heard other families say they spent the night; there were people who never left the hospital except to go home to shower. They'd return within hours to sit with their loved ones. Staying the night had never occurred to me, as I knew I had to get home to feed our dogs. I needed rest, too. I would get seven hours of sleep and do my routine all over again the next day.

Because of the frequency of her vasospasms, on Monday, August 4th, Karen was scheduled to have a scan at 4:00 pm. It took a team of five or six people to gather Karen and her machines and push her bed into the operating room. The medical staff pushed her bed as fast as they could; her heart rate had dropped to 50 beats per minute, and if they didn't get Karen to the operating room fast enough, a vasospasm could close an artery and cause a stroke, damaging her brain further. People hurried to flatten themselves against the wall as she was rolled into the OR.

At 6:20 p.m. Karen was showing signs of distress. The arteries in her head had spasmed, so she was given Verapamil, which dilated her arteries to provide more blood flow to the brain. A neuro-radiologist slowly fed the drug through a catheter and threaded it up to Karen's arteries, trying to relax the arteries in spasm. A code blue was called.

Karen had flat lined.

A technician and Karen's nurses, Alison and Michelle used CPR and brought her back to life. At 6:30, Karen's heart rate was back up to 84.

While this was happening, I was in the hospital's patio area on a hot green metal bench reading *Twilight,* unaware of the fact that she had flat lined. This was where I went to be alone. When Karen's machines went crazy--or when she went to the Angio Suite for a procedure--I would bolt outside into the hot summer sun. The green patio furniture offered a safe and comfortable place to sit and think.

From this vantage point, I could hear the double doors opening and closing and cars coming and going. People talked, and doctors rushed from the parking lot to the hospital. The Coke machine in front of me beckoned, and I fumbled for change in my shorts, which I had paired with a T-shirt and colorful tennis shoes. I owned fifty pairs of tennis shoes in colors that matched every outfit.

The sliding doors opened, admitting another family into the outdoors. I checked my watch and decided to go back into the SICU. At the desk, I asked Tracy, the unit secretary, "How much longer for Karen? She's been in there a long time."

Tracy called the Angio Suite. "A few more minutes" was her response. The waiting game made me tired and anxious. My left eye began twitching.

When Alison came to find me thirty minutes later, I knew something was wrong. The nurses had never come outside to sit and chat with me. Alison was a favorite nurse. She was kind and caring, with a soft but confident tone of voice. She showed

Karen so much love. She had long talks with her while she worked on her, saying things like, "You have to live, Karen; Susan's waiting for you."

Alison sat beside me on the green metal bench "Susan, I want you to know that Karen is alive."

Okay, when she went down the hallway, she was alive, so I didn't think she would come back dead. I could tell bad news was on the way.

"Karen coded in the OR. We were able to resuscitate her with CPR, and we're getting her settled back into her room now. I want you to come in and see her."

I picked up my book and Diet Coke, rising to my feet. I was shaking. Alison had a concerned look on her face as she watched me stand. It was hot outside, but I was in no hurry to go back to the SICU. I was afraid. *How is Karen's petite body going to handle another battle?*

I slowly followed Alison back into the SICU. Would Karen flat line again? It had happened in the OR. I couldn't begin to picture this, and I didn't want to.

When we reached her room, all I could say was "Wow." She looked awful, her face orange and as large and puffy as a cloud.

I was afraid to express how grave she looked lest it curse her survival. In those next several days, I wouldn't let anyone say the word *vasospasm* around me; afraid it could cause one. I wanted only positive words, good thoughts, and loving feelings surrounding her. My OCD wouldn't allow me to let the rituals go, creating irrational thoughts. They filled my mind, repeating themselves continually in my head. "Karen could die; don't say 'vasospasm' in her room ever again" I repeated countless times. I somehow believed my continued repetitions would ward off danger.

I never asked Alison or Michelle, the two nurses who were with Karen in the OR, what the orange hue on her face was.

I didn't want to know. She was alive, and that was all that mattered. I needed to believe that Karen would live and our lives would return to normal. As much as I wanted "normal," something was telling me that we would have a new normal—nothing was ever going to be the same again.

That evening, I bent over her swollen features and said, "Night, Bear. I'll see you in the morning. I love you."

This was another ritual—saying certain phrases every time I left the hospital. If I didn't say them, I was certain Karen would die. The urgency of our situation overpowered me; I hoped that if I always told Karen I would see her in the morning, I could protect her from death.

That evening I left the SICU and made it outside the locked double doors before I began to cry. Everyone had left for the day. None of my family, Karen's family, or our friends were there. I stood by the outer set of double doors, tears pouring down my face. Brandon, whom I had met on day two when we stood in a circle and prayed for his wife, found me.

"Susan, what's wrong? Is Karen ok?

"She just coded in the OR."

"But she's alive, right?"

"Yes."

"Then that's all that matters. All we can hope for is another day. In there, every second matters, and there will be rocky times while Karen is in the SICU. Melisa has been through so much too. Up one day, down the next. Always remember, Susan, the doctors and nurses know what they are doing. Focus on the fact that Karen's alive."

Nodding my head in acknowledgement, I went to my car. I activated my Bluetooth to call Jim and tell him what had happened; he too said there would be bumps in the road. Each day got harder when something else went wrong with Karen. My strength was dwindling. *Would I have the courage to stay, or should I just wrap things up, divide our assets, and walk away?*

"She made it through another day," Jim reminded me. *Is that all we're hoping and waiting for? Karen making it through another day?* I wanted to know that she would make it through many more years. Jim seemed stern, though I know he was trying to help me see the entire picture.

By the time I left the hospital each night, I was beyond exhausted and just wanted to get home and be with the dogs. Mom's house was on my way home, though, so I stopped and talked to her for a few minutes that night before driving to Irvine for dinner, where I halfheartedly enjoyed another night of sushi alone.

When I drove through the locked gates of our community, I thought about how double doors and gates seemed to be everywhere. Was it a sign? Karen was behind locked doors in the SICU, I was on the other side of those locked doors until I was buzzed in, and the gates to our community were locked until I used my remote to get in. Either my OCD was at work again or God was sending me signs that I had to work harder to always get through the locked doors and gates emerging in my life.

I pulled into our garage and climbed up the stairs. Waiting for me were three very happy dogs that barked and wagged their stubby tails. I fed them and gave each a chew bone. All three followed me to our bedroom, where I put my pajamas on and climbed into bed, lingering in the dogs' furry embraces after they climbed in with me.

Unable to sleep, I walked over to the double sink. Karen's bath towel hung on the bathroom bar, unwashed after her shower five days ago. I couldn't wash it. What if she didn't live? I needed to hold on to her smell as long as I could. I held the purple towel to my face and inhaled deeply to savor her scent—her scent that I needed to hold deep within my soul not only for this moment, but perhaps forever.

I folded the towel perfectly and placed it back on the rack where I would see it every night when I came home. I then glanced into our closet and looked at Karen's many pairs of pointed black shoes. I stared at her size zero clothes.

I only had her clothes, shoes, and one bath towel to hold onto. *Will the scent on her towel last forever? What if it begins to fade? Is she going to fade too?*

I prayed each night when I climbed into bed, going through the same prayers repeatedly. Begging to God seemed more relevant in Karen's hospital room than on my drive home or in bed. Perhaps the hospital was where I felt the greatest danger.

Chapter 5—Numbers

The next morning, Michael called. He went to see Karen every morning at 6:00 am. "Her color is back," he said. "Her numbers were stable all night. The nurses said that was a good sign. They'll do a brain scan this morning to see her progress, but also to make sure there was no damage from the flat lining. I'll come and see you after you get here." If I wanted to see the doctors, I knew I had to get to the hospital by 8:00 am.

"Thanks." It was going to be a tough day.

I left the house and went to Coffee Bean to get another blueberry tea latte and scone. This was my morning OCD ritual.

I tried to maintain consistency in a world of chaos. I felt I had no control of anything--as if I was just a spectator. At Coffee Bean, I felt safe, comforted by my friends and the smell of coffee. Our coffee club of 19 met every weekend, and a gentle word or smile from any one of my friends could comfort me.

Greg, one of the guys in our group, walked over to me, saying, "You look like you could use a massage. Sit here." I sat, and for ten minutes, someone took care of me for a change. Greg had large, strong hands, and the massage was exactly what I needed.

I arrived at the hospital soon after. After using Purell hand sanitizer—my new best friend--I went to Karen's room and peeked in. She was in a supine position as usual, all her machines surrounding her. She didn't move at all. It would be another month before the doctors could take Karen off her coma-inducing medication in order to wake her up. There was no guarantee that she would in fact wake-up. Brain aneurysms came with no guarantees.

The doctors said she might experience a natural coma even after they took her off the medicines and machines. *Please don't let her be in two comas. Anything at all but that,* I repeated in my prayers. I was aware I was begging to a higher power because life around me was pointing to death. At that point, I was grasping at straws; I felt deep down that God was listening to me. I'd learned to pray in church as a small child, and my mom continued to remind me that praying to God needed to be a part of my life. I took Mom's words to heart.

I waited for Dr. Kim outside Karen's room so we could talk. I believed Karen could hear us, and if bad news was delivered, I didn't want her to know about it.

Outside Karen's door, he said, "Susan, her blood pressure is erratic. It's 206 over 108. I called another doctor—Dr. Gee, a neurologist. He thinks there's a possible issue with Karen's anticonvulsant medications. They might be causing thrombocytopenia, a condition marked by low blood platelet levels."

He paused. "Dr. Gee and I have different opinions about her medications. It's also possible that one of her medications could cause increased bleeding. If there's one thing Karen doesn't need, it's bleeding more. After talking, we agreed on a medication that won't have the side effects others have had."

"What about the brain scan that was taken earlier this morning?" I asked.

"I saw a small blockage that caused a tiny stroke, but left no damage. That's a good sign. For now, we wait. That's all we can do." Dr. Kim stood at ease in the hallway. I guess he did this every day, so he probably only looked at ease. "We told you on the first day this would be a marathon, and right now, Karen has only left the starting gate."

I walked over to stand beside Karen's bed, the machines beeping. The many machines still overwhelmed me no matter how many times I walked into the room, but perhaps the stillness of the room was just what I needed. The overhead lights were always on, and I had wondered why but never asked.

I stared at the machine that was breathing for Karen. It was difficult to think that a machine could keep someone breathing. The room was freezing, the sub-zero temperature warding off infection. After thinking about all this, I talked to Karen and sang silly songs. I sang the Beverly Hillbillies' theme song because we used to sing it together in the car. I both prayed she was hearing me and believed she did.

Later I went outside and sat at the green patio table, Sue came by and sat with me. We took turns visiting Karen. Every time the sliding doors to the hospital opened, we turned around, unsure of what we would see. We laughed about how we had muscle strain from turning our heads so often. Sue and I wondered if we would acquire tics from turning around so much.

After taking breaks outside, I would always go back to be with Karen as much as possible. Alone with Karen into the late afternoon, I heard only machines and the movements of the nurse who was always in the room. She would be changing out tubes and bags of medicine. I never tired of being with Karen. I felt, that night, that I was in it until the end--whatever that meant.

In about a week, Karen's blood pressure began stabilizing, though she had developed a fever. Vasospasms were still happening too often, sometimes occurring twice a day. This created havoc for the team because they would have to quickly wheel Karen and her machines to the OR. These were extremely crucial moments in trying to keep her alive.

On August 5th and 6th, Karen was transported to the operating room several times a day. Fluid was building up in her lungs, a result of her being in bed for so long, and it was decided that the countermeasure was to make her bed shake. When they pushed a button, the bed would shake hard and fast for some time, making it look like things were out of control.

Nurse Lynda had nicknamed me "the bolter" because anytime something went wrong with Karen; I booked it outside until the problem was resolved. Lynda always came outside and brought me back to Karen's room after the event was over. She laughed each time I did this. Since Karen's vasospasms happened often, the nurses were always prepared and knew what to do. I felt better to be able to go outside and let the nurses do their jobs.

When Sue Mordin arrived each morning, she visited Karen and then came outside to sit with me and work on her crossword puzzles. Because of this routine, I never felt alone, soothed by her presence. We took turns going in to see Karen and discussed anything new about her condition with the nurses. On any one of these long and arduous days, my hopes would inflate one minute then be crushed the next.

Karen was such a sweet person, and my family adored her. She was kind, caring, and loving. We always went to family dinners together, and my two-year-old niece, Becca, couldn't pronounce Karen's name, so she called her "Pancake"--a nickname she had for the last year.

Later that day, when Sue was with Karen, Dr. Kim walked toward me from the parking lot. He told me that Karen was not a textbook case and that he was waiting for the ball to drop. I was not prepared for this, and I didn't understand. The vasospasms, the blood pressure concerns, and having only a one percent chance of living--wasn't that enough?

I went into Karen's room. Respiratory therapist Felipe was there. He opened his arms to me. "Susan, Dr. Kim is a great doctor, he knows what to do." He smiled at me. "My mom had a brain aneurysm and recovered here as well. She lived. I understand exactly what you're feeling. However, I know that Karen is going to make it. We are all working so hard to help her live."

This moment resonated with me forever. Felipe was a kind man, always and positive. It certainly felt like Felipe truly cared not only about Karen, but also about me.

When I arrived home that evening, I sat on the bed with our dogs, lost in thought. Nothing would ever be the same again for Karen and me, and I was seeing that more and more clearly as time went on.

My mind continued to wander. *Will Karen ever be able to walk up our 31 stairs again? Can we still travel? Will I be the one feeding the dogs all the time? What if she can't work anymore?* I quickly put an end to these horrible questions; I needed to stay positive. I no longer debated whether I would stay or leave at this point. I had an agreement with God and Karen, and I was determined to maintain my commitment.

I reached over to pet all three of the dogs. Benson sat next to me, resting on my papers. He never left my side the entire night; he knew something was wrong.

Michael called the next morning, as usual. I learned Karen had been rushed to the OR at 4:00 am as the result of more vasospasms. We were faced with another difficult day. Kris Machingo was one of the main nurses at night for Karen. She gave her heart and soul in working with Karen, and she was the night nurse who went to the OR many times. She was responsible for saving Karen's life when the rest of us were home sleeping.

I took a shower, fed the dogs, and went to Coffee Bean. I updated my coffee friends, ate my ritual breakfast, and headed to the hospital, where I no longer had to introduce myself to the secretary who buzzed me in. Once there, I was greeted by the nurses and Dr. Marquez, Karen's pulmonary doctor, who said, "Her body has to be cooled down again. She's the first person at Mission to ever be cooled down twice, but we can't risk the chance of worse vasospasms occurring."

Mary Kay Bader also chimed in, asserting, "Absolutely keep her body cooled. Though we're pushing the absolute limits with her body, it has to be done."

If Karen could have talked, would she have told me to just let her go? I wanted to believe that she kept pulling through repeated trauma to assert her will to live.

Three days later, Karen was rushed to the OR with yet another vasospasm. I was told that this time, larger amounts of Verapamil were injected into her cranial arteries. Dr. K, the neuro-interventional radiologist, identified a severe right anterior cerebral artery and left anterior cerebral artery vasospasm. He injected Verapamil into both areas to help open up the arteries. Dr. K. then used silk sutures to close the groin wound where the catheter was inserted. He told us he anticipated repeat episodes and trips back and forth to the operating room that day.

Jim, Sue, and I took turns writing in the *Caring Bridge* online journal, and that day, we updated it several times. Friends and family all around the world signed in to read about Karen's progress and leave messages.

On August 8th, Jim wrote, "Karen is having a good morning after a rocky day yesterday. We should all take time to appreciate what we have and make every day a special day. Karen has shown us this through her courage."

Though his words reminded me of how I took much for granted, I just wanted another day with my Bear--one more day to say, "I love you." We had shared so many wonderful memories together during the past four years. We went to Hawaii every summer; we drove to Big Sur and stayed at the five-star Post Ranch Inn. Money was not a big concern for us, and we loved visiting nice places.

I often sat next to Karen's bed and wondered if we would ever go on another vacation. I remembered the soft, balmy Hawaiian breeze on Karen's face and the clear, shimmering water of the Pacific, which was something she talked about for many years after. In an infinity pool with a Diet Coke in one hand and a book in the other, I looked at Karen, who smiled and said, "Booie, you are in paradise! You're happiest right here with your book, drink, and the island beauty."

On Sunday, August 10th, Dr. Nwagwu sat in a chair at the bottom of Karen's bed as we talked. "Karen puzzles me, Susan. Her numbers jump all over the place. We seem to get one area calmed down and then another issue arises. Her blood pressure has been too high all morning. When I get one number down, another number jumps up."

"Do you think any of it is related to the Enbrel and methotrexate that she was taking before the aneurysm?" I asked.

"I don't know," he admitted. "I'm going to have to research some of that. So far, we don't think that has a bearing on anything she's dealing with right now. Her numbers must remain stable in order for us to warm her body back to normal temperature."

I remember that Sunday morning so well. I chose to go home early to be with the dogs and watch football. Guilt ate at me. I had never missed a day at Karen's bedside, but every day I thought, I should have stayed longer with Karen. The nurses told me I needed rest too.

The following morning, the doctors wanted to warm her body. I had doubts. Every morning, Karen's body seemed to react differently. It was hard to believe that anything would ever be normal again.

The doctors gave the nurses the directive to begin the warm-up process once again. They had given this directive many times before, so I don't think many people believed it would work. However, Karen's numbers had stabilized, and the staff thought she might be ready for the next stage of recovery. It seemed like every time Karen took one step forward, her body took two steps back. We were only on day fourteen. Some families were on day 50 or 70--lengths of time I couldn't even imagine.

Karen and I had been together for four years by this time. Gay marriage was legal in California, and a colleague of mine offered to get his ministry license online so that when Karen woke up, we could marry. Peter Boyd was a wonderful man who also taught in the English department at my school.

On Monday morning, I learned that though Karen's numbers were steady, the warming process hadn't been initiated. I was in a quandary, unsure if it was or wasn't taking place. Karen was on hold. The doctors were still watching her numbers, which still weren't stable. The reality was that her body couldn't survive a hypothermic state forever. I sat with her all day, going in and out of her room. I talked to her, held her beautiful hands, and prayed and cried while she slept.

"Bear, can you hear me? I need you home. The doggies need you to come home too. Can you please wake up?" I wanted to believe that Karen heard me. In some part of me— lover's intuition, perhaps--I knew that she could hear me. I was beginning to wonder how much more her body could take.

Rationally, though, I knew Karen couldn't actually understand what I was saying. Her coma meant she wouldn't be cognizant for at least another two weeks. As I reflected on this, I was graced by the presence of Lynn, a religious woman and dear friend who would come over in her motorized wheelchair and sit for hours at Karen's bedside. She took note of everything that took place in room 12. I knew that Carol and Bob were in town the coming weekend even though I never saw them. They knew I was with Karen every day, so they visited at night. Lynn told me what time Carol arrived, what time she left, and what she said. Lynn also noted that Carol was mostly reserved when she was in the room. Of course, people don't often show their true colors in front of people they don't know. Carol had no idea who Lynn was, but Lynn had become one of Karen's many guardian angels.

Chapter 6—Warmth

After two weeks of my new lifestyle, I had to return to work. I was unsure how I was going to teach one hundred eighth-grade honor students and make sure I was following the curriculum, because test scores needed to be high and every teacher was being scrutinized.

I took one day to set up my classroom for the new school year--an almost impossible task because my OCD told me I couldn't break the ritual of being at Karen's bedside. It never bothered Karen that I suffered from OCD, as everything in our home had its place. The remote control was a big issue for me; I could never have it pointed at me. When we would watch television in bed and Karen would put the remote down, if it was pointed at me, I would ask her to turn it around, and she would. It was refreshing to have a partner that allowed me my idiosyncrasies.

Upon arriving at the hospital on Tuesday, August 12, I was greeted with more bad news. Karen's erratic blood pressure had resulted in another vasospasm, though the scans showed no additional brain damage. The doctors decided to leave her body temperature low to stabilize the spasms; there was a delicate balance between allowing her brain to heal and putting more stress on her entire body.

Dr. Lempert was back in town and was talking to the other doctors about another procedure they had planned for the next day. That Tuesday was therefore filled with anxious waiting. But hadn't every day been about waiting?

I sat with Karen throughout the day. She seemed to be stable, but I had learned that in our new situation, Karen could go from stable to being in danger in mere seconds.

Though exhausted, I wouldn't have done anything differently. I ate at the same restaurants, saw the same people, wrote e-mails, updated Karen's online journal, and slept with the dogs, then got up the next morning and did it all over again.

Karen and I used to walk the dogs in the evening. She would wear flip-flop sandals and handle Madi, our youngest; I had the two boys. I used to tease Karen about her flip-flops. How could she walk a dog in them? I always wore my running shoes even though I wasn't a runner. We would walk around the neighborhood where we lived, commenting on the homes and landscaping. Karen loved to analyze landscaping.

She worked harder in our home than I did, but we shared equal responsibilities with the pups. Now all the work was on me, as Karen was fighting for her life. As I sat at her bedside, I realized what Karen had done for our home and me. I prayed to God that He would return her to me-- the sooner, the better.

August 13th became a day of celebration. As I stood by Karen's bed, the nurses came over and told me the doctors had given them the directive to warm Karen up! I'd been hearing this for days, of course, but her numbers had been stable the entire night, so there was a good chance that she was actually ready. There were three critical days when vasospasms were concerned; Karen had almost moved beyond the initial vasospasm timeframe, having endured more vasospasms than other Mission brain aneurysm patients had ever experienced. Though this was good news, she was still hanging on by a thread.

When her body was warmed up, all hell could break loose, as a vasospasm could be on the brink of occurring. The chance of Karen having another stroke also increased day by day.

That evening at home, I received a call from a new doctor, Dr. Cho, who said he would be performing a tracheostomy on Karen to relieve the pressure of some of the many tubes in her body. This would be a new step in the direction of recovery. I knew in my heart that with the way things were going, it was risky to rely on hope. I also didn't fully understand what it meant to have the tracheostomy.

When Karen and I decided to buy our first home together, it was a big risk. We had been together for only one month, but we still went for it. I believe that we must take risks in order to get ahead in life, and the process of warming her body up was just another situation in which we had to take risks and see what happened.

Early the next day, August 14th, as Karen's body slowly warmed, she had another vasospasm. She was rushed to the OR, initiating a code blue at 10:14 a.m. She was given CPR, and by 10:20 a.m., the code was over. She had survived another near-death experience, but her brain had gone six minutes without oxygen, so it was possible she had suffered brain damage. At this point, I could hardly think straight. My nerves were shot; I felt as though Karen and I were both hanging on by a thread.

When she was wheeled back to her room, I saw that a cold towel had been placed over her eyes, which were so badly swollen that she hardly looked Japanese anymore. It hurt to look at her, as her face was a round, abnormally colored ball of puff, and she looked like she was in pain even though I knew she wasn't.

Though she coded in the OR, they continued to warm her up. It was imperative that she be able to maintain a normal body temperature. She wouldn't survive otherwise. I watched and waited even though the warming process was nothing to see, as it was all taking place inside of Karen's body. While I looked at my partner, I wondered what damage had taken place after this coding.

Karen was a brilliant woman who commanded great respect in all areas of work and life. We loved watching Jeopardy, and she would beat me every time. Would brain damage prevent this from ever happening again? I wondered if she had lost her brilliance. Waiting, again, was all I could do.

On the morning of August 15th, I was greeted with the best news; Karen's chart said "Overnight: no new events!" Dr. Kim had even used an exclamation point. He must have been overjoyed to see a break in what had become one of the toughest cases the Mission Hospital SICU had ever seen. He smiled a rare smile as he spoke to me, and I cried out of excitement. The room seemed quieter than normal, but perhaps that was just my imagination. I didn't bolt outside to the patio, so the machines' beeps were welcomed that incredible morning.

I understood Dr. Kim's exclamation point to mean success--at least for the day. At that point, I would take any exclamation point. Nevertheless, I still acknowledged that the threads of hope I hung onto were in fact only threads, knowing that one instance of overnight success was not the same as Karen sitting up and talking to me. We were only on day 19, whereas there were people in the waiting room talking about their experience 90 days in. There were no guarantees in this wild world of brain aneurysms. Every day offered the gift of something new--good or bad. Though I'd been told there was brain damage, I never let my mind linger on what brain damage would look like if Karen pulled through.

Lifting Karen's hand, I placed it on my arm. I wanted her to be able to put it there herself. Her intense need for care, her

touch, and her smell--even though it was that of the hospital--
led me to one realization: Karen and I would be together forever. I wanted to feel her touch, kiss her lips, and let her know
that I was there to stay. I believed she felt this and that this was
why she fought so hard to live.

As Karen continued to recover, her blood pressure remained erratic, and she needed a diuretic because her body
was retaining many fluids. Often enough, nurses would
literally run to the supply cabinet and get a vial of Lasix,
which Karen's body seemed to crave. I wondered how such
a small body could take in so many medicines and bottles
of liquids.

I stayed the whole day, talking and singing to her. Television does us such a disservice when portraying a patient
waking up from a coma. I originally thought that Karen could
easily wake up and return to her life. Then I learned about
the Glasgow Coma scale, which provides a numerical way of
quantifying the state of a patient. Karen was at level 1 on the
scale, and it would take weeks for her to even open her eyes. I
was learning something new every moment.

I kept thinking about how I wanted us to walk up the
stairs to the Tree House at Post Ranch Inn in Big Sur, where we
had stayed four different times. It was something Karen and I
both loved to do, marveling at the splendor of the mountains,
trees, hills, and water. Once inside, we sat there quietly, sali-
vating at all the beauty God had created.

As I walked into room 12 on Saturday morning, Karen's
nurse Alison looked over at me and gave me a hug. I was surprised when she began to cry. "You know I'm doing everything
in my power to keep Karen alive," she said.

Alison had been with Karen for days on end. I said, "I
know you are. I've never doubted your dedication and love.
Why are you crying?"

"I just want Karen to live. You're so dedicated to her." I felt so proud at that moment. There didn't seem to be a way to know if I was making the right decisions and doing everything I could, but at least my love was evident to other people.

"She will, Alison--she will." How ironic that I was comforting the incredible and caring nurse who knew so much more than I did. Alison became one of the most important nurses who cared for Karen, and she was inspirational to me. It seemed like we had already built a deeper connection. I looked over at Karen. Her skin was soft, but there were scratches beginning to form on her small face because of all the white tape holding down the tubes in her nose and mouth. I whispered in her ear, "I love you, my Bear." Somewhere in her deep coma, I believed she could hear me. My teacher voice is loud and distinctive, so I knew she would recognize it.

Alison said, "I had a talk with Karen this morning. I told her that she had to live and that she needed to make a move today to show us that she was going to turn the corner."

Alison put so much of her effort into Karen's care, poring over her charts, calling doctors, running to get medicine, changing tubes, cleaning Karen, and generally being attuned to her every need. Karen definitely demanded all of Alison's attention in the SICU that was for sure. I wondered if Alison thought about her after she went home, though I never asked if she did. Maybe I didn't want to know. I knew one thing for sure: Karen was in the best hands possible with Alison.

The mall was across the street, and I needed a break where I could sit, think, and not look at the machines keeping Karen alive. I purchased a box of cookies from a café to take to Alison--such a small gift for someone who tried to give me the biggest gift ever: Karen's life. Alison thanked me for the token of appreciation and said, "She's showing some improvement already. Her body is back to a normal temperature, and her color is great this afternoon. Perhaps my little talk with her this morning worked." That was a good sign. We hugged and both wiped away a few tears. I went home finally feeling hopeful that Karen might turn the corner.

On the way home, I thought about our relationship, remembering when Karen and I were physical with one another. I remembered how much fun that was. I wondered if the sexual part of our bond would return or if it would be gone forever. Again, brain injuries offered no guarantees one way or another.

On the morning of Sunday, August 17, I hoped Alison would be on duty again, but the nurses' schedules changed depending on what patients needed, the nurses' expertise, and the nurses' schedules. Alison was there with Karen that day, praise God. She had worked three twelve-hour shifts in a row with my Bear. Karen was considered high-maintenance, yet many of the nurses fought to be on her shift. This always amazed me. The nurses worked their tails off for Karen. I felt that Alison was whom Karen needed most, though.

There were two high-profile cases in the SICU at that time: Karen and Adam, who was 24. Adam had entered the SICU on August 12. He had been riding a bike and wasn't wearing a helmet. The bike stopped suddenly, lurching Adam over the handlebars and head-first onto the asphalt. His girl-friend called 911, and Adam was rushed to Mission Hospital in critical condition.

Adam was just down the hall from Karen. His head injuries and lung issues were as life-threatening as Karen's issues. His brain had swelled so severely that he had to have a craniotomy, which meant that part of his skull was cut off. I became good friends with Adam's mom, dad, and sister. We sat together, cried together, and occasionally laughed together. Karen was 16 days ahead of Adam; his family was just beginning to get acquainted with the number system in the SICU.

When she was healthy, Karen's entire job involved dealing with numbers. She had to negotiate with clothing manufacturers for the best prices in order to maximize sales. How serendipitous--her life now depended on numerical negotiations with God and Buddha while in a coma.

On Sunday morning, Alison turned the oxygen level of Karen's ventilator down to 55. It had been at 100 since day one, so we both celebrated this major step with smiles. Her Licox measurement was also in the mid-20s all day, which was another good sign.

"We make clinical decisions based on the Licox measurement. It also told us that Karen's heart wasn't pumping correctly on day one," Mary Kay Bader had told me.

When the Licox number dropped, Karen was in danger, death looming ahead. Several times when the Licox measurement had dropped, I bolted outside the room, heart racing and palms sweating. All the numbers meant something when added together. I wanted to know as little about the numbers as possible. They were the doctors' and nurses' job to monitor. My job was to be with Karen and to love her. That was all I could handle.

Before her aneurysm, Karen and I spent all our time together after work each evening. Our weekends were filled with weekend trips, dinners out on the town, and tranquil evenings at home with one another and our dogs. Our relationship felt right in so many ways. With Karen in her coma, I often pondered why I had ever thought about leaving her two years before. We had parallel lives, and our values were the same--no smoking, no drugs, and no alcohol, for example. That was hard to find in many other relationships I had been in. I desperately missed my Bear.

The next morning, Karen was to have her tracheostomy. It felt as if new procedures were constantly coming up. *Will tomorrow be the day I can let my guard down?* I was exhausted. School would start soon. I had believed--hoped-- that Karen would be out of her coma by the time I went back to work. I had no idea how I would balance teaching, doing chores at home, taking care of the dogs, and watching over Karen.

When I arrived at the SICU on Monday, I was told the tracheostomy would not take place. Karen had to be taken back to the Angio Suite for a vasospasm medication touch-up. The little ray of light I had seen the day before had already dissipated so quickly. Were we headed back into the dark abyss of fear once again?

Karen had had a clinical drop in her Licox measurement and was still being medicated for small vasospasms. I thought, at this point, that it wasn't just a matter of how much more her small body could take, but also how much more could I take. Emotionally, I was drained. Physically, I was exhausted. I felt like a robot at times, just going through the motions day after day. However, by the time I left Karen's side that Monday, her Licox measurement was back up to 24--a safe number. I could breathe a bit easier on my way home.

Home was where I found solace. Spending time with our dogs and sitting in front of the television was peaceful. I didn't have the energy to do more than that. I was known as a strong person with a lot of energy, but the mental fatigue and stress were causing me to break. I was even losing weight even though I made sure to eat two meals a day.

For the next few days, Karen was taken to the Angio Suite daily to have CAT scans, some of which showed changes and some of which didn't. I knew the scans revealed more informa-tion about how Karen's vasospasms were healing.

On August 23, day 29, great news arrived: no vasospasms were evident. Hallelujah! Karen was doing better. She had begun to move her head, tongue, and hands. My brother, Sue

Mordin, and Karen's nurse, Heather, were all-present to see this monumental moment!

Dr. Marquez walked in, exclaiming, "Oh my gosh, Karen moved her hand! I saw it move!" How great it was to see one of Karen's doctors as excited as we were. She would have another CAT scan at 4:00 a.m., and if the results were decent, Karen would have an oxygen-monitoring Licox device removed from her skull. However, none of us knew the extent of the damage that had already taken place in her brain.

Heather chose to work another shift the following day, as she wanted to be with Karen when Dr. Kim removed the Licox. Heather had worked endless hours with Karen and had become another favorite of mine; she was bright, sweet, and caring, and she seemed to love Karen. Though quiet, I knew she was rooting for Karen as much as I was.

When I walked into the SICU the next day, Heather gestured for me to run over to Karen's room.

"Susan, watch, this!" Heather pinched Karen, who scowled. Karen could feel what was going on!

"This is a great sign. At least we know she's in there under that coma, ready to come out."

Dr. Marquez entered the room, and Heather went to check on other patients. "This is such great news for all of us," he said. "Since she's now responding to the nurses, we want to begin waking her up next week. I must remind you, though, that this is a very slow process. We must all be patient. It can and probably will take about two weeks for her to open her eyes." He smiled. "I also have to remind you that she could be in her own coma under this medically-induced coma we've kept her in since day one. We won't know until we lift the medical coma. For now, though, let's all rejoice in how far she's come."

Another coma? I had heard this weeks ago, and I didn't want to hear it again. *Please don't let it be true.*

Heather poked her head in and said, "Here comes Dr. Kim. I think he has a present for you."

He walked into room 12 with a smile. "Susan, here's Karen's Licox! I put it in a baggie for you. I thought you might want to keep it." His rare smile proved that this was an incredible day for all of us concerned about Karen. He was right--I did want to keep the Licox as a memento. It was one of the instruments, which made Mission Hospital a great hospital for treating brain injuries. I had learned that not every trauma unit knew how to use a Licox on brain-injured patients.
I thanked him profusely and said I'd cherish it forever. "It's one of the tubes that saved Karen's life," I said cheerfully. Dr. Kim smiled, and someone took a picture of us with the Licox in the baggie.

"It is, and I think that at this point, we can say she's truly turned the corner," he said with another big smile. I felt at this moment that Dr. Kim and the entire staff in the SICU were heroes.

Chapter 7—Movement

After the news had spread that day about Karen's progress, she had many visitors. Everyone who read my *Caring Bridge* journal entry wanted to see Karen. As she began her journey back to us, she moved her head, arms, and hands. These were magical moments, and we had waited a month and a half to see them.

When Sue Mordin came in at 9:00 am, Karen had her arm across her belly. Sue asked Heather, "Why is Karen's arm across her belly?"

"Karen decided to lift her arm out of the arm rest and put it on her belly all by herself! She's telling us she's more comfortable this way."

At this point, I was getting ready for school to start, so I got to witness her movements mainly on the weekends. Sue visited Karen every morning and texted me with updates. At 2:40 p.m. every day, I rushed out of work and raced down the freeway to be with Karen.

I was excited to be with her and wanted to see for myself everything she was doing. However, no matter how eager I was walking into room 12, Bear was usually sound asleep! All her physical activity in the morning literally exhausted her.

I would sit in the chair by Karen's bed and watch her sleep. The bedside chair was soft, with a comfortable seat, and the little window behind Karen's bed seemed to illuminate her body more than it had before. Her room had become so familiar to me by this point, with its Purell smells; even the beeps of the machines all seemed a bit quieter than before. At least I knew she was waking up and could move parts of her body. Though this gave me relief and hope, there were questions I still didn't know the answers to: would she walk? Would she be able to swallow and eat? Would she talk? No one could answer these questions--at least not yet.

Even through the darker, scarier moments, I had been positive and hopeful, and several times when I witnessed the difficulties of her condition, I thought about how she was taking baby steps in trying to come back to us.

I went home to our cozy condominium, where three cocker spaniels loved me to death no matter how exhausted I was. We ran up the stairs to our third-floor bedroom, where I changed into my pajamas and sat at my computer to answer e-mails. I was also on the phone until 9:00 p.m., talking to friends and family who were calling to check on me. One of my colleagues, Julee Blair, called every night at 9:00 p.m. to see how I was doing. This became one ritual in my life I could count on.

That night, I took a lavender bubble bath, lining the bathtub with candles. I reflected on all the times Karen ran my bath water and called me when it was ready. I wondered, as I lay in the tub, if Karen could ever do this for me again. I missed her so much. Even though we were lacking a sexual relationship, I relished living with Karen and treasured everything we shared. Her condition reminded me that I truly felt I had found my soul mate.

The Democratic convention was on that night. Karen and I had enjoyed watching it together in the past. For any feminist, Hilary Clinton's 2008 presidential campaign was enormous news. We used to watch all the primary races together, but now it was only the dogs and I. I prayed that God would give Karen back her life so she could experience history in the making alongside me.

On August 27th, the new school year had begun, and I was going to meet 100 new, needy eighth-graders. As an experienced teacher who had won the Teacher of the Year award in 2007, I was fortunate that my lessons were already prepared, as I had dozens of binders of lessons.

My days began at 5:45 a.m. when I rose, fed the dogs, showered, dressed, and went to Coffee Bean in order to arrive at school at 7:00 a.m. As soon as I unlocked my classroom door, students began to file in. School didn't begin until 8:00 a.m., but students loved to be in my classroom early each morning. Regardless of whether they came alone or in groups, I was always ready to be with them.

I walked down the long cement corridor leading to room 14, balancing my blueberry tea latte, briefcase, and purse. When I got to my door, I realized I didn't have my classroom keys. I put everything on the ground and fished for the keys in my purse, picked everything up off the ground, and unlocked the door. I flipped on the lights, ready to begin my day.

Despite my chipper attitude and experience, I wasn't fully prepared for the first day of school. My heart and soul were back at Mission Hospital in room 12 with Karen. In changing my routine, my OCD had been exacerbated, and I didn't know how I would balance the many elements of my new life. Everything would be different this year.

Last year, I had agreed to teach an extra class to sixth-graders. There was no curriculum for this writing class, and I wouldn't have a conference period--a cherished break for teachers--for the entire year. I spoke to the principal and tried to get out of teaching this extra class given my new circumstances, but it was set in stone; one doesn't fool around with the school's master schedule once it's set.

To make things worse, they had asked me to take on a student teacher for the year, which my principal ironically thought would relieve some of my stress. Adding a student teacher to the most stressful school opening of my career was actually the worst mistake he could have made. It was one more person I had to be in charge of, and not only was it another person in the classroom, but someone who was relying on me for teaching knowledge and mentorship. If my OCD had a voice, it would have screamed that my world was crumbling--and school had only just begun.

I readied myself at my desk, students filing in to begin their day. Some were in jeans and sweatshirts others donned shorts and polo shirts. Everyone had his or her shirt tucked in and wore a belt--a dress requirement at our school.

I typed the agenda and put it on the overhead. The students liked to know what they would be working on in my class each day.

My hair is a spiky, silver, and purple work of art, and teaching tattoos grace both of my arms. Perhaps it is my "dare to be different" attitude that draws students into my classroom. Though new students sometimes expect me to be mean because of what they've heard from old students, they quickly learn that I'm strict, not mean. The students know what I expect and soon understand that I'm a caring teacher. I'm proud of my Teacher of the Year award for good reason; I demand a lot from each student as I prepare him or her for honors English in high school.

I had wanted to be a teacher since high school, at which point I thought I wanted to teach deaf students. I worked hard and earned an academic scholarship to attend my dream school, the University of Southern California. I was the first in my immediate family to attend college and was jubilant when I was accepted. However, after only one year at USC, I decided I was tired of school and quit, wanting to experience life and earn money. I lost my scholarship and never looked back.

I went into banking, following my father's footsteps. After that, I became a professional bowler, and the highlight was a trip to Japan to open bowling centers. I wasn't making much money bowling, so I returned to banking and decided it was time to go back to school. I still wanted to be a teacher and needed to find out how to make that happen.

I went to junior college and then transferred to Cal State Fullerton, earning my English degree and my teaching credential. I also earned my master's degree in educational counseling from National University. It took me sixteen years to earn both degrees, but I did it. I have taught eighth grade ever since.

Karen had studied biological sciences at Cal State Dominguez Hills. She graduated with her degree in biology but decided she wanted to work in clothing manufacturing. We met when I was in my 13th year of teaching and Karen had been in the clothing manufacturing business for nearly 20 years. Like most couples, we'd had a few problems during our four years together, but her ruptured aneurysm had become the biggest battle of our lives.

Karen's sister Carol had told family and friends I would just walk away--that I didn't have the stamina to stay. I knew deep down, though, that my mom and dad had raised a caring and stubborn daughter. I had the determination, love, and sense of commitment that was necessary. How ironic it was for Carol to think I would walk away when it was she herself who abandoned Karen. I never left Karen's side.

Even though I had no idea what I would be facing with her in the future, I loved her, and my commitment to our relationship was solidified as a result of the brain aneurysm. I felt reawakened to the love I had for her. Out of the eight partners I had had in my lifetime, Karen was the soul mate I wanted.

On day 31, Karen received her tracheostomy, which would allow her to breathe more easily. We all celebrated this next step in her rehabilitation. What a difference it made! When I came to see her after school, most of the tubes were gone. Her face, without mounds of wires and tubes, lifted my spirits. I wept with happiness. Karen's attempt to come back to me was overwhelmingly rewarding. Her body, while still enduring the trials of survival, was moving toward recovery.

There was a certain brightness to the room that had never been apparent before, and it seemed the light was radiating from Karen this time. It was a moment I will never forget. Heather was on her lunch break, so I ran to another patient's room, where I found Michelle, another SICU nurse. I told her the great news, and she ran back to Karen's room with me. She cried too! Full of joy and hope, I kissed Karen's face and just knew she would wake up.

Again, television creates a false sense of reality where comas are concerned. Of course Karen wasn't ready to wake up just because I kissed her soft face. She was still on coma-inducing medications that she was being weaned off little by little. I had to take a deep breath and let my disappointment bring me back to reality.

As I wiped away a fresh set of tears, I had the thought that Karen was never going to just open her eyes and begin talking and walking like nothing had happened. I hung onto the good news but kept this piece of reality on the backburner.

A bit later, Karen was able to take a few breaths on her own for her respiratory therapist, Felipe, who had become my rock in times of doubt. We were undoubtedly still running the marathon that I had been warned about thirty days before.

In those days, I was in a hurry to see Karen after school. Every day offered new insight into her progress.

One morning, Dr. Nwagwu, Karen's neurosurgeon, saw her move. I know he was as excited as I was because he was a caring doctor. Our friend, Sue, wrote in Karen's journal, "We certainly are watching a miracle take place." She was so right. Karen was a miracle, and each one of us was experiencing this miracle firsthand.

Karen was given a feeding tube three days later, marking a milestone in her 34-day recovery. Another IV pole was positioned to the right of her bed, and a bottle of tan-colored liquid was hung on it. It contained all the nutrients her body needed. Television dramatization aside, it seemed as though she was truly beating the odds. With the feeding tube in place, she was beginning to be weaned off all her coma medications. At this point, the entire waking-up process was in full force.

Because I was anxious to watch Karen slowly awaken, I was elated when the weekend came. When I walked into Karen's room on Friday, August 30th, I turned on her iPod and played soft Christmas carols. Even though she was Buddhist, she loved Christmas carols. I had been playing Christmas carols so frequently that one of the nurses said, "Susan, do you think we can put on some other music? It's only August, and the Christmas carols need a rest!" I laughed, a bit embarrassed. I had been so focused on Karen's needs that I wasn't considering anyone else's.

Of course, we started playing something different, which I decided would be relaxing piano music. With the Angels game on the television, I held both of Karen's hands in mine. They were soft and warm, and I fell asleep.

When I woke up, Karen's hands were moving! Her mouth was slightly open, and she was trying to wiggle her tongue.

She turned her head toward me now and then. My body was warm with delight knowing that Karen was moving, if only for a moment.

I went across the hall to a room where another brain aneurysm patient was staying. I knew her daughter and husband well because we had spent so much time waiting together. I asked the daughter, "May I see what your mom is doing since she is waking up from her coma?" I was welcomed in. I watched Mrs. T. as she sat up in her bed and tried to say a few words. I was quiet because I didn't want to interrupt her recovery. The daughter and I exchanged a few words, and I thanked her.

I went back to sit with Karen, confused. Mrs. T. didn't look very good. I'm not sure what I expected to see, but she certainly wasn't bubbly or talkative. In fact, the experience scared me more than it helped me.

Kris Sisterhen of Karen's day nurses said, "Get in Karen's face and talk loudly to her." Well, talking loudly was never an issue for me. I was given the gift of a booming teacher's voice and would have probably been able to wake everyone up from his or her coma in the SICU! I leaned in closer. "Bear, you're in Mission Hospital, and you've suffered a ruptured brain aneurysm." I paused, thinking of the right words. "Bear, it's Boo. You're healing and recovering. There is nothing to be afraid of." I told her this repeatedly because the nurses said she needed to know the truth. I was never one who got tired of talking, but by the end of that day, I was pretty talked out.

I have to admit that I wasn't sure how these words would help Karen. If she were still in her coma, would she even know what I was saying? Was she able to comprehend even one word? Could she really hear me telling her where she was?

Of course, Karen did not respond in any sense, but I wanted to believe she could hear me. The nurses had said it was imperative that only positive words be said in the room.

"She hears what we say and will react with body movements," they stressed. I posted this idea on her *Caring Bridge* page. I knew that Carol would read it, but the SICU staff would not let anyone negative near Karen.

I went back to work after having a blessed weekend watching Karen continue to improve. It was great to be in my classroom where I had control of something. OCD wanted order somewhere in my life, and I could feel the need for rituals rising inside of me repeatedly. I counted tiles wherever I was. I wouldn't say certain words like "vasospasms" or "die" around Karen, fearing it would be bad luck. I needed control somewhere, and since I was virtually helpless in room 12, I looked to classroom 14 to offer control to me five days a week. While I taught, I kept my phone on my desk in case the hospital needed to get in touch with me.

During the middle of my lesson on Monday, day 36, I heard the theme from *A Summer Place* playing--my ringtone.

My heart skipped a beat. I excused myself from the kids and answered the phone. Karen had been making such great strides in her recovery. I couldn't imagine why they were calling me--unless it was to tell me the worst.

"Susan, it's Lynda from the SICU. You need to hurry and get down here. Karen is sitting up, and she opened her eyes for the first time." I rushed back into class and told my students. They cheered and clapped for Karen. I was tearing up. I had been waiting for this moment.

I called the front office and told them that I needed to have my class covered. In the teaching profession, an administrator or another teacher must cover a class in such situations because the kids can't be left alone. I also had to get the seating charts out and put the lessons for the day on my desk.

I ran through the office and out to my car, my purple L.L. Bean briefcase thudding against my hip. Speeding down the freeway, I arrived at the hospital in 14 minutes, no traffic to deter me—and there she was, her eyes wide open! It was the first time I'd seen Karen's eyes since the morning the brain aneurysm ruptured. I screamed and cried. Six terrible and exhausting weeks had gone by, and finally I was seeing the beautiful brown eyes of my love.

However, something was wrong. Her eyes were covered with a gray film. It looked so odd that I wondered if she could see at all. Still, they were Karen's eyes, and they were open! She looked confused, and I wasn't sure that she knew who I was. It didn't matter. I believed she would know me in time.

Though Karen wore glasses, the nurses said she wasn't ready to wear them. Everything was new to her, and there was doubt that her eyes would recognize anything, especially with the gray film covering them. I remembered standing in the circle of prayer for Melisa during the first week of Karen's recovery and later finding out that Melisa was blind.

On day two of Karen's aneurysm, the nurses taped her eyes shut because they wouldn't stay closed. It was important they stayed closed or they would dry out. It was so difficult for me to see Karen's eyes taped. She seemed fragile, and of course she was, but her not being able to keep her eyes open or closed was concerning to me.

Years later, I found out that Dr. Nwagwu thought she might have been made blind by her trauma. Dr. Nwagwu had never seen a patient coming out of a coma that had film covering his or her eyes.

Friends started flooding the hospital. Once I posted the great news on Karen's journal, people came by in droves. Sue, Peter, Michael, Mandie, and Becca my little niece and I all squeezed into Karen's room, where we stood in awe. I cried frequently, and others cried too. We had all waited and worried, wondering if this day would ever arrive, and here we were, looking at her with her eyes wide open. She turned her head slowly from left to right as each of us said hello to her. I know she didn't recognize us yet, but she heard us and could respond with movements—just as the nurses had said. It was certainly a promising beginning.

When the staff took off her white beanie, we saw that her hair was beginning to grow back. Dr. Guu came in and said, "This is one of the happiest days of my life. She's come so far in her recovery. She still has a long road in front of her, but many of us wondered if we would ever see this. I'm so happy for all of you."

Her doctors wanted her to rest as much as she could.

By this time, I felt like a member of the SICU staff. I used to kid with Dr. Nwagwu by telling him that Sue Mordin and I were ready to become neurosurgeons! We could speak their language.

I decided that it was time to write to Karen so that she could read my notes someday in the future. I got on Caring Bridge and wrote:

Dear Bear,
I knew you could do it! You are filled with strength and a desire to continue to be a large part of this world. Sharing our retirement years has always been important to both of us. I can't wait until you are fully awake so I can tell you all that happened during the entire month of August while you slept. It's hard to believe that you missed the summer Olympics in China, something you were so looking forward to, and the beginning of Hillary Clinton running for President of the United States. Today I got to see your brown eyes, your head moving left to right, and your hands moving all over the place. Your tongue was moving too, trying to lick a small piece

of skin that was on your lower lip. Your tongue moved slowly knowing something was there but not sure how to get to it. You are doing things that we all take for granted. I love you; Bear, and I promise I will be by your side throughout this journey and for the rest of our lives. You are my Bear, and I'm blessed to have you.

Love, Boo

Chapter 8—Team Karen

Labor Day weekend proved to be eventful as well. Karen was urinating and having bowel movements on a somewhat regular schedule. When I walked into her room after school on September 2, I noticed a new bag hanging off her bed. I asked the nurse what it was for, and she said that Karen was having so many bowel movements that they decided to use a catheter. I never knew that you could have a catheter up a rectum. Even though this was a promising development, it was tough to see.

Karen's doctors made their rounds. When I saw them, they each made comments about her recovery. Each doctor said it looked like she had turned the corner and that her recovery was commencing. Even just the start of the marathon had been quite a journey.

School had been in session for a week. My lessons were prepared, but I still had to take papers home to grade. That part of my life wouldn't change. OCD kept me in check, and I was actually thankful for the order it created in my life.

When I was eleven and on a family vacation, I had been locked in a bathroom at a gas station in Denton, Texas. I think I was only in there for 10 minutes, but to my child self, it felt like a lifetime. I screamed and screamed, scared to death. My Grandpa heard me as he came out of the men's bathroom. He told me how to turn the lock, and in a moment, I was free. This incident marked the onset of my OCD. The ritual of reading and having to re-read billboards became a constant. Counting tiles and touching objects with my left hand and then switching to my right hand in order to feel balanced were also particular rituals that emerged. Some would find them exhausting, but not me. The rituals and the order they created was one way I survived my first weeks of school that year.

A woman in charge of insurance at Mission Hospital came to Karen's room to talk to me, shattering the euphoria of the good news. "You need to think about moving Karen to a sub-acute rehabilitation center." Insurance would only permit so many days in the SICU, I learned, and the room cost over ten thousand dollars a day. That meeting sent me over the edge. A sub-acute rehab would move Karen out of Mission Hospital and put her in another facility.

Standing outside of Karen's room, I cried. I was scared. I wasn't going to let insurance dictate where Karen needed to be moved or when the move should take place. Karen was fighting so hard to live, and the doctors and nurses were busting their butts to keep her alive; insurance was not going to demand anything.

I took a moment to breathe and consciously feel the impact of the previous five weeks. I was tired—exhausted, really--and my emotions were fragile. When I let myself visit the recesses within my soul, I was amazed by how much my life had changed forever. It's one thing to know this subconsciously and a very different thing to fully experience and embrace it.

After my discussion with the insurance representative, I stepped outside to reconnect with myself. It was a warm August afternoon, and the heat was welcome because the SICU was always so cold. I sat on the hard green metal chair, looking around at the patio where I had spent endless hours with family and friends. This time, I was alone. I've never liked being alone; I enjoy having people around, and I relish talking, but everyone had gone home for the day.

My emotions vacillated between highs to lows, with no in-between. I didn't have Kleenex, but I didn't care. The tears kept flowing, and I kept wiping them away. I moved to the slightly more private green bench next to the soda machine and let my heart fully take over. I wasn't one who cried often, so the release was good for me. I felt my entire body purge itself of tension.

When I regained some control, I got in the car and went to Coffee Bean—my happy place. The rich smell of coffee that permeated the cafe re-enforced the safe feeling of this special place.

Peter Mordin and his daughter, Diana, met me there, offering strength. We went outside with coffee and sat at a green table with green wrought-iron chairs, the trees surrounding us offering a hopeful sense of life. In seeing another set of green metal chairs, I wondered what significance the color green had for me. It seemed to be everywhere. None of the green metal chairs in my life were comfortable, that was for sure.

I often looked to Peter for wisdom. He was a lawyer, so there were definitely times I needed his practical advice. Around us, people were coming and going, eating dinner and moving through their daily lives, oblivious to the fact that we were discussing everything that had happened recently with Karen. It was odd to watch the world rushing forward when my world had felt like it was on hold for the longest time. Though I tried to stay strong, school duties were adding more pressure to my life. I was thoroughly exhausted and wanted to take Karen home but couldn't. I sat with the Mordins for over two hours, discussing my many feelings.

Peter said we could go and look at the two facility options for Karen, but I wasn't ready to see her leave the nurturing womb of the SICU. I went home and spent the evening thinking it over. Peter understood insurance, so I knew I could trust him to lead us in the right direction.

When I went back to the hospital the next day, Dr. Nwagwu was with Karen. I told him about the discussion I had with the insurance representative. He said not to worry; Karen wouldn't leave the SICU until she was ready. As it turned out, that is exactly what happened. Karen remained in the SICU for quite some time.

Karen's room was cozy, which I knew she would've loved. We decorated her door with pictures of family, friends, and our three dogs. The frigid air in her room was difficult to withstand at times, but that was just the nature of the SICU. Karen hated to be cold, so sometimes I would ask the nurses to put another blanket on her or wrap a towel around her hands to keep them warm. I don't think she knew if she was hot or cold, but I wanted to take care of her needs in my own way. The nurses were always kind; when they put blankets on her, I knew they were doing it more for me than her. I trusted the staff and made efforts to stay out of their way especially when they were working on Karen.

Heather, who spent a lot of time taking care of Karen, later said, "Susan, you always stayed out of our way, which we appreciated. You are there for Karen, but you let the doctors and nurses do their job." I was glad to be recognized.

After each weekend was over, I went back to teaching. I controlled the lessons, the environment, the students, and their education, which was very rewarding.

The school day seemed long, but I enjoyed the stability it provided me--possibly because my job was the one area of my life that hadn't changed. Still, I couldn't wait for another weekend.

When I arrived at the hospital on Friday, September 5th, I was told that it was a 'status quo' day, which I learned indicated that it was a great day in Karen's recovery. It meant that everything had stayed the same and there were no new worries.

In a life of trauma that was constantly changing, it was a relief to see that Karen's world inside room 12 was beginning to stabilize.

When I went to Coffee Bean on Saturday morning, my coffee club was sitting outside. I took 10 minutes to sit and talk with everyone about Karen's progress. The idea that I used to sit with these people for two to three hours every Saturday and Sunday, but was now limited to about ten minutes, was yet another sign of how my life had changed.

Room 12 was waiting for me, and I was greeted with more great news upon my arrival. Karen had been taken off the ventilator during the day and put back on it for the night. The nurses told me that this was a big day in her recovery. As she slowly came back to life, the nurses again insisted that only positive words be said in front of her. She heard what was said and reacted with body movements; I felt she was noticing our positivity.

On Saturday, Karen burped when I was with her. I didn't know that a burp could be so amazing, but it was, as it was another step in her recovery. Little by little, she was coming back to us, and I was beginning to believe that she would be normal again one day.

I went home that night and pulled several pairs of Karen's pajamas out of her dresser. She loved her pajamas, so I wanted them ready for her when she came home. I was thinking ahead. Way ahead I would soon find out.

I went back to school Monday feeling elated about the big strides Karen had made over the weekend. I shared her progress with my students. I had always referred to her as my best friend, but they had pretty much figured out that we were partners.

Halfway through my class I received a phone call from the SICU again. It was Friday. This time it was from Karen's day nurse, Kris. "Susan, Karen said her first word. Hurry and get here!" I told my students the fabulous news, and they all clapped. Once again, I got coverage for my class and ran to the parking lot.

When I got to Karen's room, Kris had Karen sitting up in her bed, waiting for me. The word Kris had referred to was "oh," which it turned out was the only thing she said all day. It was enough for me to know that her voice was ready to come out.

After I updated *Caring Bridge*, everyone scurried over to see this miracle in action. The SICU was packed with friends and family wanting to see Karen's eyes and hear her speak. She slept a lot but was able to look in the direction of whoever was speaking.

Karen's hair was growing more under her white beanie. I could tell that she would need a haircut soon. When I told our hairdresser, she offered to come to the hospital and cut her hair for free. It was heartwarming when people did things like this for us. Karen's cousin brought food for me one day too. Karen and I were always doing things for other people; I mentored students from my classes, we hired one of their mothers to be our housekeeper, and we gave the kids clothes, electric blankets, and even furniture. I was glad that people were doing things for us in this situation.

Though many stood around Karen's bed and wanted to talk to her, limits were established. She couldn't have a lot of stimulation and was exhausted after about 10 minutes of interaction. Some in the room tiptoed outside to the patio after she fell asleep each day, but I stayed with Karen and Kris because I didn't want to miss one minute of Bear returning to me.

Times like this reminded me how much I loved Karen. I missed her presence in our home. I wanted to sit across the table from Karen at our favorite sushi restaurant in Irvine. We used to talk about our day at work over dinner. I thought about all of this as I sat and watched Karen sleep.

Sitting next to her bed that day, I felt guilty about the times I had taken our relationship for granted in the past. Karen did so much for the both of us at home. We had a hand-made river rock stone fountain in our backyard that was about five feet high and five feet wide. It was stunning and soothing. Every month Karen took her cleaning kit outside and scrubbed this enormous fountain from top to bottom. Seeing her on the precipice of life and death made me understand just how important she was to me.

After Sue Mordin had heard Karen speak her first word, she wrote in the *Caring Bridge* journal: "Yesterday was awesome! It was a special moment seeing you sitting up with your eyes open, tracking people and reacting to sounds and names. We knew this would happen and prayed so hard for this miracle. To hear your doctors and nurses say such amazingly positive things about your progress makes us smile."

I wasn't sure if all this progress meant that Karen was still in danger of being in a natural coma. I had learned a little each day about being in a coma but had never really figured out where the line between the dark abyss of death and the light of recovery was drawn.

September 6th, I walked quietly into Karen's room and was greeted by her big brown eyes watching me intently. I bent over her face, and our eyes locked. Then she immediately fell asleep! I wanted to talk to her, but her stamina was minimal. The nurses told me she slept a lot and would continue to do so. This was just part of the process of waking up from her coma, I understood.

I needed events like the ones that had just taken place— Karen being taken off the ventilator, opening her eyes, and saying her first word. They had rejuvenated me so much.

One of Karen's co-workers, Aileen, updated *Caring Bridge* with: "Karen, I'm not sure you realize what a powerful effect you have had on so many of us, reminding us all how to have hope and to believe in miracles. I can remember the first days after your trauma when several of us at work, instead of complaining that there was so much left of the work week, would speak of how appreciative we were that we could work; we were so happy to be able to help you. Your strength and perseverance, along with Susan's, have reminded us how important it is to never give up. Because of you, we have a positive outlook--a gift I think Susan certainly has been blessed with. You remind us to always stay positive. Even though this is a difficult time, Susan you are a wonderful hostess to all who come by to check on Karen."

When I read the journal entries each evening, I was proud of how I handled myself day in and day out. The people in our lives who stood beside me and came to see Karen every day, or at least a few times a week, made me feel like I had a team supporting me. Sue Mordin had named us "Team Karen." Karen had so many people praying for her recovery.

On Saturdays and Sundays, I tried to be at the hospital by 8:30 a.m., anxious to see what Karen would do. On Saturday, she had another outstanding day. When I arrived, she was awake, so I spoke to her. To my amazement, she began making faces at me! She smiled, her eyes tracking my movements. She scrunched up her face.

Dr. Kim came by to check on his prize patient, greeting her in his usual way. Karen actually waved to him. I think he was the happiest I had ever seen him. He asked her to hold up two fingers, and she did!

I liked helping Karen hold things. She wrapped her beautiful long fingers around an item, and I said, "Work through it, Bear." Her lips moved to repeat my words, though no sound came out. Every day was a miracle, and I was honored to experience each one.

Because there had been so much improvement up until this point, I wasn't ready for a bump in the road on Sunday morning.

After I had been in the room for a few minutes, I noticed Karen was gasping for air. I yelled, "Something's wrong!" Without a word, the nurse on duty paged the pulmonary doctor. It took maybe a minute for Dr. Marquez to arrive and determine Karen needed a breathing tube change, as it had recently been switched and was not working, as it should. She was doing so well that the respiratory therapist thought the recent change would be a step forward, but instead, it created a problem.

Dr. Marquez substituted the smaller trach tube for a larger one and asked Karen, "Do you feel better now?" She nodded. I was happy to see her oxygen level improve right away.

I felt the SICU staff were as excited as I was in seeing Karen continue to improve, but they had to keep their expectations realistic. Her friends were overzealous about her small but amazing strides, and everyone, including me, wanted recovery to happen immediately. Brain trauma recovery doesn't work that way, though. I had learned that setbacks would happen, but this breathing tube setback still scared me. It was difficult seeing Karen having a hard time breathing.

After this event, I thought I would go outside to sit in the warm sun. Each time I started to leave, though, Karen grabbed my arm. She didn't want to sleep; she wanted to be with me. I was thrilled to spend the whole day right next to her.

At one point, she put a finger in her left ear and right nostril. I never knew I could be so excited to see someone put her finger in her nose. This is something she never would have done before her injury. She was a woman with high standards and impeccable manners, so it was quite funny to see her with her finger in her nose.

I took Mom to the hospital with me later that day. She hadn't seen Karen in a few weeks and she wanted to participate in her progress. My mom loved to dress to the nines. In her fancy jeans, off-white sweater, and gold necklace, she looked stunning. I always felt at peace with Mom by my side.

She strode over to the right side of Karen's bed, pulled up a chair, and looked intently at her. I didn't say a word. I had a feeling that Mom was conversing with God and Karen at the same time. When she reached out and put her hand on Karen's arm, my heart swelled. This moment brought back so many memories of when I was little and Mom used to take care of me. Karen was close to my mom too. She always called my mom "Mama," and I was always touched by their love for each other.

Karen had about 14 visitors over the course of the weekend. One of Karen's cousins brought sandwiches. Others just brought themselves. Brian, Karen's cousin came with his partner Mark. It was great to see them both. I felt as if they were on our side. Brian loved Karen and I knew she would be elated to know he was at her side.

I stood in the hallway so Karen's room wouldn't be over-crowded, watching her carefully for signs of exhaustion. I needn't have worried, though; when she got tired she closed her eyes and fell asleep in an instant.

I thanked everyone for their constant support, but had to remind them that the nurse limited visitors to two at a time. Over stimulation could impair her healing. She needed rest more than anything. It was difficult for me to post this in her online journal, but Lynda, who was Karen's nurse that day, said it was imperative to Karen's outcome that visitations be limited. Of course, I was allowed to be at the hospital as much as I wanted, but everyone else's presence had to be kept to a minimum.

Sue Mordin was also given permission to have unlimited time with Karen. Sue continued to be my eyes and ears while I was teaching. Her morning texts meant so much to me.

It was becoming harder and harder for me to go back to school each day. Even though I loved my students, Karen was making so much progress that I wanted to spend every waking moment with her. I missed many of her movements because most of them happened in the early part of the day. By the time I arrived each weekday, Karen was exhausted and sleepy.

On September 8th, Sue wrote on *Caring Bridge*, "What a wonderful present you gave Peter and me today on our wedding anniversary, Karen. Thank you! How could anyone have the right to ask for more? We talked to you and again you moved your hands and arms. You are and always have been a genuine and heartfelt friend, and to feel the spirit of our friendship once again was more deeply moving than we could ever put in words. We all believed deep down that this day would arrive, and it did! Thank you, God, for giving us back our friend. Even Dr. Nwagwu, who was in the room with us said, 'Phenomenal. You never get used to it.'"

Where was I when all this took place? I was at school, teaching!

Aileen Berger, who had worked with Karen for many years, was at the hospital often. She had gone in to see her on the same day after Sue and Peter had left. Aileen got a smile, and she was even able to hold Karen's hand. She wrote that she was over the moon and got goose bumps when she read Sue's post.

I loved our *Caring Bridge* journal because I was able to access it from my school computer on my breaks; I could see who was visiting Karen and how she was responding. Each positive, exciting report made me long to be in room 12, not room 14.

Chapter 9—In the Sun

On September 9th, the 44th day of Karen's journey, I was given the best news ever. Kris said Karen was going to get in a wheelchair to go outside for 15 whole minutes! My favorite number is 44; I was a huge Lakers fan in the early seventies, and my favorite player was Jerry West, who wore jersey number 44. I love the coincidence of my favorite number aligning with this day of Karen's journey.

The double doors that held Karen in so tightly and safely were about to open for her. She would get to feel the warm summer sun on her skin.

Everyone was cheering Karen on. She was moved to the wheelchair, and an oxygen tank was placed on the back. I stood next to Karen, tears dripping down my face and goose bumps covering my arms.

Michael was there to share this moment with me. While the staff was getting everything ready for Karen's first ride outside, I taught her how to count to five with her fingers. She repeated each number slowly and responded to my questions confidently.

Though this day was a huge turning point, I was also really beginning to realize how much Karen had lost due to the brain aneurysm. She had been a math wizard who handled millions of dollars at work. She had often sat at our dining room table for hours doing figures on spreadsheets that I hadn't ever learned how to do. After the aneurysm, though, she had to learn to count all over again.

I still believed she would be able to recover and be the person she was before all this. I never let myself travel into the dark abyss of thoughts about how bad it could have been and instead tried to stay in the moment. The dark abyss would mean death, so I never let my mind enter that realm of inescapable horror. I kept myself in the light by praying that each day would bring Karen closer to her former self. My heart couldn't smile, but it at least never let go of the possibility of life. Still, amid the joys, it was sometimes heartbreaking to see how much Karen had lost.

Kris got Karen situated, we were ready to roll. The SICU double doors opened wide. Karen's friends and family—plus staff members, like Mary Kay Bader--stood outside, waiting for her to come through the next set of double doors. As Kris pushed Karen, I thought about how proud I was that she was able to hold her head up--a miracle in itself. Then a smile emerged on her face. Though it was a half-smile, it meant that she had not lost the ability to move her facial muscles.

Once she was outside, I maneuvered her wheelchair over to our car and asked, "Bear, do you know whose car this is?" She smiled her half smile again and replied, "Yours." She knew my car! Perhaps this wasn't such a remarkable thing because of my personalized plate, but in that moment, it didn't matter.

I asked her what she was thinking. Unsurprisingly, she didn't answer. She hadn't seen natural light since the morning I rushed her to the hospital, so I'm sure she was basking in the moment. Her world had been dark until this day.

The light was so beautiful on her features that I relished the miracle taking place. The light from above meant that God was opening the door a crack. This milestone gave me reason to believe that anything was possible.

Fifteen minutes later, Kris wheeled Karen inside and put her back in bed. Sleep was especially crucial since this was the most activity Karen had consciously experienced in 44 days. It was a beautiful beginning, but it exhausted her.

Karen was starting to really come back to us, and not long after her sojourn outside, Lynda asked me to bring Madi, one of our cocker spaniels, to the hospital. She actually begged me to go back home and bring her to the SICU to see Karen.

I had bought Madi for Karen 3 years before when she was diagnosed with rheumatoid arthritis; I thought she needed a reason to get up every morning. Work was one thing, but having to get up to walk and feed a puppy was an additional motivator.

I drove home, got Madi, and drove back to the SICU. I knew therapy dogs were allowed because a lady had brought her beautiful black therapy dog in to see Karen the first week she was in her coma. I never thought they would encourage me to bring Madi in to see her.

As I drove down the 405 freeway, I was excited; thinking about what Karen would do or say. Then doubt set in. *What if she doesn't remember Madi?* There was a good chance she wouldn't. Madi meant so much to Karen. She followed Karen to every room in our home, and the two slept together every night. Joshie and Benson were my boys, but Madi was Karen's girl. I was frightened that Karen wouldn't remember her baby.

Madi was our wildest dog. She liked to bark, run all over the place, and give kisses. I parked in my regular parking spot that everyone seemed to leave open since they knew I liked to park there. Even the parking attendant guy knew me by name.

I walked Madi to the internal double sliding doors, where I was buzzed in immediately. Lynda had Karen in a sitting position when I came in. I put Madi on Karen's bed, and she sat right next to her. I was so excited that I began talking rapidly, exclaiming, "Bear, its Madi! Remember your puppy?" She stared at her, saying nothing. Slowly she reached out and touched Madi's back. Madi sat so still that I knew she could feel something was wrong with Karen. I told her, "Talk to her, Bear! It's your baby girl." I wanted Karen to jump up, call Madi's name, and wrap her arms around her faithful puppy.

However, that didn't happen. She sat there quietly, one hand on her back her fingers gently rubbing the soft fur on Madi. At least the two of them were together again.

Finally, Karen lifted her right arm and stroked Madi's warm, soft fur. I could see that their eyes were filled with love and devotion. When I think of all the material things we want and the many details of life we take for granted, such as brushing our teeth and turning on a light switch, I try to remember this day when Karen and her dog, Madi, were reunited in touch and love. Every moment in our lives is precious, and this reunion proved that to me more than anything.

Madi sat next to Karen like a queen. She never barked, and she let everyone pet her. It struck me as what a true therapy dog would do. I know that somewhere deep inside, Karen felt Madi's love.

Not long after seeing Madi, Karen hit another bump in the road. When I was at work, I was informed that Karen's lungs were filled with fluid, causing shortness of breath. Another cat scan was ordered, and the staff decided to remove the fluid through an ultrasound-guided thoracentesis. Dr. Konstantarakis, the interventional radiologist, needed to insert a large needle into Karen's lungs, and the nurses needed verbal consent from me for her to have the procedure. I gave the verbal consent over the phone for the nurses right away, though I was nervous.

When I arrived at the hospital after work, the nurses told me that 60 cc's of fluid was removed and that this allowed Karen to breathe easier once again. I breathed easier too—until Dr. Guu sat me down.

He said, "Susan, Karen is recovering well. However, you must know there will be days where she will take one step forward and two steps back. That's just the process for a brain trauma patient."

"Why does recovery take so long?" I asked.

"When a patient has a ruptured brain aneurysm the magnitude of Karen's, we never know what the outcome will be until they come out of their coma and begin the rehabilitation process. Karen is very fortunate to have lived at all. Most people would have died. From what I have seen so far, I think she will recover well, one small step at a time."

He smiled. "Remember the marathon I told you about on the first day? You just passed the starting gate. However, do you remember where we were 7 weeks ago? Karen has made fabulous strides in her recovery."

I loved Dr. Guu. He was honest and caring. He always gave me a dose of reality first but ended our conversations with positive comments.

When school had been in session for two months, I was able to connect well with my kids, teaching with the authority and care that I always had. Essays were written and turned in, novels were read, and portfolio work was unfolding. My routine was set.

At home, I turned my thoughts to Karen. I had to compartmentalize my two lives. Because of the Paxil that I took daily, I was able to remain calm when I worked. It was imperative that I be able to live in these two vastly different worlds. I realized that I was the only breadwinner now and that we had gone from two hefty salaries down to one. It helped that I had a therapy session each week as well. Dr. Kaplan helped me to live within the walls of each of my two worlds. We talked about how I would handle my thoughts and I undertook a lot of introspective work. She remained my rock.

September 10th was another outstanding day for Karen. When I arrived at the hospital, she was sitting in her wheelchair. Many of her nurses came to her room to see her, and she put on quite a show for them.

Karen wouldn't stop gleefully bouncing her right leg. I asked her, "Bear, why are you bouncing your leg so much?" and she replied, "Happy." Alison and I cheered for Karen. She remembered our finger counting activity from the day before, and we did it several times. How often have all of us taken our counting ability for granted? On this day, I was amazed that Karen could count to five, and I will always remember her skinny fingers rising one at a time as we counted together. My heart smiled as I watched another small miracle take place.

Chapter 10—Small Steps

Karen was evaluated for her next level of recovery on September 11th: the Mission Hospital's unique Progressive Care Stroke Unit (PCSU). At this point, she was mouthing words but not full sentences, and was able to recognize faces, yet unable to say names. She wasn't in any pain, but she became tired easily. She was able to follow commands.

The doctors and nurses noted that she seemed depressed, but this was normal for brain trauma patients, and she could be put on an SSRI to combat depression. She was mouthing fewer words than before, and her smile seemed to have become a frown. I think that deep down, she knew something was going on but was unable to communicate this to me. Since I took an SSRI for my OCD, I was 100% in favor of Karen taking medication if needed.

Later that evening, I learned that Karen was going to leave the SICU--the womb that had held her so tightly and safely for six and a half weeks. She was ready to move to the next unit of rehabilitation. She was a bit agitated and depressed that evening, so she was started on Prozac.

I remember that she took her finger monitor off, so I had to put it back on, telling her that it monitored her pulse and needed to be kept on. She nodded, understanding. I then turned her iPod on, and we listened to Ella Fitzgerald, one of Karen's favorite singers. She did some arm dancing and hand clapping. Her movements encouraged me, as they indicated that many of Karen's limbs were working.

Friday, September 12th was one of the hardest days, as I wasn't ready to see Karen moved out of the SICU. I taught all day and rushed to Mission Hospital. When I walked into room 12 I was greeted by an empty bed. A room once filled with so many machines that you could hardly walk around was now empty. I got an eerie feeling. Was the room waiting for its next arrival? Would another patient be worse off than Karen?

I looked at the bed and the light shining through the small window at the back of room 12. The tube once affixed to Karen's skull that emptied the excess blood into a bucket behind her bed was gone. Only the bed and a monitor were left. The room seemed colder than it ever had. This had been home not only to Karen, but to me as well. I knew everyone in the SICU; everyone knew me. *What will happen in her new room?* I was told she would have a nurse that would be in charge of three patients at a time. What if the nurse was with another patient when Karen needed her? Karen didn't know how to press her help button. *What if Karen has trouble breathing?* Who would be there to save her? I couldn't stay overnight at the hospital; I had to take care of the dogs and teach each morning.

I ran down the hall to room 133, Karen's new home. I met several of the nurses and the charge nurse, who seemed nice.

I walked over to Karen and said, "Bear, you're in your new room. How does it feel?" There was no response. She just stared at me. She had been mouthing words just a few days ago; what happened? My shoes felt glued to the linoleum floor. My heart was aching; I knew I had to go home in a few hours but wanted to just sleep on the chair at the foot of her bed. I panicked.

One of her nurses came in and explained how the PCSU worked. She let me know right away that she had three patients to care for and could not be with Karen every minute like the nurses in SICU.

"What if Karen needs something? She doesn't know how to call you!" I screeched.

"We do a great job here in the PCSU and I think Karen will be ok." *Just ok? My God, does this nurse have any idea what we have been through?*

When she left, I told Karen I would be right back and ran down the hall toward the SICU as fast as I could. Karen's former nurses came over and wrapped their arms around me.

Laurie Roberts was the first to reach me; she was a kind soul who knew me well. Alison also came running over with hugs. They told me that every time a patient leaves the SICU, it is harder on the family than the patient. They both told me it would be okay and promised they would go and see Karen in her new room. I walked back out the double doors and down the shiny hall, my head hung low. When I walked into Karen's new room, she was fast asleep. This time, I was the one suffering.

I left the hospital that evening with a heavy heart. On my drive home, though, I tried to remember that going home to rejuvenate was advantageous for me.

I couldn't wait to return to the hospital on Saturday morning. I maintained my routine of going first to the Coffee Bean and then the hospital; it worked for me, so there was no need to change things. I had to keep my order.

When I arrived, Karen was awake, her gaze on the wall opposite the bed. As I quietly walked over to her, her little brown eyes lit up. Her lips formed a sweet smile. No words were exchanged--just a great deal of love.

Often we are afraid of silence filling a room, but I knew Karen so well that I knew no words were needed. We used to laugh at how we could finish one another's sentences or thoughts; we would sing songs together, stop quickly at a certain word, and notice that one person would pick the song right back up and sing the next line or two. We loved moments like this. We were often in the car when we would sing together. Would we ever get to sing together again?

A nurse came in and said Karen had a good night. Sitting in a wheelchair for an hour had been Karen's therapy for the day. The nurse told me that the therapist was going to move Karen's legs and arms and try to have her sit on the edge of the bed. I was there to witness it all.

I guess I hadn't really noticed Karen's legs in the SICU because they were always covered with blankets and cooling pads. I knew she had lost weight, but what I saw on this Saturday shocked me. Karen's legs were so skinny. They looked brittle— like they could snap in half. I was afraid to touch them. What if they had to remain perfectly still in order for Karen to live? I wasn't going to jeopardize any small success Karen had already made. She always had beautiful legs, but now they looked as if they would crumble if anyone so much as touched them.

Karen sat in her wheelchair for an hour, and Sue and Peter came by to visit. We sat around Karen and talked as if she could jump right into the conversation. I continued to count and recite the alphabet with her. Peter talked to her like he used to about his work. I handed Karen a marker and small whiteboard that Peter and Sue's daughter Diana gave her. Karen took the dry erase marker in her hand, turned it repeatedly, and looked at us, not saying a word.

Since I use dry erase markers every day in my classroom, I took the fact that Karen remembered what it was for granted. I had to show her how to hold it correctly, instructing, "Bear, put two fingers around the middle of the marker. Now take your other hand and push the marker down just a little." This was difficult for her. I nudged the marker a bit to make it rest between her thumb and pointer finger. It worked.

I had learned so much about what I took for granted and what Karen had lost. I studied her face as she continued looking at the marker and playing with it. Sue explained to Karen what it was and how to use it. Watching Karen try to keep her grip on the marker as she made a small line on the board was gratifying but horrifying. My heart sunk. I never thought that something as simple as holding a marker would be an issue.

She became tired easily, and after an hour had passed, the nurse came back in and said it was time for Karen to nap. We watched the nurse put Karen back to bed. I kissed her and told her I would be back later that day. She waved at Sue and Peter and quickly fell fast asleep.

As we walked to our cars, I wondered who would speak first. "Well," I finally said, "I think we're seeing progress. I'm not sure what I was expecting, but for Karen to sit up for an hour is a miracle in and of itself."

Peter looked at me and smiled, saying, "Small steps, Susan. Very small steps are valuable for Karen's recovery. Today we saw something we thought we would never see, and that was Karen sitting up in a wheelchair. I'm quite excited about her progress today."

I loved Peter and Sue. Peter always seemed to be the voice of reason.

We got into our cars and left the hospital. As I made the drive home, I thought about Karen's recovery. I'm not sure what I had been expecting. I thought she would be walking at this point, but she wasn't there yet. I had to try to settle for Karen sitting up in a wheelchair for one hour while holding a dry erase marker and trying to understand what it was.

I visualized us in Big Sur again, climbing the stairs to our tree-house room and being surrounded by nothing but God's beauty. Mountains and hills of green were to our left, and the glistening water of the ocean sparkled on the other side of the road. *Will Karen ever be able to walk those stairs again?*

I went to dinner with my mom and stepdad that evening, and we all went to see Karen afterwards. This was the first time Karen was awake when Mom came to see her. Karen's eyes lit up when I told her Mama and Jim were here. She clapped her hands together for them, which was something I was teaching her to do. Then she gave them the queen's wave that Sue Mordin had taught her. My parents were thrilled to see what Karen could do.

We left, as Karen got ready for bed; she was tired because of how many visitors had come by that day. I left for home with a smile on my face, as I knew each day was a little better and that we were seeing Karen making small strides.

That night, I took the dogs out for a walk. Walking three dogs seemed easy to me after watching Karen begin to recover from her coma. The gardeners had just mowed, so I smelled the sweet aroma of cut grass. I even took a phone call from Julee Blair, my buddy, while holding all three leashes.

As we walked around our neighborhood, the dogs and I took everything in. Joshua, Benson, and Madi loved to smell every tree, and that was fine with me. I noticed every flower and eucalyptus tree along the immaculate streets of Irvine, our planned community that Karen and I loved. This tranquility only intensified my longing for Karen to return. We had walked down these streets with our dogs so many times together. I wondered if we would ever do it again.

Work was a therapeutic release too; I could feel my breathing soften when I entered room 14 at my school. I knew Karen was being taken care of at the hospital, so I tried to put all my energy into teaching between the hours of 7:00 a.m.-2:35 p.m.

On Monday, September 15th we celebrated day 50 of Karen's recovery. Of course, when I arrived at the hospital, she was asleep. She had sat up in a regular chair earlier in the day and done physical therapy in the morning, so she was exhausted. I watched her sleep, kissed her sweet face, and left to have dinner.

When I came back the next day, I got a "hello" and "doing well" from Karen. At this point, Karen was being evaluated for the next phase of rehabilitation: the Acute Rehabilitation Unit. If she qualified, she would continue her recovery at Mission. It was something we all wanted for her; we could sense that in the PCSU, she was getting bored.

It seemed like everything was going well, but a bump in the road revealed itself on Saturday morning. When I walked into Karen's room, Sue greeted me. She talked quickly, her face had a strange look. I went over to Karen, kissed her pale face, looked at Sue, and asked, "What's wrong?" Sue replied, "Karen's dehydrated!"

Everyone in the SICU had worked tirelessly to lead Karen to where she was in her recovery. What could have happened? Just another hurdle I thought.

Dr. Guu, who was still Karen's internist, was called in immediately. He said Karen was dehydrated. He put in orders to get her hydrated immediately with an IV.

I sat next to Karen's bed and talked to her softly. I assured her, "You were dehydrated, but Dr. Guu is going to help you get better." I got a half smile. Karen didn't talk the rest of the day.

When I got home, I sat on the sofa with the dogs and cried. I knew there would be bumps in the road. I just wanted Karen home.

It was a long night for me. The dogs cuddled with me on the bed, and I took in all their smells, felt their soft fur, and vented to them. They were my calm in the midst of yet another storm.

Monday morning while I was at work and Sue was sitting beside Karen, a speech therapist arrived and put a small voice button over Karen's trachea to gauge her speaking abilities. As Sue wrote in Karen's journal, "Karen was able to say over 30 words this morning, albeit they were a little raspy. Whose voice wouldn't be a little raspy after 52 days of no voice and suctioning?"

When I saw Karen late that afternoon, she was sound asleep again. The speech therapist tried to wake her up, but she couldn't. Michael walked into the room and said hi to Karen, who opened her eyes and said, "Hi, Michael!" She knew my brother well and responded to him every time he entered her room.

I showed Karen a *National Geographic* magazine that I knew she would love. I pointed out a fish, and she repeated the word "fish." Then she closed her eyes and fell asleep again.

I loved Friday afternoons when school was over, as I got to spend a lot of time with Karen over the weekend. When I got to the hospital, Diana was asking Karen to write a few words on a small whiteboard. She handed a red dry erase marker to her, as that was her favorite color. Karen took the marker in her hand and rolled it around. Unassisted, Karen wrote the words "hi" and "bye," which were the first words she had written since her coma. Miracles were taking place every day in Karen's new world.

Here I was teaching my eighth--graders how to write er-udite essays using SAT vocabulary words and figurative lan-guage while my partner was learning to write words like "hi" and "bye." What a dichotomy. Karen was brilliant before her aneurysm, and I had long considered her one of the brightest women I knew. It hurt me to see all of this. She had no idea what had happened, and even though I kept explaining it to her, she couldn't comprehend any of it. *Is this all there is going to be for Karen?* A question I frequently asked myself.

When I arrived at the hospital the following Monday afternoon, I walked into Karen's room and there she was, fast asleep. I sat in a chair and waited for her to wake up, because I knew she needed her sleep. When she woke up, I gave her a facial with hospital lotion. Karen hated it. She made a funny face.

The next morning, I brought in her Aveda face cream, and she smiled. It was hard to believe she could tell the difference so soon, but she could. I got the whiteboard out and made a tic-tac-toe game. I marked the first "X," and Karen marked her "O." She played the entire game with me with no hiccups. How did she even remember the game? I had no idea.

I left for dinner but came back afterward, excited because the real Karen was emerging, and I wanted to be there. I bent over her and told her that I had onions on my hamburger for dinner. I asked her, "Bear, can you smell the onions?" She rolled her eyes, dropped her head to the right, and sassily closed her eyes as if she were passing out from the smell of the onions! What a character. I doubled over laughing; Karen had a big smile on her face. I still treasure this moment today.

I tried putting on Harry *Potter and the Sorcerer's Stone*, which is one of Karen's favorite movies, but she fell asleep and began to snore. I kissed her goodnight, and left.

My students asked about Karen each day, and I was excited they cared about someone they didn't even know. I had a pacing guide to follow, so I had to keep the fast pace up even if I was exhausted. I had tests to give the students because our district required them, and we were preparing for the big state test given in May. I knew I was privileged to teach gifted students, and I took my job seriously.

Their essay-writing abilities were of extreme importance. I would craft high-school-level prompts for my students because they were so bright. When I handed out their weekly prompt every Thursday, students would dissect it with passion. After 30 minutes, they were allowed to ask questions. I loved essay-writing day; I enjoyed seeing effort and elation on the faces of my 115 students. A strong thesis statement was a sure way for a student to get a "good job" comment from me.

On Mondays, the kids brought their rough drafts back, and we critiqued them. I would ask a volunteer to come up to the front of the room and place his or her essay on the projector. The class would then discuss what was good or bad about the student's essay. I loved this method because the students learned from their peers' mistakes. Each week I told them, "No one here is ready for Harvard University. Therefore, you aren't allowed to berate someone's work unless you can offer a better way to write his or her essay."

Though the students took some time to adjust to this format, they came to realize that if the class assisted with their essays, they had a better opportunity to earn a higher grade. All of a sudden, kids raised their hands right and left because they understood the benefit of the lesson. I treasured these moments with my kids because I could see immediate improvement.

On September 20th, Mom went with me to see Karen. When we walked into her room, she was doing physical therapy with Vicki, one of the best therapists at Mission. Vicki had Karen sitting up and leaning on one arm in order to push herself up in the bed.

I asked if we could take Karen outside in a wheelchair, and everyone was accommodating. There was no oxygen tank on the back of the wheelchair this time, marking another monumental step in her recovery.

When we wheeled Karen over to the SICU, all the nurses came running over to greet her. They cried along with Mom and me. What a joy for the nurses to see Karen sitting up after they had worked so valiantly to keep her alive. To this day, they are my heroes.

We took Karen outside to the warm, inviting patio. It offered shade, but I could tell that Karen wanted sun. I wheeled her into the sun and she closed her eyes, basking in the warmth. My heart melted. We both loved the sun.

We had returned from Hawaii just three weeks before Karen's brain aneurysm ruptured. I took the sun for granted as I lay by the pool, looking out at Waikiki Beach, sipping my diet coke and reading a book.

In the light of the sun, I noticed that her usually dry lips seemed more supple and that the tape marks on her cheeks were no longer as evident. Could it be that Bear was coming back faster than we anticipated? My heart was betting on it. Many of the hospital staff on duty that day came out to take pictures of Karen. I believe that she had surpassed Princess Diana as the most photographed woman in the world! I was glad that Mom could be with me for this experience.

Mom consistently offered safety and love. When she was with me, I felt anything was possible. She didn't go to the hospital often, but when she did, I could always feel her love embracing Karen and me. Mom had been the rock in our family when my dad passed away at the age of 55. Dad had never gone to the doctor and always seemed healthy, but he was a high-functioning alcoholic—a bank manager and family man.

I have memories of Mom ironing all of Dad's work suits. He was always dapper when he left for the day, wearing a different suit each day of the week. Perhaps I get my meticulous ways from my father.

Some of my most fond memories of my father are from our vacations. We loved to go camping. Dad would stand on the edge of the lake and fish for hours, Mom sitting in a chair with her fishing pole close by. Michael would fish alongside Dad, and I would be back at the campsite in a hammock, reading a book. Lake Cachuma in Santa Barbara, California, was Dad's favorite camping site.

Michael and I each remember that we had a wonderful childhood. Every night at dinner, the four of us sat and talked about our day. I loved the idea that we had special rules and traditions that we respected even when we grew up. We were taught not to talk when others are talking, and when we were through eating we had to ask, "May I please be excused?" Consistency and politeness were my parents' parenting style, providing safety that allowed Michael and I to become competent adults. We loved our family.

Nevertheless, alcohol took over my dad's life. In one weekend, his entire body shut down, and he went into full cardiac arrest. At the time, my brother was in the United States Navy and was stationed in the Indian Ocean. My mom had never lived alone, so this was a particularly horrific time in her life. When Dad passed away, I called the Red Cross to have them get in touch with my brother, and it took two days to get him home.

My father's early death was a crushing blow for all of us. Every holiday, all of our camping trips, every family function, and even our family rules and traditions changed when there were just three of us. Without Dad, who would change a light bulb for Mom? She was short and would have to use a stepstool. What if she fell? No one would hear her. Our family dynamics changed in ways none of us had ever expected. Perhaps this was a lesson I had to live through for Karen and me as well.

The Navy allowed Michael to stay at home with Mom for 30 days. I was in college when Dad died but lived only 30 minutes from home. The two of us were with her constantly, helping make plans for Dad's memorial service, maneuvering bank account changes, and taking care of all the paperwork involved with a death.

The day Michael had to leave to go back to the Indian Ocean was devastating. I drove the three of us to Los Angeles International Airport, and we walked my brother to the terminal, this was 1989, pre 911 security. In his Navy uniform, Michael looked as handsome as ever, and I remember him kissing us both when his plane was ready to leave. He left us with his head down, and he turned to give one last look before he boarded the plane. I took Mom's hand and we both cried. Our family unit was broken, and Michael, now the man of our family, was leaving. I would be responsible for helping Mom grieve and get back on her feet.

Karen was only allowed 10 minutes outside, so Mom and I took her back to her room earlier than we wanted to. The nurse got her back into bed, and I put her covers over her, making sure she was cozy. She was asleep in minutes.

We left and after I dropped Mom off at her house, I went home to see the dogs. Our little cocker spaniels' tails were wagging as fast as they could when I walked up the first flight of stairs. It was hard to believe the boys hadn't seen Karen in almost two months. I hoped they would remember her, but even more than that, I hoped Karen would remember them.

I ate dinner at a restaurant near the house, picked up my sister-in-law, and went back to the hospital. We stopped at the mall across the street from Mission where I bought Karen a giant yellow duck pillow.

At the hospital, Karen was wide awake, and she smiled when we came in. She wrapped her arms around her gift and said, "Hoot-n-Nanny, my new duck!" We had no idea where the name came from, but from that day forward, the duck was Hoot-n-Nanny.

I asked Karen to write the duck's name on her whiteboard. She was able to do so without any help at all! I felt we were seeing a new Karen emerge daily, and I was filled with confidence once again, sure, that normalcy would prevail in our lives.

The next day, however, was a reminder that there is no normalcy where this kind of recovery is concerned. I was told Karen had an infection, which is common for patients who are in the hospital for long periods. I had to put on a mask and yellow gown when I visited her. She was exhausted, so she didn't talk much; she was happy to be in her bed napping. I was very glad when the nurse told me later that evening that Karen's lab tests didn't reveal further evidence of infection.

Though still tired, the physical therapist came in to work with her; Karen looked up and said, "No!" We took this as a sign of Karen asserting her independence. She worked hard each day and needed to work harder in physical therapy, which she was doing in order to progress to the Acute Rehabilitation Center.

Adam, the young man who joined Karen in the SICU on August 12, was being rehabilitated too, and he had joined Karen on the same floor. They were in a race it seemed, to get to Acute Rehab first. Adam's family and I kept in touch, often comparing notes on our loved ones. Though Adam was admitted to Mission two weeks after Karen, he seemed to be creeping ahead of her in rehab. My stomach churned when I thought about this. I wanted and needed Karen to be in first place. I loved the Bulloughs, who were like family, and I of course wanted Adam to succeed too--but not more than my Bear.

In retrospect, I should have celebrated Adam's progress, but selfishness and jealousy had reared their ugly heads. I pasted a smile on my face when I was in Adam's room with his family and then slowly walked back to Karen's room with tears streaming down my face. Inside, I was screaming, my OCD not able to deal with the fact that Karen might be in second place.

When I returned to work the next day, my kids embraced me in smiles and attention, allowing me to lose myself in teaching. Standing in front of the students with my voice bellowing a new lesson filled my heart with joy. Watching students understanding a concept I taught was beyond rewarding, and knowing that I was changing their lives for the better was the fuel that kept me going. I knew that in the near future, I would be taking on a new teaching challenge in taking care of Karen. Despite her progress, her mind was probably equivalent to that of a young child. I knew I would become her teacher as well.

I tried to keep my school life and hospital life separate, which was a nearly impossible task. My OCD helped me most of the time, but there were days when my energy was depleted and I couldn't separate my two lives in the same way I usually did on my drive home. Exhaustion came into play when I had a demanding day of kids needing me even a tiny bit more than was typical, meetings at lunch, or parents calling to talk about their child's grades.

I never took papers to the hospital to grade; I made sure that was strictly for home. When I taught, I tried to focus solely on teaching, and when I was with Karen, I put all my energy into her. To this day, it surprises me how I separated my two worlds most of the time yet still had energy for our three dogs when I arrived home. School was truly a safe haven for me. It was a place where I had all the answers; in the hospital, on the other hand, every minute could mean something knew.

Chapter 11—Rehab

I had an ineffable feeling that Wednesday, September 24th—day 59--would be the greatest day in Karen's recovery. When I walked into her room in the afternoon, she was sitting up on the edge of her bed.

She was put into her wheelchair, and I wheeled her down the hall to meet Adam for the first time. As I pushed Karen into Adam's room, she looked all around, finally resting her eyes on Adam. "Hi," she said with a straight face.

Adam, wearing a helmet to prevent further injury, replied, "Hello," and that was the end of the conversation. For the Bulloughs and me, though, this was a moment of glory. Two people, both with head traumas and still fighting for their lives, were meeting one another. My jealousy deteriorated in this moment, and for perhaps the first time, I was completely pleased that both were in recovery.

When I took Karen back to her room, the speech therapist was waiting. Karen looked up at her and said, "Hi." The therapist smiled as she walked over to Karen and began asking questions that required only one-word answers. I stood next to her wheelchair and was thrilled to hear her "yes," "no," and "maybe" responses. This went on for about 10 minutes before Karen started losing focus.

When the therapist left, I was so pleased with Karen's work that I excitedly handed her the whiteboard and red marker, telling her I loved her. She wrote on the board "4-ever!" Words can't express what a moment this was for me. I thought back to how I longed to have Karen tell me she loved me the many days I sat at her bedside. For six weeks, only my voice had been saying the loving words we once so often spoke to one another, but now Karen was returning my love. I stood there with tears running down my cheeks; sure, that nothing could top this moment. Then the head of acute rehab walked through the door.

"I have great news for the both of you. Karen, you will be transferred to Acute Rehab tomorrow, and this will be your final stage of rehab at Mission before you get to go home."

I was so happy that I jumped for joy and reached over to give Karen a hug. She was finally on the last leg of her recovery. It was the first time someone actually had made home seem like something other than a distant concept.

I took that Thursday and Friday off from work because I wanted to be with Karen as she made the new transition. On day 60, it happened! She was wheeled to the Acute Rehabilitation Unit, where she would learn how to function all over again. This meant re-learning how to walk, eat, dress herself, and handle personal hygiene. Of course, this would be accomplished with several therapists at her side.

We sat together and sang the theme song from *The Beverly Hillbillies*. I held Karen's hand, and she held mine. I sang while her lips shaped a word or two, and for me, this showed tremendous progress.

Dr. Kim walked in and said, "She will fly through this area!" It was so encouraging to hear those words from one of the neurosurgeons who had helped save Karen's life. Dr. Kim told me back in July that this was a marathon, and I don't think he ever thought Karen would make it to this point in recovery. He had given me such frightening news that first day, and here, 60 days later, Karen was doing great.

I knew there was a God.

Strict rules were to be followed in rehab. Only two visitors were allowed in the room at once, and everyone had to leave by 8:00 p.m. The only weekday visitors allowed were Sue and I. Karen would need to get used to her new area and to the intense therapy schedule.

Peter came on Sunday, and we took Karen outside in her wheelchair together. She was the star. Her sense of humor was just like her Auntie Matsy's. Auntie Matsy had a dry sense of humor, and Karen was beginning to show shades of that dry humor herself. Her facial expressions made us laugh; she would curl her lips into a half smile, looking in different directions. I wondered if she was experiencing the world differently--like everything in sight was new to her. If she didn't understand what one of us said, she would squeeze her lips together and look puzzled. She raised her eyebrows, and I reached over to touch her lips and smile. Of course, everyone wanted to see her, hug her, and talk to her.

When I took a break on the patio later on that day, Heather, Karen's SICU nurse, found me. "Susan, I want to hear Karen's voice," she said.

I thought this was an odd request until I realized that the SICU nurses and doctors had never heard her talk! Every day they were with her, she had been in a coma. I resolved to make sure all the SICU nurses would hear Karen's voice as soon as was possible.

On Karen's second day in Acute Rehab, I left school early. When I got to the hospital, I learned that Karen's endurance was low, but this wasn't surprising for someone who had just spent 60 days in a hospital bed. She was able to sit on the edge of her bed and get in the wheelchair with assistance. I was able to take Karen outside to the garden for a short time, which we both loved. I would initiate conversation, but as was usual for her those days, she responded with one or two words--"yes," "flower," and "red" were a few of her go-tos.

Is this going to be my new life? In seeing these glimmers of progress, I constantly wondered about what the future held. I knew Karen was still in rehab, but I was a bit worried about her limited vocabulary. What if we couldn't have our dinner conversations anymore? Karen had planned our vacations, so what if I had to take that over too? I took her back to her room, where she was placed in her bed. She fell fast asleep.

Karen's new schedule was grueling, but in order to go home, she had to do all the necessary work. The therapists told me that Karen might be able to walk again in two weeks.

Seeing Karen struggle with her weakness and endurance was difficult to see. I stood in the exercise room watching every move that she made. There were machines all around us, and big plastic balls lined up against the walls. Nothing looked easy even to me.

Karen wanted to move her skinny legs but couldn't. She wanted to lift her arms around me and give me a big squeeze, but she couldn't. She had been such an independent woman before her aneurysm. I wanted to help her if she couldn't do something like lift a ball, but the therapists told me I had to let her do it on her own. This was the only way she could regain some type of independence.

Karen had a runny nose. I walked over to wipe it for her, but stopped myself, remembering I shouldn't. I got a Kleenex and handed it to her. "Bear, take the Kleenex and raise your hand to your nose to wipe your right nostril." She did it! Such small actions were monumental. She was tired from the events of the morning, and I said I'd let her sleep. In less than five minutes, she was out like a light, tucked in her cozy bed with all her blankets and Hoot-n-Nanny.

On Sunday, many visitors came to see her. All of Karen's visitors were amazed at her progress. Karen recognized most people who came in to see her, but names eluded her. She touched her baby cousin's hand and even said a few words to her family.

When everyone left, Karen and I played hand games. She loved to slap my hands and create rhythm. As she sat in her wheelchair, we danced with our arms.

I went back to work with a happy heart. My students were learning, and I had hundreds of papers to grade to keep my mind busy; I was motivated by kids needing me for this or that and lessons needing to be planned and taught, such as those for *Johnny Tremain* and the Holocaust. The lessons would ensure great test scores for my students.

When I stood in front of these young scholars, my world was calm. It's hard to believe that looking out into the faces of 40 middle school students could have a calming effect on anyone. As thrilling as it was to watch Karen regain her speech, I wasn't in control of her success.

I had joined the MacArthur Fundamental School staff 12 years before Karen's brain aneurysm incident. I had made a few close friends, but overall, teachers were so busy that at it was difficult to be close to more than a handful of people. Julee, who was across the hall in room 22, was a friend I talked to on my classroom phone when something pissed me off. We were sounding boards for one another, good friends and while Karen was in the hospital, it was Julee, who called to check on me nightly at 9:00 p.m. She was the sole person from school who truly showed how much she cared.

Naturally, many faculty family catastrophes had taken place throughout the years. We signed cards; collected money, prepared dinners, and made sure stuffed animals were given to any involved kids.

Our school nurse, who had been at MacArthur several years, lost her husband at the same time Karen was hospitalized. I loved this kind and caring soul, who was dedicated to the faculty and, most importantly, the students. The office did a great job raising funds to support her.

Around this time, I walked in the office one afternoon and saw a large manila envelope being passed around. When the envelope came to me, I was devastated by the blatant reminder of how little regard the staff had for me. I opened it up, looked at the office secretaries, and yelled, "Really?" No one has done one thing for me!" I ran out of the office and to my classroom, my cheeks burning. Not one person on the entire MacArthur campus, save Julee, offered anything to help me out. Not even one card.

In an English department meeting one day, a card was passed around for a noontime school aide. We were asked to sign the card because the woman had donated a kidney to help save her husband's life. However, I didn't sign the card. I couldn't. All I could feel was the tremendous pain from the thought that a noontime aide was more important than I was. I got up and walked out of the meeting. My own English department had never sent me a card. Forget the dinners or money--just one card would have made me feel supported, acknowledged, and thought about for the few seconds it took to sign one's name.

When I had previously asked the entire staff if anyone could be on-call to cover my class given my situation with Karen, out of forty-five teachers, only three offered to help. In this way, my safe haven became slightly hostile. I focused on my kids as much as possible, which usually helped.

Karen was well into her recovery in the Acute Rehabilitation Unit. Around the time she started her new regimen, I took a day off work because I wanted to watch her go through one day of therapy. There was a board on the wall of the unit that listed the patients and what therapy they would have with which therapist. It looked like a grueling schedule to me, and I had seen that Karen was in store for three hours of work in the morning.

I got to the hospital early so I could be sure to see everything. Karen's first physical therapists specialty was occupational therapy. It was her job to see that Karen dressed herself. Then she would help begin her workout in the small Acute Rehab gym area.

"Karen, put your pants on," she instructed, watching Karen. "No, put your left leg in last. Your right leg is weaker, so put that one in first." she was the expert, so I just watched. Though it was still morning, Karen was tired already. She would have occupational, speech, and physical therapy every day except for Sunday. If she were struggling so much after putting her pants on, how would she ever manage the three hours still in front of her?

Next, we went to the workout room. I listened to every bit of the therapist's instructions.

Sue also went to witness Karen's therapy, and one morning, Dr. Guu stopped by and told her, "I have no doubt that Karen will make a full recovery. She will have disabilities, but overall, things should be fine." A brain scan had been ordered for Karen early that morning, but it was only done as a check-up. Everything was healing well.

A week later, on October 1st, I took another day off work because I wanted to see more of Karen's therapy. She worked hard, and before noon, she was able to nap.

That afternoon, I went with Michael across the street to the mall, where we had lunch. He was a man of few words, but he talked a good deal about Karen and rehab. My brother knew the CEO of Mission Hospital, who had heard all about Karen. I think most of the hospital knew who she was.

When I returned to her room, she was asleep, so I sat in a chair next to her bed. A woman walked in quietly with her little terrier therapy dog. The dog jumped up on her bed and howled loudly enough for the whole floor to hear, but Karen slept soundly through the whole thing. Everyone kept telling me that sleep was good for Karen's brain. She was certainly a champion sleeper!

That evening, Sue posted on *Caring Bridge,* "Susan, you have been the most wonderful partner ever to Karen. You could have walked away, but you didn't."

I was touched. I knew that when I learned how bad her condition was on day one, I could've turned around and walked out. Even though we had talked about separation just a month before her aneurysm, we had concluded that we loved one another and wanted to share our lives together forever. Karen's hardship solidified my commitment; I would not leave her side.

I was Karen's first partner and the first person she had moved in with. Ours was a special bond. Naturally, I wanted her to live, and even beyond the vows we had made to each other in achieving domestic partnership, I wanted to be there for her until I left this earth.

I had no doubt that Karen would have done the same for me. Memories flooded my mind as I sat there watching her sleep. She would cook, clean, and go anywhere that I suggested. We loved to travel, and she was a great traveling partner. She filled our water bottles with iced tea for road trips, packed a lunch for us, and always shared the driving with me. Even on days when my OCD demanded the remote face the television, Karen was accommodating. She loved Christmas just as much as I did, and we decorated our Christmas tree together each year. We hung our stockings and filled them with excitement--just like two kids would do.

A week into intense therapy, the heads of Acute Rehab, the therapists, and the nurses met with me. Karen had been in the hospital for 67 days and, according to everyone, was just now starting down the road to real recovery. Dr. Guu said it might take at least another 67 days for her to achieve a state of normalcy. Karen needed to work hard, but she became tired very easily. We talked about a sub-acute rehab option whereby she could recover at a slower pace and not exhaust herself. I was actually quite happy about the possible move; it sounded like Karen needed a slower paced therapy program. I believed she would make better progress. After I expressed my feelings, the staff said they would determine the next step in Karen's therapy plan and keep me informed.

The next morning, Sue sat with Karen in her room, and they communicated and smiled at one another. Karen spoke a few words, and Sue handed her the whiteboard and red pen. Sue asked Karen to write down her thoughts and feelings. Karen wrote down names of loved ones, including our dogs. She wrote that she was happy, but I didn't believe it. I couldn't imagine anyone feeling happy after everything she had been through.

Sunday, October 5th, was the 70th day of Karen's journey. I sat with her and talked about my students and the dogs. Though I tried to get her to interject a word or two, she was quiet. She was so tired. It became clearer to me every day that she was not in the right facility, as I felt the rigid therapy was wearing her down. She talked less, slept more, and didn't seem to smile much. Karen was shutting down, depression beginning to seep into the dark abyss that she had once climbed out of. I could see and feel her sadness.

I went home so Karen could sleep, and once there, I watched football on our big screen television. I loved the

Dallas Cowboys and thought it would be good for me to take a breather. The dogs, excited I was home; climbed all over me, three little stubby tails wagging faster and faster. I handed them each a rawhide bone to chew, and they were content.

After the game, I napped, and then went online and looked at Care Meridian, a sub-acute rehabilitation facility that had been recommended for Karen. It was beautiful: a large house in a country setting that made it look like a soothing retreat. I printed out the information I needed and put it in a folder in preparation for a meeting that would occur the next Friday.

I went back to work feeling calm and hopeful that Karen would be transferred to a good place for her. I took the following Friday off work and asked Sue to go with me to the meeting.

Karen was awake around the time the meeting was scheduled to start, but I didn't think she should go; she needed to rest. She wouldn't understand what was going on anyway, and she didn't need to know that we were going to move her until it was officially planned. In my mind, the decision had already been made.

Sue met me at the hospital and together we walked into the large conference room. Most of the chairs were already filled. The only other time we had been in a conference room was the first week when we met with Mary Kay Bader.

The meeting began with the therapists' reports. The head nurse said, "I think we need to be honest, Susan--Karen isn't doing well in Acute Rehab. I think it's time to think about sub-acute rehab. You need to look at a few facilities and decide which one would be best for Karen."

I stood up and with tears running down my face, and said, "Get Karen ready to be transferred tomorrow morning. She will be going to Care Meridian." I was ready for the change and I looked at Sue and said, "Let's go."

I knew it was going to be difficult to leave the hospital that saved Karen's life. But if she was going to continue recovering it would have to be a program that offered a slower pace.

We walked out of the meeting and went to Karen's room. Sue's daughter, Diana, was sitting with her. "What happened?"

"We're moving Karen to Care Meridian tomorrow.

Sue concurred that I was doing the right thing. We tried to explain all this to Karen, but I could see in her eyes that she didn't know what we were talking about. The longer she'd been in the Acute Rehab Unit, the less she'd talked, and I believed she felt tired.

Though the safe incubator of the SICU was not the same as the cavity of acute rehab, Karen needed a new venue, and I believed somewhere deep in her mind that she sensed something was going on.

October 7th was day 72 of our journey, and I hoped Karen was ready for a big change. I took the day off work and nervously explained to her that we would be leaving that afternoon. Sue and I had discussed our concerns about Karen's mood and hoped she would become happier quickly.

There were so many reasons I was anxious about moving her. The SICU would no longer be right down the hall, the nurses I loved so much would not be close by, and the beloved Bullough family would be left behind. So much had happened in the last 72 days that it was difficult to process all of it.

I gathered everything in the room I had brought for Karen's comfort in Acute Rehab—her iPod, DVDs, and toiletries--and packed it in a small red rolling suitcase. My OCD was kicking into high gear due to my stress and anxiety. It was choking every move I made, wrapping itself around my brain like the tentacles of an octopus. I checked her closet and then re-checked it twice because with OCD, my number 3 ritual was paramount, though I couldn't say exactly why. Everything would be perfect if I did things in threes. Ever since the onset at age 11, I was compelled to do things in threes. When I was in college working on my degree in English, if I didn't feel I had read a paragraph correctly, I would go back and read it three times. If I didn't do things in threes, the fear of something bad happening would overtake my being. No one really knew about my OCD except for Dr. Kaplan. Without her, I wouldn't have known how to understand and manage it.

While packing Karen's things, many of her nurses and doctors came to see her off and say goodbye. Bittersweet tears flowed from many eyes. She gave a small smile to each person who came to say goodbye, though she still had not spoken a word in the past few days.

When the ambulance came, attendants pushed a stretcher with yellow handles into Karen's room. 73 days earlier, I would have run out of the room in a panic. I had never understood my fear of stretchers or ambulances; perhaps I always thought they would take *me* away somewhere instead of the person who really needed the help. Karen's experiences over the past few months had helped me break through the medical aspects of my anxiety. My familiarization with Karen's hospital equipment and her disability, coupled with my father's death and my Mom's widowhood, had become a central part of my acceptance of my fears. Though I had not been ready to call 911 on July 28th, as we prepared to transfer Karen to Care Meridian, I was ready to follow the ambulance I was trusting to safely transport her.

While I followed her through the halls of the hospital I knew so well, I took time to take it all in-- the smells, the periods of chatter and silence, and the details of the emergency room where our time had begun. Mission had not only been Karen's home for 73 days; it had been my home too. The very doors that had once sucked Karen and I in were now open wide, allowing us to embrace our new path.

Chapter 12—The Move

They carefully maneuvered Karen into the ambulance parked in front of the hospital. After she was secure in the ambulance, I got in my car to begin the journey to Care Meridian. I was by myself; a few friends had gone on ahead to see the facility before we arrived.

When we got to Care Meridian, which was nestled in the remote area of Trabuco Canyon, we pulled into a long driveway. I parked alongside the ambulance, and then went in ahead of Karen and the attendants.

I looked over the large stucco and brick building in front of me, the windows hung with beautiful flowered curtains. Inside was a living room with a couple of sofas and a large wooden dining room table. A small kitchen stood off the dining room with an opening so everyone could see what the girls were making in the kitchen. In doing my research, I had learned that every meal was homemade and that the workers would go shopping weekly for fresh food. Karen wasn't eating because she still had her feeding tube, but when she could, she would have great food.

A secretary greeted me with paperwork, which I read and signed. Karen, in the meantime, got situated in her new bedroom.

After I completed the paperwork, I was given a tour of Care Meridian. It was incredible. There were separate men and women's quarters, a big bathroom, and a cozy living room.

I was led to Karen's bedroom, where I was asked to unpack all of her clothes and belongings. Wearing regular clothing, I was told, was an important part of her recovery. Finally, Karen would be out of the hospital gown that had been her only outfit for 72 long days.

I breathed a sigh of relief. We were in a home--no longer in the sterile hospital where machines were beeping and tubes were hugging every orifice of her body. There were curtains hanging in the bedrooms, regular beds, a dining room table, and even a fireplace in the living room. Karen's room had a bed with a flowered comforter, curtains bright as life, and even a television. I could feel the warmth throughout the room.

I was told that Karen's initials needed to be written on everything in black marker because laundry was done communally. OCD rebelled against the ugliness of this task; her pajamas, bras, jeans, new iPod, and mini sound system would all be marred by permanent black marks. Though it rattled me, I did it anyway. Despite this minor institutional touch, I felt that Care Meridian was truly a home where Karen would flourish.

Karen was tucked into her new bed, Hoot-n-Nanny wrapped in her arms. I bent over and gave her a gentle kiss. It had been so long since I had seen her in a regular-style bed, all warm and cozy with her duck tucked within her skinny arms. I believed in my heart that I had made the right decision in moving her to Care Meridian.

The first day of the move to sub-acute rehabilitation was over, and I went home. It had been a long, emotional day.

When I arrived after school the following day, the directors came into the room to tell me about how Karen was doing. She'd had her first real bath in 73 days! She had been wheeled into the bathroom and placed on a board so she could be lowered into an enormous bathtub. They said she loved her bath.

When she was dried off and dressed, she was wheeled into the living room. She had been given a newspaper and a copy of *Reader's Digest*. Although she wasn't able to recall what she read after the fact, she read the paper from beginning to end.

Karen's activities director reviewed her schedule with me. At 1:00 each day, she was put to bed for two hours. After she was put into bed, I peeked into her room and saw that she was still awake. She grinned at me, her cheeks pink with happiness. Less than 24 hours after we had left the hospital, I already felt the welcome difference in her.

Karen's second full day included a visit from Sue in the early morning. Sue continued coming for the daily morning visits the entire time Karen was at Care Meridian. When I arrived that day, I was thrilled to see Karen having another bath. Thin and dressed in street clothes that hung off her body, I wheeled her outside onto the Care Meridian grounds. Roosters crowed in the distance, beautiful gardens and large oak trees surrounding the walkways. Karen had been into gardening before the aneurysm. It was no surprise, the surroundings made her smile. Though she still had but few words, her face spoke volumes.

I pushed her around the lush gardens, handed her my iPhone, and showed her which button to push to take a picture. She pushed it. Another miracle--Karen took a picture! What an incredible moment it was.

"Bear, you took a picture!" I exclaimed.

She gave me a big grin and said softly, "I did!"

Our happiness was dampened when Carol called Care Meridian later in the day. The nurses had been informed about the problems we'd had with Carol at Mission, so at the nurses' station, I was handed a portable phone. "Hello, this is Susan," I said.

"I know who you are. I want to talk to my sister."

"She can't have a conversation yet, but I'll put her on speakerphone so she can hear you."

"No, you won't put her on speakerphone. This is a private conversation."

With a growl in my voice and a slow step in my gait, I went into Karen's room with the phone. I said, "Karen, it's your sister."

She looked at me without a word. I held the phone to her ear, but still Karen uttered not one word, and her expression did not change. I therefore placed the phone to my ear and listened to the entire one-sided conversation. "Karen, this is your sister. We are thinking of you and love you. Come to visit Florida when you get well." When she said goodbye, I hung up, and the nurse and I had a great laugh.

Karen's happiness outweighed the annoyance of Carol's phone call, and for the remainder of that wonderful day, I felt reassured by how kind and comforting the nurses and staff were. I stayed with Karen until bedtime and drove home with a smile.

The following day, I noticed something different: Karen's PICC IV had been removed. It had been inserted into Karen's arm on her first day of treatment at the SICU as a form of intravenous access. I had previously tried not to notice the details of medical equipment like this too much, as the less I knew, the better off I was. Details were the doctors' and nurses' job; my job was to love Karen and be there for her emotionally. We all had specific jobs, and I followed the rules of my job emphatically.

The other big change I learned of was that Karen's trach tube was downsized from a "six" to a "four" by her respiratory therapist. Visible progress was happening daily. As she improved, the trach tube, which had been downsized in order to let the surrounding tissue close and heal. On her third day at Care Meridian, it had been downsized again so that it would be easier for the staff to remove it when she was ready.

Karen's new speech therapist, also named Carol, saw her that day as well. I was pleased to see that she was diligent, firm, and gentle. She was incredible, and I had full faith in her. It was Carol's job to get Karen to say one or two words so that she could eventually talk again, and at first, this seemed like a tough task; though Karen had talked back in Acute Rehab at Mission Hospital, she had not spoken much recently as a result of her depression.

Carol talked softly, and Karen smiled. When she worked to form words, her lips were animated and earnest—fun to watch. She struggled to say just one word such as "yes" or "no," but I knew she could do it, and I also knew she would soon say more. With her apparent need to talk, Karen interacted with the whiteboard she'd been too tired to use our last few weeks at Mission. I asked her how her day went, and she wrote the words *fantastic and wonderful*. I couldn't believe she remembered such expressive words; my heart smiled.

Karen had a flood of visitors on weekends, and I was always there too, of course. Early on Saturday morning October 12th, my family came to visit. I had even flown my niece, Ami, out to be with us. Ami and I had been close when she was little; she was the child I never had, with blonde hair and the biggest brown eyes. As an adult, she had a can-do attitude and was ready to pitch in right away. She was something solid for me to hang onto. I was a sounding board for her when she had disagreements with her dad, and so I loved that she could support me during this time. I looked forward to her help, as I needed someone to share the driving and to help with occasional errands.

When Karen saw Ami, she smiled and said, "Hi!"

When it was time for therapy, we were invited to participate, instructed to form a circle around Karen. Her therapy was to hit a balloon over to each of the six of us. Since it didn't have far to go, the light balloon was easy for Karen to smack, and we were all delighted to see her active interaction with us.

After the balloon task, Karen was given a lightweight ball to kick to each of us. This proved to be much harder for her, and she grimaced each time she had to move her legs, as they hadn't been used for months. Her muscles had atrophied, so this was particularly demanding work, but she did it—sometimes with a smile.

The last part of her therapy that day involved Karen being put in a harness and using her fingers to move beads from one side of a bar to the other. Though it was exhilarating to watch, it also was difficult to see, as this and the other tasks seemed intended for children. My own fingers tingled, as I wanted to move the beads for her or hold her hand. I knew she had to persist; this was necessary work, and I could not intrude.

When it was time for Karen's nap, everyone said goodbye, and Ami and I followed the nurse and Karen into her bedroom. We sat on the side of her bed and talked for a short time. Within a few minutes, only Ami and I were talking, as Karen was fast asleep.

Chapter 13—Big Steps

On October 10th, Sue texted me at school. She said that Karen had just taken 10 steps using a therapy machine. I didn't want to cry in front of my students, so I held in my emotions, but I couldn't wait for school to end.

Karen's physical therapist, Dan, was a tall, patient man in his mid-fifties. He had recently led Karen in taking three steps using a new machine. She was strapped into a jump seat in standing position, and Dan wrapped tape around Karen's right tennis shoe so it would slide easier on the carpet. Now that I'd heard she had taken 10 steps, I felt she was truly learning how to walk again.

When Karen arrived at Care Meridian, she was still using a feeding tube. Their goal was to get her off her feeding tube and eating solid food. The same day she took 10 steps, her ability to eat solid food was tested with applesauce, and she swallowed it with no problem, passing on the first try! This was major for her recovery.

I handed Karen the whiteboard, telling her to write anything she could remember about our home, and she wrote her birthdate, our home address, and the names of our three dogs. Karen's interaction with the whiteboard was vital for me. I no longer took for granted the small things we shared.

I longed to have her home where we could be the family we were three months earlier, going on vacations to Hawaii every summer, taking fall trips to Big Sur, and having dinner at nice restaurants each evening. It still hadn't fully sunk in that our life would never be the same. I still believed deep down that Karen would heal and that our lives would go back to what they were before. I believed in my heart --or needed to believe-- that Karen would reclaim enough of herself to allow for normalcy. I was so busy teaching and spending time with Karen, though, that I never really thought about what this idea meant.

After less than a week in her new home, Karen progressed at a pace no one anticipated. She smiled frequently, and when I arrived after work, she was often awake. I could feel her love when I walked into the room.

Karen kept Hoot-n-Nanny tucked under her arm every day—her form of security blanket. One morning when Sue came in and turned on her iPod, Karen played drums on the duck. Only later would I understand that the drum playing was a kind of tic. Karen, who had always been so proper, was playing drums on her duck pillow's back.

At this point, I had settled into a work routine that allowed my students more access to me. I'm known at school as a teacher whose door is always open; I let kids come in at 7:15 in the morning and again at lunch so they can talk to each other or do homework. Even though I was exhausted frequently, with periods so loud that I couldn't even hear myself think, I really felt like a teacher.

Since I'd won the Teacher of the Year award the year before, many of my students wanted to get to know me better. I loved to tease my kids, so I would tell them to give me some quiet time and go to another teacher's room. They always responded with "But we love you, Ms. Davis, so we want to stay in here." We were like a family in room 14.

Now that Karen was at Care Meridian, I wasn't fearful when my phone rang. Sue was my key to peace of mind; she sent me a text after Karen ate breakfast each day. It was comforting having Sue there to give me a bird's-eye view of Karen's morning. On Karen's 79th day, October 14, 2008, Sue wrote on *Caring Bridge,* "We all know that miracles happen, and it's awesome watching one take place. Karen is progressing at a pace beyond anything we could imagine."

On the 80th day of Karen's rehabilitation, I sat with her for dinner. I watched intently, as she considered taking up her fork. I could tell she didn't remember how to hold a fork, so I took it from her long skinny fingers and showed her how to hold it properly. She held it in her right hand and stared at it.

"Karen," I said, "this is your fork to eat with."

She stared and stared, then scooped up a small amount of mac and cheese. As she slowly raised it to her mouth, her hand stopped. She turned the fork every way she could, observing her food.

"Bear, it's mac and cheese. Go ahead and put it in your mouth!"

About 5 minutes later, the mac and cheese finally went into her mouth! I stood up and applauded.

Karen pursed her lips and said, "Good." For the first time in 80 days, she was eating solid food--mac and cheese and strawberry yogurt.

I helped her spoon up the rest of the mac and cheese, but she was able to eat the yogurt on her own. The mac and cheese looked delicious, and although I was offered some, I didn't want to take what was meant for the patients. Karen and I both loved yogurt, which was thick and creamy. Nothing about the food looked institutional.

Once shown, Karen quickly remembered how to use a fork. After that, Karen would pick up her fork and slowly choose a piece of food off her plate. She'd bring the fork closer to her face and inspect it. If she heard a noise in the dining area, the fork went down back to the plate, and the whole process would start over. It took Karen two full hours to eat her breakfast with Sue cheering her on. Karen was also given Ensure each day; she drank one in the morning and another in the afternoon to help her put on weight. She was an astonishing 83 pounds at this point, so putting on weight was very important for her recovery.

Less essential to her recovery but still a milestone were the events of day 81. When Sue arrived in the morning, Karen was at the bathroom vanity in her wheelchair, putting on lipstick! Karen liked lipstick, but not to the extent I did. When I walked in after school and saw Karen's pink lips, I ran over and kissed them. They were stunning-- perfectly colored with the pink lipstick I had bought her months before.

Sue told me that she put on Tim McGraw's song "When Stars Go Blue" for Karen. Dan came in and asked his patient if she would like to dance; with his help, Karen was able to stand, and they danced together, her arms tightly wrapped around Dan's body. With small steps and Dan's support, she was able to move her feet on the floor-- a beautiful moment for Sue to experience. When I was told all about the dance, I think my smile was bigger than the moon.

On *Caring Bridge,* Sue wrote, "It was so sweet to watch Karen move her feet and enjoy the music." For almost three months, we had all seen Karen in a bed where she couldn't move. She was a miracle.

The next morning, she walked with limited help. She took only a few steps, but she walked by herself, and I was able to watch a video Sue had taken for me.

When I went to visit the following Saturday morning, the staff told me I needed to take a day off and go to the movies. The director said, "Find a movie that will make you laugh."

I thought this was silly. *Why in the world would I want to go and see a funny movie? There still isn't a great deal to laugh about.*

"You need to take a break, Susan. A break would be good for you. Take some time to be alone."

I said, "I would never do that." I didn't like people telling me what they thought I should do. I wanted Karen home, but until she left Care Meridian, I would be at her side every day. I understood the importance of taking care of myself too, but I was better being with Karen than I was at being at home without her.

Care Meridian, the staff asked if I would be willing to be filmed for a video they intended to put on their website, and I told them I'd be honored. They whisked me away to a stunning home high on a hill where I imagined rich people lived. A camera was set up in the backyard, and other people were being filmed upon our arrival.

I was asked questions about Care Meridian and what I thought about Karen's care. Years later, I looked up "brain aneurysm survivors" online and found myself on You Tube, labeled "partner of a brain aneurysm survivor." I was honored. Being able to support Care Meridian, the facility to which we owed so much, was an exciting and valuable way for me to take care of myself.

Karen had spent only one week in her new rehab home, yet I knew we had made the right decision for her. It took me more time to get to Care Meridian than to Mission Hospital, but still I never missed a day.

Whenever I came in, the staff greeted me as I walked through the door. Karen was always either in her bed or sitting in her wheelchair in the dining room. When she saw me, I'd ask, "What's up?"

Karen would often reply by singing, "What's up, pussycat, whoa." Before long, she had the staff singing the line every day too. Karen was learning to talk, had learned to swallow, and now was singing. Hearing her sing was one of my favorite parts of my visits. On our road trips, we used to sing to an array of music while Karen drove; she had a fabulous voice. Three months into rehab, Karen was learning to walk, but there was no driving in her near future.

What I liked most about Care Meridian was the kindness of the staff, the cleanliness of the home, and the rest requirements for each patient; no visitors were allowed for a period of two hours each day while each patient was in bed. The timing of the rest period was also perfect for me because I usually arrived at 3:00, when Karen was wide-awake from her nap. She would be in her wheelchair and ready to sing to me when I came around the corner.

I was beginning to really think that life was going to be normal again.

We had always had music playing at home-- Ella Fitzgerald, Celine Dion, Johnny Mathis. Sue said Karen wanted to listen to music. She even did a bed dance for Sue. Her arms moved up and down as she drummed away on Hoot-n-Nanny, keeping a steady beat. Sue wrote, "This journey is exciting, and it's wonderful watching the metamorphosis of our Karen. She is turning back into a beautiful butterfly."

I truly felt like I was living two lives by this time, teaching all day then being a loving partner in the afternoon and evenings. My stamina was strong, though, and seeing Karen's progress motivated me even more.

I kept a picture of Karen on the dashboard of my car. The photo was taken while we were vacationing in Hawaii in July- -just weeks before her aneurysm ruptured. Karen had her hand modestly covering her mouth, smiling like she always had. I had looked at that picture every day on my way to Mission Hospital, and now I was doing it on my way to Care Meridian. I needed that Karen back. I missed her. Whether I would ever get that Karen back was uncertain, though.

I was grateful to Sue, who had also written, "Susan, you are an awesome partner. You have been at Karen's side through this journey and, as I think I have said before, most people could only dream of having the support you have given her. You are a star." It was touching to know others saw how much I loved my Bear.

When Karen's second weekend at Care Meridian arrived, I slept until seven, then showered and went to Coffee Bean. Karen had loved a Coffee Bean drink called "Mucho Mango," so I called Care Meridian and got the okay to take one to her.

When I got there, Sue and Peter were with Karen. We took her outside to the patio, which was surrounded by gorgeous oak trees, flowers, and chirping birds. When I brought out Karen's drink, her eyes got as round as saucers, and we all laughed.

At lunch, the three of us went in to sit with Karen while she had a ham and cheese sandwich, fruit salad, and carrot slaw. She proudly showed us that she could use her fork properly. She enjoyed everything on her plate except the carrot slaw, which we encouraged her to eat but still made her face contort in a squeamish way. Karen was a mere 84 pounds, having gained one pound at Care Meridian up until that point. We would cheer each time she gained a pound. I myself had lost fourteen pounds since her aneurysm ruptured, which was a positive for me as well.

It was hard to believe that summer had passed and Karen had missed most of it. Fall was upon us, and at least she was learning how to read a calendar and identify the days of the week. Holidays were designated on a calendar in the Care Meridian dining room, but Karen had no idea what day or even month it was. I had been a positive person for the past 83 days, but I occasionally became overwhelmed when I realized the disabilities she faced. I never cried in front of Karen because I always wanted to be upbeat for her. However, there were plenty of times when I felt every part of my soul aching to have my old Karen back. Without her, OCD overtook me more. I ate less; I clung to our dogs more and pulled my eyebrows out with my fingers, which is something I had struggled with since childhood.

As I drove to work one foggy fall morning, my thoughts were flooded with ideas about what Karen would do that day. My lessons were planned and my students knew the routine, but in Karen's world, though there was a routine, there were no expectations of solid outcomes.

Within a few hours of being at work, I received my morning text from Sue, who had been with Karen for over an hour. Sue was absolutely my morning lifeline. She told me that Karen had walked 15 feet that morning, carefully placing one foot in front of the other. More progress! Never having raised children, I hadn't fully realized the difficulty Karen faced in learning the seemingly simple task of setting one foot in front of the other. Like with other parts of a normal life, I had taken it for granted.

After I arrived that afternoon, Karen got ready to eat dinner: cabbage rolls and orange Jell-O. I hated cabbage rolls. I didn't know if Karen liked them or not because we never made them at home. There wasn't a morsel left on her plate, though, so I wondered if being on a feeding tube for three months made things taste better.

Karen was filled with a fierce determination Sue witnessed every morning. By day 84 she was taking steps all the way down the hallway, assisted by Dan. Dan suggested that Sue take Karen outside, so she positioned herself behind her wheelchair, "ready to push her out into the sun-soaked afternoon," Sue told me. "Dan jumped in suddenly, saying, 'No more pushing Karen. She has to push herself in the wheelchair.'" Sue stood back, and Karen gripped the wheels, slowly pushing herself out the door. She sat there soaking up the sunlight, eventually closing her eyes and falling asleep.

Karen opened her eyes instantly when she heard my voice. My nieces and I talked and laughed with Karen until the sun began to set.

When everyone left, I went to see the nurse put Karen to bed. She was tucked in safely with the bedrails up on both sides. I handed her Hoot-n-Nanny and said, as I always did, "Bear, I'm going home to feed the dogs and cuddle with them for a bit."

"No, don't go!"

This was the first time in two months that Karen told me not to go. I pulled up a chair and sat with her until she fell asleep. Her dark eyes closed, her lips pressed together sweetly. Though she looked vulnerable and fragile, I thought about how she was a fierce competitor. She had beaten all the odds. I stood and went to the door but turned to gaze at her one more time--my love, my partner, and the one I would take care of forever. I wiped away my tears and walked slowly to my car.

The next day, I stayed into the evening and watched a movie with Karen on her DVD player. She loved the Harry Potter series, and though I knew she didn't understand everything she was seeing, she had read the books and seen the movies before. Her therapists said that hearing words and seeing moving images would help stimulate her brain. Beyond that, I think she just enjoyed having me there to watch a movie with her.

The next day was a big day for us. Karen was going to a different hospital for a procedure. She needed to have a scan for her lungs, to see what they looked like from all the aspiration. When the Care Meridian staff asked me if I wanted to ride in the ambulance with her, I thought I was going to faint. No one knew I had a phobia of ambulances. Anxious thoughts raced through my mind. *Am I going to have to face this fear in front of everyone? Will I have another panic attack?*

When I first began therapy with Dr. Kaplan, I told her about my phobia and said, "Don't ever *flood me* and have an ambulance show up here outside your office. If you do, I'll run, and I'll never come back." *Flooding* is the appropriate term for overexposure to one's phobias as a way to combat fear. That was 16 years ago; I couldn't believe I had been with Dr. Kaplan for so long an had never faced this phobia. It seemed easier to just not face it.

I was faced with a decision: letting the attendants take Karen without me, or trying to act like it was no big deal to join her. The stretcher was rolled into Karen's room, and I stood there in shock, anxiety wrapping itself around my body. My legs became weak. My heart raced.

The men were gentle in lifting Karen out of her bed and onto the yellow stretcher. I trembled from head to toe. When she was strapped in, one of the nurses looked me in the eye and said, "Susan, do you want to ride with her?" This was the second time they had asked me; the first time, I hadn't answered.

I focused my attention on Karen. I had been by her side for 88 days at this point. How could I choose to not go with her? I looked at the nurse like it was no big deal and stilled my rattled nerves enough to say, "Yes, I will go."

With wobbly knees, I followed the attendants out to the ambulance. They got Karen in and asked, "Would you like to sit in the back with her?"

Dear God. What if I have a panic attack back there? What if I pass out in fright? Then the trip will be about me. It was all about Karen, and I couldn't take anything away from her recovery.

I looked at the kind attendant, gritted my teeth, and lied, saying, "Yes, I would like that." I took the step up into the ambulance and sat on the hard metal seat next to Karen's head.

As we rolled down the road, I began to worry about Karen and not myself. I talked to her the entire way there, full of nervous energy. She said few words in response, yet this was still a form of therapy for me.

Later, back at Care Meridian, the doctor informed me that Karen had great test results. I was pleased about this, but I was even more pleased that I had been set free from a phobia that had plagued me since I was a small child. I had created my own form of flooding, I realized. I was going to be just fine.

Karen rode the stationary bike the next morning, and this time; Sue didn't have to assist her. Karen made the pedals go around on her own. Sue did help her with activities at the dining room table, which were done as a way to increase use of her hands; on this morning, she made pompoms. Sue pushed yarn through the holes of the cardboard template, and Karen pulled the yarn through, using all her fingers. Hearing this news from Sue, I thought about the many times we would wind something like a hose or piece of yarn and never thinking it was a big deal. In Karen's new world, it was an enormous task requiring all her effort and concentration.

Before her aneurysm, Karen was a big movie fan. The staff put on *Father of the Bride*--one of her favorites. I was interested to see how much of it she remembered.

Sue sat through the movie with Karen not once, but twice. I knew she didn't mind in the least.

Meanwhile, my life continued outside of Karen's world. I was supposed to attend a conference at UCI the upcoming Saturday but was torn about whether I should attend. I hadn't missed a Saturday with Karen in ninety days. When I didn't show up, would she think I had abandoned her? Would Karen even know that it was a Saturday morning and her Boo wasn't there? Would it jinx her rehabilitation?

I called Sue and explained my dilemma. She said, "Go to your conference. Peter and I will be there with Karen." I don't know what I would have done without the Mordins. They gave endless hours of their time to Karen and to me. We were not long-time friends, but they had proven how generous, caring, and committed they were through all the days of our ordeal.

Knowing Karen was in the hands of the Mordins, I went to the conference but didn't learn much. I wanted to be at Care Meridian, so my mind was not on the conference. When we were given a bag lunch, I took mine and left.

I got to Care Meridian when Sue and Peter were outside with Karen, having a great time. Peter hadn't seen Karen in a week, so he was amazed by how she had progressed. She rode the little stationary bike for him. As they talked and laughed together, I felt such joy and gratitude for their friendship.

I tiptoed up behind Karen in her wheelchair and pressed my lips against her soft black hair.

She turned her head and yelled, "Booie!"

My day was complete.

Karen's determination to get better could be seen during her daily workouts. She was in her wheelchair in the exercise room kicking a ball with another patient, which Sue had texted me about while I was working. Peter came in and was asked to help both Karen and the other patient, John. Peter said that Karen was having a great time laughing and working hard on her legs. She had always loved Peter, so I think she was showing off for him. Sue also texted me to say that Karen was later strapped in a standing position on a piece of exercise equipment and asked to do ten standing squats, which completely exhausted her.

She was at the dining room table when I arrived that afternoon. Sue and Peter left, and I sat with Karen while she ate all of her minestrone soup, crackers, and fruit salad.

That evening, we received the news that Karen would get her trach tube removed. I was asked if I wanted to do the honors of taking it out. I said that I would rather let Sue do the honors. Sue agreed to do it in a few days.

After a day of exercise and visitors, Karen was ready to nap. With Hoot-n-Nanny tucked safely in her arms, she fell asleep quickly. I kissed her and quietly walked out of the room.

While I was busy preparing my students for the state test, Karen's strength was being tested on the Golvo walker. The next morning, Sue was directed to the exercise room, where Karen was strapped to the Golvo with Carol the speech therapist in front, guiding the frame, and Dan behind Karen, positioning her hips. She was asked to count each step she took aloud. Karen's voice was low and raspy because of the trach tube and relative lack of use.

One-hundred-fifty steps later, Karen had walked the entire length of the hallway twice, also remembering her numbers! When asked how many steps she had taken, Karen replied, "One-five-o!"—just one example of how her humor was also coming back. Sue said everyone cheered and clapped, and I bet there were not many dry eyes. Mine were certainly moist when I heard the news and saw the video of this milestone.

When I came in that day, I greeted Karen with my usual, "What's new, pussycat?"

She replied on cue, "Whoa whoa whoa! Pussycat, pussycat, I love you!" The nurses who were around sang with us.

I asked Karen if she remembered the *Beverly Hillbillies* theme song we used to sing, and she sang every word. Sue and Peter shook their heads, chuckling in amazement. Karen was gradually teaching us how beautiful the human brain is and how, even after devastating trauma, it can slowly recover.

I was so glad I was at school the next morning. Karen would have her trach tube removed that day--another major event in her recovery. When I had been asked again if I wanted to take the trach tube out, I again said--probably too loud-ly--"No thank you!" For some reason beyond my understanding, people are thrilled to take these out. Not me!

A text from Sue appeared on my phone. The trach tube was out, but it had been removed in an unexpected way. Everyone had gathered in the room, and Sue was handed surgical gloves in preparation. As the Velcro strap holding the tube in place was removed, Sue stood next to Karen, waiting for instructions. All of a sudden, Karen coughed, and the trach tube flew out like a projectile! Laughter filled the room. Sue had been so excited to remove Karen's trach tube, but after all the build-up, she had done it on her own. That's my girl!

I left work a bit early because she had to have an MRI that day. She would be transported by ambulance to Mission Hospital for the procedure. When I was younger, I had three previous MRIs of my brain—an awful experience. It brought out the claustrophobic aspects of my OCD, so I had a difficult time completing the tests. I wanted to be with Karen to support her. I chose to ride in the ambulance with her again, this time with no problem at all.

Once in the procedure room, I sat to the side so I would be out of the way. They laid Karen down and placed a blue ball in her hand. The attendant was sweet, saying, "Ok, Karen, if you feel anxious at all, squeeze the ball and I'll stop the test." She nodded.

She was then maneuvered into the MRI scanner, and the test began. Karen squeezed the ball. The attendant walked over to her, asking, "Are you anxious, Karen?"

"No," she replied. The test began again. Karen squeezed the ball again. The test was stopped again.

The attendant's voice came over the speaker, asking, "Karen, are you nervous?"

Karen said, "No!" I think that she was squeezing the ball accidentally.

After what seemed like forever, the test was complete, and I helped Karen get dressed. Taking in all that had happened, I wondered if this was an indication of what it would be like to live with Karen and her brain injury. She was so childlike and naïve now. Would she be an adult when we got home?

When we returned to Care Meridian, exhausted myself, I could only imagine how tired Karen was. When her nurse tucked her in for a nap, I knew I had to get home to try to relax. It had been a long day for me too.

I handed Karen her duck, which she held tightly in her precious hands that I loved. I kissed her and told her I would see her the next day. Before I finished my sentence, she was sleeping. I drove home thinking about how fortunate we were. Slowly Karen was coming back, and many of us had been blessed to witness her rebirth.

Chapter 14—Freedom and Fear

Work was still going well for me around this time. I was deep into teaching writing to my students and enjoyed our lessons. I was editing thesis statements, giving SAT vocabulary exams, listening to kids' problems, and basking in my educational purpose for seven hours a day. I graded 100 essays a week and delighted in seeing the elation on students' faces when they received a good grade. Their smiles and high-fives warmed my heart. As a teacher, nothing, is better than to see a successful student bright and early in the morning.

Beyond giving me a safe haven of purpose and intention, work filled me with peace, encouraging me to provide lessons about forgiveness and acceptance. Many years ago, I had been dubbed the "Holocaust teacher" because I taught a two-month unit on the Holocaust every year that culminated with a trip to The Museum of Tolerance in Los Angeles. I was proud of my unit, as I had students from years ago return to tell me that it was their favorite school experience of all time. I have taught over 2,000 students so far, and I'm glad to know I have made a difference in teaching acceptance.

People sometimes asked me how I could balance my two worlds. "One day at a time" was my usual answer--one day at a time. It was interesting that both of my worlds required extreme acceptance and tolerance.

On day 94, Karen went with three other patients to a nearby park to feed the ducks. She was pushed in her wheel-chair and was later allowed to walk around a small part of the park, holding onto the railing with a therapist holding her gait belt on her side. During this first real outing, Karen took small, slow steps, smiling the entire time.

I brought in a Baskin Robbins mint chocolate chip ice cream cake for everyone at Care Meridian that afternoon, as mint chocolate chip was Karen's favorite ice cream flavor. They served it for dessert that evening, and it was all gone by bed-time.

Outside on the patio at Care Meridian that day, I received a call from Jim, Karen's former boss, who informed me that Ray's group was closing its doors. Karen was officially unem-ployed.

When he ended the call, I started to cry. What would we do? We had two homes, and I couldn't afford the mortgage and taxes on both. Money had not been an issue for us before because we had both had solid jobs. My insides crawled with fear, this idea of Karen being unemployed more powerful than my fear of what would happen next in her recovery. She was in the hands of brilliant doctors and staff who were caring for her, but without her income, I had no idea what we would do. Though I may not have fully known in the past 94 days just how much everything was in my hands, in that moment, I felt the weight of responsibility profoundly.

Halloween was upon us. Care Meridian decorated all over with bats, ghosts, and witches. The next day I visited, Karen sat at the dining room table with the other patients and drew a face on a small pumpkin. She took a foam brush and covered her pumpkin with paint, smiling in her usual way. Sue helped decorate pumpkins for the other patients who were unable to hold a brush, which made me feel grateful that Karen could use all ten fingers.

Sue gave Karen a pen and notebook, telling her she wanted her to start writing in it. The first word she wrote was her father's name. Sue asked, "Who is that?" and Karen responded, "Dad." It was a special moment.

By this time, I was able to have conversations with Karen when I arrived in the afternoon. Her vocabulary increased day by day, and she was able to stay awake even after taking 150 steps in her Golvo.

I sat with her as she ate roast beef, fish, tacos, and much more, truly enjoying the food. Since she was eating more and taking her meds orally, the doctor said, she would have her surgically placed J and G eating tubes taken out. We couldn't wait for this day to come; these were the last tubes Karen had in her body.

She cruised through October enjoying the daily activities with Sue and the other patients. Though she couldn't remember what she had managed to do each day, I always asked her about it.

On a cool fall morning, I took Karen outside in her wheelchair. The wind was softly blowing, and leaves were rustling in the trees. The fall colors were simply beautiful.

Karen eventually said, "Booie, let's go back inside. I'm cold." I wheeled her back into the living room and got her settled in front of one of the movies Care Meridian provided. I took a soft blue blanket, draped it across Karen's lap, and got Hoot-n-Nanny for her. Karen smiled and said, "I love my Duckie. He keeps me so warm." As I sat and watched Harry Potter with her, I again wondered if this Karen had become truly childlike.

November 4th, 2008, was day 100 of Karen's recovery. Even given conversations with other families experiencing trauma, I never could have imagined that Karen's recovery would have taken this long. It was a big day for us, and we were excited about all the progress Karen had made and would continue to make. One thing we talked about was that in recovery, we found Karen had a side many had never seen before; she was a comedian. Her one-liners were better than those of most comedians on television. Sue once said to Karen, "Time flies like an arrow; fruit flies like bananas," and laughed.

Karen immediately responded, "Poop falls to the ground" and smiled. After a moment, she exclaimed, "The laws of physics and gravity require that poop fall to the ground!"

Karen's long-term memory was also beginning to kick in. When she had a bologna sandwich for lunch, she belted out the entire Oscar Meyer song, "B-O-L-O-G-N-A!" To record such small but meaningful steps, we asked Karen to start writing her own journal entries. Here is her first entry on Day 108, exactly as she wrote it:

> *Hello! My weight is now 89.3 lbs. I am a bit tired but otherwise have no big issues. Thanks to everyone for all their support while I was incapacitated. Now I'm back, ready to go home with Boo, and can't wait to see our Madi, Josh, and Benson. I'm looking forward to catching up on the latest chitchat and all! Please don't forget to feed Boo, Josh, Madi, and Benson. Thanks so much for keeping us in your thoughts. We will remember to update you as often as needed.*
> *Love, Karen*

The fact that Karen came up with a word like "incapacitated" overwhelmed me. She had been a gifted individual before her brain injury, and I was finally seeing moments of clarity shining through her childlike state. It was amazing to watch Karen grow back into herself.

The next evening, our hairdresser, Faith, came to cut Karen's hair free of charge for the second time. This was a wonderful moment for Karen. Haircutting experiences were one of the few situations I could recall Karen showing even a bit of vanity. "Booie, do you like my haircut?" she would ask each time she got her haircut or styled.

Her hair looked so cute in the new style Faith gave her-- cropped around her ears, with a little touch of messy spike— and I told her so. Her smile lit up the room. It touched me that someone was willing to come and do something free for us. Karen had touched so many lives, and everyone was rooting for her. Later, Laurie, one of Karen's nurses from Mission Hospital, came and gave her pumpkin ice cream. She ate the entire cup.

Karen had always been aware that I loved fine jewelry. On day one of her brain aneurysm journey, I lost one of my diamond earrings in the commotion. As we talked at Care Meridian one day Karen observed, "Booie, you lost a diamond."

I looked at her, amazed. "You remember I had a diamond in my right ear?"

"Yes. And it's gone." After being in the dark abyss for 102 days, I couldn't believe that she had noticed I was missing an earring, especially since I wore two earrings in that ear. I had been trying to understand the idiosyncrasies of brain injury, but relied mostly on firsthand experience, as reading about it was difficult. Seeing such special, interesting behavior from Karen, I realized that while going home to read about someone else's trauma was something I couldn't have handled several days ago, this had changed.

After weeks of great success, Karen wasn't sleeping much, which I didn't understand. She was exhausted from her physical therapy but didn't sleep well and stopped eating as much. Her feeding tube was still in, and they were using it to give her Boost so she would get enough protein.

After school on day 116, Karen vomited. Perhaps it was a little bug going around or just pure exhaustion. When they put her in bed, I noticed a small yellow fleece blanket with dragonflies neatly folded at the bottom of the bed. Sue had made it for Karen. Sue and Peter's gifts of time and small touches like the yellow blanket soothed us both on a day like this one.

I hadn't recently had to deal with insurance calls, as Care Meridian took care of everything for us. The next day, however, I was called into the office of Care Meridian's assistant manager. She said, "Susan, the insurance company has informed us that Karen has ten days left to stay here; then she'll have to move to the next phase of her rehabilitation." I asked her what that meant. "It means she'll have a new home to live in where she can learn how to become more independent. It's a fabulous home and facility."

I didn't understand why she had to move. I had believed she would finish rehab and then could go home. I fretted about the idea of another facility, new people for Karen, and a new drive for me. I just didn't think it was necessary.

I looked down at the desk, dejected. "I don't want her to go anywhere but home." I could feel my face getting red, and I thought about how my left ear was also turning red—a quirk of mine.

"There is an option to take Karen home. We'd have to send Dan out to do a home visit to make sure it's safe for her."

I was told that in the proposed facility, Karen would have her own bedroom, learn to make her bed, help to cook in the kitchen, and do more intense exercise. I visited the facility, trying not to rule it out completely. Though it was another facility, I liked, I couldn't imagine Karen doing so much on her own. She wasn't ready.

After talking with the Mordins and the staff at Care Meridian, I decided I wanted Karen home and that she could be an outpatient at the new facility, not a live-in. There was just one problem: who would take care of her when I was teaching? I decided to make a few calls.

Karen continued taking her small steps around Care Meridian with the Golvo while I planned how to make our home suitable for her. We had over 30 stairs in our condominium, so I wanted to order a chair lift, but I was advised to wait. I'm proactive, not reactive, so I called Access to Freedom, which installed a chair lift at a cost of seventeen thousand dollars that I had not planned for. Thankfully, my mother gave us a loan. The lift was installed on November 18, 2008, and yes, I did take the first ride on it.

I also had the hardwood floors ripped out and had carpet put in, as it would allow Karen to walk more easily and eliminated the possibility of slipping. After I had made these changes, Dan came over and did his inspection of our home. He found everything to be in order, and his only concern was that our three doggies would get in Karen's way. I promised to do my best to ensure the dogs would not be an obstacle so we were cleared.

In the middle of preparing our home to receive Karen, I got another phone call from Jim, Karen's former employer. I was told clearly that she no longer had insurance, which meant that she would have to use COBRA, an insurance that takes the place of her original policy from her work. It didn't seem like too big of a deal, and the paperwork was completed with no problem. Little did I know that the worst was yet to come.

On day 118, I wanted Karen to write her own *Caring Bridge* journal entry. I had my laptop with me, so as she waited for dinner, she wrote:

> *Hello Everyone,*
> *How's everyone done? I'm at Care Meridian with Sue, Peter, and Boo. I am using Susan's laptop for the fits me (oops). I forgot to mention that I am practicing walking, healing, and H typing. The past 118 days have been full of surprises along with support. I truly miss my 4-legged, furry buddies and my 2-legged buddy.... By the way, I want to mention that there are people who work here and hav been offering their good wishes.*
> *Love, Karen*

I didn't know how to feel. This was my partner who, four years ago, had captured a piece of my heart with her erudite writing. Her emails were eloquent and deep. I read the entry again. Should I be happy that she could write at all? Should I be discouraged because this was what her brain injury had left her with? She had come so far in 118 days, but I found myself expecting more.

I tapped into my OCD and ruminated for a while. What could I do that would allow me to accept what might be permanent? Could I count tiles again? Would that put everything back in order? How about incorporating the number three into more of my daily thoughts?

I went outside to the patio to think while Karen was put to bed. I didn't use a journal for myself-- and didn't want to read to relax because I couldn't focus for long. I sat in the hot steel chair in the sizzling heat of the afternoon and looked out at the manicured grounds that surrounded Care Meridian, watching the chickens run around. Unfamiliar noises from animals made it feel like a farm. For the first time, I fully allowed myself to feel what I had lost--the woman I had fallen in love with four years ago. Nothing would ever be the same again.

Thanksgiving weekend became another turning point for us. Sue and Peter went to see Karen and were shocked to find that she wasn't there! She had been taken to see Christmas lights with other patients. When she returned, she was holding a cup of coffee, and when Sue went over to greet her, she almost spilled the coffee. We all made a mental note that Karen wasn't always aware of what she was doing. Sue and Peter said she chatted with them and filled the room with her infectious smile.

Sue and Peter had left by the time I arrived. Karen was asleep, as the outing made her extremely tired. I stayed and talked to the staff, hearing about the Christmas lights. Then, unexpectedly, the head director came out of her office with great news-- Karen was going home! The target date was December 3rd.

When Karen awoke, I told her the news. She said, "Well, Booie, it's just like Dorothy said--there's no place like home!" That was the best thing I had heard in months.

Care Meridian provided a lavish Thanksgiving meal for the patients. I wanted to share Thanksgiving lunch with Karen, but I needed to be at my mom's house by 3:00 p.m. for our family dinner, so I stopped by for a quick visit. When I walked in, Karen was at the dining room table, and her nurse approached me. She said, "I think you need to peek under her pajama top."

I couldn't imagine why. I carefully lifted it, and my eyes bulged. The G and J tube had been removed! Four long, arduous months of tubes, lights, and machines, and finally she was free of all of them. I sat beside her, tears dripping down my face.

"Booie, why are you crying?" Karen asked.

Though I knew she wouldn't fully understand, I said, "Bear, for 123 days, you've had tubes in your body and machines that have kept you alive. Today is the first time I get to see you without any of that."

She smiled in her usual amiable way.

I ate a small portion of turkey with Karen and the other patients. Sitting there with Karen, I thanked God for all He had done for us.

By 2:30 p.m., Karen was done eating and had been tucked in for her cozy nap. Her nurse left, and I sat her duck in her arms, kissed her, and said I had to get to my mom's. She seemed to understand. I waited until she fell asleep, which took all of five minutes.

It was a quiet drive to Mom's, allowing me to reflect on the joyful idea that though I had parted from Karen on a holiday, she would be coming home soon.

My mother is the best cook, and there is no shortage of food on any given holiday. By the time I arrived at her house, the Thanksgiving meal was ready, and everybody was there waiting for me. We offered prayers of thanks for our lives and for Karen and her recovery.

After the meal was over and the pumpkin pie had been devoured, I called Karen's nurse to see how she was doing. She gave Karen the phone.

She sounded quiet. "I feel lonely, Boo."

My heart sank. I had never heard her say this during her time away from home. "Bear, I'll jump in the car and come back."

"No, you stay at Mamma's and finish your dinner. I'll be fine." Though I felt guilty, the fact that Karen remembered I was at Mom's was amazing in itself.

Mom knew how I was feeling. She always knew. "Honey, Karen's fine. You know the nurses there take great care of her. It will be her bedtime soon, so she won't even know you were there if you went back to visit. I think you need to know that you give Karen everything she could possibly need, and you still got to spend part of today with her. Now you're here with us. Try to relax and enjoy these moments as well." I did.

That weekend, our friend Elly drove all the way from Colorado to help me bring Karen home. Instead of using the Golvo, Karen used a regular walker to assist her with walking, and she was able to take 52 steps with Elly watching.

Despite this progress, eating was still a problem for Karen. She inspected every morsel of food on her fork. We weren't sure what she was inspecting it for, but if someone made a noise while she brought the fork to her mouth, she'd put it back on the plate then pick it up to start the process all over again. I suppose this was her kind of OCD. Karen was still not gaining weight; in fact, she had lost another pound. At this point, she weighed 88.4 pounds, her legs and arms as skinny as a baby bird's.

When I got to Care Meridian the next day, Karen had just returned from another outing, this time at Downtown Disney. I visualized Karen's face there--all smiles, eyes soaking up everything around her. As she told me about her trip, she gripped a cup of coffee, appearing to enjoy the warmth of the cup beneath her thin fingers. Though she chatted up a storm, the little details of the trip eluded her. Short-term memory loss was still prevalent in nearly every conversation.

Two days later--December 3, 2008—we were finally going home. 129 days had passed, and we were ready. Elly and I had prepared the house for her arrival, and I was so excited that my nerves warped my insides. After five months of code blues, doctors, nurses, hospitals, and tubes, I finally got to bring Karen home.

I wondered if she would remember our condominium in Irvine, as we'd lived in two others before this one. *What will her reaction be?*

For a short time while she was at Care Meridian, Karen had a roommate, Linda. Linda had far worse health complications than Karen. She couldn't walk or talk and she never knew where she was. For all of Karen's great progress, strangely enough, she never appeared to know she had a roommate. Even though they shared a large bedroom, Karen had never mentioned Linda. This added to my worry.

Despite being worried, I was filled with excitement, a wide smile on my face the whole morning. I even felt I was breathing more easily than I had been for the past several months.

Worry came and went throughout the day. *Will it be an easy transition once I bring Karen home?* She talked, but she didn't initiate conversation. She could barely walk, and only with assistance. Even though I'd had a chair lift put in, there were still eight stairs Karen would need to navigate: three to get onto the chair lift and five more to fully reach the top floor.

What about bathing Karen? She couldn't raise her legs into a bathtub. I was bringing her home in a few hours; why hadn't I thought of all this before? Was I overwhelmed, perhaps? Time had seemed to stand still for so long, but on this day, it felt like everything was happening so quickly.

I thought about the doctors and nurses who saved Karen's life. I remember Lynda, who was with Karen on day one, telling me, "This is the easy part, Susan. When you take Karen home, the difficult part begins." For five long months, this was impossible to comprehend. As we prepared to take her home, though, I was staring 'the hard part' in the face, and I had little idea what to do.

I drove to Care Meridian for the very last time, taking time to appreciate the trees and the California wildflowers wrapping around their trunks. I looked at the Silverado Canyon sign for the last time, reflecting on how I had driven there every day for almost three months.

As I parked my car close to the front door where Karen would exit one final time, the trees seemed to whisper tranquil words of good luck. I took a moment to appreciate the white lights that lit the walkway, which were soft but helpful; they were so different from all the colored lights at Mission Hospital. The wind rustled through the leaves, allowing me to stop and take a deep breath. This was my new life, and I wondered if I was prepared for it. It didn't matter what I thought, though. Tonight was our night, and whatever happened would happen.

The front door was already open when I walked into Care Meridian for the last time. Always a festive home, it was decorated for Christmas. They had adorned the walls and halls a month in advance so the patients could enjoy the decorations. Karen was sitting in a wheelchair in the living room.

"Hi, Bear! Are you ready to come home with me?" She nodded, but I had to wonder if she really knew what "home" meant. Karen had no idea she had been at Mission Hospital and didn't remember what had taken place. She still didn't fully understand what Care Meridian was or know why she was there. I was nervous about her remembering our home.

I had the thought that I wanted her to jump out of her wheelchair only to realize shortly after that she couldn't jump.

Elly was standing next to me. She ran over to hug Karen, asking, "Do you know who I am?" Karen nodded shyly. Perhaps she was nervous or couldn't find the words to express her happiness.

As the team filled the room for Karen's departure, tears flowed. The living room of Care Meridian emanated warmth, love, and safety. Soon the door would open and Karen and I would enter our new reality. What would it mean for her? What would it mean for me?

Outside the classroom, I had never been responsible for anyone but myself. Now my partner was my full responsibility. She had been tucked safely in the womb of the SICU and swaddled in the protection and love of Care Meridian; now it would be my responsibility to take care of her. Anxiety crept through my body, OCD taking hold as well. I counted tiles in the living room, using the number three to ground me.

Hiring a caretaker would be first on my list of many things to do because Elly would return to Colorado after one week. How would I get Karen to the bathroom? *Breathe. Bask in the moment; you're taking Karen home!*

Elly began taking Karen's belongings to her SUV. I was amazed at how much one brain-injured patient had acquired in two months. Karen had new clothes, shoes, all her medicines, a wheelchair, and DVDs, along with her iPod and speakers.

The living room at Care Meridian was filled with joyful people who had taught Karen how to walk, talk, and eat. They were eager to say good-bye to her. I followed the nurse who was pushing Karen in her wheelchair, and at my car, everyone kissed and hugged Karen, wishing her well.

"Bear, do you know whose car this is?" I asked.

She glanced at my license plate, "ITEEECH" and nodded. "Yours!" It relieved me to see that she knew.

One of her nurses carefully put Karen in the car. I reached over to put her seatbelt on, which made me realize again how terribly underweight she was. She looked very different than she did five months ago when she'd crawled into the backseat of my car. Never once did I think about a seatbelt then.

We waved good-bye, and I started the car. Elly followed us with all of Karen's belongings. The breeze had picked up, and the temperature had dipped. I reached over and pressed the button that would heat Karen's seat.

"Bear, we're going home! Are you excited?" Karen nodded. "Do you remember our home?"

"No," she replied.

I talked fast because my anxiety was boiling over and all I could get from Karen were one-word responses. She seemed methodical with her words. *Does she have a word bank?*

I wanted her to talk so badly. I was ready to scream, "Please talk!" but didn't dare scream at her, as the resulting guilt would have been too much for me to handle. My OCD also told me that she could die if I screamed at her. That was one thing I knew I could count on was my OCD. It would not leave my side anytime soon. That was a strange kind of mixed blessing. As much as it fed my anxiety, I also needed it to keep me in my own box of boundaries and safety.

We eventually pulled into our gated community. I pressed the opener and the gate opened just as slowly as it had five months earlier when I was in a race against time to get Karen to the hospital. Karen sat quietly in her seat, not talking at all.

Just like that, we were home. We had made it. Karen had made it, and a completely new chapter of our lives had just begun.

Chapter 15—Home

I got out of the car and walked over to Elly, asking, "Now what do we do?"

"I think we need to get Karen inside; then I'll come back down and get all her things."

Elly and I reached in and lifted Karen out of the car, Elly on one side and me on the other. Karen was silent. Was she overwhelmed? Was she frightened about being home? As we walked down the long driveway, we stopped at the door. We were about to face our biggest hurdle: the stairs.

"Elly, you take the lead. Take Karen's left arm; I will take her right arm. I will stay one stair behind you."

"Okay," Elly agreed.

"Bear, are you doing ok?" I asked. Karen nodded.

No one had taught me how to maneuver Karen up and down stairs.

We made it up the first two stairs and got Karen onto the chairlift. We strapped her in and sent her up. I was shaking, praying that she wouldn't fall off the lift, but it stopped at the second floor without incident. Elly and I had to lift Karen off and walk her up three more stairs to the next chair lift. We had still not heard one word from Karen--nothing.

We made it up the next few stairs, but it was a struggle for all three of us. We strapped Karen onto the lift and sent her up to the third story. A solemn look was on her face.

"Bear, do you remember any of this? Does anything look familiar?" She shook her head. The dogs were crated, and I thought that maybe once we got Karen settled in our bed and I could let the dogs out, she would remember our home.

I could feel the tears welling in my eyes, but I couldn't break down. Not then. It was an evening for celebration.

When we finally reached the third floor, getting Karen on the bed was the next step. I unstrapped Karen from the lift, and Elly and I each took one of her arms, slowly walking her to the bed. Karen's legs were so frail that I worried they would break. We successfully got her to the bed, where she sat down. No words were exchanged.

I breathed a sigh of relief.

Elly and I put her in pajamas. When I took her to the bathroom, the toilet was too low for her, so we had to help her sit and stand. After bringing her back to bed, we put pads under the sheets in case Karen had an accident during the night.

It was a huge relief to have Elly with us. She was physically strong, which I needed, but I needed her emotional strength as well.

Elly stayed with Karen as I ran downstairs to let the dogs out of their crates. Of course, they bolted upstairs. Madi jumped up on the bed and went right to Karen. She kissed her face and rubbed up against her. A smile slowly broke over Karen's features. Elly and I just stood there, tears dripping down our faces.

Benson and Joshie jumped on the bed too, sniffed Karen, and then lay down at the foot of the bed. All was right in their world. Elly kissed Karen goodnight and went downstairs to attend to clients, as she was a travel agent and needed to continue working from our home. I got ready for bed and crawled in next to Bear. Five months after her aneurysm ruptured, our dogs finally next to one another in our cozy bed with our purple sheets, surrounded us. I could feel the warmth of Karen's body--something I had missed for five months. It was 9:00 p.m., and I knew Karen was exhausted.

"Do you want to go to sleep?" I asked.

"Yes, Booie."

She had said more than one word! I was so happy. I gave her a big kiss goodnight and turned off the light. In that moment, I felt that Karen being home meant that everything would be okay.

I kept waking up every hour and glancing at Karen's chest to make sure she was breathing. I was becoming increasingly scared that something would happen now that I had her home. She slept without one peep, her chest moving up and down like it should. I knew everything was okay.

All of a sudden, I heard a loud thud around 1:00 am. I jumped up and saw right away that Karen wasn't on the bed. She had fallen and was flat on the floor. I screamed for Elly, who flew up the stairs. Karen was on the bedroom carpet, her soft brown eyes staring up at us. "Bear, are you hurt? Did you hit your head?" She said nothing. "Elly, let's get her up on the bed."

We lifted all 89 pounds of Karen back on the bed, tucking her in. "Bear, do you hurt anywhere?"

"No," she replied.

"Elly, should I call 911?" I asked, somewhat hysterical.

"No, let's wait a bit and see." Elly was more rational than me, thank God.

We sat on the bed and watched her close her eyes and fall asleep. I knew she hadn't hit her head on anything, but she had still fallen a distance of a few feet. Was there internal bleeding? I cried. It was my first night in charge of my Bear, and I had failed.

Elly did what she could to comfort me, and then went back downstairs. I stayed up most of the night watching Karen sleep. It seemed like I was reliving the last several months.

The next morning I called Laurie, one of Karen's former nurses, and asked her if she could come and help us out. She came over around 7:00 a.m. having an SICU nurse with us made me a little more relaxed. She assessed Karen and said there was nothing wrong. However, she said that we needed to buy a bed rail, higher toilet seat, and bathtub bench. *Why didn't anyone tell me this?*

Laurie went right to work with Karen, helping her change her clothes and then putting her on the lift. Elly cooked a fabulous breakfast of eggs, sausage, and toast. It was great having Karen at our dining table once again. She ate slowly until there was nothing left on her plate.

When she was done, Laurie took Karen to the bathroom to brush her teeth. Elly and I sat and made a list of things I needed to purchase. When Karen came out of the bathroom with Laurie, she had a little smile on her face.

"Bear, you're home and sitting in our living room!" I exclaimed.

"I am, Booie. I love Laurie and Elly."

We handed her the newspaper, and she began reading. I had no idea how much she understood, but she was looking at the newspaper and seemed to be enjoying every minute of it.

Elly stayed with Karen while Laurie and I went off to shop for items I should have had in the house before Karen came home. *Where is the manual I need in order to make sure Karen never gets hurt again? What page would have told me that I needed to buy these items before I brought Karen home? What food should I buy?*

I wondered if Karen's tastes had changed. The ladies at Care Meridian knew what the patients should—and could—eat, whereas I wasn't given food directions.

I also still didn't have a caretaker in place for when Elly returned home. I had spoken with one of the certified aides, Lizzy, from Care Meridian Sub Acute, but we hadn't worked out details. One thing I knew for sure was that Karen could not be left alone.

OCD mode kicked in hard and fast. I had to teach, take care of the dogs, do the shopping, pay the bills, grade papers, do the laundry, and learn how to take care of my disabled partner. There would be physical therapy, speech therapy, and neuro-psychologists to evaluate Karen, neuro-surgeon check-ups, a neurologist to meet, and medicines to keep track of.

My prayers for the past five months had been about Karen living. At this point, I was ready to pray for myself. Our lives had been significantly altered, and nothing would ever be the same again.

Dear God, where is my manual?

Chapter 16—New Steps

I had an even greater appreciation for the nurses at SICU and Care Meridian after I brought Karen home. Elly, Laurie, and I worked our tails off, lifting and walking with Karen nonstop. Our toughest challenge was the stairs not covered by the lift. Because our condo had wrap-around stairs, it was less expensive to have the lift not wrap around the stairs from bottom to top. However, this fact sure took its toll on our bodies. It took three people to manage Karen, and I knew this was only the beginning. I wished I had paid the extra five thousand dollars it would have cost to have the chair lift built around all the stairs—a lesson learned for sure.

I had been in contact with Winways, the organization that would be handling Karen's outpatient therapy. Since she would be an outpatient there, Elly would drive Karen there and pick her up while I was teaching. Karen would have seven hours of occupational, speech, and physical therapy. I knew she would be exhausted when Elly brought her home.

While I taught, I was able to concentrate because I knew Elly was with Karen. Elly and I had been friends for over 15 years, and she was extremely dependable. When I returned home from teaching, I felt my day really began.

Christmas was just around the corner. Lynn, who had sat with Karen many days in the SICU, sent us a beautiful wreath for our door. Karen and I loved Christmas, and I hoped it would continue to be a special time for us.

At that point, I was feeling the stress of Elly's imminent departure. I knew she had to get back to Colorado, where the snow was already wreaking havoc on the roads. I needed a fulltime caretaker for when Karen was done with Winways, and God answered my prayers once again.

Lizzy, one of Karen's assistants at Care Meridian, was leaving the facility and looking for a new job. Liz loved Karen, and I had seen how she worked with her for the past two months. She asked for 16 dollars an hour, and though I knew it had to be done, I had no idea where I was going to come up with that kind of money. We had just lost Karen's income, and at that point, it wasn't looking like she would ever work again.

Before Karen's aneurysm, I had applied to an MFA program so I could continue writing a novel I had been working on since 2003. I enjoyed writing because I had control over the lives of the characters I created. I was thrilled when I was accepted to Fairfield University for the inaugural MFA creative writing program beginning in December 2008. It was a low-residency program, which meant that I'd do independent study at home with a mentor, but would fly to Connecticut twice a year and spend nine days on an island with other writers. Karen's aneurysm had meant I had to put my dreams on hold.

I kept thinking about the program as Karen was learning to walk again. I didn't get to attend the inaugural residency. Dr. Michael White, the founder and director of the program, was kind enough to offer me delayed entrance so I could enter the program the following summer. Because Karen's condition made that impossible too, my MFA program was put on hold indefinitely, and I had no idea if it would ever happen for me. Everything was about Karen.

She progressed in therapy at Winways, but we could all tell it was too much for her. After even just 50 minutes of therapy, she was exhausted. In a group meeting with all the therapists, we concluded that if Karen was to continue healing, she had to endure therapy. I was glad I was teaching; having to deal with so many details about Karen's progress was difficult for me.

Elly left on a Friday morning in December, and I had two days on my own with Karen before Liz started helping us. I was frightened, as I had always had someone else with us. I phoned Mom and Jim to come help us. I got Karen up and dressed her, then put her on the chair lift. We had breakfast, and then I put her back onto the chairlift in order to get her to the car. Mom and Jim arrived and helped me get Karen down to the garage. Karen had therapy, so I had to drop her off at Winways and then pick her back up afterward.

When we got back home after a long day, she was able to get out of the car with my help. However, once we entered the house and tried to go up the initial three stairs to the lift, we fell. I burst into tears, not knowing what to do. I didn't want to hurt Karen, whose legs were tangled with mine.

I called Michael, who quickly drove over and let himself in. I cried again, when I saw him. Michael lifted Karen onto the chair lift. At the top of the stairs, he helped Karen off the lift and into her chair in the living room. Karen looked exhausted. I couldn't stop crying.

Michael stayed a couple hours with us, and later that afternoon, my niece, Mandie, came over to help me get Karen into bed. When she left that evening, I felt so alone. How could I pay for a full-time caretaker? When Liz came over the next day, I agreed to her rate request. I would just have to use

Karen's retirement funds for her caretaking. It was 2008 and the market had tanked; there was nothing else we could do. We had two house payments, but at least one of them was supported by rental income. Money had never been an issue for Karen and me before, but that was changing quickly.

Karen's first appointment with one of her neurosurgeons was Monday, December 11th. We got Karen to the facility only to find out that Dr. Kim was at a Mission hospital doing emergency surgery. I therefore decided to take Karen to Mission Hospital to see everyone. It was like a party. Even Dr. Kim was able to stop by to see the woman whose life he had saved.

We went to Dr. Kim's office the following week, and Karen had a good check-up. I talked to Liz about doing full-time work, and she agreed to do five days a week, twelve hours a day. I could breathe again, relieved that I was able to go back to teaching and feel confident that Liz was taking care of Karen. I also hired Michelle, who had been our barista at Coffee Bean, to be Karen's weekend caretaker. She was studying to be a nurse, so I thought it would be a great match. She ended up staying with us for six years!

Winways continued to be too difficult for Karen, so I found a new rehab center, Rehab Without Walls that sent therapists to our home. Karen had been doing more walking at Care Meridian and seemed to have lost some of her mobility at Winways. I felt that Liz knew what Karen was capable of doing and would supplement her Rehab Without Walls work. It was becoming clearer to me each day that a three-story condo was not the ideal, but there was no way that we could move given our circumstances.

I was so happy when Christmas vacation came. Karen was feeling so happy one evening that she asked me if we could get in the car, roll the windows down, and drive around singing Christmas songs! Liz got Karen ready, and off we went. With the heater turned on high, we were able to take a drive and sing on a cold winter evening. After the drive, we took Karen to get Japanese food, and we had a great dinner together. Karen still had to be pushed in her wheelchair, though, and her walking was not improving much.

When Christmas Eve was upon us, Liz put Karen in bed, and I made the mistake of handing her the remote control. She turned on *Star Wars* and turned the volume all the way up. I didn't even mind much, though; it's funny what we can tolerate after a trip to hell and back. Then she changed the channel and found the Mormon Tabernacle Choir, which was singing beautiful Christmas music. Within an hour, Karen was asleep.

Day 151 was Christmas Day! In the last five months, I had really learned that life was the greatest gift of all. There was no need for presents under the tree, as the supreme gift, for me, was Karen.

I continued to discover what my new place would be in our home. I constantly wondered whether I was going to be a partner, a caretaker, a therapist, or just myself.

The day after Christmas, I got Karen up, and we were able to handle the chair lift and five steps on our own. I sighed a big sigh of relief when we found the underlying cause of the second floor. It felt like a Christmas miracle! I jumped up and fist pumped, so happy that Karen and I were able to do this on our own. When Michelle came over, I was able to leave with Mom to go shopping--one of our favorite pastimes. The day after Christmas was a family ritual for us, and I was elated that we could continue it.

I shopped differently than I had before Karen's aneurysm; I wanted to find things that could further her recovery and make her happy. I found a hand-held game console, so I bought that along with two games.

After a day of shopping and food, Mom and I went home, I was feeling anxious about Karen and Michelle and wanted to get home to see my Bear. I dropped Mom off at her home and went on to ours.

I was delighted to find Karen and Michelle watching television and laughing. What a joyous sight that was! I felt tears gathering in the corners of my eyes.

Michelle had Karen ride her exercise bike for 20 minutes, and when the timer went off, Michelle went over to get the bike and put it in the back room. When she tried to get Karen off the bike, Karen said, "I'm fine. I still want to pedal a bit longer."

When I handed Karen the bag with her present, she looked carefully inside. She pulled the game system out and knew immediately what it was but didn't know how to use it. Michelle took it from her, opened the package, and put in the first game, which gave Karen items to find. The second game had puzzles that I knew would stimulate her brain. We found Scrabble, Boggle and hidden items underwater on the screen that Karen would have to find. Some of the games were timed some were not.

Michelle did a great job on her first day as a caretaker; I felt we had found a gem. My nerves were still on edge at this point, but I knew I needed to trust my caretakers because I had to teach; I also needed to be able to do things for myself on weekends. Life was, as always, a balancing act difficult to undertake.

It seemed like Karen had many tests still to take at Mission. Whenever we went to the hospital, we headed into the SICU first so Karen could see the many nurses who saved her life. So many came over and talked with her because they wanted to hear her voice. We were told about new patients in the SICU with head injuries, and the nurses asked us if we could talk to their families. Karen placed her hand gently on each patient's arm. She said, "Hi, I'm Karen. I looked like you do. You will get through this."

There were many tears. One family told Karen, "You give us so much inspiration and hope." We were so glad to help. This was our way of thanking the SICU staff, who had given their all to save Karen. We wanted to give back, and we knew this was one small way we could.

I bought a new 42" television for our bedroom and a 50" one for the living room. Karen was so excited about the one in the bedroom, saying, "Booie I love this TV so much that I may never leave home!" She also enjoyed playing with the remote, switching stations every couple of minutes. At first, I wasn't sure if she would remember how to use a remote, but she certainly learned quickly.

Friends brought us dinners, which was a saving grace. Our friend Aileen had her son bring us homemade chicken soup, and Lisa brought over a casserole dish that lasted three nights. I felt the love our friends had for us, and I was so appreciative. Cooking was something that had become difficult for me because there were so many other things I was in charge of.

On December 30, 2008, we took Karen to get a pedicure. Karen was meticulous about her toes; she frequently had pedicures before her aneurysm, and her toes were always painted red. She was known in the SICU as the patient with the prettiest toes.

At the nail salon, we put Karen in a chair and handed her a magazine. After everyone who knew her said hello, she quietly sat and read. Karen's smile was limited to the corners of her mouth, but I knew that she was having one of the best afternoons of her recovery.

That afternoon, Liz and I decided to take Karen to Downtown Disney. Downtown Disney couldn't offer a better environment for Karen; the sights and sounds were what she enjoyed the most. As we pushed her around, she smiled and laughed, my heart filling with joy. I always believed she would live, but I'm not so sure I knew we would share a day at Downtown Disney again.

With New Year's Eve upon us, I couldn't decide if I was happy or sad that we were leaving 2008. I had almost seen Karen lose her life, but then again, she got a second chance to live. I was able to experience medicine at its finest, and I had learned that miracles really do happen. Karen didn't remember anything that had happened that year. Even now, she is surprised when I tell her she was away from home for five months. When I show her pictures of her hospital stay, she can't believe the person in the pictures is herself.

New Year's Day was uneventful, and I had learned that sometimes, uneventful days are the best days. I made a spaghetti dinner, Caesar salad, garlic bread, and fruit salad. Karen ate everything on her plate. Her appetite had certainly returned, and she was gaining weight, which was great because I had been given a direct order to fatten her up. After dinner, we watched football games, and then Michelle and Karen watched movies. Karen loved movies, but I was never a movie fan. I was able to go upstairs, read, and write, sure, that Karen was safe with Michelle.

Our home had always been filled with music, and we were lucky to have a surround-sound Bose system. When I came home from running errands one afternoon, I heard music playing. Karen was singing the words to every song, and though her singing amazed me, the doctors had told me Karen's long-term memory was intact and that she would begin drawing upon her memories. She had no idea who the president was or what day of the week it was, but she could belt out any Ella Fitzgerald song.

On January 3, Michael came over to help me with Karen. We were trying to coach her to walk on her own. Karen loved my brother, who used a soft tone when he spoke to her, so I felt confident that he could help us.

Michael helped Karen stand, bringing her walker over to her. She actually took steps across our small living room floor by herself! It was day 160, and Karen had taken her first solo steps! I sat on the couch crying. I was filled with emotion and didn't hold back, allowing myself to cry on the sofa.

As the days passed, Karen continued to practice with her walker. Someone had to be at her side at all times in case she toppled, but she was making strides.

What used to take 15-20 minutes could be accomplished in about 5 minutes. Her size seven blue-tennis-shoes were getting things done. When the caretakers worked with Karen, she would sometimes move her arms like she was dancing! We had to tell her she needed to master walking before dance again.

Liz had to leave early one afternoon, so Karen and I were left to fend for ourselves. Sue's daughter Diana was kind enough to bring us dinner. After dinner was over and the dishes were clean, I was able to get Karen onto the chairlift. I got her ready for bed, and by 6:30 p.m., I had her all tucked in. When I got the dogs on the bed and put on *Jurassic Park*, Karen was in heaven. I felt as though I had just finished a marathon, so I allowed myself to sit at my desk and write as a reward. It was at that moment that I realized we would need caretakers for a very long time.

January 7th, 2009 was Karen's Auntie Matsy's 90th birthday. We loaded everyone in the car and went to IHOP for lunch. It was so nice to see Karen sitting next to Auntie, and we had a great time. They had always shared a close bond.

Though we had fun, Karen tired easily when out of the house, so we went home to let her take a nap. Liz walked Karen to the bathroom but let go of her hand, and Karen took her first three steps on her own, no walker in sight! What a moment that was. 164 days after her aneurysm ruptured, Karen was finally able to walk three steps alone. To us, three steps were incredible.

I thought about the past five months and how difficult they had been. It seemed like every once in a while, Karen and I would get a window of great progress. Those small windows kept me going and remaining positive. I knew she still had a long way to go, but every new milestone was a reason to celebrate.

Karen had a doctor appointment with Dr. Kim the following day. I was excited for the two to talk, as I felt like a proud mom showing her off.

When we walked into Dr. Kim's office, Karen's face lit up. "Hi, Dr. Kim!" she exclaimed. "Thank you for saving my life!" She would reiterate this many times to the doctors who had worked with her. I couldn't imagine what it must be like to save a life; I had my own small part in helping Karen since I initially drove her to the hospital, but these doctors and nurses absolutely did the rest.

Dr. Kim was warm and kind to Karen. He asked many questions, some of which Karen could answer herself. Overall, Dr. Kim was overjoyed with her progress, saying, "You have come so far, Karen. Your progress is amazing. You have Susan to thank for that." I was a bit embarrassed because he was the surgeon, not me. Dr. Kim insisted that getting Karen to Mission was the first step and that by staying by her side for over five months, I had enabled her healing.

Karen was exhausted from talking to so many people, but when we got home, she was able to take four steps completely on her own. Then she stood by her chair in the living room for 14 seconds, barely wobbling! Another record. I was jumping all around the living room, tears of joy coursing down my face. Karen sat down in her oversized chair, jubilant. These were bits of progress, that made each day worth the struggle.

During this period of Karen's recovery, it seemed like we were running a different kind of marathon that involved intermittent hospital visits. The next morning, in fact, we were at Mission Hospital at 7:00 a.m. for Karen's blood clot filter to be removed. Dr. Lempert, who was in the operating room when Karen's aneurysm ruptured, had been instrumental in saving Karen's life. He happened to see her that morning and remarked that she looked great. Karen was thrilled to meet him. She loved pleasing the doctors and nurses--even those she couldn't recall.

Karen and I met several more families in the SICU during this time. Almost every time we visited the hospital, the nurses would ask me to have Karen meet with a new family whose loved one was experiencing some form of brain trauma. Sadly, we met a few families whose outcomes were not good. A young girl in her twenties lost her dad. We visited her several times, so my heart was broken when I heard he had died. Karen and I understood that not everyone was able to be successful. This reinforced for me how fragile life is and how miraculous her recovery was.

Time continued to march on; small setbacks occurred, but major successes pushed us forward. Rehab Without Walls had come to our home twice a week to work with Karen, but it became quickly apparent that paying almost twenty-five hundred dollars a week for this specific type of therapy exceeded our budget.

Lisa Foto, who had showed up on day one with the photo album, had a friend, Jane, who was a physical therapist; we were able to hire her for a month. She was excellent with Karen. Her voice was soft but firm, and her patience in showing Karen how to get in and out of her chair helped in so many ways. I think it was her voice and caring control of Karen's body that set her apart from other therapists. Her schedule was also perfect for Karen's needs.

Jane, who had her own busy practice, couldn't keep Karen as a special client forever, and I needed someone who took our insurance. I was learning the ropes of insurance coverage and had come to understand that I would have to fight to get properly priced services for Karen. Teaching full-time only to come home, relieve the caretakers, and make what felt like endless calls to insurance companies and therapy facilities, was beginning to take its toll. However, I was still able to compartmentalize my teaching and my labor of love for Karen. I had to in order to be effective in both areas of my life.

One of the most difficult parts of this entire journey was looking at my Bear and realizing she could do very little on her own. She had been a person who helped run a million-dollar-plus company, but now she couldn't even call the insurance companies or make her own doctor appointments. These realizations were some of my darkest moments. How could our lives have changed so quickly? Would Karen *ever* return to 100 percent of who she once was? We were only six months into her recovery, and though the doctors had told me her rehabilitation would take at least 18 months, what else could I realistically expect?

My world took another turn for the worse on January 21, 2008--Karen's 178th day of recovery. My stepfather had a heart attack while I was teaching. My mom, who was at Saddleback Hospital with Jim, called me and asked if I could leave work to be with her. The front office quickly sent a teacher to cover my class. Saddleback was right before Mission, so as I drove the same route I had driven 178 days before, my mind raced, and my nerves were on the precipice of exploding.

When I arrived, my Mom was in the emergency room. The doctors and nurses were running tests on Jim, I learned quickly. I asked Mom, "Where's Michael?"

"He's at Mission in the emergency room with Mandie! She had severe stomach pain." When my sister-in-law reached Mission to be with Mandie, Michael came to Saddleback to be with us. Thank goodness that the two hospitals were only 10 minutes apart from one another and Mandie's condition wasn't serious.

In the meantime, Karen was having a great day with her Michelle. They were at the movies seeing "Marley and Me." Karen was walking much more and had even walked up the 15 stairs in our home. Though Michelle was at her side, she did it herself!

A doctor came to talk to us about Jim. There were more issues at play than just the heart attack. He was bleeding internally, so he needed a blood transfusion, and two spots on his lungs had been discovered. Things were not looking good. Mom, as the rock she always was, asked plenty of questions, but she leaned on Michael and me to help with decisions. This was her husband--her true soul mate.

Chapter 17—Therapies

On day 183 after Karen's brain aneurysm ruptured, we were back at Mission for her first angiogram, which would be performed by Dr. Nwagwu. After Karen was given anesthesia, Dr. Nwagwu would put a wire up her groin, past her lungs and heart and go to her brain. It would show him if the aneurysm was sealed and make sure there were no new aneurysms forming. We had two neurosurgeons from day one, Dr. Kim and Dr. Nwagwu, and we needed to choose which one would be Karen's primary surgeon to satisfy the demands of Karen's insurance. We chose Dr. Nwagwu because he had a gentle demeanor. I know we would have been fine with either doctor, though, as they had both played a significant role in saving Karen's life.

We arrived at Mission at 7:00 a.m. that day, and the procedure took place at 9:00 a.m. I was rattled. The last time Karen was in the OR felt like a lifetime ago and yet oddly also like it was the other day. I couldn't go through anything like that again. All the nurses reassured me that Karen would be fine--that Dr. Nwagwu did these procedures all the time. Everyone there knew Karen; all the technicians had been with her for the two and half months she was at Mission. It was overwhelming to see the love they gave her. When Dr. Nwagwu came out to talk to me pre-surgery, I hugged him, and he told me he would come talk to me again when he was done.

I sat in the waiting room while Karen was having her procedure. I paced the floor, tried to sit still, pretended to read a book, and repeated this sequence. Yes, OCD was alive and well, buckling my insides. It seemed like an eternity before Dr. Nwagwu reappeared, but within an hour, the door opened, and he walked through. "Susan, the brain aneurysm that we coiled 183 days ago is clean as a whistle, and the rest of the blood vessels in her brain were pristine!"

I hugged him and collapsed into the nearest chair. I had been told that once a person had a brain aneurysm, they could have a mirror aneurysm later on. Fortunately, Karen didn't have one. Dr. Nwagwu was a busy man, so he left shortly after delivering the news. I'm sure he was off to save another life.

When I visited Karen's recovery room, she was in her bed, as she had to lie still for eight hours. She couldn't raise her legs or her head, and she had to be still until she was released. Karen was never able to do anything the easy way.

Suddenly, a rash began forming all over her body. From her head to her toes were red blotches. The nurse wasn't sure what was happening. As she was investigating and calling Dr. Nwagwu, I called Karen's internist. Everyone's efforts allowed Karen to be diagnosed with an allergy to the dye that was used in the angiogram. Benadryl was administered immediately. She complained, whereas she had never complained about anything before. I felt helpless--there I was, waiting again. At least Karen was awake and I could talk to her. She was released at 7:00 p.m., marking the end of a long 12-hour day for all of us.

The next day, Karen's rash had cleared up. She slept a lot that afternoon, and we put on movies so she could stay in bed for most of the day. That night when Lizzy got Karen ready for bed, she discovered that she had another rash--this time on her face. Perhaps it was left over from the day before. We gave her Benadryl, and it cleared up immediately.

January 28th was Karen's 6th month aneurysm anniversary. I told her, "We need to celebrate."

She looked at me incredulously, saying, "Booie, it seems like it's only been 5 or 6 weeks." I laughed and told her I felt every minute of the entire 6 months! By this point, Karen could help with basic household tasks, so she helped me make cookie dough balls. She told me that she wanted to go to Downtown Disney, and the fact that she could recall Disney was amazing. I took her to Downtown Disney along with Lizzy.

The next day, she wanted to go to Fashion Island for lunch. We sat on the patio and shared a lunch in the beautiful Newport Beach afternoon sun. It seemed like Karen's stamina was improving, but when we got back home, she was exhausted. She took a three to four hour nap every afternoon.

Insurance was not cooperating, so the caretakers and I would do our own therapy with Karen until we could work something out for facility therapy. Each day, we had her doing thirty minutes of word searches, pedaling on her little exercise bike, and walking up the stairs. I myself was beginning to reap the benefits of Karen's success. Now more than ever, I felt she was in great hands with her caretakers, and it certainly made going to work easier for me.

Karen's days were filled with lunch dates, little trips to Target, and trips to places that she remembered. While at CVS waiting for a prescription to be filled, Karen looked at Lizzy and said, "I'm hungry. Let's get a donut," so they went next door and got a donut and a cup of coffee. Karen still wanted more afterwards and asked for a second donut, which they shared. I was so excited that Karen was eating and asking for more.

It had been over 7 months since Karen had seen her rheumatologist, Dr. Charles, at the UCLA Medical Center. The last time I talked to Dr. Charles was on day one. Dr. Guu had told her that Karen had a ruptured brain aneurysm and probably would not pull through. When we saw Dr. Charles, there were tears everywhere.

The only issue with Karen, in Dr. Charles' assessment, was that Karen's arthritis had flared up since she had been off most of her medicines. She thought that overall, she was doing well.

In the midst of all this, I was trying to fit in time for my writing. Having put the novel I started in 2003 to the side, I hadn't written the entire time Karen was in the hospital, with the exception of writing for the *Caring Bridge Journal.*

UCLA had an upcoming Writer's Studio event that I wanted to attend, but it was 4 days long, and I was reluctant to be away from Karen for that long. Everyone pressured me to do it, though, so I did.

The first day was outstanding. I was in a room with writers, which was rejuvenating. I felt I was finally doing something for me.

I stayed at an elegant hotel my first night in Westwood--the "W." I was in my room writing when I felt, all of a sudden, that I had to go home in the morning. I couldn't go back to the event; I needed to be with Karen. OCD-fueled thoughts tore through my head. *It wasn't fair of me at all to think about myself after all Karen went through.* I emailed the workshop facilitator and said that for personal reasons, I needed to go home. I packed my things up and went downstairs to get my car. It was raining hard.

I decided right then that I needed Coffee Bean. On the corner, I saw a Coffee Bean, so I went right in and ordered my other favorite drink--a Hazelnut Ice-Blended—and walked back to my car with the rain pouring.

I drove home as carefully as I could. Driving between home and Los Angeles wasn't my favorite thing to do by far, but I needed to get home to Karen. We were 193 days into our journey and it was still too difficult for me to be away from her.

When I walked through the door, Karen's face lit up with happiness. "Booie! You're home!" I was—right where I needed to be. Karen kept asking for more and more hugs. I knew I had made the right decision to come home.

We started watching *Jeopardy* and *Wheel of Fortune* together every evening. Karen loved to answer the questions, and it seemed like her long-term memory was coming back a bit. She answered questions I didn't even know, and I told her I was glad we weren't competing for money! I'd always been good at playing along with *Wheel of Fortune*, but Karen was giving me a run for my money!

I was still trying to nail down what we would do about Karen's rehab situation. Rehab Without Walls was not very expensive, but was also becoming ineffective. The therapy they set up for Karen was to go to the store and buy some flowers for our home. They asked her questions she couldn't answer and then were surprised that she had short-term memory loss! In my mind, we were done with them.

Karen had a visit to see Dr. Nwagwu on day 198. When she walked into his office, he couldn't believe she didn't need her wheelchair. The prognosis for someone surviving a level 5-brain aneurysm rupture, according to Dr. Nwagwu, would be, at best, a bedridden or vegetative state. Having had a level 5+ aneurysm rupture, Karen was a true miracle. We were told that her third month angiogram was clean, and so was her sixth. Her next marker would be one year.

After receiving a great report, we went over to Mission to visit Karen's nurses in the SICU. As we were buzzed through the double doors, the nurses came running over to see Karen---hugs and tears galore. Everyone kept hugging Karen repeatedly, and she smiled from ear to ear. When we left Mission and got outside, Karen asked, "Booie why does everyone make such a big deal out of my visits?" I looked at her and smiled, saying, "Because you survived when all odds were against you. These fine erudite nurses kept you alive minute by minute, and you certainly gave them the challenge of their careers."

Around that time, I had an epiphany about how to improve Karen's balance. I had fought dizziness for over 20 years, and I had just seen a news special on dizziness. A doctor in San Diego who claimed he knew how to cure it was interviewed. I had tried many doctors in the past, but I was eager to visit him.

Within one hour, he had diagnosed me and given me the name of a few therapists who could help me improve; in a few months, I felt much better, and a year later, I was free of dizziness, having been to a balance therapist who was fabulous in helping me. I realized that a balance therapist could best address Karen's balance.

I set up an evaluation. Karen weighed in at 96 pounds, so she was definitely on her way back to normal. Jackie, who would be her therapist during the months ahead, hooked Karen up to a harness. She walked all around the therapy room, which she claimed was like walking on the moon.

Karen was then tested in England Physical Therapy's balance machine--the same machine I was tested in seven years prior. It was the same type of machine that NASA used for recording astronauts' balance. I remembered how difficult it was for me, and I couldn't imagine Karen being able to do it at all, but as usual, she defied expectations and had no problem! She was able to finish the entire test. After her assessments were completed, a therapy plan was set in motion; Karen would continue her therapy with England Physical Therapy for years to come.

Valentine's Day fell on day 200 of Karen's recovery. We never liked Valentine's Day before; we both thought that love should be celebrated every day and that there is no need to give your partner flowers or candy just because society says you should. I knew then, more than ever, that I was blessed to have Karen in my life every day and that we should acknowledge our love on a daily basis. We went out for an early lunch and stayed at home the rest of the day. Quiet and uneventful days were especially valuable for both of us.

Liz and Michelle set up lunches for Karen when our friends were available. Karen was taken to Las Brisas, a famous restaurant in Laguna Beach, on a beautiful sunny afternoon. I heard that the food was great and the view was something to behold. I was busy teaching while they had a great time. I would later tease Karen about this. I felt I did some of my best teaching that week, glad about Karen doing so well.

By day 206, Karen felt pleased to be affiliated with an excellent physical therapy office, and had great caretakers who happily showed up for work every day. At this point, my stress levels seemed to be lower, and my OCD had settled down quite a bit. Both were indicators of how well both Karen and I were adjusting to our new lives.

Karen was walking all over our townhome, eating like she had before, and carrying on conversations with anyone and everyone. It was heart-warming for me to think that after seven months, she was doing many of the things she had done before. I knew Karen still had a long way to go, but having conversations with me, every evening was amazing.

The Academy Awards were on the 208th day of our journey. We got cozy on our bed and watched together. Impressively, she could name actors from years ago that I couldn't name. Her long-term memory was still intact. I looked over at her and teased, "I thought you had a brain aneurysm! You can remember more of these actors than I can."

She smiled at me. "Oh Booie, I'm just lucky I remember who they are."

Perhaps luck was part of the equation. I think we both knew that there was a higher power controlling this entire journey. We were given a second chance at a future together, and I knew I would be by Karen's side through it all.

Chapter 18—200 Days and Counting

My step-dad, Jim, who was age 81, had been diagnosed with terminal lung cancer. We were all devastated. What would Mom do? Everything she did was with Jimmy. He was such a kind man, and as Karen always said, "Jimmy is the salt of the earth."

Day 215 was March 1, my fifty-first birthday. Karen wanted to see Jimmy, and he was excited to see her too. Our family met at Mom's for cake and presents. Although we were glad everyone was together, it was difficult for us to celebrate in our normal loud ways. I reflected on the dichotomy-- Karen getting her life back while Michael and I watched our step-dad losing his battle with cancer. Life definitely had its twists and turns.

I was proud of Michael, who helped our mom and Jim a lot. Though Karen and I lived 10 minutes away, I was busy taking care of her after her caretaker left each evening. I couldn't leave her alone, so I would often depend on Michael to help our parents out. I went over to Mom's as often as I could when a caretaker was with Karen.

Karen started itching all over again, but this time, she didn't have a rash. She asserted, "Booie, I wish I could turn my skin inside out." I knew she was miserable because she was complaining. I figured that the itching was due to all the medicines that had been pumped into her body over the course of the past seven and a half months.

We kept going to the doctor, but nothing helped. Karen became a bit agitated. She was tired, and so was I. She accidentally tried to use the wrong remote control for the TV, so I couldn't get the television to turn back on. I also found myself having to repeat things to her three or four times. I knew it wasn't Karen's fault; it was the residual effect of brain trauma.

I called Mom to talk about these issues; she always seemed to have the right answer.

"Honey, Karen is human too. We all have rough days, and she's going to have them too." I thought about how I was calling my Mom for support when she was at home taking care of her dying husband. Life just didn't seem fair sometimes.

Karen loved therapy. With England, it seemed like we had finally found the perfect match. Every time she went, she would go on a treadmill, walk with a harness, and balance on a board. Each day when I arrived home from teaching on therapy days, I would ask Karen about her day, usually needing to remind her that she had gone to therapy.

When I asked, "How was therapy?" Karen would reply, "Oh Booie, it was great, and I just love Jackie."

"What did you work on today with Jackie?"

"I don't remember."

I would ask her caretaker what she did, and she would often give me the report for the day.

At a certain point, I knew it was time to secure a lawyer to get our affairs in order. Having been reminded that Carol tried to have the doctors and nurses pull the plug on Karen, I knew we needed to have legal papers drawn up.

I met our lawyer at my Coffee Bean, where I had him draw up documentation regarding our domestic partnership. When it was finalized, Karen and I both signed the papers. It was a huge relief to know that we were legally connected so no one could come between us.

We went to Mom's the next day--day 222 of Karen's recovery. She hadn't seen Jim in a while. He wasn't looking great, but he was still sitting in his favorite chair, talking and laughing with all of us. We had no idea that death was looming.

Karen got to see Dr. Nwagwu for her 6th month checkup the next day, and I was happy to witness their love fest. Though Karen smiled from ear to ear, I never knew who was happier—her or Dr. Nwagwu. Dr. Nwagwu was always so informative, saying, "You don't have to worry about Karen developing another brain aneurysm because she is monitored so closely. Sometimes patients develop other aneurysms after the first one, but that doesn't look likely for Karen at this point." She stood so Dr. Nwagwu could check her, then she walked over to the table and stood on the little black stool.

"Please don't fall!" yelled Dr. Nwagwu.

"I won't," replied a confident Karen.

He was amazed by everything his prize patient could do.

There was a conference in Washington D.C. at the U.S. Holocaust Museum. I applied to go and was accepted. The conference would start on March 11, 2009 and last four days. I was unsure if I was leaving at a time I should have stayed home.

Everyone told me to go, saying the respite would be good for me. Everyone kept using that word--"respite." I never understood why until years later. I was traveling alone for one of the first times in my life. It was only the second time I stayed in a hotel by myself. It was going to be a form of therapy for me.

I went to Mom's the night before I left. Jimmy was in his chair as usual, and we had a nice talk. It was hard to leave.

I told him, "See you when I get back." I just knew I would.

I lasted two days in Washington D.C. before returning home. I missed Karen too much and knew she missed me. Even though we talked on the phone twice a day, it wasn't the same as being there with her. Jimmy's health was failing, and he was in a hospital bed at home.

I flew home on March 13th. Karen was so excited when I walked through the door. I unpacked and sat with Karen and the pups, feeling drained. When I called Mom, Michael answered the phone, telling me, "Jim is in the final stage of life. I'm here with Mom almost all the time. The hospice nurse has been great."

"How's Mom?" I asked, concerned.

"She's hanging in there, but it's tough on her. She just doesn't want Jimmy to suffer."

I told Michael I would be over the next morning after Liz arrived.

The next morning, I went to Mom's and stayed for quite a while. Jimmy was asleep and had no idea I was there. Mom, Michael, and I sat in the living room and talked, sharing great stories. I left to go home so Lizzy could leave. After Karen was tucked into bed, the call came.

"Susie, Jimmy just passed away. Mom and I were talking, and I looked over at Jimmy and saw he was no longer breathing. I told Mom he had passed on, and she said he hadn't. When we walked over to him, though, we saw he had." He sighed. "Mom is in the kitchen crying. Do you want to talk to her?"

"Yes." Michael went and handed the phone to my mom.

"Hi, Mom. I'm so sorry, but Jimmy isn't in any pain now. You two shared a beautiful 15 years together. I can't come over because our caretaker left."

"It's okay, honey. Your brother is here with me. He called the hospice to tell them. It's just so difficult."

"I know, Mom. We all loved Jimmy so much. I'll take tomorrow off work and come over as soon as I can. I love you, Mom."

"Love you too, honey."

We were all worried about Karen living through the first month of her brain aneurysm and never once would think that Jimmy would lose his life to cancer. This was the third husband my mom had lost—my dad, a man she met in her neighborhood and married, and Jimmy, whom she had met at bingo in their mobile home park. Mom often told me that while she and my biological father grew up together, Jimmy was her true love and soul mate. They shared more in 15 years than many share in a lifetime.

Karen was walking up the stairs at this point, so I decided to have the chairlift taken out. On day 232, I had the chairlift removed. We had our railings put back on the stairs, and I was glad that Karen could walk up the stairs holding a handrail.

March 21st was Karen's 56th birthday and day 235 of her recovery. It was a particularly special day because there were times people wondered if Karen would see another birthday. I planned a party at Coffee Bean for her, and several people attended—people from Karen's old company, family, and friends.

Everyone was thrilled to celebrate with my Bear. Karen didn't like being in the spotlight, but we knew we had to have some type of celebration for her birthday. She received all kinds of gifts, but the best gift of all was the hugs everyone received from her.

The next evening, my family, the Mordins, and Lynne all met in Laguna Beach for an Italian dinner at one of our favorite restaurants, Salernos. Our friends were always at our side and we were all were excited to celebrate another year of Karen's life. We had watched over her in her most harrowing moments on the edge of death, but she had recovered in a way many were never able to.

On Sunday, I asked Karen to write her own Caring Bridge entry:

> *Day 236 of my journey.......SURPRISE, this is Karen. I am feeling so much better and would like to say HELLO and THANK YOU FOR ALL THE WONDERFUL BIRTHDAY WISHES.*
>
> *It seems like only yesterday that I was introduced to* caring bridge. *I've been wondering how it would feel to be typing my first caring bridge message...I'll be back tomorrow with more...*
> *Love, Karen*

I felt it was important for people to know where Karen was in her recovery. This was her second message on *Caring Bridge,* but it didn't matter if she thought it was her first. She still knew how to write, mistakes and all.

That evening she was dancing with Lizzy in the living room. I came downstairs and muttered, "Bear, do you think you could master walking before you ballroom dance?"

She laughed. "Booie, the rhythm helps my walking." Who was I to debate the issue?

Karen was able to peddle a stationary bike in therapy on day 237. She also sat on a big blue ball trying to steady herself. She had surpassed all her original goals in therapy, amazingly.

Karen never complained; in fact, she was excited each time she went to therapy and got to work with Jackie. I marveled at her stamina, commitment, and demeanor. I'm not sure that most of us could do what Karen continued to do on a daily basis.

I finally had to let her know that she had to get a California ID card because her driver's license had been suspended the day her aneurysm ruptured. They sure don't waste time making sure you don't drive! I could see a somewhat puzzled look on her face, but we discussed it, and she realized why she couldn't drive. She went with Lizzy to get her ID card. I couldn't imagine how she felt about not driving.

On day 244, Karen was back in the astronaut balance machine in therapy. Looking back at where she was on day 44 of her recovery was amazing; back then, she was taken outside the double doors of the SICU for the first time. Two-hundred days later, she was balancing on one leg and showing off her great humor. She scored a "39" on her balance test and needed to achieve a "69" to be considered at a normal stage. However, she was able to balance on one leg for 60 seconds.

In the middle of Karen's recovery, I tore my meniscus in my right knee. I had surgery to repair it by Dr. Ryan Labovitch who was not only handsome but an extremely bright orthopedic surgeon. He loved to tease me and vice versa. He thought my purple hair was amazing. Even though I was again having knee surgery, I couldn't have a better surgeon than Dr. Labovitch. Now the caretaker would need caretaking in the evening! As we celebrated, Karen's balancing on one leg we now had to focus on another recovery: mine.

Thankfully, I healed quickly and was back on my feet in four days. I had to incorporate physical therapy into my daily routine and it became challenging but I did it. Just another bump in the road for us but we were successful.

We continued to play along with *Jeopardy* and *Wheel of Fortune* nightly. I looked at Karen one evening after she answered another question correctly on *Jeopardy* and said, "Bear, I was the smartest one in this family for five and a half weeks. Now that you are recovering, you are the smart one again!"

"Oh Booie, that's not true. You're smarter." I truly didn't think I was.

I finally ventured away from our house during my spring vacation. Since Mom loved to play the slot machines, I took her to the casino about two hours from our home while Karen stayed with Lizzy. It felt good to go out with Mom, and I knew she needed a break as well. But after we had only been there a little while, Mom started thinking about the times she would go to the casino with Jim. I knew she had to get through the "firsts" before she would feel all right again.

While we were there, Karen called me, exclaiming, "Booie, I had a blast in PT today!" I thought how lucky I was because she loved her PT and didn't argue about going to her appointments.

Karen received her driver's license in the mail soon after. I told her, "You cannot drive. They made an error sending you this." She had to go back to the DMV, which is never fun.

On day 253, I asked Karen to write another *Caring Bridge* entry. She shouted, "NO!" That was the first time I heard a negative remark from her. She also told me for the first time that she missed work and was feeling sad.

I felt bad for her. She had been on Prozac for several months and had been taken off, as per her doctors' directions. They thought it was causing the itching she experienced for so long. Sure enough, after a few weeks of not taking Prozac, the itching stopped, but her sadness intensified. I felt fortunate that Karen was able to express negative feelings at all.

One evening when we went to bed, Karen looked pensive, staring off into the distance.

I asked, "What's wrong, Bear?"

"Booie, I don't want to die."

"Why are you saying that?"

"Because I've had a couple of these things."

I knew she was referring to her aneurysm. I informed her that she had only had one, and that she was in the process of healing; the doctors were monitoring her closely and she would be fine. She thanked me, turned over, and fell asleep within minutes. As she slept quietly, I watched her for a few minutes, filled with warmth. I knew I was doing my best to help my Bear recover.

I walked over to my desk and began to write. I was taking two on-line classes--one at UCLA and one at UC Irvine. Writing was my relaxation for the day.

We all shared a wonderful Easter dinner at Mom's. She was the best cook. This was our first holiday without Jimmy, but we still shared stories and laughter. Mom was busy in the kitchen with a glass of red wine. Our little niece, Becca, was two and a half, so she was our main source of entertainment for the evening. She put smiles on all our faces as she danced around.

I returned to teaching after our Easter break. It felt good to get back into my routine.

I had quite the scare when I arrived home from work after my first day back. Karen complained of a headache and nausea, which took me right back to day one. I felt like Pavlov's dog, having been trained to react. I ran to the bathroom and grabbed a Tylenol, which I gave her along with an apple. Within a short time, she was fine. I think that she was actually just hungry. I remembered, after the fact that Dr. Nwagwu had said because Karen was monitored so closely, she was not going to develop another aneurysm at this point.

On day 262, we were blessed to see Adam and the Bullough family. We all met at a restaurant nearby and talked about the road Karen and Adam had travelled. We shared all the difficulties our two families had been through during an incredible dinner.

Karen and Adam sat next to one another, which was beautiful to behold. As we talked about their experiences, Karen and Adam listened intently because neither one remembered what they had been through. It was certainly a time to be grateful.

After this, I wanted to take Karen to Mission to see some of her nurses again. She still had no idea how much they had gone through to save her life.

On day 264, we drove to Mission, and Alison was the first one we saw. She ran over and hugged Karen happily. Then Heather came over, hugged Karen, and cried.

Chuck was one of Karen's nurses in SICU. He was all smiles when he saw Karen, and I was glad to see him. Chuck and I had learned how to converse comfortably about Karen when she was in her coma; he had a stern personality, but I was a delicate flower at times. It was great to see Chuck.

Mark, Karen's respiratory therapist, also came over. He gave Karen a big hug and stood back, just staring at her.

Heather asked, "Who did your beautiful make-up, Karen?"

"I did!" she replied.

This was another great moment in Karen's recovery. The nurses and therapists had given all they had to save Karen's life, and we were eternally grateful. They watched in awe as Karen talked and laughed with them.

After many hugs and tears, I took Karen to the waiting room to show her where we had waited day after day. Several people were in the waiting room, which looked just as it had 264 days ago. I introduced Karen to everyone and told them that she was a miracle. People recognized her from her pictures on the Wall of Fame, clapping for her. It was a beautiful moment for us.

As Karen continued to improve, I decided she could do some chores around the house. We made a list and determined that she would help the caretakers with dishes and cleaning counters. I also asked Karen to lick the envelopes and place stamps on each one when I paid bills. She never complained; in fact, she enjoyed the opportunity to help. I was noticing that Karen's focus was not that great. I thought that there was a bit of ADD present. She did as asked, but she would often be distracted by the television. I would refocus her, and we'd continue; then she would become distracted again.

Finally she looked at me, saying, "Booie, you never yell at me."

"What good would yelling do? I'm just happy you're alive! I can handle telling you five times a night that it's Monday. It's really no different than repeating my lesson 10 times a day in my classroom."

While this was true, deep inside, it still pained me that Karen wasn't one hundred percent of who she once was. We were only on day 266, and though she had come so far, I knew it would take years for her to approach what she once was, if ever.

Open house was coming up at school, which meant I had to schedule two caregivers for the day--one for ten hours and then another for four hours. Even though it was a 14-hour day for me, I relished our school's open house. It was a time to showcase my students' work and to hear compliments about my teaching from parents. I felt such gratitude on open house nights, which always validated why I taught.

I knew enough about my students with ADD to compel me to finally consult a neurologist about Karen. I felt it was time to have her checked cognitively.

Dr. Ingalls, a neuro-psychologist, tested Karen a bit while we were in his office, commenting, "You are functioning at a very high cognitive level considering where you were 279 days ago." He asked Karen the date and she replied, "July 2, 2009."

"Well, you got the year correct!" We all giggled, as it was May.

Karen still couldn't drive, but Dr. Ingalls told us that in time, he thought that could be a possibility. Dr. Ingalls was a brilliant man, and I liked him working with her. He gave us different ideas about what to implement at home. He wanted Karen to return later so he could test her cognitive skills further. She would be taking an EEG test that monitored brain activity, which I was happy about. He also reminded us that she should not be left alone because of her impaired safety judgment.

On the evening of day 297, Karen and I were chatting about our days. She looked pensive. She sadly said, "Booie, I know I'm disabled. I wouldn't blame you if you left me because I don't want you to feel saddled with a disabled person." That hit me from left field.

"Bear, I haven't stood by your side for the past 10 months to leave you now. I'm not going anywhere. I will admit that these past months have been difficult for both of us, but I know we were given a second chance to share our lives with one another. I will never leave you."

She responded, "Good!" One thing I was always guaranteed was that our nights were never boring.

Day 300 of Karen's recovery was Memorial Day, so we went to Mission to celebrate and take a strawberry pie to the SICU. It didn't seem like we could do enough for this staff of heroes, so we tried to be content with small efforts.

When we arrived, many of the people that worked with Karen were there--Dr. Kim, Dr. Lempert, her nurses, and more. The doctors came over and hugged us, and the nurses were still awestruck. I looked around the SICU and saw several patients who looked just like Karen 300 days ago. Being there reminded me how fortunate we were that she had survived her ruptured aneurysm.

I felt for the families that were there that day. They too had a long road ahead of them. I wondered how many had begun to count in days. I think that was one of the most difficult things I had had to do, but I got through it, and others would too. It was all just part of the recovery process.

It was time for me, I decided. After 300 days, I felt I needed to find me again in this large dark abyss of brain recovery. I wanted to attend Fairfield University, which still had my application on file. I spoke to Michael White, the director of the MFA program. He was such a kind man, and he welcomed me warmly.

Eventually it was decided that I would spend the next two years flying to Connecticut for a low-residency program on Enders Island. I was simultaneously excited and worried.

Karen's aneurysm had been located behind her left eye, so I thought it was time for her to have her eyes checked. Dr. Taubman, our optometrist, performed Karen's eye exam. When she came out of the exam room, I was greeted with fabulous news: her eyesight had not changed! Another milestone had been successfully passed.

Karen's personality had certainly changed as she recovered, however. The doctors had told me that this was normal, whether for better or for worse. Karen became hysterically funny. She was prim and proper before, but post-rupture, she would say anything that came to her mind, asking questions like "Booie, how come your eyebrows look like a lawn mower has just run over them?" Karen now had no filter due to where her damage was on her frontal lobe. I suffered from Trichotillomania, a hair pulling disease where I would use my fingers to pull out my eyebrows. It was amazing that Karen could remember I had done that.

She danced around the house and sang in the shower, but she couldn't cry, whereas she was a crier before her aneurysm. Every sweet commercial, especially during the holidays, would make her cry. Now nothing could bring her to tears. The doctors said it was normal and that she would cry again one day. There were still so many questions without answers.

On day 320, we decided to go to Mission to say hi to Karen's nurses again. I had the thought that I was eager to show her off to everyone like a proud mom. As usual, everyone rushed over to give Karen hugs. She walked down the halls on her own, laughing and chatting with everyone. It was hard to believe her one-year recovery anniversary was the following month.

When we left, I drove us to Laguna Beach, which was a short drive from Mission. We enjoyed a quiet dinner with just the two of us, talking about how fragile life is. I knew how fortunate we both were that we were able to share a lovely dinner in a beautiful beach town at our favorite restaurant, Sundried Tomato. At times like this, our life could seem almost simple. I taught, and Karen recovered; we loved our tiny townhome, and we had three wonderful dogs. Life was good.

July approached, and I booked a trip to Oahu, where we would stay at the same hotel Karen and I had vacationed the year before. I hoped it would all be familiar to her. We brought Liz, and my mom.

As we all enjoyed the breath-taking views and walked on the soft gentle sand of Waikiki beach, where the warm water delighted our feet, I still wrestled with the idea of leaving Karen for my writing program, which I would do right after we got back home. We hadn't even celebrated her one-year recovery anniversary yet. How could I fly 3,000 miles across the country and be away fulfilling my dreams when Karen was still recovering? It seemed so selfish of me.

I stood on the balcony of our hotel room, gazing out to the ocean with sunlight glistening on each wave. I was torn. Dr. Michael White, still head of the MFA program at Fairfield University, and I shared many conversations when I was on that balcony. I was going, and then I wasn't going. I couldn't make up my mind, and I just wanted someone to tell me what to do.

Finally, I called Michael one last time from our balcony, and the conclusion was that I couldn't go. I had waited five months to get Karen home; how could I leave her and be so far away? So once again, I didn't go.

I knew that we were going to need to sacrifice the two town-homes we owned, as we couldn't pay two mortgages. I was directed to an attorney who specialized in bankruptcies, but we were given poor information and lost quite a lot. We bought a home that was next door to my brother and his wife and around the corner from my mom and nieces. The deal was made in July 2009, and shortly after, we moved into our new home.

Karen walked out the front door of our new home one day to get the mail. She didn't know our new address, so we told her she couldn't go out the front or back door without someone with her. I asked Dr. Ingalls if Karen would remember that we told her this, and he replied, "No, she won't. Someone must be with her 24 hours a day."

We hired a new caretaker for Karen--my niece, Mandie. Lizzy moved on to a fulltime job at a nearby hospital. Mandie lived right around the corner with my Mom, and Karen loved her. Mandie stepped right up and helped, suggesting that we make stop signs for the front door and back door, organizing all of Karen's medicines with a pillbox, and ordering Karen's rheumatoid arthritis shots and pills. Organization was key to Karen's success as well as mine.

Mandie being around more often meant that Becca, our little niece, came over too. She was three years old and loved being with Karen, whom she nicknamed Pancake. Becca would crawl in bed with Karen when I was ready to go to work, and they would watch movies together. When I came home, they would be on the loveseat in the living room, watching television. Karen and Becca were a fabulous pair.

In the blink of an eye, it was day 365! One year ago, Karen's and my life changed forever. We celebrated by bringing food to the SICU and having lunch with everyone there. Karen's nurses, doctors, secretaries, and therapists were all there. What a day of celebration it was! We had so many memories of difficulty and joy, having watched a life almost end and then bounce back and come alive all in one year's time.

Karen's angiogram was set for August 3rd, so we went back to Mission. This time she was given medication prior to surgery so she wouldn't have a rash. A 45-minute procedure meant an 8-hour stay in the recovery room. Naturally, I was nervous.

It was mentally exhausting to watch the team wheel Karen to the operating room. My level of anxiety was still the same as it had been a year ago. Dr. Nwagwu came out to talk to me about the procedure and, of course, I cried. He stressed that everything would be fine and that Karen would be safe, but my nerves were still hanging on by a thread. Because the procedure took so little time, Dr. Nwagwu came out even sooner than I expected and confirmed all was well. The aneurysm was sealed, no new aneurysms were seen, and Karen was in recovery.

I gave him a huge hug before he walked off to save another life.

There was always a "however" when it came to Karen and her recovery it seemed, but on this day, she fully came alive.

Karen was hungry after the procedure, so we ordered breakfast for her. An hour and a half later, she was hungry again. The staff brought her lunch, and an hour after that, she wanted a cookie, and so they gave her two cookies. Then Karen was bored and wanted to take a walk. She took off the pulse monitor on her finger and began swinging it around. I think we were seeing the full effect of her ADD.

When she had to go to the restroom, I was allowed to take her. I walked in to help her stand and noticed she had pulled off the entire surgical packing around her incision! It was not supposed to be removed until the next morning.

Five hours later, we were allowed to take Karen home. I hoped that her familiar surroundings would allow her to calm down.

That evening, Karen began breaking out in a rash again. This time, it was all over her body. We took Karen to her internist, who gave her prednisone for the itching and antibiotics to reduce the appearance of the rash.

The next morning, the rash was mostly gone, but it remained on Karen's legs, which looked nasty. Karen felt fine except for the itching. She washed dishes, remarking, "Booie, it feels good to participate in house activities again." I couldn't have been happier.

Chapter 19—Challenges

On August 7ᵗʰ, I received Karen's neuro-psychological report. Her IQ was normal, but this concerned me. She'd had a brilliant mind before her aneurysm ruptured. Her highest scores were for visual puzzles, which meant that she was integrating the left and right sides of her brain well and her visual cortex was working well. She could also analyze and differentiate between different stimuli well.

She had also performed well when it came to naming things. She scored in the superior range in that category, and her speech was pronounced fluent too. Dr. Ingalls noted that he believed Karen had suffered three types of brain injury: a ruptured brain aneurysm, a small stroke, and reduced supply of oxygen to the brain.

In an unstructured environment, Karen was very distracted, and memory and learning were revealed to be weak areas. She had trouble taking experiences from her short-term memory and transferring them to her long-term memory, which perhaps was a result of a lack of cranial oxygen after the aneurysm ruptured.

As Dr. Ingalls reviewed her results, I glanced at her to see if she had any facial expressions that might allude to her feelings, but there were none. I realized that all the details of this report probably would not remain in her memory, so they wouldn't affect her feelings; they would affect only mine. I knew there had been a great deal of brain damage, but hearing these facts from Dr. Ingalls' perspective was heartwrenching.

While reading a story for the first time, Karen could remember only minor details. I was beginning to see the bigger picture: I would be an English teacher not only at school, but also at home, teaching my partner.

Dr. Ingalls was thorough in his testing and documentation of reported findings. He suggested that Karen avoid driving for at least two years. He recommended that in order to communicate, she use a PDA, a voice dictation system, and Post-Its. He also recommended that she attend college classes to aid with her mental rehabilitation. This was all valuable information for me; I was able to determine where she was cognitively and speculate about what plan of action we would use.

When we left Dr. Ingalls' office and got into the car, I asked her what she thought about the meeting.

She said, "Well, Boo, this is the deck we were dealt, so we will just deal with it."

I was amazed by Karen's outlook. However, Dr. Ingalls also reminded me that she had no idea of the magnitude of what had taken place in her brain. He framed this as a positive, though, because it would help her to not become depressed.

Many people asked me if I was overwhelmed by Dr. Ingalls' findings. Of course I was! The brain aneurysm had turned our lives upside down and depleted us of a great amount of money. Karen's life was always the most important part of this entire journey, and I had made decisions I felt were best for her regardless of cost. She was my constant companion, and no matter where she was on the brain injury spectrum, I had resolved to always take care of her and love her for a lifetime.

Karen would have nothing to do with attending college. Dr. Nwagwu talked to her about her decision.

"Why don't you want to attend Coastline College?"

"Because there is nothing they can teach me."

"But how do you know that if you don't give it a chance?"

"I know that I would be bored, so I'm not going to attend."

The best part of the entire discussion was Karen keeping up with Dr. Nwagwu's conversation. He eventually agreed with her; she would be fine without attending the program. We were doing a great job at home with her, and she had exceeded expectations for a level 5+ brain aneurysm rupture.

On August 13th, 2008, Mission Hospital set up a reunion for six survivors who had been in the SICU. I decided I wanted a tattoo dedicated to Karen and her team at the Mission SICU. Sue Mordin's son was a tattoo artist, and he did the tattoo for me free of charge. He tattooed Karen's brain on my left arm for all to see. On top of the brain image were the words "Karen," and "Mission Hospital SICU" was below.

Sue had sat and waited with me hour after hour, day after day, month after month. The event was filled with excitement, memories, and love. Lisa Foto, Adam, and Karen--three of the most serious cases of Mission's history--hugged each other, and Adam even played his guitar. My tattoo was a big hit as well! Many people wanted a picture of it, and someone even sent a picture to the Mission CEO. It was a day that will forever be safe within my heart.

Our new home had one level, which was fantastic--no stairs to deal with. I could sit in the office that I had built right off our master bedroom and feel at peace.

When I was in there writing on a Saturday evening, Karen walked in to say hi to me. She tripped over one of the dog's beds and hit the floor. I quickly called Dr. Kim, who was on call at Mission that night. He told me to take Karen to the hospital and said that he would order a CAT scan as soon as possible.

When they took Karen into the trauma area, I just stood there, nearly paralyzed. My eyes searched every room until it locked on trauma room 2, where Karen had been one year before. The nurse asked me questions, firing one after the other. I hadn't even heard the first one.

My brother Michael stood next to me, gently prompting me with "Susie, you need to answer the nurses' questions."

I turned toward the nurses, saying, "Sorry."

The CAT scan concluded that there was no bleeding, which meant I got to take Karen home. Had I failed? We were in our new home and things were supposed to be easier, but Karen had fallen. I wasn't used to having to watch her every second because she was usually tucked in bed by the time her caretaker went home. Did this new accident mean that I couldn't write? Would I not be able to use the office that I had had built for myself?

I received a call from Dr. Kim the following morning. He went over Karen's report with me. There was no bleeding, and while the aneurysm remained coiled, she had had a minor concussion. He reassured me that with enough rest she would be fine.

Karen seemed unfazed about her accident, but she did start crying again, which I took as a good sign. "I miss driving, Boo," she told me, "But in two years I know I can drive again, and I want a Mini Cooper."

"If you can drive in two years, you may have any car you want," I said with a weak smile. I highly doubted that Karen would ever drive again.

Mom began to help with caretaking to help us save money. My mom and I are alike, as we like things done in an orderly way. Karen, however, didn't like how strict Mom was. She called Mom a nag twice, refused to eat lunch once, and once refused to get dressed when I arrived home from school. However, I knew Mom working with her was for the best.

Mom bowled twice a week, so Karen had to go to the bowling alley with her. Everyone there knew Karen's story and enjoyed seeing her and talking to her.

One afternoon, my cell phone rang while I was teaching.

"Hi, Booie. What are you doing?"

"I'm teaching. What are you doing? Whose phone are you using?"

"I'm in the restroom, and I don't know whose phone I'm using."

"Bear, where's Mom?"

"She's bowling."

"Ok, hang up and get back to Mom."

I called the office for a sub and headed to the bowling center. My heart was racing, and I had no idea what was going on. When I arrived, I ran into the center and found Karen and Mom sitting behind the lanes, sipping sodas.

"What are you doing here?" asked Mom.

"Karen called me from the bathroom. Did you know that?"

"No."

"Bear, whose phone did you use?"

"Mamma's."

"I'm here because I had no idea what was going on." Boy was I relieved!

I needed a vacation in a place where cell phones don't get service--perhaps the beach or the mountains. Books and pens would be all I needed to take. But how could I leave Karen?

As time went on, I gave her more autonomy. I would let her walk into the kitchen to get her meds out of the cupboard. On Saturday nights, Karen had five pills to take, four of which were her RA meds.

One particular Thursday, I asked her how she was doing, and she said, "I'm fine, Booie, I'm taking my meds. I took my 5 pills."

I flew out of the bedroom. "Bear, it's Thursday! You only have one pill!"

"Oh, I thought it was Saturday!"

"Are you kidding me? I told you it was Thursday when you went into the kitchen! Bear, really?"

"I'm sorry, Booie. I forgot what day you said it was."

I got her back on the bed and began phoning the pharmacist, UCLA, and my Mom. I knew Dr. Charles at UCLA would tell me if Karen was in an overdose situation with her RA medications. I was told she should be fine but that I should keep a close eye on her, as she could bleed, vomit, or get an infection. I was on my last nerve. It had been fourteen months and still I felt that we needed more help.

I apologized to Karen for yelling at her.

"You yelled at me, Booie?" she asked, perplexed. I don't remember!" I guess the best part of the brain injury was that if she and I argued or I yelled, she never remembered—but I still felt guilty.

I still saw Dr. Kaplan, my therapist, once a week. She was my rock. She told me repeatedly that I had nothing to feel guilty about. She felt I had done everything right, including saving Karen's life by getting her to the right hospital. It would take years of conversations with Dr. Kaplan before I would ever let go of my guilt surrounding Karen.

I concluded that I truly did need a break, so I scheduled a five-day trip to Colorado, where I could spend time with Elly.

I can't say that it was relaxing for me because she was having relationship issues with her partner, which overtook our conversations. However, I was able to see the Rocky Mountains with her and experience the great outdoors. I missed Karen, and after a short time, I was certainly ready to go home.

I thought things would settle down more, but they didn't. To make things worse, I received all the paperwork regarding our condos in the mail. We had a short sale for one condo, and lost ninety thousand dollars. We had to give the other home back to the bank because our renters were moving to Chicago, so we lost one hundred twenty-five thousand dollars on that home.

I therefore worked on all the paperwork in my office shortly after I returned home. At one point, I turned around to see what Karen was doing and found her on the bedroom floor wrapped in a blanket, the dogs next to her. I ran over to her.

"Bear, what happened? Did you fall?"

"No, Booie, I didn't fall. Did you hear a thud?"

She had me there. I didn't hear a thud. She must have slid down the end of the bed with her blanket and found that she was quite content sitting on the floor with the dogs. The world of brain injury offers such an array of challenges.

Karen was still regressing, forgetting more and more things. Dr. Nwagwu ordered another CAT scan because he needed to rule out hydrocephalous, a condition that caused water to accumulate in the brain sac.

Soon after, it was November 26, 2009--Thanksgiving. Karen was having difficulty remembering any directions at all, she got tired more easily, and her gait was more haphazard than normal. If the CAT scan did in fact reveal evidence of hydrocephalous, it would mean another brain operation. I didn't know if I was ready for that.

Around this time I was challenged by the lack of support from many of Karen's family and friends. Everyone had filled the SICU waiting room and were so concerned about Karen surviving before. Now that she had been home for a while, it was rare for anyone to call her. The Mordins came over, and Trish and Chuck, Karen's cousins stopped by, but where was everyone else? Everyone had our home phone number; I had it posted on Karen's journal a while ago.

I finally got mad enough that I wrote a post about my feelings on *Caring Bridge.* I would learn later that somewhere near ninety percent of a brain trauma sufferer's friends and family members leave him or her and never return. Karen didn't realize it, but I did. I cried because I thought it hurt her.

On December 3rd, 2009, we received the news I was dreading; Karen's brain ventricles were enlarged and she had hydrocephalous, so she would need surgery to have a shunt placed in her brain and a box placed in her tummy. A drain would go from the brain through her neck, draining into her stomach.

Normal procedure meant that she would spend only one day in the hospital, but Karen had been anything but normal in her recovery. Dr. Nwagwu said she would recover in the new SICU tower that was just opened. We had been there for the open house of the new tower, but never once did I expect Karen to have to recover there.

On December 7th, her surgery was postponed, as she had a urinary tract infection and an issue with her EKG for which she had to see a cardiologist. Her new surgery date was scheduled for December 15th.

Karen was tired all the time, was eating well but not enough, and had lost 3 pounds. Her memory wasn't working well, but she constantly laughed and was always in a good mood. When we were getting ready to have her stress test with her cardiologist, I joked to Mom, "Soon they're going to have to give me a stress test!"

When December 15th came, Karen's surgery was cancelled again. She had a reaction to an antibiotic given to her for her urinary tract infection; it was responsible for the worse rash I had ever seen. Her nuclear heart scan was normal, so her cardiologist cleared her. She was put on prednisone, and her surgery was rescheduled for a few weeks later.

The prednisone was exactly what Karen needed. Her rash cleared up, and she ate everything put in front of her. I called her neurosurgeon's office and discovered that her surgery was to take place on January 5, 2010.

As we got closer to the day of her operation, I became more frustrated. I gave Karen directions six times one evening, yet she couldn't do any of the things I had asked of her. I knew it was the hydrocephalous, but my nerves were shot. I apologized to Karen so many times for being upset, although she didn't remember.

When January 5th finally arrived, Mandie and I took Karen to Mission. Upon arriving, we found Michael was already there, working. Trish and Chuck came and stayed with me in the waiting room. I thought about how we are all just prisoners of time.

Karen was still a star at Mission, of course. While we were waiting to be admitted, people came over to say hello. It was amazing just how many people knew her, but then again, she had been at Mission for almost three months.

Dr. Nwagwu came out and announced, "We will be shaving Karen's hair." I was sad, as it was so beautiful once again--black, thick, and styled in the cutest haircut. Trish suggested that they shave it all the way off in the back so it would grow out evenly, and Dr. Nwagwu said that would be fine. He explained what would be done and then left. I had trusted this man for the past 18 months; there was no reason not to trust him now.

They wheeled Karen back through the double doors. I was transported right back to July 28, 2008, and OCD came rushing back to rest on my nerves. Sometimes OCD was my best friend, and other times, it definitely wasn't. I counted tiles again, plagued by thoughts. *Will Karen survive? What if something goes wrong? Is this a routine surgery? How many surgeries of this type has Dr. Nwagwu performed?*

We all waited once again. Time ticked slowly minute by minute.

When Dr. Nwagwu reappeared, he said, "She did great. Everything went well. She has a horseshoe cut in the back of her head where I put the device. She has many staples too, but I will take them out in a couple of weeks, and the incisions will heal. I cut her hair like you asked. I think you will see a major difference in Karen's recovery now."

I jubilantly hugged the man who had once again saved Karen's life. Without this surgery, Karen could not have continued to improve. In fact, death was the ultimate result if her shunt wasn't put in.

I walked to the room where Karen would wait during her recovery, and everyone else went home. Alison had just ended her shift, so she stayed long enough to see Karen. It felt so good to have one of my favorite nurses by Karen's side.

When Karen was wheeled in, there was a cute white beanie on her head. We were told she would spend two days in the SICU, where she was monitored 24/7.

Brandon, whom I had met back on July 28th, happened to be at the hospital for a meeting. He ran to the cafeteria and brought me back dinner--a hamburger and fries. I ate at Karen's bedside. She awoke relatively quickly and chatted with us a bit. I knew she was tired, so I stayed only until 9:00 p.m. that evening and then made the drive back home. I knew Karen was safe.

The next morning, I was back at Karen's side. She was wide awake and eating breakfast. Dr. Nwagwu came by and checked out his girl, commenting that everything looked great. He wanted her to spend one more night in the SICU. Another hurdle had been surmounted.

Chapter 20—A Caring Bridge

Over the course of the coming months, Karen's progress was amazing. She was doing things in therapy she had never done before--walking over blocks, turning and stretching, and even throwing a ball onto a trampoline and catching it behind her back. Karen had arrived!

Life continued. I taught, Karen recovered, and we always knew how fortunate we were that she had made it. On April 18, 2010, I wrote my last *Caring Bridge* entry:

> *Day 630! Tomorrow I will shut down the Caring Bridge site for Karen Kozawa. Everyone's words of support are now saved in a binder for Karen to read one day. I want you all to know that our journey could not have been possible without your support. You all know who you are. I close this site with love and admiration for each one of you who participated and gave endlessly of yourself. Karen continues to beat all odds and is making strides every day. I was blessed to be able to think quickly on July 28, 2008 and drive Karen safely to Mission Hospital, which is the only place where she*

had a chance of surviving. Mission Hospital will always remain number one in our hearts because of all they did to save my Bear's life.

It is difficult to close a site that became a means of sharing Karen's struggles and strengths during the past 630 days. Thank you again for participating in the marathon that the neurosurgeons said I would undertake. I never jogged, and I never ran; I walked every step beside Karen. It was worth every mile we both endured.

Love,
Susan and Karen

Epilogue

Six years later, I found the courage to apply once again to Fairfield University and the MFA program--this time for Non-fiction. I trusted all my caretakers and I knew they would take great care of Karen. I knew I had given Karen all I had inside of me for the past six years and would continue to do so for the rest of our lives. However, it became clear that I didn't want to lose myself in the abyss of brain trauma and recovery, and it had become more than apparent that I needed to climb out of this dark place and find myself.

The past few years, I had taken classes through the UCLA Extended Education program. Writing from home and taking these online classes worked for a few years, as the interaction with other writers was exhilarating. Lynn Hightower, a teacher at UCLA, had impacted me the most. I frequently vacillated between the option of finishing the novel I had put on hold and the idea of writing a memoir-- one that could possibly help others who endured devastating brain trauma.

I had eighty pages of my memoir written when I applied to Fairfield the second time. I wrote Michael White, who was as supportive and caring as he had been years before, and I went through the entire application process again.

I wasn't used to traveling alone, so I needed to be assured that I could fly across the country on my own and leave Karen back in California with her caretakers. I needed to convince myself that she would be safe. Once again, Dr. Kaplan became the wind beneath my wings that convinced me to soar. She worked tirelessly to form a plan that would assist me if I were accepted.

In April of 2014, my acceptance letter arrived. My program would begin in July, and I would travel back east for nine-day residencies in July and December. I had three months to put everything together. My dreams were coming to fruition, and although I was nervous, I knew I needed this more than I ever had.

Coordinating our caretaker schedule took a great deal of work, as it involved making sure Karen had someone for every minute I was back east. I put Mandie in charge of everything. I packed the freezer with food and left money in case the caretakers wanted to go to the movies with Karen and left a list of phone numbers.

When I kissed Karen good-bye, I reflected on the idea that my departure was harder on me than on her. She knew I left daily for work but always came back each night, so I wasn't sure she would even fully understand what my trip meant. I kissed her several times and hugged her little frame. Then Mandie took my luggage to her car, I kissed the puppies, and I was off.

While I wasn't nervous about flying, I was apprehensive about changing planes and then getting to my hotel, where I would stay alone. What if my driver didn't show up the next morning? How would I get to the island? There were so many firsts for me, but then again, hadn't the previous several 6 years been anything but firsts?

The flight from Orange County to Atlanta, Georgia was wonderful. A nice young couple was sitting next to me, and we talked the entire flight. When we disembarked in Atlanta, my OCD went into full throttle. The airport was huge, and I needed to run to another part of the airport to catch my next flight, sweat dripping down my face. At fifty-six, I was learning to expand my world.

When I finally found my gate and sat down, I breathed a sigh of relief; at least I was halfway to Connecticut.

We arrived at midnight. OCD my best friend came right along with me and this time it raged and rankled through my mind, making me unsure about how I would get my luggage and take it to the Sheraton, especially given that I had a fractured foot at this time and couldn't walk well. Luckily, I saw an attendant who helped me with my luggage, guided me into an elevator, and walked me to the Sheraton. I thanked him profusely and gave him a big tip. I had arrived in one piece.

I took a deep breath as I walked into my room. My room looked out onto the airport's runways, which was stellar. I called home to tell Karen I had arrived. Everything was calm back at home, and Karen was happy to hear from me. At first, I couldn't sleep that night, but I eventually did.

Morning came quickly, and before I knew it, it was time to leave for Enders Island. My driver was early, the ride was beautiful, and in an hour and a half, I was standing on the island.

We had a little dorm room with two beds and a desk, and I learned to share a bathroom with women of all ages—a first for me because I had never stayed in a dorm in college. We ate breakfast, lunch, and dinner together in the dining hall. Everything had a schedule.

I couldn't believe that 6 years after Karen's horrific brain aneurysm, I was allowing myself the opportunity of a lifetime to find myself and become a writer. I missed Karen terribly, and this trip was difficult for her as well, but we did it. We both survived the separation twice a year as I continued to return to Enders Island, writing on the east coast and then returning home to the west coast. I met so many wonderful teachers, writers, and staff on the island. As I sat in a gazebo gazing out at the Sound, I realized that Karen was not the only one who had been given a second chance; I had also.

I finished my master's degree in creative writing, Non-fiction, in July 2016. The graduation ceremony was emotionally overpowering. I didn't have my family there to share it with me. I figured I began this on my own; I needed to come full circle and complete it on my own. The next morning I packed all my belongings, had one last breakfast on the island and hugged my friends and teachers. My driver had arrived. I climbed in the backseat of his black Town car. He softly shut the door. As he began driving slowly off the island, I watched out the back car window. Seeing the sunrise on the sound, the trees softly swaying in the light breeze, and knowing that I had completed what I once had set out to conquer so many years ago was bittersweet.

I was overjoyed that I had completed my MFA, but I was not ready to leave the program. There were conferences across the United States that I could participate in, but I knew they wouldn't be the same.

Five months later, I applied again to Fairfield University—this time for the Master's program in fiction writing. I wasn't ready to let go of the school that had given me back my life. I would again be able to travel from the Pacific to the Atlantic, stand on the edge of the Long Island Sound, gazing at the glistening sunlight bouncing off the water, and know that I too had been reborn.

Karen has since regained her long-term memory, her ability to critically think, and she takes piano lessons. We've traveled to Hawaii several times, we continue to play Jeopardy nightly, and I still lose to my Bear. No one ever thought any of this possible. We are truly blessed.

On April 14, 2014, Karen and I were married.

Acknowledgements

Susan M. Davis

I have earned a Masters of Fine Arts in Creative Nonfiction at Fairfield University. It was a joint effort that included many people and a coffee shop.

First, to my wife, best friend, and soul mate, Karen Kozawa, who had to endure the horrific ruptured brain aneurysm. Her recovery and determination to live gave me the encouragement to pursue my MFA and write our story. Without her, this book would not be possible. She remains my daily inspiration. I love you Karen Kozawa.

To my mom, Joyce Myers, who taught me the love of reading, taught me right from wrong and gave me the courage to be myself.

To our doggies, Joshua, Benson, Madi and Miles who gave me hugs and love when I needed them most.

To my niece Mandie, who has been an endless caregiver for Karen as I traveled 3000 miles to study the craft of writing. Without her, this would not have been possible.

I would also like to thank Lynn Hightower, whom I met through UCLA Extended Ed. Writing program. She encouraged me to write and continue to write and supported me to enter the MFA program. She was the first of my mentors. And to Barbara Abercrombie from UCLA Extended Ed. who offered writing retreats in the mountains of Lake Arrowhead where I learned to be critiqued without tears.

A special thanks to Coffee Bean store (#64) in Irvine, California who offered me a safe place to write every weekend.

Michael White of Fairfield University, creator of the MFA in Creative Writing program. Michael never gave up on me, though I vacillated so many times in choosing to become a student in this fabulous program. A heartfelt thanks to my teachers in the program, Da Chen, Kim Kupperman, Rachel Bausch, Adriana Paramo, Sonya Huber, Bill Patrick, and Eugenia Kim, with their guidance and superior words of how to write a memoir of value. Their devotion to the written word is what makes this program outstanding.

An extra special thank you to Eugenia Kim who endlessly poured over my Memoir with edits and more edits. She is one special person.

Thank you to the mother of our MFA program, Elizabeth Hastings, whose dedication to the student's keeps us all in place. She always had the answers in assisting my travels from California to Connecticut.

Last but certainly not least, thank you to my therapist, Dr. Susan L. Kaplan, who taught me how to believe in myself, to know everything was possible by taking small steps, and whose love and dedication has carried me through so many obstacles, and in ultimately supporting me in making this dream possible. She is truly the wind beneath my wings.

About the Author

Susan M. Davis graduated from California State University Fullerton with a degree in English. She has been an 8th grade English teacher for 27 years. She is a former Teacher of the Year. Susan also has a Masters of Science in Educational Counseling. She just completed her MFA in Creative Writing Non-fiction from Fairfield University in Connecticut. Susan resides in Southern California with her wife, Karen Kozawa and their 3 Cocker Spaniels. Her favorite color is purple. If you know her, you will know this.

"Many veterans are traumatized by what they went through in war, but others, like Daniel (and perhaps the author himself), wonder "What will replace the thrill of combat?" For the main character of Samuels' book, the answer is in the title."

– ForeWord Reveiws

A credible, instantly appealing and meaningful read.

– Kirkus Reviews

This is a well written work of fiction that explores many issues common to returning veterans spiced up with a number of compelling twists.

– VHPA Aviator

PAGE PUBLISHING, INC.
New York, NY

First originally published by Page Publishing, Inc. 2015

ISBN 978-1-63417-653-8 (pbk)
ISBN 978-1-63417-654-5 (digital)

Printed in the United States of America

Contents

Acknowledgements

I am the last person I ever thought would write a book. I had a lot of help and encouragement. My good friend and neighbor Diane Chamberlain, a famous author herself, was a great inspiration and always there with words of wisdom and encouragement. Along with her partner, John Pagliuca, they were instrumental in getting this project started and completed. My good friend and fellow veteran Dennis Rogers worked on the manuscript and kept it flowing. At first he said "not another war story" but told me "you have a story to tell and I can tell a story" which became very true. His lovely wife HollyAnn became a tremendous help with her computer and editing skills. My actual crew chief Ken Rucker and gunner Galen Elders are the reason I survived the war and am here today to tell any stories. Thank you one and all for all the kind words and support.

Preface

As a helicopter pilot in Vietnam, I learned about camaraderie, combat, and courage. I also learned how addictive life on the edge could be. While that heady feeling of invincibility served me well in the military, it left me adrift in civilian life.

That's when organized crime found me and offered to feed my dark and dangerous addiction.

Society may scorn thrill junkies like me, but not the mob. Organized crime not only seeks you out for its own advantage, it embraces and rewards your willingness to push yourself to your limits and beyond.

I was there. I saw it. I lived it. And I walked away.

I was a pilot for the mob.

Chapter 1

"Badger One-Five, this is Two-Seven. Are you up yet?"

No answer.

"One-Five, this is Two-Seven. Are you up yet?"

"Roger, Two-Seven, this is One-Five. I'm right behind you. We had a few adjustments to make."

"Roger that, One-Five, stay as close as you can, and I'll see if I can get us safely out of this mess."

"Roger, Two-Seven, just keep your lights on as long as you can. I can't see shit in this soup."

"Roger, One-Five."

It was one of those nights in Vietnam that pilots hate: low ceiling, low visibility, and a steady, miserable rain. There was no moon above and no lights below. We had a hell of a time flying straight and level. When it is dark in Vietnam, it is dark. We should not have been flying that night.

I'd gotten the call at 2130 hours. A squad of paratroopers from the 101st Airborne Division was with a platoon of South Vietnamese soldiers at a listening post near the Cambodian border. They were west of Tay Ninh in the III Corps area.

An American captain radioed that his position was under heavy attack by a battalion-size force of Viet Cong fighters armed with mortars, small arms, and satchel bombs. I figured he was young, probably twenty-three or twenty-four, and he sounded scared. I was in my eleventh month in Vietnam, and I'd heard many a young and scared soldier on the other end of the radio.

He needed help, and he needed it now—or he and his men would die.

It may have been a night pilots hate, but it was exactly the night the VC loved. They had great respect for United States air power and artillery, and they knew that if weather conditions kept us from controlling the skies, they had a better chance of controlling the ground. A perfect night for killing Americans.

I told the young captain there was no way we could rescue him and his troopers before sunup. The weather was just too bad to fly safely.

He tried to hold his composure when he said, "Listen to me closely, we will not last till sunup!"

There was no real decision to make. This was a combat zone. American soldiers were in trouble and needed help if they were to live. The only real question was how fast could we get there?

I told him to hold on—we'd be there as fast as possible.

I flew my own Huey helicopter gunship and was also the leader of a two-ship fire team. It wasn't just my life at risk. I had responsibility for two gunships, four pilots, and four gunners. They should have a say in this decision, too.

I hurried to the flight line where the other guys waited. We were on standby alert. The troops cynically called it "graveyard duty." I quickly ran the available options through my mind. The Air Force, Navy, and Marines all had jet fighter-bombers—the aptly named "fast movers"—but the bad weather kept them grounded. If they couldn't see the target, they couldn't hit the target.

Artillery? I checked, and there was nothing close enough.

Ground reinforcements? It would take too long for troops to get there traveling on foot, and even if they made it, by the time help arrived, there likely would be no one alive to rescue.

That left us.

I briefed the crew on what kind of suicide mission this was likely to be. They listened with one ear while strapping on their gear and untying the blades. I never got a chance to ask for volunteers. Not that it would have made any difference. We were combat flyers. This is what we did. The pilot of my wing ship was Chief Warrant Officer John McNeill, an excellent pilot, and I was glad he was with me. We didn't have to check anything further, we got our orders and we knew what had to be done.

The flight from Long Thanh to Tay Ninh was usually about forty minutes as the crow flies. The problem was that because of weather, the crow was grounded, too. We had to fly by what experienced Vietnam pilots called IFR—"I Follow Roads."

Because of the weather and darkness, the highest we could fly was four hundred feet, and the fastest speed we could maintain was fifty knots, which is slow, low, and dangerous in a combat zone. My crew chief, Kurt Rose, and my gunner, Gabe Elton, hung off the side of the ship watching for the road, the ground, and anything else that might be in our way.

We reached the firebase at 2300 hours. It looked like the Fourth of July. Tracers, white phosphorous grenades, and mortar explosions were all over the area. The beleaguered base from five miles away was lit up enough to make it the only light around on this nasty March night.

I called the young airborne captain on the radio and told him we were there and asked where he wanted us to start our assault. He almost cried from relief when he told us to start our gun runs on the outside ring of his barrier wire and work our way in. He put up flares for us to see the enemy positions. Where we should attack first was a moot point: enemy troops were all around the base camp. He was surrounded by hundreds of Viet Cong. He and his men didn't have much time left, just like he'd said. It wasn't even midnight. They could never have lasted until daylight.

"One-Five, this is Two-Seven, are you ready?"

"Roger Two-Seven, we are locked and loaded."

"One-Five, we are going to start our runs from east to west and break south so we don't fly right over the enemy strength."

"Roger Two-Seven, we're right behind you. The rain has slowed so we have some visibility."

The ceiling had lifted to above 1,000 feet by that time, so we had little sky in which to maneuver. Ideally, we would start the run at

1,600 feet and break it off at 700 feet. But all we had was a thousand feet of dark sky, so we had to make it work.

I rolled in first and started firing the rockets. Gunship pilots have to control the rockets because the rocket mounts don't move. The attitude, altitude, and direction of the aircraft determine where the rockets will hit. In simple terms, you don't aim the rockets; you aim the helicopter—the better the pilot, the more accurate the rockets. After eleven months of flying and shooting rockets, I had gotten pretty good. It wasn't like I had to hit a particular spot. I had a whole area to fire into because the enemy was all over.

My copilot was in the left seat and controlled the mini guns, the Gatling guns mounted on each side of the aircraft. They were on flexible mounts, so the shooter could accurately aim them. Every fifth round in the belt was a tracer round that glowed when it left the barrel, so you could watch it all the way to the target.

A Gatling gun can fire five thousand rounds per minute, and a good shooter can put six rounds in a twelve-inch box from four football fields away. The weapon was awesome, and we needed an awesome weapon that night. Unfortunately, the minis could shoot only in ten- to fifteen-second bursts because the barrels would get so hot they could melt and jam. One of a gunship pilot's worst nightmares was a gun jam during a firefight.

We made three or four passes over the target, altering our pattern and avoiding the heavy fire the VC threw at us from the ground. I had fired all my ammunition, so I grabbed my M-16 rifle and fired out the window. The M-16 ran out of ammunition, and I used my .38 pistol. We fired everything we had—so had my wingman, John McNeill. It looked like the VC were running back to the tree line for cover.

I radioed the captain we were out of ammo and dangerously low on fuel. We would be back as soon as possible. The VC were running, but they would return the moment we left the battlefield.

"Hotshot Six, this is Badger Two-Seven, hold tight we will be back ASAP."

"Roger Badger, my men and my kids are counting on you."

"Badger One-Five, this is Two-Seven."

"Go ahead, Two-Seven; this is One-Five."

"One-Five, what's your status?"

"We took a few hits but no blood, just a little shrapnel and a whistling blade." A "whistling blade" meant a round had gone through the blade. It wasn't immediately critical, but it could get worse, depending on where the bullet went through.

"Same here, One-Five. No blood, just a few hits. How's your equipment?"

"So far so good, Two-Seven. We might need to adjust one of the minis when we get on the ground."

"Roger, One-Five, we're going to try to get to Tay Ninh and hope refueling is open, and they have some ammo we can get our hands on."

"Roger, Two-Seven, I'm right behind you, but we don't have much time. Those VC are going to regroup once they see us gone. What do you figure the count so far?"

"Not sure yet, One-Five. I know we got plenty of them, but there was plenty left."

We landed at the helicopter base refuel area at Tay Ninh. It was about 0030 hours. No one was around. We didn't need any help to refuel, but the pros do it in far less time, which was something those Screaming Eagles on the ground didn't have much of.

McNeill and I agreed we should not shut down our helicopters while we refueled. We didn't want to take a chance on some unforeseen mechanical problem with batteries or anything else keeping us from heading back to the fight as soon as possible. The last comment the captain made about his men and kids really got to me and kept my blood pumping at full speed. Refueling with the engine running was not all that dangerous as long as you were careful, but rearming the weapons was another story.

As I was landing the ship I turned to the crew.

"I don't have to tell you how important it is we get back to the fight ASAP. Don't cut any corners, just be careful, and we'll win this thing and kick some ass."

"Roger, sir," they said as they got out and started to refuel and rearm. We had done this so many times during the last year we all knew what to do when so many lives depended on us.

I told the copilot, "Simmons, you stay in the cockpit, pull all the non-essential circuit breakers, keep the engine at idle and monitor the gauges. We don't want any sparks or misfires." He gave me a thumbs up. I got out and started loading the rockets.

We were refueled, rearmed, and ready to go in twenty minutes. Not bad considering the dark night and no help. The crew chiefs and gunners we had were the best in the platoon. We were back in the fight in less than an hour. Sure enough the VC had regrouped and were hard at it again.

We started the same gun runs as before, only this time they had an ugly surprise waiting for us. They had concentrated quite a few automatic weapons and rocket-propelled grenades in one area, so we flew into a hail of fire before we realized what they were doing. Luckily for us, they were bad shots. There were a few more hits and a little blood on that first gun run but nothing serious.

This was a new tactic for the VC. In all my previous firefights, once the gunships showed up, the VC pulled back and often retreated. That night, they were counting on the bad weather to limit what we could do. That, and they had an overwhelmingly larger force. The concentrated fire position they'd set up was a smart and effective tactic. They were determined to take this firebase. But I was just as determined that wasn't going to happen and the captain and his men would go home safely at least from this firefight.

"One-Five, this is Two-Seven. You still OK?" As I was talking to McNeill, I suddenly felt metal particles in my mouth, and my head moved slightly to the right. As I was spitting them out. I thought, "What the fuck is this?" I wiped the pieces of metal with the back of my hand and looked around for the cause. "Holy shit!" Right in front of me, in the instrument panel, there was a hole. A bullet had come right through the front of the ship. It sprayed small pieces of metal into my mouth as it grazed my helmet and went out through the roof. Now that's destiny!

"Roger, Two-Seven, that was hell. Where'd they learn that?"

"I don't know, One-Five, but I want you to get as high as you can and run at that position from the south. Keep your lights on and guns blazing. I'm going to come at them low level from the east with my lights off and be on them before they know what hit them."

"Roger, Two-Seven, it sounds a little suicidal, but it might just work if you can get a good shot off at that altitude."

"Roger, One-Five, just make sure you break off your run before the target. I don't want to get shot down by my own wingman."

"Roger, Two-Seven, I'm climbing."

"One-Five, after this is over, remind me to tell you what just happened, I think I'll get drunk tonight."

"Roger Two-Seven make sure your rocket sight is fine tuned to those sucker's frequency."

McNeill climbed into his position. I followed him, turned north, cut off all our lights, and started to dive. I had to come at them right above tree top level just as McNeill broke off his gun run. Timing was crucial. We would both be hung out to dry if this didn't work.

I had briefed my crew on the plan before I told McNeill, so once I saw him turn toward the target and start his run, I told my crew, "Get ready—here we go."

He dove at the target with guns blazing and flew into a firestorm of bullets. I could see the tracers flying all around his ship. He was taking a hell of a beating. This plan had to work; all our lives depended on it. We only had one chance. McNeill's gunner keyed his mike that he was hit but he could still keep firing. Just before he broke off his run, and while the VC were still looking in the same direction waiting for the second ship, I came at them from a different direction and at low level.

It took them a while to adjust their fire to an assault from another direction. That gave me just enough time to get a good bead on them and put three rockets right into the middle of their group. My adrenaline was at full peak. I was sweating. My ears were burning with the deafening sound of the machine guns and the rocket explosions, but I kept a tuned ear to the sound of the engine. A change in the sound of the engine was the first indication of a pending disaster, and I was pissed. A few minutes ago if my head had been turned or if the wind had shifted I would have taken a round right in the face. "Not tonight you little cocksuckers!"

After I fired the rockets, my copilot continued his barrage with the mini's. I was so tuned into the target and doing as much damage as possible on this run, I couldn't pull out in time, so I was forced to fly right over the target. This was a big no-no, but it gave Rose and Elton a chance to finish off anything left moving with their M-60 machine guns. They were on full rock 'n' roll, standing on the skids, and firing straight down. Both of them were tuned into the mission, too. They were firing full automatic and screaming as loud as they could at the enemy. They were pumped and on target. Nothing could have survived that run.

Meanwhile, the main force was still attacking the American base. But now we were free to use all our firepower on the attackers. Within a few more minutes, though, we were out of ammo again and had to break off and re-arm.

"Hotshot Six, this is Two-Seven, we are out of ammo again. Be back as quick as we can."

"Roger, Two-Seven, after that last barrage, the incoming has slowed down."

"Roger that, Six, we have ruined their day as best we can. Still, keep your head down, there are plenty more to deal with when we get back.

"Roger, Badger, we'll be here."

We made it back to Tay Ninh and had to sit down a minute to catch our breaths. McNeill looked at me, and I looked at him. We both knew we had defied death once again, and we were going to win this battle after all. All four of our gunners looked exhausted and their arms were burning from the strain of firing their machine guns, but they still knew that we were saving lives! No way were we finished yet! We were back in the air in twenty-five minutes and on our way back to the firefight.

We decided this time we would come at them from two different directions again, but both from higher altitude. He would dive and break right, and I would come from the opposite direction then dive and break right, too. This way there was no chance of a mid-air collision. The rain had stopped, and the clouds were getting higher. It was still dark, but we were used to it by now. We both climbed to 1,900 feet and started in at them again.

We had plenty of time on target from that altitude. We could see the VC on the ground, and they were in total confusion. They didn't know which way to run. We had all their exits covered. This was the end of the battle. We had broken their will to succeed. They knew they were beaten and started to retreat, what was left of them anyway. Bodies were all over the battlefield. We made one more gun run into the retreating force as they tried to escape back into Cambodia. One of the tactics they used was to take as many dead and wounded off the battlefield as possible so we wouldn't know how badly we'd hurt them.

They knew exactly where the border was and counted on us to not follow them in, since Cambodia was strictly off limits to US forces at this point. We didn't like the rules, but we didn't make the policies. Hell, all we wanted was to not have to meet the same enemy over and over again.

"One-Five, this is Two-Seven. Do you have a map?"

"Yes, Two-Seven, I have a map, but it is too dark to read it."

"Roger, One-Five, same here. You know, we can finish this here and now or see these little suckers again in the future."

"Roger, Two-Seven, lead the way."

So we went where we had to go to do our jobs, policy or no policy. Rules be damned, at least that VC battalion would not attack another American base or take another American life. We did what had to be done.

By the time we returned to the firebase, the sun had started to come up, and we could see a relief column of 101st paratroopers streaming toward the base.

It was about 5:30 a.m. March 13, 1969, one month before my twenty-second birthday.

"Hotshot-Six this is Two-Seven, your reinforcements are right down the road. They'll be there in twenty. We're heading back to our base. It was a pleasure working with you."

" Badger Two-Seven, the pleasure is mine, but that's not enough. You have to land so we can thank you."

I told him there wasn't room to land in his area but I could tell, he was serious about us landing. I would try to land in a flat area two hundred meters north of his position.

"One-Five, did you get that?"

"Roger, Two-Seven, you have to do it. He wants to thank us. Give him a kiss for me and my guys, and I'll stay up here and watch your ass."

"Roger, One-Five."

I landed in the field. Rose and Elton got out and stood guard with their M-60s. They looked battered and bloodied, but they stood proud knowing what we had all done that night. I didn't think there were any VC left around to contend with, but I still felt naked with my gunship on the ground. The copilot kept the aircraft running at an idle, and I got out to meet the captain.

He came limping on to the field. He had taken a round in the leg and one in the hand, but he still had a huge grin on his face. His sergeant and the ARVN executive officer were with him. The ARVN commander had been killed in the battle. The captain had sixty-five ARVN troops at the start of the night, but twelve had been killed and twenty-one wounded. His squad of Americans had started with eighteen men. Three had been killed and eight wounded.

The captain dropped his M-16, threw his arms around my neck, and started to sob. With tears in his eyes, all he could say was, "Thank you, thank you." His name was John Matthews, and he was from Iowa. He asked my name, where I was from, and what unit we were with. The other two shook my hand and then went to the rest of the crew and did the same. We wished them good luck, told them to keep cool, and call us the next time they were planning a party. We loaded back into our ship, and took off.

The fact that we were almost out of ammo and low on fuel made the takeoff easy. Once in the air I told the copilot to fall in behind McNeill, and off we went.

"One-Five, you lead the way. I'm exhausted."

"Roger, Two-Seven, another job well done by the Badgers. We'll sleep well tonight."

I felt good knowing that the children and grandchildren of these guys would one day run around raising hell because the eight of us were on a mission that dark and rainy night.

We finally landed at our base and shut down the helicopters. I counted fourteen bullet holes in my ship, and McNeill had nineteen. All the bullets missed critical spots.

Rose had shrapnel wounds from hot brass and exploding rounds. Elton took a round right through his calf muscle. He never said a word when it happened. Somehow, it didn't bleed much; it just burned like hell, he said.

Like it or not, this time they were getting the Purple Heart. On previous missions they never wanted me to say anything or put them in for the Heart when they came back bleeding. They were too proud and said the other guys that were really hurt deserved it more.

McNeill was OK. Flying Plexiglas cut his copilot, and both his crew chief and gunner were cut and bruised. His gunner took a round through his flak vest, through his shirt and grazed his side. They were getting Hearts, too. Usually, whenever we returned from a mission, the pilots take off, and the crew stays behind and cleans up the ship and does maintenance. I told them all to leave everything as is and get some rest. I would get someone else to do the work. They'd done an excellent job and helped keep us alive. They deserved some rest too.

After I checked in at operations, I told them I would fill out the reports in the morning. I must have looked like hell, so they said OK. That was unusual.

I couldn't even wash or undress. I just took off my boots and fell on my bunk. I was filled with that warm feeling I'd come to expect every time I came back from the edge. It started one night back in flight school when we were practicing escape and evasion, and I made it to the safe zone. It was good. Life was good. Flying was good. Vietnam was good; it was my destiny to be there.

I was twenty-one years old and in love with the excitement of war.

Exhausted as I was, I couldn't sleep. I started thinking about all my close calls, all the times that death or serious injury were inevitable, but I survived them with mere scratches. That night of escape and evasion training back in flight school might have been the first time I'd felt the rush, but the first time I'd been shot down was the real beginning of my love for the dangerous life I was leading. Could it really have been only nine months?

Chapter 2

The road that led me to the sweaty jungles of Vietnam and later to the menacing people and places of organized crime began in an ordinary town in Bergen County, New Jersey.

It was the summer after high school, a summer filled with hard work and plenty of fun. Girls, cars, beach parties, all the things that make up a great summer for a teenage boy. Next was college—what you were expected to do in the world in which I lived. It didn't matter if you *wanted* to go to college. You graduated from high school and you went to college, period.

My high school grades were just OK, Bs and B minuses, mostly. It kept me out of trouble in high school, but grades like that didn't impress many colleges. Like most high school boys, I thought less about algebra and social studies and more about football, girls, wrestling, girls, baseball, girls, my car, and what's up for the weekend. There was not much time left for studies, but I got by, just barely.

I applied to a few colleges with help from my advisor. My mediocre grades, dire financial position, and size—the fact that no matter how much I enjoyed playing sports, I was simply too small to play anything at the college level—kept my list of college possibilities short.

I hoped to find a school to study hospitality management. I liked the idea of running—and maybe owning—bars, restaurants, or hotels. I had worked in a few of these places as a teenager, and I liked what I saw.

My aunt, my father's sister, made quite a bit of money in the hospitality business. She left some of it for me in her will. It was enough to at least get to college. The idea of going into hospitality management was partly to thank her for her help.

My parents weren't interested in my college career. Neither of them went to college, and they were in no position to help me financially. My father was basically an absentee father. He was at the house every day, but he might as well not have been for all we had in common.

He was quite a bit older than my mother when they got married. My mother's family was poor when she was growing up during the Depression. My father was successful when they met and showed her things she had only dreamed of before. The age difference between them didn't matter much at that point, only the nice things he could give her and nice places he could take her. My sister came first, two years before me. By the time I came around, his burnout had started, and it got worse every year.

There was no one to play catch with when I got my first baseball glove. When I was four or five years old, I got a set of electric trains for Christmas, an expensive set of American Flyer trains. Naturally, I was too young to play with electricity by myself, so I waited for someone—my father—to show me what they could do. I waited and waited, but he never did. One day I tied a string around the expensive little engine and started pulling it along the floor. That was cool and better than nothing when you were five years old.

When my father got home, he hit the ceiling at the sight of me dragging an electric train across the floor with a string. He took the train set away from me and said I wouldn't get it back till I was old enough to appreciate how special it was. Hell, I was a kid. I didn't want to appreciate a toy train; I wanted to play with it. I decided right then that if I ever got that train set back, he would never see me play with it. And he didn't. I still have those trains. They're in mint condition.

By the time Little League came around, it became such a hassle to ask for a ride to practice or the games that I eventually stopped asking. My father never abused me or hit me. He just did nothing. My mother tried to make a difference in my life, but my father essentially abandoned her, too. I became independent early in life. No matter what I did, I did it on my own, with no help from my father.

These days my father would probably be diagnosed as severely depressed and placed on medication. In those days, he just wasn't there for me or anyone else. He was a failure as a father, a husband, and a businessman.

I joined the Boy Scouts the spring I turned eleven. As summer approached that year, all the meetings were dedicated to discussions and planning for summer camp—Camp NoBeBoSco. Two weeks of hiking, swimming, campfires, merit badges, and fun. I had to sit and listen to all the other boys making their plans to go to camp because there was no way I could get the sixty-eight dollars from my parents to pay for it. I was depressed about that and did not get to go that first year. Once I hit twelve, I got a paper route delivering the *Bergen Record*.

It was a six-days-a-week paper, and then I had to collect from customers to pay for the paper. It took a lot of free time away from playing and sports, and at times I hated it, especially on the kind of cold, snowy days we got in the winter in the northeast. But that paper route gave me things I'd never had before, freedom and money in my pocket. I didn't get an allowance. The chores we did around the house were part of the deal, so I was told.

Things were a lot different the next year when the talk turned to Boy Scout summer camp. I was right there with the other scouts because I could pay for it myself. I didn't need my parents. I went to camp for the next three summers, two weeks at a time. It was on my own dime, and it felt great. I even had spending money for souvenirs and ice cream. That paper route was a great learning experience and taught me the value of money. When you were spending your own, you were more careful with it.

When I got into junior high school, my friends on the block and I decided to lift weights to build us up. We thought the girls would like us better, and it would help us in sports and on the beach. In the eighth grade, I asked Santa to bring me a set of weights. Santa was especially good that year and brought me a starter set of Billiard weights. I fixed up a corner of our basement to lift. I made a makeshift bench and hung pictures on the wall of heroes. The weights came with a color brochure demonstrating the proper way to lift and do the basic exercises. The man in the brochure was Bruce Randall, Mr. America 1958 and 1959. He had a nineteen-inch neck, twenty-one-inch biceps, a fifty-four-inch chest, thirty-four-inch waist, and thirty-inch thighs. He was my hero. I never wanted to look exactly like him, but he was a great role model. The other guys on the block,—Donny Boy, Billy Mack, Herbie, Davey, and John—all got weights, too, and had different brochures with different pictures. They all agreed Bruce Randall was the best.

JFK got elected in 1960 and took office in 1961. He immediately started with his famous speech about what you can do for your country and went right into his president's physical fitness program. It took the United States by storm, and everyone got involved. We started lifting and exercising all the more. In 1962 our Fourth of July parade had the theme "Fitness America." We all went to the parade, as did the whole town. We stood on the street watching when the main float came by featuring a bodybuilder and a few female bodybuilders all lifting weights and posing for the crowd.

Right there in front of me was Bruce Randall. I'd know him anywhere. His body and dimensions were engraved in my memory. The other guys all recognized him, too. We yelled and cheered and paid respects to our hero. He had a barbell, Billiard of course, with one hundred pounds, and curled it one handed and pressed it above his head with each hand. We followed him to the end of the parade.

The guys wanted to invite him to our block—and all agreed I should be the one to ask him. I was nervous about doing so, but did not want to miss this kind of opportunity. We went up to him for autographs, and I told him I had Billiard weights and his brochure that I worked out with. He commented what a good choice I made and wished us all luck.

"Mr. Randall," I said. "I have no idea what your schedule is, but we would love it if you could come to our clubhouse and talk to us for a few minutes and have a hamburger." After all it was July fourth and the word of the day was barbecue!

He finished signing an autograph, took a long look at me, and said, "I really appreciate the offer but my sponsor has me on a tight schedule and I'm riding with them." My heart dropped along with my jaw, and our disappointment was obvious.

"I'll tell you what," he said. "Give me your phone number, and if I can arrange it, I will give you a call."

That was better than a no, so we were excited. We left the parade site talking about the fact we did not have a clubhouse, so if he did come, where would he come?

We decided that since my house was in the middle of the block, my garage was the best choice. I told my mother and sister, and they thought I was kidding. We begged my father to back his car out of the garage. The request annoyed him, but he did it anyway at my mother's urging.

An hour later my sister answered the phone.

"Hello, is Daniel there? This is Bruce Randall, Mr. America."

My sister said, "Yeah right, and I'm Cleopatra."

I took the phone and told him not to pay any attention to my sister. He had about an hour he could spend with us. Where did I live? I thought I would wet my pants. I gave him my address. He would see us in one hour.

Now we had to make my garage look like a weight-lifting clubhouse. All the guys brought equipment from home to decorate the garage. In one hour it looked acceptable, not that it mattered to Mr. America. He came with his friend and two of the girls from the parade. The girls were gorgeous and built, but he was the main attraction. He came in a suit and tie and looked strange, out of place. He talked to us for over an hour about lifting properly, taking good care of our bodies, and staying healthy.

We hung on every word. My mother, my sister, and a few neighbors came over and listened, too. He thanked us for the invitation to stay and eat, but he had to get to his next stop.

That was one of the highlights of my childhood and left a lifelong impression on me and on my friends.

We kept working out all through high school and playing sports. All the high schools had the President's Physical Fitness Test, and the top ten at our school were listed on the wall at the entrance of the gym for all to see. As a sophomore I was number nine, and as a senior, number three.

I never considered myself especially strong, but I held my own in most contests. In the middle of sophomore year, I made the varsity football team as a defensive lineman. I was not that big at 165 pounds, but I was fast and tenacious. As a junior and senior, I was starting right-side defensive end. I was 180 pounds by then and loved sacking quarterbacks and hitting guys trying to go out for a pass. I loved defense.

During practice one day in my senior year, Coach Gasparino asked me to fix a helmet. The chinstrap had broken off, and the helmet had to be squeezed back together. I grabbed the helmet in my two hands and squeezed as hard as possible. The helmet went back to the right position, the coach handed it back to the player, and practice continued. I still don't know why he picked me. I was not the biggest guy on the team by any means and not the strongest, but I did the job.

Our freshman football team went undefeated. I played defensive right end as a freshman.. During my twelve years in public schools in three different states, I never had a black kid in my class or in the school. My only association with black kids was on the sports field when we played other schools. Hackensack, one of our big rivals, had a bunch of black athletes, and they were very good players. Fast, very fast.

As defensive end, I had to protect the outside to make sure no one got around me to the sidelines to run downfield. We were ahead 6–0 in the third quarter—we had missed the extra point. The quarterback rolled out to his left, my side, and started to set up for a pass. I had him in my sights and got ready for the sack I was going to make. All of a sudden he pitched the ball to his running back and away he went for the touchdown. I was committed to the QB and couldn't catch the runner. The guys behind me on my team got faked out, too, and were waiting for the pass. They tied the game and missed their extra point also. I was really upset, thinking it was my fault that they scored. The coach said it wasn't.

Hackensack always had a good team, and we were neck and neck in most sports. My sister's class, two years ahead of me, was county champs in football and state champs in basketball.

When I was a senior, when the chips were down and each player had to dig deep to come up with the best they had, our football team was undefeated after six games. The next game was against Hackensack. As usual they had an excellent team with a great running back that could run and catch the ball, too. He was tall—six-two, fast, and black. At the half, it was 14–7 Hackensack. That running back was all over the field making yardage every carry. When he lined up on my side, I hit him hard on the line to stop him. They went to the other side. Sometimes he would recover from my hit and catch the ball anyway.

During the halftime briefing in the locker room, the coach told us what to do and do it harder and better. We cheered, yelled, and split for the field for the second half. The coach called me over to the side. He waited till all the other players and coaches left the room.

"Daniel, the team needs your help if we are going to win this game and go to the playoffs. That number forty-two has to be stopped and stopped hard. We don't have anyone that can keep up with him on a straight run. Do you remember when you played Hackensack as a freshman?"

What was this? He was not my coach when we were freshmen, and that was four years ago. What did he know? I had a lot of respect for Coach and thought he did a great job with the team. We were winners and enjoyed the game but I didn't understand what he was saying.

"I think they are going to run that same play, the pitch out, around your side, so I want you to be ready. In the meantime, I want you to stop number forty-two. I don't want you to break any rules or cause any penalties, but I want you to stop him this quarter." Do you know what I am saying? Do you know what I mean?"

My head was spinning with what he did mean, but I didn't want to ask.

"Yes, Coach, I know what you mean, and I will do my best."

"I know you will, Daniel; I know you won't let us down. Go get 'em!"

This was strange. First off, he never called us by our first names and to my knowledge never called one of the other guys over like this. At least they never told me he did. What was I suppose to do? Stop number forty-two. Hell, I'd been trying to stop him all day, but it hadn't worked. He wanted me to do something else, something I hadn't done yet and do it without a penalty.

I loved this team and the guys on it. I always tried to do my best for them. Now I was being called to do something extra—just like with the helmet in practice. Why me? How far was I willing to go for the team?

We received the ball at the start of the second half. They held us to four downs, and we punted. Now I was on the field and had to perform. The first three plays went to the other side; they got one first down and were marching. The first time number forty-two lined up by me, I faked going to his outside without hitting him. It was a hot day in October. I was sweating, my heart was beating fast and I needed to move now, time was running out.

He went eight yards and caught a pass, first down.

The next time he lined up by me, it had to be the last. I felt it was going to be another pass to him, so at the snap, I faked going to his inside. Before he got straight up, I took my left forearm with an elbow pad and hit him square under the chin and kept driving. It was a solid hit. I felt his teeth move.

He straightened right up. I kept driving forward, my arm in his throat and my shoulder in his chest, back six yards, and then he fell backward to the ground.

The QB rolled out to my side, had no one to throw to, and tried to run, right into my arms. No gain.

Forty-two was down. Time out. The medical crew carried him off the field, and he didn't come back into the game. I felt a rush, but it was unsettling. I did not want to hurt him permanently, just for this game. It was a clean hit, even if it was a bit ahead of the snap. The team needed an edge, and I helped them get it. The end justified the means. That's how I made it work in my head.

We won 21–20. The team was excited. The coach complemented everyone on a good job. He glanced in my direction one time. I thought I saw a wink, but nothing was ever said about the incident that day or ever.

I never told any of the players. If he ever talked to one of the other players like that, I never heard about it. That's the day I found out exactly how far I would go for the team.

We lost the last game of the season and did not make the playoffs.

I also learned that the only person I could really depend on in life was me. That attitude became a problem later on.

I wound up going to Florida State University. It had a good program in hotel management and an affordable out-of-state tuition plan—at least for one year in my case. So off I went, in my own car. The car I bought with my own money, tuition money from my Aunt, and money for room and board that I earned myself.

I remember saying good-bye to my mother after I was all packed, and she said, "Where are you going again, and when will you be home?" She did the best she could under the circumstances, but she had trouble getting through each day on her own.

College was about what I expected, nothing special. My first challenge was a fake ID to get me into bars. The drinking age in Florida was twenty-one, and I was eighteen. All the really cool, good-looking girls were in the bars, and that's where I needed to be. I had learned at an early age to get the things I wanted, even if the rules had to be bent a little, so I scored a fake picture ID fairly easily.

I met a guy named Les who had been in the Air Force and was now back in college. He was a drummer at a local pub and introduced me around to all the right people. I'd played the drums from the fifth to the ninth grade until I had to choose between the marching band and football. I did the right thing because I had a great four years on the football team.

That first year in college I took accounting, English, sales, physical education, introduction to front office management, economics, and band. I wanted to stay on good terms with Les, and he said the college band needed help, so I joined. It gave me more drum practice, even if it wasn't exactly the experience I needed.

A drummer job came open at the local Bunny Club. It wasn't a high-class Playboy Club or anything close to it—just a local bar with go-go dancers and a few girls who danced topless.

Les took me to try out for the job. The bandleader sized me up and said, "Sonny, you don't belong here. This place will eat you alive."

Les told the guy to give me a chance. I played OK for the marching band experience I had .

"Look Jake, I'll work with the kid till he gets comfortable and you can pay him a little less in the beginning."

The band leader knew Les and took his word. After the audition was over, two of the dancers walked over to the bandstand.

"Who's the new drummer Jake? He's a lot cuter than that last old fucker you had. The girls will love him."

Now I knew I was in heaven!

That was it. I got the job. The bandleader was obviously desperate. Next thing I needed was drums. The drummer who quit, the old fucker, took his set with him.

Les took me downtown to a music store, introduced me to the owner, and left. I explained my situation, and based on my future salary of seventy-five dollars a week, I told the owner I could pay off the drums in two months. The deal was made, and off I went with my first set of red Pearl drums.

I had to fake a lot since most of my drum career had been spent playing marching band music like John Phillips Sousa. Not exactly the kind of tunes you could dance to or even do bumps and grinds to. But at eighteen I had already developed a talent for bullshitting my way through things, something I wound up doing a lot of in the future. Rather than saying I couldn't do something or didn't know how to do something, I said sure, I can do whatever it is, and I worried about the details later.

The bandleader was a real character who showed me more about nightclub life and flirting with older women than music. He tried to teach me how much women loved sex and how they would do just about anything to get as much as they could. At first I thought he was talking about men. After I watched him work the crowd for a few weeks I started to believe him. He was not all that attractive but he was a real chick magnet. That job lasted until he got caught with the club owner's wife. The club owner got really mad and fired the entire band. I could never understand why he didn't get mad at his wife because, from what I found out, she did that sort of thing a lot.

I lost that job and had to take the drums back to the store where I bought them. I'd made quite a few payments on them and the storeowner tried to get me to keep them. But I decided I wasn't ready for nightclub life just yet and wanted to concentrate on girls more my age. I was developing a real taste for the female anatomy, and I figured I should at least give college a working chance.

My experience at the Bunny Club helped me grow up a lot and taught me that I needed a profession, an education, or something that would get me to the places I wanted to go in life. Unfortunately, I wasn't sure if college was the answer right then. I was too busy thinking beyond college, and I felt like I needed more excitement in my life.

The year went by fast, and soon I was on my way home, knowing I would not be back the next year. Getting home felt good for a while, but college kids don't do really well at home after being on their own—not me anyway.

Besides, I found myself paying a lot of attention to the news about the war in Vietnam.

Chapter 3

It was 1966. The news was Vietnam. The six o'clock news on television dedicated at least ten minutes every day to the war. The front page of every daily newspaper had at least one story or report about the war. No matter who you were or what you were doing, you couldn't get away from the fact that the United States was involved in a military conflict on the other side of the world.

The draft was alive and well that year, and the war in Vietnam was of special interest to those of us who were male teenagers and eligible to be called up. People like me. I was never big on current events before, but war news caught my attention.

My trip home from college was uneventful. I spent the first week visiting friends and spending time with family and my girl. Things were pretty much the same as when I left. My sister was married with a year-old kid, my little brother was eleven, my father was older, and my mom was still doing the best she could with what she had. She was glad I was home. And I was still in love—or so I thought. I was still dating my high school sweetheart. We'd been dating since junior year; naturally she was the best looking girl in the class.

Her name was Suzanne and she was beautiful!

My year in college had left me almost broke, so my first order of business was to find a job. After being cooped up in classrooms and a smoky bar, I liked the idea of being outside, so I decided to find a job in construction or some related field. My cousin owned a construction business in a nearby town, so he was the first person I thought of. Actually, he was not a real cousin, but he was married to my mother's first cousin, so he was considered part of the family. I asked my mom to give him a call for me, which she did, and set up an appointment.

His name was Michael Pagliotti. As my good luck would have it, Mike had just won two big contracts and needed help. I went into his office to meet him, and we talked a while about school and my plans for the future. Mike understood why I had dropped out since he never finished college, either. He had taken over the family construction business when his father died and had educated himself with classes in blueprint reading, engineering, and drafting. It wasn't a college degree, but it was enough education to make him a successful businessman with a growing company.

Mike hired me to drive trucks, make deliveries, and take care of equipment, supplies, and tools. I was, essentially, to be his eyes and ears at the many different job sites where he had crews working. And if I didn't have something pressing, I was to fill in on jobs where they needed an extra hand. We agreed I would start the next week.

I arrived at his office at 8:00 a.m. the following Monday. I thought I was on time, but he had already been there two hours. We got into his new Cadillac, and he drove me around to his various job sites. He was building the new public library in Plainfield, a four-story apartment building in Elizabeth, a portion of a new amphitheater in Holmdel, a seven-story apartment building in Caldwell, and a few smaller jobs scattered around central New Jersey.

My education in how the construction industry works in New Jersey began immediately: the unions controlled everything.

The first week I was challenged to show my union book at every job site. The Teamsters had a lock on all truck driving jobs at union-controlled construction jobs, but since I was a company man working on a summer job, they let me go. They really had no choice since they had no jurisdiction over what I was doing for the company, but they just wanted to bust my balls to see if I could take it.

I took it well, and after a while I began to give as good as I got. They seemed to like that, so soon I picked up a nickname: The Kid. All of the top guys on any job had nicknames, so clearly I had been accepted.

The labor union system in New Jersey in the sixties was simple, efficient, and strict. The foreman of each construction specialty was the top dog of that trade. The shop steward, who was the official union representative, also had a lot of power, sometimes even more than the foreman. He could stop all work on a site if union rules were being broken.

The supervisor, sometimes called the project manager, was a company man and not a member of any of the unions. He was in overall charge of the project, and it was his job to work with the unions and the foremen to get the job done. The owner of the company was usually well respected because he was not only the reason the crews had jobs, but he also brought the payroll—in cash—to them every Friday.

Private debts were paid on payday, borrowed money was paid back, and new loans were made. Kickbacks went to the right people, and everyone was happy—simple, clean, and no paper trail. Once I figured out how things worked and who was in charge, the rest was easy. I occasionally delivered the Friday payroll to a few jobs and that earned me respect. Respect was a big factor on the job, and once you knew whom to respect, you could figure out what to do.

I learned right away that I could play their game as well as they could.

The rules on the job were simple; you did your work, kept your head down, and your mouth shut. Since I was a company man and the boss's cousin, the union guys let me work right next to them, digging, raking, carrying, loading, etc. However, since they were all union, they made a lot more money than I did. When I brought this up to my cousin after a few months, he was not real impressed. He explained my job was steady, I didn't have to worry about missing work on bad weather days, and I got company benefits. What the hell—I was having a good time, so I didn't push him for more money.

Besides, I enjoyed being outside with the guys and getting to meet interesting characters who taught me a lot about how things actually worked in this new world in which I had found myself. I came to realize that things that might seem strange or even illegal to the rest of the world were perfectly normal in the construction business in the northeast. It was my job to learn how to deal with these new rules. As I watched a few side deals unwind, I figured as long as they didn't involve my cousin, his job, or his property, the rest was none of my business. I figured right away that I should sit back, watch, and learn.

The chief "shy", the big guy who loaned out the money, was somebody I wanted to get to know better. His brother was killed in Vietnam, and I wanted to know his feelings about the war. He didn't want to talk about the war, but he appreciated my interest in his brother and his opinion. After a few weeks of working and talking to him I overheard two guys talking about trying to scam him out of some money and using another guy as a patsy. I didn't like the sound of that, so I passed the info on to the shy. His name was Roberto, but he wanted to be called Bob.

Next thing I knew, the two guys planning the scam were off the job, nobody knew why.

"Kid I appreciate the tip," Bob said. "How about you give me some money, I'll put it with mine and get you on the street." Whoa, I never expected this. If I gave him money and lost it, there was nobody to complain to. But, I figured, what the hell, give it a try.

"You give me some money and we'll split the vig." The vig is the interest on the loan. Bob was good with math. Everything he did was in his head, he never wrote anything down.

I gave him some money and entered my first venture into loan sharking. After a few weeks the vig started piling up and I was making money. One of the things I hadn't planned on was his cut.

"Kid, since you're just starting out, I'm only gonna charge you ten points from your end, this is a good deal."

The deal meant I had to give Bob ten percent of my split of the vig because he was who he was.

I was getting ready to say he never explained that part, but I decided to keep my mouth shut.

One Friday he said to follow him into the supply trailer. I always had my guard up around him and his people even if I didn't know what I would do in case of trouble. In the supply trailer we met up with one of our clients, who just happened to be late on his payment.

Bob said, "I'll ask you one more time, where's my money?"

The guy was ready to wet his pants and started to stutter when Bob just hauled off and smashed his face. The guy had a broken nose and a cut lip. "You have till Monday."

We left the trailer, Bob said, "No sense hurting him so he can't work, just make it so people know what happened, get it? Will you be ready for next time?"

Now wait a minute, putting this money in my pocket and spending it was good, but collecting it like that was another story. I didn't think I was ready yet, but I just looked at him and nodded my head.

I hadn't had too many dealings with the law.

I vaguely knew that if you broke the law, something bad would probably happen to you, but I wasn't sure exactly what. I hadn't even learned yet that sometimes the legal system doesn't work at all. I didn't understand that sometimes the guilty go free. And sometimes the innocent are punished. And sometimes the law doesn't show up at all.

I heard about an attempted payroll robbery at a job site near one of Mike's projects—a robbery about as smart as a tourist taking food away from a hungry lion at the zoo. The incident never made the six o'clock news, and the foiled robbers just disappeared. No one knew anything.

My first view of mob justice. I learned, "No sense getting the law involved when we can handle it ourselves."

One of the most important rules on a union job site was accountability. If a rule was broken on the job, it was dealt with on the job. If someone got caught stealing, he paid a stiff price. Sometimes that price was a lot heavier than the value of what was stolen. The punishment didn't always fit the crime, but it was a rough justice that worked. The police were never called. You could do what you pleased away from work, but on the job you were loyal to the people you worked with and for. I immediately understood the whole concept of loyalty and accountability, and I liked it. I was comfortable in a world like that.

The notion of unquestioned loyalty became part of who I was. But it might have become too big a part of my character.

Chapter 4

I went to a Christmas party with a bunch of high school friends that year. It was good seeing them, but most were still in college, and that was all they could talk about. I realized that night there was a growing distance between us. We were all the same age, but in my eyes they seemed like big children.

It was different with Tommy, one of my good buddies. He had joined the army when all the rest of us had gone to college. Now he was a helicopter pilot, and that, to a bunch of students and dropouts like me, seemed cool. His stories were great, even though he was going to Vietnam to fight in the war. I truly believed in why we were there—or, to be more accurate, like most Americans I believed what the government told us.

This was 1966, and the Cold War was serious. Russia was rattling sabers; China was threatening everyone on its side of the world, and democracy had to make a stand someplace, didn't it? So why not in Vietnam? It seemed a long way from the United States, so what harm could come from a little war so far from home? It wouldn't take many more years to learn the sad and savage answer to that naïve question.

I grew up watching John Wayne and Audie Murphy war movies. War didn't look so tough. If they could do it, I could, too. Besides, Tommy was going to war. He may have been stronger and six months older than me—he was one tough dude who I always wanted on my side in a fight—and if he could fly a helicopter in combat, I sure as hell could, too.

I did not want to make construction a career, especially not working with my hands and back. Maybe as a union negotiator, or the boss, or at least some guy in a suit, but definitely not out in the hot sun with tools in my hand. I was still not ready to go back to college. That was just too boring to even consider at that point in my life. I needed excitement. I was ready to do something different. I thought a lot about military service and being a pilot. Now that was cool and exciting.

I looked seriously into the military. I'd always wanted to be a marine—at least when I was watching movies about marines—so naturally I went to the marine recruiting office first. The recruiter said the marines would love to have me as an infantryman, a grunt, a ground-pounder, a finely trained gung-ho killing machine. But, unfortunately, their pilot training required a college degree. Oh, well.

I next looked at the Navy. Naval officers flew jets and traveled around the world. But, like the marines, you had to have a college degree to become a pilot. Even the air force wanted a sheepskin before it would let you fly one of its precious airplanes.

I started to resent these college kids.

The Army had helicopters, and the best news was they would take high school graduates into the pilot program. But first you had to pass the entrance exam. I found out you could take the exam before enlisting so you would know for sure if you'd been selected into the flight program. I also found out they were not taking any draftees into the program. You had to be regular army, an enlisted volunteer, not some reluctant draftee. I was nineteen years old and a college dropout. I had to act fast if I was going to enlist before I was drafted. My chances for flight school would vanish the day I received a draft notice. Colleges loved to notify your local draft board that you were officially eligible to be drafted as soon as you quit school.

My school record was not all that great. I didn't do well in stressful written tests, so I had to figure out a way to pass the test before I took it—or I was shit out of luck. Cheating was out of the question, however. This was not some high school or college social studies test. This was the United States Army. Crib notes or copying from somebody's paper wouldn't get it.

Then it came to me. I lived in New Jersey, but I had friends who lived in New York, so why couldn't I use their address and take the test as a New Yorker? If I passed, fine, and off I go to the Army. If I failed, at least I had gotten a look at the test and would know what to study before I took it again back in New Jersey. How would that hurt anyone? I would get what I wanted—an adventure—and the army would get a fantastic and good-looking pilot.

Me.

I went down to the Army Induction Center on Whitehall Street in New York City. The place was jammed, what with the draft, and the new recruits overran the army staff running the place. I signed in using my name and a friend's address in Manhattan and told them I was there to take the flight school test. Their whole attitude changed. I went from being treated as just another sad-sack draftee being force-fed through the military grinder like so much sausage to a fine young American who wanted to join the Army to serve his country. I liked that.

They escorted me through the whole process. First came the physical. If you couldn't pass the physical, there was no sense taking the written test. That took half a day. It was a full day for everybody else, but I went to the front of every line. I was not popular with the other guys waiting in line, but they'd just have to live with it. After a lunch break, I got the test results from my physical and, of course, I'd passed with flying colors. The recruiting sergeant was as excited as I was. Future helicopter pilots were apparently worth more credits on his monthly quota than future riflemen, and he was already counting on me to make him look good.

Then came the hard part—the written exam. Since I was the only flight candidate at Whitehall Street that day, I was alone in the exam room. Nice enough room with desks and chairs, no windows, no pictures—just me, the test, and a monitor. The test was about things I had never heard of before, which was pretty much what I expected. There were questions about reciprocating winds in a down draft, cyclic sticks, collectives, VFR, and IFR.

What the fuck was all that about? How could anyone know this crap before flight school? Then came the part about weapons. Who knew 60 mm rockets, .30 caliber rounds, or the effects of recoil? And what the hell was "bore sight"? The only weapon I'd ever seen was when a guy got pistol-whipped on a construction job for being disrespectful to a superior. I did see another guy get shot while trying to steal a truck, but that didn't seem to have much to do with flying a helicopter. My flight career was passing before my eyes, and it was a depressing sight.

Keep cool, keep cool, I kept saying to myself, *remember the plan. If I can't answer the questions, then at least remember the questions for next time. And don't forget, there will be a next time.* So I just concentrated on the words I didn't know and the specific parts and phrases I had never heard of.

Needless to say, I flunked the test, not horribly, just not well enough to pass. The recruiters were upset, but I left armed with enough information to get me one step closer to my next goal, so all was not lost.

I spent the next few weeks looking up the words I didn't know from the test and reading about flying helicopters, which apparently were very different from airplanes, not that I knew anything about flying airplanes, either. When I thought I was ready, I returned to the army recruiting office, this time in Newark, New Jersey, to repeat the process. This time I knew what to expect. The Army did everything the same no matter where you were. I breezed through everything.

The physical was a snap, of course. After lunch came the flight-school entrance exam, and this time I was ready. There was one other guy taking the test with me, and he seemed as nervous as I'd been the last time. This time I was cool. I still don't consider what I did as actually cheating because, to me, the end justified the means. I didn't rush through the test, but I finished well before the allotted time was up and well before the other guy.

My test got graded right away, and my score of ninety-two made for a happy day. The recruiter asked if I was already a pilot because a ninety-two was quite an impressive score compared with the other scores he'd seen since he'd been there. I told him no, "I just studied up on flying."

Everyone who joins the Army has to go first through basic training. You have to learn how to march and fold your clothes the army way and run and take orders and field strip a weapon and salute before you get to do anything else. The fact that I passed this entrance test only guaranteed me a slot in flight school and nothing else. I still had to work hard to earn my wings. If I flunked out of flight school, they'd give me a rifle and send me off to Vietnam as a grunt.

I was ready to go. I'd already made up my mind that flying helicopters was what I wanted to do, so what was the point of waiting? The recruiter explained the difficulty of scheduling me for basic training and flight school, but I wanted to go now. I must have seemed anxious because the recruiter asked me if I was being chased by anyone or if I was running from something.

I told him no, I just wanted to get going before the war was over. Don't worry about that, he said. Go home and wait for us to call you when a class becomes available.

I'd already developed a tendency to be impatient, so the waiting got to me. Finally the call came telling me to report back to the recruiter in Newark. The news was not good. There were no flight school classes available for at least four to five months.

I couldn't believe my ears. The television said every day the war was escalating. The government was drafting people every month. And I was supposed to wait four or five months to go to flight school? I guess I appeared a bit annoyed because the recruiter's words were not real kind when I left the recruiting station. I was pissed. How could I change a decision I didn't understand or agree with? I was ready to go—now!

I decided to walk a bit. Not being familiar with Newark, I soon found myself in a part of town where I shouldn't have been. Two young guys about my age came up to me and asked for change to get coffee. I considered myself a tough guy at this point in my life. I'd played four years of football, had wrestled for three years, and been in numerous fights along the way. I knew these guys were looking for more than change for coffee.

I braced myself, took the proper stance, and got ready. Next thing I heard was the whoosh of something rushing through the air. I turned my head just in time to see a club speeding straight toward my head. I caught a brief sight of two other guys I hadn't seen before and then the lights went out.

I came to in an emergency room. People were touching my head, and boy, did I have a headache. Luckily, someone had seen the whole thing and called for an ambulance. They cleaned up the considerable amount of blood and put nine stitches in the back of my head and sent me off for X-rays. All head trauma results in concussion—they needed to see how badly I was hurt. After all the paperwork and a few hours of observation, they were ready to release me. I was nineteen years old, this was Newark, New Jersey, and my injury was not life threatening. They'd seen a lot worse every day.

My injury may not have been life threatening, but it was certainly life altering. Besides losing what little money I had in my pocket, my ego was deeply bruised, and that hurt more than the nine stitches in my hard head. I thought a lot about the incident, trying to figure out where I went wrong and what I could have done differently. I decided that neither I, nor anyone close to me, would become a victim ever again.

After I healed for a day, I went back to work and wore a hat to cover the bandage. I didn't feel comfortable talking about it to anyone; somehow it seemed like what happened was a weakness and should have been avoided. Explaining my head bandage to my family had been hard enough. I couldn't wait till I had to explain it to my friends. What a ration of shit I was going to take.

I wasn't politically involved in those days, but I knew Mike had been active in politics. He knew a lot of important people, and I remembered having seen Washington types around his office. Pictures of him with high-powered politicians were on his wall. I didn't have a grasp of how important and widespread political favors were, but I was quickly learning.

I told Mike about the delay in my plans. I asked him to speak to his close friend, a congressman from New Jersey, and to ask him to intervene on my behalf. Hell, I'd heard about guys who were calling their congressman to get them out of the draft or into the National Guard or Reserves to keep them out of Vietnam, but my request was different. I wanted in.

Mike listened intently. He tried his best to talk me out of going into the army. He explained how the family would give him hell if he helped me get into the service. I listened, but I needed excitement in my life. I was ready to do something different. In the end he said he would talk to the congressman for me.

The next Monday I was getting ready for dinner when my mother said there was a call for me from Washington. It was Mike's friend the congressman. He thanked me for thinking of him. He told me what Mike had told him and asked if what he'd said was correct. I told him Mike had it right; I wanted to join the Army, I wanted to become a pilot, and I wanted to go to Vietnam. And I wanted to do it now!

After a brief pause, he said that in his whole career as a politician, he had never had such a request. He said it would be an honor and privilege to help me in my quest. He thanked me for my dedication to my country. He asked me once again if I was ready to go. I said I was, and he told me to pack my bags because he just happened to be a member of the House Armed Services Committee.

On Thursday, a mere seventy-two hours later, I received a call from an army colonel. He told me a flight school class was available and asked if I would be able to report the next Monday? It was just one more lesson in how things actually got done in this world. Who you knew made all the difference.

My family had mixed feelings when I told them I'd be leaving in a few days. My mother was concerned for my safety, but at the same time I think down deep she was proud of me. My sister, who was married at the time with a son of her own, was torn. She was not an antiwar hippie exactly, but she was a borderline liberal. She seemed more interested in the part about the congressman and my increasing ability to navigate the system. She was concerned about my soul and wished me luck. I asked them to tell my father for me. To hell with him.

The hard job was telling my sweetheart, Suzanne. At nineteen, I thought I was in love, but I wasn't sure yet. For now flying was my priority, and young love would have to wait. She drove me to the recruiting station in Newark on Monday morning. We said another good-bye there, but it wasn't too bad since we knew I would be home in ten weeks after basic training.

I walked into a room with a bunch of other guys being inducted into the military. The man in charge was the same recruiting staff sergeant I had dealt with earlier. The last time we met didn't end too smoothly, so when he saw me walk in, he said, "Well, well, look who's here. Men, we have a celebrity with us today. Come on up here so everyone can see you.

"This individual thinks he's special. He thinks he can manipulate the system and get whatever he wants. Who do you know that can change things for you?"

I never had to deal with this asshole again so my only comment was, "I don't know anybody. I guess I'm just lucky."

"Bullshit," he said. "You think you're special, don't you? Get in the back of the line, you'll be the last one processed today."

This guy felt overruled in my case and evidently didn't like it very much. Some enlisted types feel they ought to run things and don't like new recruits or anybody else who rocks their boat or interferes with their operation. I was going in; I had a flight school date set, and there was nothing he or anybody else could do about it.

He was right, though. I did feel special. I had a guardian angel.

A young captain with no campaign ribbons swore in the whole group later that day. The song "You're in the Army Now" kept running through my mind.

We loaded a bus to Newark airport then an Army transport plane for Louisiana. Our destination: Fort Polk.

God help us all.

Chapter 5

Fort Polk, a leftover from World War II and just outside Leesville, Louisiana, is truly a place time forgot. It featured thousands of identical two-story wooden-frame barracks with no insulation or air conditioning, which had been built by Depression-weary workers who flocked to new jobs at military bases gearing up to fight World War II.

All flight school candidates were sent there for basic training. Two hundred recruits were in my basic training company, one hundred flight school candidates, and the rest a mixed bag of draftees, volunteers, and reservists doing their mandatory six months of active service.

The first few days were typical army: hurry up and wait, run everywhere, and wait some more when you got there, picking up uniforms, shoes, boots, and web gear, all the things a well-dressed army private needed.

Next up was the infamous basic training haircut. The stitches in my head had been removed only a few days before, and the scar was still quite tender. I was standing in line waiting my turn in the chair, and I noticed right away that these barbers (butchers?) had no finesse and less patience. They had a quota of heads to mow, and nothing else mattered.

When my turn came up, I politely showed the man my scar, told him it was fresh and still quite sore. Next thing I felt was a sharp pain in my head, and I saw blood dripping down my face when I looked in the mirror. This seemingly pleasant gentleman whom I spoke to politely one minute ago, either did not hear what I said, did not understand, or did not give a shit.

My reaction was admittedly severe. I never considered myself a violent person—at least not at this point in my life—but I figured that of his three choices, he decided to not give a shit, and that pissed me off. I got out of the chair and threw this asshole into the mirror. The mirror broke as he bounced to the floor. Within two seconds, my arms were pinned behind me by two military policemen, and I was dragged out of there.

After spending a few hours at the MP station, a major listened to my story and inspected my head. He learned I was on my way to flight school after basic training, so he read me the riot act about this kind of behavior not being acceptable in a future officer and gentleman. I did not get another chance to speak, but he did send me back to my unit by way of the infirmary for a new bandage.

I had to pay for the mirror as punishment. As a private, that was one month's pay. On top of that, I had to pull a week of KP after my training days were over.

Welcome to the Army. Did I make a mistake, or what!

My instant reputation as a bad ass, a wise guy, a troublemaker, and a guy who wouldn't take any shit got back to my unit even before I did. Drill Sergeant Manzano immediately called me into his office. He was a Cuban with a strong accent that was hard to understand for a kid from New Jersey. Evidently the barber was also from Cuba and didn't speak much English, either. He could understand sign language, though, so I figured he got what he deserved. And I'll bet he understood it, too.

My next four weeks in the Army were not at all what I had bargained for, thanks to Sergeant Manzano. He made sure I was as miserable as humanly possible. Enduring basic training and Drill Sergeant Manzano at the same time was a true test of my desire to be in the army.

I coped by pouring myself into learning everything possible about the military. I got in good physical shape and learned the basics of hand-to-hand combat. I paid special attention to the combat training because it fit right in with my vow to never again be a victim. My previous combat experience came from street fighting and learning collegiate-style wrestling. This was different. This was for keeps. This could be life or death. I intended to pursue the hand-to-hand combat part of our training.

The Army drives a single phrase into your brain: "The spirit of the bayonet is to kill." A few of the new recruits simply could not bring themselves to say it. That was the beginning of their demise. These drill sergeants, combat veterans all, did not take pity on conscientious objectors or anyone else who did not conform to what they considered the army way. Those poor bastards were singled out for unrelenting abuse, and I had to pity them. They simply did not belong there.

The rest of basic training was standard. By the fourth week I figured out what the army wanted and fit in a little better. I kept my mouth shut, did what ever they told me and didn't make any waves. The seventh week was a field trip to the woods of Fort Polk to simulate what it was like in the jungles of Vietnam. After dark I pitched my one-man tent—right in a patch of poison oak.

I am highly allergic to poison oak and wound up with a terrible case, taken to the infirmary, and pulled off training for four days. Even the medics and doctors couldn't believe how bad a simple case of poison oak could be.

When I came back to the company after missing four days of training, I had to stand in front of the company commander, a young lieutenant whose name I'll never forget: Blackthorne. He had the power to recycle me, an Army term for being sent back to a newly formed basic training company and starting the process all over again. Or he could simply send me back to my platoon so I could graduate on time. If he recycled me, I would miss my scheduled flight school class that I worked so hard for. That would leave a real bad taste in my mouth for the Army and result in a seriously bad attitude.

I was nervous standing there in front of him, and he knew it. The lieutenant made it as hard as he could for me. My entire future rode on his decision, and the asshole enjoyed his power. He went over my whole file, test scores, PT scores, everything. I was in great shape physically, except for the poison oak, so all my PT scores were in the top of the class. My written test scores were high, also.

I sweated while standing at attention in front of this lieutenant. He finally proceeded to tell me how my start in the Army was rough, beginning with the ugly haircut incident, but it looked like I straightened out. Since I was going on to flight school, he was going to make an exception in my case and let me continue with my class. What a relief. What a nice guy, huh?

What a prick is more like it.

I found out later that his decision was not an exception to army policy, and he didn't have to make me sweat like that. He just enjoyed my predicament and his power over me. I silently wished I could meet him some time in the future in a role reversal. The world is round: what goes around comes around.

I graduated from basic training with my class, on schedule, with high grades and a promotion to private E-2. I flew back to New Jersey for two weeks' leave and some hearty partying. Suzanne was waiting at the airport and I was glad to see her. It was May and the weather was turning warm, so we spent time at the shore and just relaxed. Neither one of us was a big drinker, so we just enjoyed being together and being alone.

I love being alone with her.

I took a day to see my cousin. I had left so quickly three months before that I never got a chance to thank him or say good-bye. I took him out to lunch, and he brought me up to date on his jobs. He admitted he missed me and thanked me for watching out for his interests while I was there. Word from the field must have gotten back to him. I'm glad it did because I'm not big on blowing my own horn. I thanked him again for helping me with the congressman and said good-bye. We both knew this might be a last good-bye, but, being guys, neither of us mentioned it.

I spent time with my mom and my sister. I told them funny stories about basic training and my travels. I kept it light and didn't tell them exactly how it all went down. They enjoyed it more that way. They got a kick about the poison oak story because I didn't go into all of the details, and they liked the idea of me being on KP duty. They thought it meant I had learned to cook, and if that made them enjoy the story, what's the harm?

My two-week leave went quickly, and soon I was on a plane to Fort Worth, Texas, to my next duty station. Soon, I'd be flying helicopters.

Or so I thought.

Chapter 6

The primary training for all future military helicopter pilots was at Fort Wolters, Texas, a large military training facility outside the town of Mineral Wells. I say "all" because not only did the Army send its future pilots to Fort Wolters for basic helicopter training, so did the Navy and Marines.

The beginning of flight school was called "preflight." It was four weeks of reading, writing, learning, and marching—but no flying. We learned maintenance, aerodynamics, navigation, and flight planning. We also learned about being an officer and taking care of the troops.

After four weeks of this unpleasant hell, we finally got to the flight line and were assigned a flight instructor. Since the Vietnam War was so demanding on helicopters and pilots, there weren't enough active duty pilots available to train new pilots. So the Army contracted with a civilian company to do much of the primary flight school training. Some of these guys were ex-military, but most of them had never been in the military or, more importantly, to those of us who were likely going to war, they had never been in combat. Their job was to teach us to take off, fly from Point A to Point B without getting lost, hover the helicopter, and then land.

That should have been a simple process, but it didn't turn out that way. These guys were cruel, sadistic, and damn proud of it. Their instructions were to weed out the weak to save the Army time and money.

The instructor took us to a staging field, miles from the main heliport, and started the training process from there.

Hovering a helicopter is hard for the beginner. Just rise three feet off the ground and sit there. *No way—it wouldn't do it!* The damn helicopter had a mind of its own. It certainly did not want to sit still three feet off the ground. I soon realized why the school was in Texas: you needed lots of room to learn to fly a helicopter.

The first week trying to hover, we were lucky to keep the sucker in an acre lot. Once we were able to pick it up and hover, then we could move around the staging area to get in position to take off and actually fly somewhere. The army gave you fifteen hours of dual time—flying with your instructor—to solo. If you didn't solo in fifteen hours it meant you couldn't cut it. You weren't meant to be a pilot or you couldn't take the pressure. You were put on probation. Then you were given a few more hours of dual time to solo. If that didn't work you were washed out of flight school.

Washed out for a nineteen-year-old kid who dreamed of being a pilot meant being handed a rifle and sent to Vietnam as a grunt, a foot soldier, a jungle junkie, an infantryman. There's nothing wrong with those guys—they are the backbone of every service, every war, and every combat operation. It's just that becoming one of them by washing out of flight school was not what any pilot had in mind.

When I reached the fourteen-hour mark, my future as a helicopter pilot was in serious doubt. My instructor yelled and screamed while I was at the controls and then hit my arm when I did something not to his liking. I didn't do well under those conditions. I wanted to get him on the ground and kick his ass with my newly learned hand-to-hand combat skills, but that was not going to happen. I learned in basic that violence to your fellow man on an Army post was not acceptable.

Finally at fourteen hours and thirty minutes, he landed the aircraft at the staging field and started to get out of the aircraft. His parting words were: "Just try not to kill yourself and wreck this aircraft. Take off, fly the pattern three times, and meet me back here."

Wow, what a send off. I did it like I knew what I was doing. I soloed, and I loved it. My heart was beating fast, and my head was swimming with all that I had learned. What a rush! When I got back to my instructor, he congratulated me. For a while there, I thought I was dealing with my father. What a scary thought that was!

The tradition in flight school was that after a candidate solos, he is thrown in the water in his flight suit. The bus taking us back to the barracks stopped at the base swimming pool, and those of us who soloed that day were thrown in.

My flight school class had started in preflight with 132 candidates. Only 125 made it to the flight line, and only 109 soloed. The rest of flight school washed out many more. The competition and training were that brutal.

We went from dual flight with our instructor, to solo, to dual flight with another student, to night dual with our instructor, then night solo, then cross-country flying all around Texas.

Picture this: the TH55A training helicopter is thirty-one feet long. It has a main rotor diameter of twenty-seven feet. The max airspeed is ninety-five miles per hour, and it can go 210 miles on a tank of gas, or approximately two hours of flight time. The empty weight is 1,000 pounds. The maximum gross weight fully loaded is 1,850 pounds. A full tank of gas weighs about 300 pounds, so that leaves enough weight capacity for two average-sized pilots and gear. It was a small sucker.

We spent the next few weeks learning to hover, take off, land, and maneuver in all conditions. First we went up with our instructor, the lovely guy who liked to yell and hit. Then we flew solo to practice what he taught each day. Each day was a new topic, and there were plenty of emergency procedures. The running joke was that the helicopter is not really designed to fly and neither are the student pilots trying to do the impossible, which was fly one. Plenty of things could go wrong, and a lot of them will kill you.

We started from day one with simulated engine failure. We practiced that three, four, five times a day. The helicopter will auto rotate, which means it will essentially float to the ground if done properly. If done improperly, it falls to the ground like a 1,800-pound rock and turns into a ball of fire. Not too pleasant a thought when you are constantly told the helicopter you are flying is going to have an engine failure if you fly enough. *Great!*

Each instructor had two to four students, depending on the size of the class and the experience of the instructor. I shared my instructor with three other candidates. When you weren't flying, you had to sit in the bleachers and watch your classmates fly the idiot pattern—hover to the runway, take off, climb to eight hundred feet, turn left on crosswind, turn left on downwind, turn left on base, and turn left on final, bring the aircraft to a hover, and start the process all over again—and then again. We called it the idiot pattern. Repetition is the key to successful learning, and it's no different in flying.

Along with the helicopter being inherently prone to engine failure, we also had to learn and prepare for hydraulic failure of the controls, tail rotor failure, electrical failure, instrument failure, transmission problems, as well as problems with fear and panic. The first four months of primary helicopter flight school were spent dealing with failures and how to turn the failures into a safe landing you could walk away from. Any landing you could walk away from was a good landing, regardless of what the aircraft looked like.

The first night solo was an anxious event. Our group of four students had gotten a new instructor two months into the course. The new guy was a 250-pound former Army chief warrant officer from Vietnam who had a severe limp, the result of being shot in the leg and crashing. He was a big Polish guy named Romazewski—and a great pilot, that was a given, but he wasn't much on small talk or war stories. He was also a good instructor, and because of him and his different style of teaching, I was able to pass the primary portion of flight school and go on to become a good pilot.

The preflight briefing before our first night solo was all about emergency procedures and how to handle them. Romazewski said, "If you are flying along and your engine fails, get the collective down, get the aircraft under control, make your emergency call on the radio with your position, turn into the wind, and turn your landing light on to find a good spot for your landing. Once you find a good spot, turn your landing light off so you don't get fixation on the light and crash into the light, get your head back into the aircraft, get to one hundred feet off the ground, flair the aircraft, put your light back on at this point, and finish your landing. This whole procedure should take approximately ninety seconds. Then make sure you secure the aircraft, walk to the nearest phone, and someone will pick you up. Any questions?"

The four of us just sat there with our mouths open and must have looked real confused. We were.

He repeated, "Any questions?"

One student had the nerve to ask a question. "I think I have it all up to the point where you put your landing light on for the first time to look for your landing spot. What do you do if all you see are trees, or water, or dark spots, and no good place to land?"

Romazewski looked him right in the eyes and said, "If that happens, just turn your light back off and pray."

What a send off. What an impression that made on all of us. We sat there in awe and quietly walked out to the flight line to our aircraft and one step closer to our destiny.

That first night solo flight was a nerve-racking experience. I decided right there and then that I was not going to enjoy flying after dark.

In the next few days, we had the opportunity to fly night dual with another student. My roommate Greg Smith and I were paired together.

Mineral Wells, Texas, the closest town to Ft. Wolters, had a drive-in movie theater. Every time we flew in the vicinity of that theater, I thought how cool it would be to fly over at night and "flash" the cars with the landing light and light up the screen during the movie. The landing light on an aircraft is one bright sucker.

Well the time came for the opportunity to try my secret plan. I was flying with Greg, whom I could count on to keep a secret. Breaking the rules in flight school came with heavy penalties, so the reason better be a good one. This plan was foolproof: no one around to see, no one on the ground could read the aircraft number, so no way to get caught.

We took off from the heliport and headed on our prescribed route. As soon as I thought it was safe, I changed direction and headed for the drive-in. As I got closer to the destination, I couldn't believe my eyes or ears. I know my secret plan was a secret because I didn't tell anybody about it. What I didn't know or plan on was how many other guys were planning the same caper. I lined up number six over the holding pattern waiting for my turn at the big screen. By the time it was my turn, all the fun was gone, and the powers were screaming over the radio for us to get out of the area. So much for great plans and secret capers.

The next highlight was dual cross-country with a buddy. Already the daily routine of takeoffs and landings and emergency procedure practice had lost excitement. Cross-country sounded fun and exciting. The night before, we went to the PX and stocked up on snacks and treats for the long flight. Each leg of the flight was two hours (max air time for the fuel capacity), and there were four legs planned. First west, then south, then east, and back home. Each stop was at a refueling point. The flight consisted of fifteen aircraft, two students each, and two chase aircraft. The chase aircraft were for any maintenance problems, and they carried extra fuel just in case.

There was not much room for error. The flight path was precise and direct. Each student flew two legs and navigated two legs. Greg and I flipped a coin, and I would fly first. Greg was a good pilot and navigator. We flew this first leg with no problem and were second to land at the refuel. It was not a race, but getting there second was cool.

The second leg was interesting. It was my turn to navigate and get us to refuel number two. As I was looking at the map, I saw a chance for a shortcut and gave Greg a heading to fly. I was also tuning the radio, trying to get some music and serving snacks to the pilot and myself. After about thirty minutes into the second leg, I picked up the map to check our progress. We were flying VFR, visual flight rules, and following the roads and terrain below us. But the ground below and the map in front of me looked different.

"What do you mean they look different?" Greg asked, trying not to scream.

He started to call out things he was seeing on the ground. Do you see that lake? How about those railroad tracks, that town over there? He gave me the controls and grabbed the map.

"We're lost," he said, annoyed.

Finally, after a few minutes of searching, we realized we did know where we were, and it wasn't where we were supposed to be. We couldn't call for help, not yet anyway. Too embarrassing. The flight leaders would not take kindly to anyone getting lost at this stage of training. It would definitely result in a pink sheet, a failing grade for the day's efforts, not to mention the harassment from the other students in the class. We made the decision. We had to land somewhere and ask for directions. There was a small airport off in the distance, but that meant calling on the radio for landing instructions and alerting everyone of our dilemma. We decided to land at a gas station we saw on an isolated road just ahead. Hell, this was 1967, and gas stations still gave out directions to lost motorists. We were just lost in a different kind of vehicle.

There was no question in Greg's mind, since I was responsible for the infraction and getting us lost, I had to get out to do the asking. Greg, an excellent pilot for this stage of the training, made a good approach and landing on to the field right next to the station. I got out of the TH55A in my flight suit and my student pilot status and walked into the station. Five local men sat around a table playing cards and smoking cigars. I swallowed my pride, walked up to their game with my map, and asked if they could help me find the way back to our next fuel stop. One of the bigger men must have been the owner, even though they were all extra-large individuals. He asked me if I was a helicopter candidate student pilot.

I said, "Yes, sir, I am," in my less-than-southern accent.

At that point they all burst out in a chorus of knee-slapping laughter. After a few minutes of me standing there in total humiliation, they finally got down to a mere chuckle. I asked, "Other than the fact I am lost, is there anything else that strikes you so funny?"

The owner said I was not the first one from the flight school to stop there for directions. "As a matter of fact, a few boys stop by every year during the cross-country phase." He showed me on the map where I was and how to get back on track. They gave me two drinks, even though I tried to decline; they said my bad day wasn't over yet, and I needed all the help I could get.

I walked back to the aircraft, briefly told Greg my experience, and off we went—heading in the right direction, this time.

After another hour of flying, and some discussion about how to explain this screw-up, we realized we were not going to make it to the next stopping point with the amount of fuel we had left. Our slight detour had become a big problem. Greg decided to make the call to the chase ship, give them our position, and request a fuel drop. Greg picked a spot in an open field and started an approach to land. Texas has a lot of big, open fields.

The chase ship landed next to us shortly after we landed, and the two instructor pilots handed us a five-gallon container of fuel to put in our tank and get us on our way. I made a feeble attempt to explain the reason we ran out of fuel, which they realized was bull and said we would discuss the reasons in detail back at the heliport at the end of the flight. They took off first after mentioning something about keeping the rest of the flight in sight from now on.

Greg made it to the next refuel point without any further problems. The next two legs of the cross-country flight went smoothly, on schedule, but we could tell from the reaction of the other students and the ribbing from the instructor pilots, we were in trouble.

The last leg we flew near Denton, Texas, the home of an all-girls school. I casually mentioned to Greg what a gas it would be to fly over the school to look at the girls.

"You've got to be kidding," he said.

Needless to say, we didn't fly near the school.

Back at the ranch, we were called into the flight leader's office to explain. I told Greg I would handle the explanation, since it was my screw-up. I could count on Greg to not exaggerate about it being my screw-up. I'm not sure how I knew this; I just did.

I had it all planned out, what I was going to say to get us out of this. The aircraft was not fully topped off when we left. The gas gauge was not working properly. The engine was not running right and burning too much fuel.

As I stood in front of this civilian contractor, the flight leader, who had the authority to end our flight careers, I decided to tell him I just screwed up and wasn't paying attention. I got us off course for a brief time. Once we realized the error, we corrected our course, called for help, and got back on course. I purposely left out the gas station part.

He gave me a strange look, as if he was expecting one of my other explanations. He appreciated the honesty, said we handled the problem correctly, no damage done, no one hurt, and a safe ending. My grade for the day would reflect the screw-up and the safe ending. No foul. As for the team of Greg and me, our grades would be passing. I found out later that quite a few teams got lost over the course of flight school, but most of them tried to talk their way out of it.

Once back at the flight line, everyone wanted to hear the outcome, so I made a good story out of it and became labeled a big chance taker.

The rest of primary training consisted of a crash course in instrument flying, just in case we got inadvertently stuck in bad weather. Practicing all the emergency procedures was still a daily event. Finally, the last week of training and the check ride—the test to see if you were qualified to move on to the next phase of flight school.

The next phase was the biggie, the part we all were waiting for. The next phase would be at Mother Rucker.

Chapter 7

Fort Rucker, Alabama, the Army Aviation Center—this was the place where the best pilots flew and where successful flight candidates graduate. This was the place where the beloved Hueys were. The Huey, the UH-1, was the ultimate in helicopter flying in the 1960s. Compared with the TH55A or any other trainer, there is no comparison. We couldn't wait to get our hands on a Huey.

But before we got to Rucker, we had to pass the check ride in Texas.

My check ride turned out to be a piece of cake. The check ride instructor pilot was a military type, a veteran. The instrument portion was a bit rough, but the rest of the test was above average. I liked flying helicopters, and I was getting good at it. So ended five months in Texas.

After a brief leave at home, I was anxious to get to Rucker and on with the training.

Driving to Alabama, I decided to stop in Washington, DC. I had never been to DC. This would be a good time to thank the congressman for helping me.

I pulled off Interstate 95 and headed toward the Capitol. It was two in the afternoon on a weekday, so I thought my chances of seeing him were good, even though I had no appointment. I found the

Capitol with no problem and even found a place to park fairly close. I walked in and up to a huge information desk. At least five women were working at that post. I asked to see the congressman from New Jersey.

Congress was in session, and committee meetings were going on. They called a number, and within a few minutes, a page, a young man a few years younger than I came up, introduced himself, and said he would escort me to the congressman's office. After a long walk down many corridors and through many doors, we reached the New Jersey section. The page showed me into a large reception area. An attractive woman, late thirties, dressed in a nice-fitting skirt above the knee and a white blouse that revealed an impressive figure, asked if she could help me.

I told her my name and asked if I could see the congressman. She said the congressman was in a committee meeting and would not be available for a few hours. He was on the Armed Services Committee, but I didn't know what else. I wouldn't have minded sitting there for a few hours chatting with this woman, even though she had a wedding ring on but I knew I had to get to Fort Rucker, I was here now and who knew if I would ever get another chance to see the congressman.

I told this beautiful woman I had seen in movies where efficient assistants interrupted important people in meetings to hand them a note, if it was important enough.

She asked, "Is this important enough?"

I told her I was on my way to Fort Rucker and then to Vietnam, and I wanted to thank the congressman for helping me. For a moment I thought I saw a look of recognition on her face. She gave me a cute smile and told me to wait. She would see what she could do.

About fifteen minutes later, the door opened, and in she walked with the congressman. I stood right up, extended my hand, and said, "Congressman, I'm Daniel."

He walked right up, shook my hand, and said, "Of course, I am so happy you stopped by."

He turned to his secretary and introduced us. Her name was Sherry. He told her I was the young man who asked for help in getting into the Army and the flight program. She extended her hand. She thought that was who I was and knew the congressman would want to say hello, so she made the effort. The congressman said Sherry had made the different calls at his direction and knew the case. He invited me into his office and offered a seat.

This office was beautiful and large, with high ceilings, dark paneled walls, and thick carpet. I was impressed. He offered something to drink.

I said, "A soft drink would be nice, some kind of juice." I don't like the bubbles in soda, so fruit juice is my soft drink of choice.

He called Sherry and made the request. He wanted to know how things were going and how his help had worked out. The only information he had gotten was from my cousin.

I reminded him of his call to me a few months before and then told him how fast things progressed from there. I briefly talked about flight school and how happy I was to be there and how well I thought I was doing.

A knock on the door and in walked another page, an attractive girl about seventeen or eighteen named Jan (short for January), with our drinks. I was beginning to like this Washington, DC, and all the fringe benefits. I was introduced to her as an Army pilot on my way to Vietnam. That made me feel proud and flattered.

After more small talk, the congressman said he had to get back to his Armed Services Committee meeting. He offered to set me up with a private tour of DC. If I thought for one minute it would be with Jan, I was ready, but duty called, and I told him I would take a rain check. He asked if there was anything else he could do for me, and I replied he had done plenty already.

He asked one more time if I was still content with my decision to finish flight school and the possibility of my next duty after that. It was fall of 1967, and Vietnam was increasingly heating up every day.

The newspapers were full of daily war news, and the television news couldn't get enough. I told him I was still solid in my conviction and thanked him again for his help and concern. He thanked me again for my service to my country, wished me luck, and walked us out the door to Sherry's desk. He said goodbye and left. Sherry called the first page, and he escorted me down to the lobby. I left the capitol that day with a good feeling about my country and my Congress. Back to my car and back on track to Alabama.

Fort Rucker was an old post, left over from World War II, and brought back to life for Vietnam. Fort Rucker was all military, no civilian flight instructors, no fooling around, just serious people with a serious mission. After all, most of the pilots and pilot candidates on this base were going to Vietnam, and in 1967 that was serious business.

Once we checked into our new flight unit, we received new equipment and uniforms and class assignments. For the next five months we spent five days a week flying and going to class. One half day was flying and one half day learning maintenance on the Huey, navigating the Huey, cleaning the Huey, and being one with the Huey.

The instructors expected you to know how to fly a helicopter at this point. We just had to transfer those skills to the Huey. The TH55A maxed out at 1,850 pounds. The Huey maxed out at 11,000 pounds. The trainers had reciprocating gasoline engines. The Huey had turbine engines and used jet fuel. The trainers could hold two people. The Huey could hold twelve to fourteen people. The Huey had real instruments and gauges—the cockpit was intimidating, to say the least. Circuit breakers surrounded the pilot and copilot. Two pilots must be in the cockpit at all times.

The controls were standard to the helicopter, so they did the same thing, just bigger and faster. Once I got over the thrill of being in a Huey, and I understood what all the instruments and gauges were for, I was able to settle down to concentrate on flying this big sucker.

My instructors during this phase were not memorable. They were non-emotional and not particularly personable, but effective, professional, and excellent teachers.

Once I learned how to hover back in Texas, I could hover any aircraft, anytime, any place. The Huey, as big as it was, was stable and easy to fly, once you learned to respect it and keep your hands still.

The first six weeks were basic flying, getting comfortable, learning all the new emergency procedures, and learning to talk and listen to more than one radio at the same time.

The next phase, and the rest of the course, was directed to group flying, formation flying, landing in groups, landing and taking off from tight areas, and learning combat tactics.

The last two weeks of flight school at Fort Rucker consisted of simulated Vietnam living and flying. One of the phases was an orientation to helicopter gunships: armed helicopters designed for assault and for the protection of other helicopters and troops on the ground.

These Hueys were fitted with machine guns and rockets. Because this was Alabama, and we could only go to a firing range with many restrictions, we could get only a small idea of what these gunships were capable of doing. The one thing that came right to my attention: I was in love! The gunship was all I wanted, all I could think of, the only way to fly. I had to wait, though; real gunships were only in Vietnam.

One day about dusk, we were put into trucks and taken out into the back woods of Alabama. The purpose was to get an idea of escape and evasion in case we were shot down in enemy territory. We were put in groups of five. One candidate had the map showing the area and how to get to the safe area. One had a flashlight, one a compass, and one a book of phrases in Vietnamese in case we encountered friendlies.

The area was planted with enemy patrols looking for us, a prison camp if we were captured—complete with a torture chamber if we didn't talk—and a safe zone for us to reach. Most of the guys I was with took this exercise as a joke, something to treat lightly. I took it seriously. I figured if I could reach the safe zone under these circumstances, I at least had a chance when it happened for real, so I was determined to not get caught and reach the zone.

We all glanced at the map and got out of the truck, which drove away and immediately a group of the enemy started shooting and yelling in our direction. The rifles shot blanks, but were still scary and nerve-racking. My group took off running in all directions. Since it was pitch black dark with no moon, we became separated. I wound up with the compass, but without the map, which was little help. I first had to get away from the enemy and get my bearings. I crawled on the ground making no sounds. As soon as I thought it was clear, I stood up and started heading west. At least I remembered the safe zone was west of where we were dropped off.

I came to what sounded like a stream and had to cross. It was dark, and I could only see five feet in front of me. I found a log going over the stream and climbed on. The log broke. It was rotten, and down I went into the stream, flat on my back on the rocks. I scrambled to the bank and was more concerned about the sound I made when I yelled out rather than the pain in my back from landing on the rocks. I lay on the bank stone still for a few minutes to make sure I hadn't been heard.

There I was, lost in the jungles of Alabama, all alone, a bad pain in my back, some bleeding from a cut on my head, and now I was soaking wet, right down to my OD (olive drab) green skivvies. It started to get cold, and I thought about getting through this ordeal in one piece and successfully. My blood pumped, my adrenaline flowed, and I was in an element in which I felt comfortable.

I can beat these odds and get home.

I thought I noticed a stream on the map with my brief glance, but I didn't know if this was that stream or another one. I followed the stream for a while. I also remembered from the briefing before we started that the enemy prison camp was between our drop off point and the safe zone along the easiest and most direct route. I was in no position to find an indirect route because I had no idea where I was. I soon heard voices, but it was too soon to be the safe zone. It must be the enemy position. Since I wasn't sure either way, I had to get closer to find out. The secret here was finding out without getting caught. I moved slowly on my belly, stopping long enough to rub dirt on my face to make it dark. I saw someplace in a movie that mud on your face kept you from getting caught. I was ready to try anything.

I heard more voices. They sounded harsh and loud. I figured at the safe zone everyone would be happy and glad to be there and quieter. Besides, it was still early in the night for many guys to have reached the safe zone. I started to back away and find a way around this undesirable location. I didn't have a watch, so I had no idea how long I'd been out there. I crawled all the way around the camp until I got a west heading again. I felt safe enough to stand up and started running west. In the pitch black with uneven terrain, I fell a bunch of times and tripped over every branch in my way.

I slowed down to get my breath and check the compass heading and thought I saw a flicker of light. My blood pumped faster as I moved closer to the light. Soon I smelled the fire—a large fire in a clearing. It must be the safe zone. There was only one prison camp, right? I couldn't be sure, so back on the ground crawling. Once I got close enough to hear the talk and see the guards dressed in US garb speaking in English. I reached the zone, so I stood up and walked in.

I must have looked a sight. No hat—I had lost it. Hair all filthy with mud and leaves. My fatigues were covered with mud and so was my face. I had many scratches. My pants were ripped and so was my jacket. They looked at me and said, "What happened to you?"

"I made it! How many guys ahead of me?"

"Just two so far."

There were sixty-five guys on the exercise that night, and I came in third. Not bad. I felt good—I didn't look too good, but I felt good. I was ready. I was ready to go.

I rode in the bus back to the barracks with the few guys who made it to the safe zone by midnight. Some more of the guys made it by sunrise. About twelve to eighteen got caught and went to prison. A few got lost and were rescued the next morning.

I lay in my bunk that night, too jacked up to sleep. A warm glow ran through my body. I had accomplished something, and I was preparing myself for the unexpected. There was going to be a lot more "unexpected" as I continued this path of flight school and beyond. Slowly I drifted off to a sound sleep. I was exhausted.

Chapter 8

We all felt pretty special after graduating from flight school. We received our wings and warrant officer insignia and Congress had deemed us gentlemen. Of the ninety-six people who graduated with our class, eighty-five received orders directly to Vietnam. The others went to stateside units or to Germany. We had logged 250 hours of flight time during our twelve months of flight school. Those 250 hours entitled us not only to fly military aircraft but also qualified us for a civilian commercial pilot's license. The Federal Aviation Administration knew our military training was far superior to any civilian flight training available.

Normally when you get orders to report to a combat zone, you get thirty days' leave. But these were not normal times. Vietnam was getting hotter every day, and helicopter pilots were very much in demand. My orders told me to report to Travis Air Force Base, California, in twenty-one days. I was disappointed I didn't get more leave time but decided to make the best of the time. I scheduled a trip to the Caribbean with Suzanne to just enjoy each other and spend as much time as possible in bed.

We planned a nice eight-day trip to St. Thomas and scheduled it so it would be time to begin my twelve-month tour of duty right after we returned to the states. I also spent some leave time visiting family and friends and getting ready for my trip to Southeast Asia.

A few days before we were scheduled to leave for St. Thomas, I received a telegram from the Army changing my orders and directing me to report four days earlier to Travis for immediate shipment to the Republic of Vietnam. I was not a happy camper, or a happy newly appointed warrant officer or a happy helicopter pilot. I had three choices: cancel the trip to St. Thomas, cut the trip short, or ignore the telegram and act like I never received it.

What was the worst thing they could do to me? The Army desperately needed helicopter pilots, so they weren't going to take away my shiny new wings. And since you had to be an officer or warrant officer to be a pilot, they weren't going to take away my shiny new bars, either. All they could do was put me on a plane and send me to some god-awful place on the backside of the world where people could shoot at me. Since that is exactly what they were going to do anyway, what did I have to lose?

We went to St. Thomas as planned. We had a great time and tried not to think about my leaving when we got back home. This was bittersweet thinking. On one hand, I thought I was in love and wanted to stay home; on the other hand, I had finished my training. I had done well, and I was ready to get on with the next step and fly in combat. I decided not to think about the rising casualty rate.

Then came the day I was to leave for Vietnam. I wanted to say good-bye to my mom and my girl at home. My Mom tried to stay strong for Suzanne and me too. She said, "There are special powers in force that are going to watch over you and bring you safely back to us." Suzanne was filled with tears and had trouble saying goodbye. I kissed her tears and said, "I will be back and we will be together again." I wanted these last memories at my house, so I asked my best friend Donny to drive me to the airport. Once we were out of sight, my Mom walked into the house and turned on the light in the living room. "Daniel is the only one that can turn off that light when he comes home," she said. The trip to the airport with Donny was filled with reminiscing about old times when we were growing up. We also talked about getting together after my year at war was over. He was married to his high school sweetheart and we had doubled many times.

"Listen comp'," he said – from his Italian roots, comp, was short for *compagno*, the Italian word for good friend. As he was driving he took a ten dollar bill out of his pocket and ripped it in half. "This half is for you, when you get home, the two of us will go out on the town just like we used to." He put the other half back in his pocket.

That's when it hit me: maybe there wouldn't be a next time. Maybe these were my last good-byes, and maybe it was my destiny not to come back. These were not good thoughts, so I had to change my direction and get on with the task at hand. My buddy dropped me off at the gate and gave me a big hug.

"I want you to watch your ass, kick some ass and come back to us in one piece." He drove away, and my heart sank a little more.

The flight to California was simple enough with no glitches. There were a few other GIs in uniform along the way, but no protesters. I had heard about the protesters, but I had not seen any in my little town. At this point in 1968, the antiwar movement was growing larger every day. The main thrust seemed to be directed toward the soldiers, something I never understood. The war certainly wasn't our idea.

I checked in at the front gate at Travis Air Force Base, which was manned by four large MPs, and showed them my orders. A staff sergeant looked at the orders, saluted me, and asked me to follow him to the commander's office. I expected something like this since I was three days late reporting.

The MP announced my arrival to the commanding officer's orderly and left.

The orderly looked at my orders, then at me and said, "Sir, you are in for it now!"

I asked him who the commanding officer was and he said Major Spence. I asked if he was a Vietnam veteran, and he said yes, and had been wounded, too. I thought to myself, this would be a piece of cake, no problem.

I reported to the major, stood at attention, and saluted sharply.

The major asked if I knew the date but didn't wait for my answer." Didn't they teach you to read a calendar in flight school? Are all pilots this casual about being AWOL? I ought to throw you in the brig for a few days to teach you a lesson".

I asked for permission to speak and explain. He said, "Go ahead."

I told him how I had joined the army to go to flight school, had passed flight school with high grades, and was now on my way to Vietnam to do my part as a helicopter pilot for my country, just like he did. I had noticed his Vietnam campaign ribbons and the Purple Heart on his chest.

Then I told him about my leave being cut short, about my trip to the Caribbean with my sweetheart, and how I didn't see the telegram until I returned from the trip.

I was convincing. Hell, I even convinced myself that what I did was unavoidable. He tried to be stern and act mad, but he started to melt and asked me what unit I was assigned to. I told him. He said they were stationed in the Delta, down in the III Corps area. He said the flying would likely be tough, especially now, right after the Tet Offensive. He advised me to not let my disregard for orders happen again and dismissed me. I'd gotten away with it.

My flight to Vietnam was not until the next day, so I was taken to a barracks where I grabbed a bunk for the rest of the night. The next morning I did the necessary paperwork and went through the out-processing ritual. I received money from payroll because I'd spent all mine on leave, grabbed breakfast, and boarded the airplane to another world. It was a civilian Boeing 707 configured for taking GIs back and forth to Vietnam.

I made a promise to myself during that flight that if I ever had a daughter, I would not let her be a stewardess on one of these flights. These guys were unreal. Over two hundred GIs were on board. Most of them acted like gentlemen, but a few acted like they were on death row, and Vietnam was worse than any penalty for bad behavior. As it turned out, some of them were right.

I was only twenty years old, but I had far more respect for females. A few times during the flight, I and a few other officers had to slow down the fun some of these guys were having. I don't think they meant any real harm; they were just entering a phase of life and experience that most people only get to read about. We went by way of Anchorage, Alaska, then Japan, then into Tan Son Nhat airport in Saigon, Vietnam. It was a long and noisy flight.

When we finally landed, we had to stay on the plane until the security police gave the all-clear signal. Quite often the VC lobbed mortar rounds in and around the airport to harass the troops. I was exhausted from the flight, but excited about what was to follow. The crowd on the plane became quiet toward the end of the flight. Everyone was thinking about what was in store for them and what combat in this foreign land would be like.

I reached the exit door and stepped outside into the bright sunlight and thought: *My God, how can people live in this heat, let alone fight a war!* It was hot. Hot and sticky. Hot and wet. The humidity in Vietnam is near one hundred percent almost every day.

We all loaded into buses and drove to the 91st Replacement Battalion area in Long Binh. Everyone was sent to a different part of the camp, depending on rank. I guess the area where officers were sent was nicer than the other areas—I couldn't tell. We all did some in-processing and then were shown a bunk where we spent the night waiting to be picked up by our respective units the next day.

We were awakened at dawn and had breakfast. I wasn't hungry, but I heard it might be the last decent meal for a while, so I ate.

Eight warrant officers from my flight school class flew to Vietnam with me, and we were all assigned to the 185th Combat Aviation Battalion. The battalion executive officer gave us a briefing when we arrived at battalion headquarters in Bien Hua. He told us there were four assault helicopter companies in the 185th. Three of the companies were stationed in various cities throughout III Corps area. The fourth was stationed in a rubber plantation in the middle of the jungle along with the 5th Armored Cavalry Regiment. They called the place Camp Blackhorse.

The first six guys were assigned to the units in the cities, but WO Vasquez and I were going to the jungle. At about 10:00 a.m., a helicopter picked us up. I was off to my new unit, my new home for a year, and my next big adventure. The helicopter made two stops along the way picking up supplies. The pilot's landings and takeoffs didn't resemble the ones we did in flight school, but I guess he was in a hurry. Welcome to the combat zone.

As we approached Blackhorse, the crew pointed out a huge open area cut out in the jungle. It was filled with tents and small buildings, a long runway, trucks, tanks, and rows of protective revetments loaded with helicopters. We landed on the runway and hovered to the revetment area to park. The pilot managed this interesting maneuver like a piece of cake.

We all got out, introduced ourselves, and the crew showed us to the headquarters tent. Most of the structures at this base camp were tents. A few hours ago I was making fun of small cities with low buildings and poor roads. This place had no buildings and no roads. Welcome to Blackhorse.

The executive officer was at the headquarters tent. We were the first replacements to the unit in quite a while. He took our orders and assigned Vasquez to the 1st platoon and me to the 2nd.

An assault helicopter company has three platoons: two slick (unarmed transport) platoons for carrying the troops into battle and one gunship platoon. The slick platoons each flew five ships on a mission. The gunships flew two or three, depending on the mission.

The XO, executive officer, told us we would go on an orientation flight to get familiar with the area and the aircraft. This unit had all "H" model Hueys for slicks and "C" model Hueys for gunships. In flight school, the best we flew was a "B" model. The "H" model was the newest and had a bigger engine, more power, and more lift capability.

The day after that would be our first combat mission as copilots. We would stay copilots till we had 300 flight-hours in country. My jaw fell to the ground. We got 250 hours total time in flight school and that took one year. How long would it take to get 300 hours in country? I must have looked perplexed, because the XO asked if anything was wrong.

Since I hadn't learned yet to keep my mouth shut in these circumstances, I proceeded to tell the XO what a great job I had done in flight school and all about my high grades. I let him know it would be a waste to keep me as a copilot for that long. Besides, I really wanted to fly gunships, so how could that be worked out?

When he asked if I was finished blabbering, I knew I was in trouble. Maybe I should have waited to express my desires. He was a major, and he went on to tell me how every pilot in this company was an excellent pilot. They had all gotten high grades in flight school, and some of them were still alive to prove it. From there he informed me that the gunship pilots were an elite group, and they would pick and choose who they wanted to fly with them. They would consider such things as experience, ability, and longevity. There was no mention of good grades in flight school. In conclusion, I would be better off if I spent my 300 hours learning from these experienced pilots, keeping my mouth shut, and maybe, just maybe, I would live long enough to become an aircraft commander. Of course, that would be AFTER I logged my 300 hours in country as a copilot.

"Any questions?"

If there was ever a time for no questions, it was that moment. "No, sir!" we all said in unison. Once we got outside, Vasquez said, "That was smart. Anyone else you want to make a good first impression on?"

We were shown our platoon area. I was to share a tent with five other pilots in the 2nd platoon. My new bunk had just been vacated that same week by a chief warrant officer wounded on a mission and medevac'd to Japan. He wouldn't be coming back.

The word got out about my blunder with the XO, and I took flak from the other pilots for a while. After my introduction to my new unit, I was afraid to ask questions. I didn't do much talking at all for the first few weeks, just listening and watching and learning. Ego and stupidity made me think I was ready to take control of this situation with my minimal training. But my check ride and orientation to the "H" model went well.

The second night at my new unit, the VC decided to put on a fireworks display for our entertainment. As I was leaving my tent to watch, the siren started and everyone ran for cover. The VC lobbed mortar rounds into the camp on a regular basis. This time they found a target, our ammo dump where the unit's entire supply of rockets and machine gun ammunition was stored. We all rushed to a bunker, a big hole in the ground lined with sandbags. Each bunker had a metal roof and was topped with more sandbags. It would not withstand a direct hit by anything too large, but it protected us from shrapnel, flying debris, and small arms fire. Each bunker was built to hold six or eight guys for a short period. During the scramble for safety that night, we wound up with nine guys.

Usually the VC threw anywhere from two to six rounds into our area. Once in a while they hit a tent, so everyone stayed in the bunker until the attack was over and the "all clear" sounded. The night they hit our ammo dump, rounds and rockets were going off for hours. You could not tell where the rounds were going to hit, so we stayed in the bunker all night. Sleep was sporadic with the guys moving around trying to get comfortable. Needless to say, a restful night it was not.

We got up at daybreak. The ammo dump had stopped exploding, and it was empty. The aircraft commanders and their copilots went out to the flight line to check on the helicopters. As long as there were enough aircraft to satisfy the mission, the work would go on. Luckily, there was only minimum damage to two aircraft.

Chapter 9

I teamed up with the platoon leader, a seasoned first lieutenant who had been in country nine months, for my first combat mission. His first words were, "After you finish your preflight inspection, get in the right seat, strap in, and don't touch anything. During this flight you are going to watch and listen with *no* touching. Be prepared—we've been in this area before and it's a VC stronghold."

I was excited, anxious, scared, and in awe of all the things going on around me. After that first day at Blackhorse, I realized that flight school taught us how to take off and land, but we came to Vietnam to learn how to fly.

We arrived at the PZ, the "pick-up zone," and immediately started loading troops. That day we were supporting a battalion of the 7th ARVN Division, which was making an assault near My Tho in the Delta. The ARVN (Army Republic of Vietnam) were all nice and clean with their uniforms and bright red bandanas to designate their unit.

We loaded the ten slicks with ten ARVN soldiers each and headed to the LZ (landing zone), a predetermined spot large enough to accommodate ten helicopters landing and taking off in formation with minimal difficulty. As we approached the LZ, the gunships started their runs, firing into the surrounding tree lines to keep any enemy heads down. My pilot told me to put my hands on the controls lightly just in case he got shot during the landing. The idea was that if that happened, I would be able to immediately take off. "Yes, sir," I said, without having any real idea what he was talking about.

I guess I grabbed the controls a little too roughly because he snapped, "I said lightly!"

My mind was a whirl of confusion. The commander gave instructions to the lead ship on one radio. Another radio had the gunships talking to each other about what they were doing and about to do. A third radio provided the ground troops with last minute instructions before the landing. Three radios all blaring at once. It was total chaos.

How did anyone know what they were supposed to do?

Our helicopter was in the sixth position, but after the first five had landed, the whole LZ erupted in gunfire. The door gunners were firing into the tree line and reporting to the pilots we were receiving enemy fire. The ARVN troops fired into the trees as they were getting off the ship. The gunships responded with rockets and mini guns, and the whole time while three radios blasted with information and instructions.

I was in the right seat, a sitting duck for any sharpshooter VC who could see me.

I couldn't believe my eyes or my ears. My first thoughts were, *What the fuck am I doing here? Whose idea was this anyway?*

I can't believe I didn't pee in my pants right then and there.

The lead ship took off and reached about fifty feet. That's when the second ship took a hit, burst into flames, and crashed back to the ground. There was no hope for the crew. They were gone. The ship to my left, the number seven ship, took off at the same time we did and immediately started to dive and yaw. The copilot yelled into the radio that his aircraft commander and crew chief were hit and bleeding badly. He was told to keep his cool and get them to the med station near My Tho ASAP. That copilot, John Stevens, had been in country for four months and was ready to get his aircraft commander status. The gunner pulled the pilot into the back of the ship because he was lying on the controls.

Even with all the confusion and chaos, the rest of the flight remained in formation, returning fire as they left the hot LZ. The commanding officer told the flight leader to hustle back to the PZ, grab some ammo, and load up with the next group of ARVN troops. The guys we just landed needed help.

My aircraft commander got on the intercom and asked if everyone was OK. The crew in the back responded right away they were OK. I thought to myself, they must be used to this by now, but I couldn't imagine anyone getting used to what I had just experienced. I finally relaxed enough to feel my body to see if all my parts were still there and if there was any liquid oozing out. I made an attempt to tell the AC I was OK, too.

He asked if I was OK enough to take the controls; he needed a cigarette. Hell, I wasn't sure if I wanted to take the controls of anything ever again. I dug deep inside and put my hands on the controls and said, "I've got it." The AC leaned back and lit up, he told me to stay as close as possible in formation and not to crash into anything.

That was my first combat mission, my very first, and what an introduction. If they say things get worse before they get better, what could possibly be worse than that? But I actually felt good. I was alive, not hurt, and able to fly this big sucker just like I was supposed to. The bad thing was, we weren't finished yet. That was just the first lift, the first flight into that hellhole of an LZ. We were supposed to take two more lifts this morning.

We landed at the PZ. The crew got out to throw in ammo for their M-60 machine guns, the AC got out to take a piss, and we started loading up the next group of ARVN soldiers. We were two ships short from the first lift, so we could only take eighty this time. We could tell by the slow movement of the ARVN that they'd heard what the first group had gone through, and they were in no rush for the same. Hell, we wanted them to hurry up so they could reinforce their buddies. I found out later that was not how the ARVN looked at it.

Our CO was flying in the command and control ship at 2,000 feet. He had the ground troop's CO with him. They decided to use a different LZ two klicks to the south this time and try to catch the VC retreating. The VC had learned that once the helicopters left the LZ, they would be back soon with more troops, so we landed at the new LZ with only minimal incoming ground fire. At least it was minimal

78

compared with the original LZ, although it is hard to call bullets coming at you "minimal" anything.

By the time we got to the LZ with the third lift, the ARVN had neutralized the main VC force, and they were scattering, going back to the villages, and pretending to be farmers. The ARVN commander decided to keep his men there over night so the main force of our flight was released back to base. Two ships were left behind to resupply the troops for the night.

The three gunships from our third platoon really had a workout. While we were ferrying the troops into the LZ, the gunships stayed on station the whole time supporting the ARVN on the ground. They left one at a time to rearm and refuel. The VC were neutralized due to the awesome power of the gunships, which were relentless once they identified the VC position. Needless to say when ground troops had good air support, they could kick ass. I learned quickly that even though the ARVN had been fighting this war for ten years or more, they were still learning.

We got back to base, assessed damage to the aircraft, and headed for a debriefing. My ship, or should I say the ship I was flying in, did not take a single hit, believe it or not. All that lead flying around, one ship and its crew going down, three other guys getting shot, and not one round hit my ship? That is destiny.

Chapter 10

Military units have traditions and superstitions. Vietnam was no different. There were all sorts of traditions with the 1st Cavalry Division, the 9th Infantry Division, and the 1st Infantry Division (known forever as "The Big Red One"). There were also plenty of superstitions. One of them involved pilots, copilots, and receiving fire and taking hits. It went like this: a new copilot thirty to sixty days in country who was flying combat missions and receiving heavy enemy fire and continuously taking hits was labeled a "Magnet Ass." The new copilot who flew combat missions but did not take many hits was labeled a "Cherry Boy." This had nothing to do with flying ability or common sense, but it was real and was used regularly. Naturally, no one wanted to fly with a Magnet Ass, and everyone wanted to fly with the Cherry Boys.

By this time I had been in country for six weeks. I was on the schedule to fly every day except four during that first six weeks. My first combat mission, we lost six crewmembers. We lost nine more in the next six weeks.

The Tet Offensive in January and February of 1968 resulted in all-out warfare throughout South Vietnam. The Viet Cong and the North Vietnamese Army were on the offensive and attacked every US and ARVN installation they found. The result was that Vietnam became a huge free-fire zone. When we were flying to or from a mission, or were on a mission, and spotted movement on the ground, we were free to fire if those on the ground did not identify themselves immediately. This resulted in friendly fire accidents, but overall, the enemy took huge losses. This free-fire policy lasted until July 1968 when we took back all the ground lost to the VC during the Tet battles.

Since our company had lost so many men, we were shorthanded. The replacements could not keep up with the losses. The situation stayed that way throughout the rest of 1968. We all had to pull our weight and fly extra time. Before I arrived in country, the powers that be decided that a pilot could safely fly 80 hours per month. The safety factors were adjusted, and the maximum was raised to 90. By the time we got things back under control, the maximum hours a pilot could fly safely rose to 120 hours per month. But what the hell, there was nothing else to do. At least you kept busy, and the time flew by.

The company flew combat assaults almost every day. The only days we didn't were the days we could not muster enough ships to fly due to the previous day's damage. During that first six weeks, I had the privilege of flying with some excellent aircraft commanders and crews and learned how to stay alive. I also had the misfortune of flying with some pilots who should not have been in charge of anything. But there were not many options since we were so short-handed. Too many losses were due to pilot error. One thing was for sure, I did not want that to be my legacy.

I learned and watched and tried to do a good job. I still could not relax or feel comfortable; I kept thinking how vulnerable I was and how I was not in charge of my situation or surroundings. The war was in charge, not me. I worried about getting to go home to see my family again.

Chapter 11

The first day of my seventh week in country, we were supporting the US 9th Infantry Division deep in the Delta in the IV Corps near Can Tho. It was an area we had been in before, and we didn't like it.

We were coming out of a hot LZ after dropping our troops. When we carried US troops, we carried eight on board instead of ten ARVN. The American troops we carried into combat were always ready to kick ass, especially the 9th Division. This day was no different.

The gunships were working on the left side of the LZ where the enemy fire came from. After we dropped off our first load of troops, we turned to the right as we climbed out, since we knew the main enemy force was to our left. At about 1,200 feet there was a loud bang, and the aircraft yawed violently to the left. The pilot and I grabbed the controls. The adrenaline started to pump, and real fear was with us. All the cockpit gauges were normal, but the helicopter was hard to control. Chief Warrant Officer Blake, one of the best pilots in our unit, was my aircraft commander that day. The crew chief told him a rocket-propelled grenade knocked off a piece of the tail rotor shaft. The tail rotor shaft connected the tail rotor to the drive mechanism and kept the helicopter flying straight. Without it, a helicopter cannot go below forty knots or else it will start to spin in the direction of the main rotor. The result can be a bad crash. We practiced this emergency procedure many times in flight school. Big difference was, the instructor was right there, and we practiced the landing on a nice, flat, paved runway, not in the middle of rice paddies and jungle.

You controlled the yaw with the throttle and landed like an airplane with forward speed in the forty-knot range because you couldn't hover. But here we were at 1,500 feet with no runway for miles, in the middle of a combat zone, not knowing exactly where the enemy was. We did know we had to get down on the ground as soon as possible and do it without turning into a big ball of burning metal and men.

Blake was cool. He made the radio call: we were hit and going down. The rest of our company's nine other slicks and two gunships were right there ready to help.

Blake told me I was too tight and to lighten up on the controls. I kept thinking to myself, *damn right I'm tight. I'm a little nervous, too.* We told the crew to strap in tight and get ready for a controlled crash. We headed for the ground not thinking of the enemy right now, just our landing. We were in the Delta, and the area was mostly rice paddies and very flat. The VC had plenty of tree lines and jungle spots to hide in, but we had to get this beast on the ground. We picked out a rice paddy that looked big enough.

It was winter in Vietnam and the rainy season. That meant the rice paddies were wet and would help to cushion our crash. Each rice paddy was about a half acre in size and surrounded by a dike about two feet high to keep in the water. We had to make sure we didn't hit a dike.

We hit the ground nice and straight at about thirty knots. We had planned on skimming the ground to a stop, but we landed nose low on my side and dug into the wet mud. The Plexiglas bubble on my side broke and filled my part of the cockpit with mud. I was buried in my seat and could not move.

At this point, the rest of the company flew around us, laying down fire to keep away the VC. The gunships blazed away with minis and rockets. It reminded me, as anxious as I was, how much I loved the sound of gunships on a run, especially the ones protecting me. The gunner got out on my side and started digging me out of the mud with his hands. Blake shut down the aircraft and unhooked the radios. The

VC felt a downed US helicopter was a huge trophy and loved showing it off. They also took advantage of any captured radios to listen in to our conversations. When possible, we took the radios with us.

We made it out OK, but being on the ground surrounded by jungle and people who would like to kill you is not for the weak-hearted. It felt good to climb into the rescue chopper and head for home.

After being shot down once and rescued a few times and watching the gunships workout, I knew what I wanted to do when my time was up being a copilot in slicks. I wanted guns!

I had been in country about ten weeks when I reached my three hundred hour milestone. In flight school it took us one year to fly two hundred and fifty hours of flying and it took ten weeks in Vietnam to reach three hundred hours. We were not sitting around playing cards. Like I mentioned, in flight school we learned to take off, land, fly from A to B, and all the emergency procedures, but we came to Vietnam to learn how to fly the helicopter. After flying in combat with some great teachers, I knew how to fly. I still had plenty to learn, but I was ready for the next step, gunships.

The gunship platoon of an Assault Helicopter Company gets to pick the pilots it wants from the slick platoons. Most of the pilots at that stage of their career in Vietnam were good at what they did; some were very good. I wanted guns, so when my flying time was getting close to the mark I started hanging around with the gunnies. Their tents were in a different section of the company area, and they kept to themselves. They were called out to combat occasionally when the rest of the company was not.

I became a member of the gunship platoon after being in country for eleven weeks and spent the rest of my tour flying armed helicopters. There was one downside, I still had to be a copilot in guns until I learned the ropes as a gunny and learned how to fly a "C" model Huey. The "C" model was designed for mobility with certain distinctions from the troop carrier slicks. The gunships tried to carry as much ammo as possible, sometimes sacrificing fuel and usually maxed out the lifting capacity of the aircraft. The "C" model would not just pick up to a hover and take off like the other helicopters. We usually had to bounce down the runway to get the needed lift to get airborne. The process took finesse and getting used to. An experienced gunship pilot was an excellent pilot.

The fact I was already a trained combat pilot, the transition to guns went smoothly and quickly. I became an aircraft commander in quick order and was given my own gunship. I flew my ship everyday it was flyable

Rose, Elton, my ship, and I became one—a fine-tuned killing machine.

We named her *The Judge and Jury*.

Chapter 12

We had an unexpected stand-down from combat missions on April 2, 1969. A stand-down normally occurred when the unit couldn't get enough helicopters in the air due to maintenance problems, the Hueys were shot up too badly from the previous day's mission, or there were not enough healthy pilots to fly them.

And then there was the good kind of stand-down, the one for a special awards ceremony. On that day Major General Curtis Burnett, deputy commander of the 1st Aviation Brigade, came to our unit to award medals.

It seems the young infantry captain from the mission the night of March 15, along with his first sergeant and four other survivors of that night, thought my team and I deserved a medal for saving their lives. Chief Warrant Officer John McNeill and I were awarded the Silver Star, the nation's third highest award for gallantry in action. The six guys flying with us were awarded the Distinguished Flying Cross.

Hell, we just thought we'd done a good job, but I have to admit we were all pretty darn proud that day. The rest of the unit seemed proud of us, too. It was a day I will never forget.

There were other awards along the way. On November 22, 1968, I had been awarded the Vietnamese Cross of Gallantry for a combined American and Vietnamese mission just outside of Xuan Loc, southwest of Saigon. The ARVN had gotten pinned down and separated from the main force. It was another hair-raising experience with bullets flying all around.

I wound up with fifteen Air Medals; each Air Medal represented twenty-five combat missions. We actually lost count after a while since every day was a combat mission. I also received the Distinguished Flying Cross, the Army Commendation Medal, and Good Conduct Medal. That's the one that confused me the most. The 75th Assault Helicopter Company was also awarded the Vietnamese Cross of Gallantry for a combined mission. By the time I left Vietnam, I had a nice chest of fruit salad.

The 75th had formed up in Texas in 1967 and stayed in Vietnam for five years. The company was eventually retired in 1972 after the American pullout started. McNeill and I were the only ones from the 75th to be awarded the Silver Star in the five years the unit was deployed. That is something I'm also very proud of.

The Army called it "DEROS" but every man in Vietnam knew what it meant: "Date Eligible to Return from Overseas." Unless there was a major screw-up by you or the Army, it meant the day you kissed the war good-bye and got on that big-assed Freedom Bird for the sweet flight home.

I had mixed emotions when I received my DEROS. Sure, I wanted to see my family, my girl, and my friends, but I had friends in Vietnam, too, and, once I went home, I might never see them again. I had to stay positive and start thinking of new adventures and start looking forward to new thrills stateside. I had about used up my nine lives in Vietnam.

My first priority, though, was getting a rifle home. It was my big war souvenir and my most prized possession. I was determined to take it back to the world with me.

This was not just any piece of battlefield junk. On one of our many missions in the deep delta of IV Corps near My Tho, we got into a heavy firefight with some hard-core VC who had no intention of giving up or leaving. Apparently they wanted to die. Which seemed like a fine idea to me.

I was on a steep gun run toward a group running for cover on my left. Suddenly, I saw a lone gunman on my right. He was leaning on the bank of a creek firing his rifle at me. We were so close I really could see the whites of his eyes. His rifle was a Chinese SKS and not the familiar AK-47 that most North Vietnamese and VC carried.

I screamed to crew chief Kurt Rose to look right, but as usual he was already there and cut the VC down with his M-60. I wanted that weapon; that SKS that had almost changed my destiny.

I turned around to look at Rose, he said, "Let's go get it."

That's the way it was with us. I'd start a sentence, and he'd finish it. I'd think a thought, and he'd say it. We were a great team and true soul mates. He saved my life at least a dozen times. He and Elton were partly responsible for my invincible attitude. As long as they were by my side, I wouldn't get hurt. They were sent to Vietnam to be by my side and watch out for me. Maybe they were part of the special force my mother mentioned.

You never land a "C" model gunship in a combat zone. Never. It is potentially suicide because you might not be able to take off again. Pick a word: dumb, stupid, crazy, your choice, not to mention being against every regulation in Vietnam and likely illegal.

I didn't care. I wanted that weapon, and I was going to have it. I circled the area a few times to make sure the hostile action had stopped. I told my wingman what I planned to do and asked him to cover me.

"Are you crazy?" he asked.

"Yes," I said, and down I went.

I hovered three feet above the VC's body. Rose got out to get the weapon. Gunner Gabe Elton covered him on the right and my copilot had his M-16 out the door on the left. My wingman laid down some fire near the area just for good measure. Rose took the rifle, the guy's backpack, web gear, and his pistol. My heart pounded and my blood was pumping. I was truly in my element. I loved the adrenalin rush.

When we got back to base, we all gathered round to check out our booty.

The SKS was in perfect condition, right down to the Chinese writing on the stock and barrel. In the stock compartment I found a small note pad. This VC kept a diary; I would have to get it translated. The bayonet was sharp, the magazine was full, and I was a happy boy. Another good day in Vietnam, plenty of excitement, a real rush, and no blood…well, not ours anyway. Rose got the pistol, Elton got the backpack and web gear, and I got the rifle.

Getting these prizes off the battlefield was tough, but getting them home to the world was going to be an even bigger challenge. The brass had sent down orders in 1968 that no weapons of any kind were allowed to be transported back to the States, especially a semi-automatic rifle in perfect working condition like my beautiful SKS. I guess the ban was a good thing for most of the vets coming out of Vietnam, but surely it didn't apply to me. I was a hotshot pilot, and I should be treated special, right?

I couldn't ship it home with my other stuff. The Army or US Customs would certainly check the baggage and confiscate the weapon. I had no choice. I had to carry it through military security and civilian airports all the way from Saigon to New Jersey. The sight of a soldier obviously just back from Vietnam walking through an American airport with a rifle slung over his soldier ought to just thrill civilians and law enforcement. The movies had already started portraying us as crazed killers.

Clearly, I couldn't just walk into a military airport with an SKS. But how about if it was an honor awarded to me by a high-ranking Vietnamese military or civilian official? Military would be more believable, but you take what you can get.

Yeah, that might just work.

I'd heard rumors there was paperwork that authorized certain items to be awarded to certain individuals under certain conditions. I asked around as to where someone could lay his hands on this legendary paperwork.

I always had a great relationship with the enlisted men in my unit. I learned early on that it was the Spec-4 and Spec-5 clerks and supply guys who ran everything and could get anything. As luck would have it, my crew chief Kurt Rose said that our company clerk, a young Spec-4 who could get any paperwork in Vietnam, had a burning desire to go on a combat mission and fire an M-60 machine gun in action. Not everyone in an aviation company is on flight status, and often those who are not wish they were. Or so they thought.

Well, I just happened to be in a position to grant the resourceful Spec-4 his fondest wish in exchange for hard-to-get paperwork that would allow me to disregard military policy and federal law and take my rifle home. Since the clerk was not authorized to fly on a mission, I couldn't just ask the commanding officer for permission to give him a thrill. This had to be done hush-hush, like a lot of the deals going down every day in Vietnam. I had no desire to put the kid's life in danger, so I had to take him on a mission I thought would be reasonably safe. That in itself was going to be tough because we got in a firefight on almost every mission we flew.

Every night after dinner, the gunship and troop-carrying platoon leaders met with the company commander and commander of the ground troops to plan the next day's mission. Our target would be wherever the intelligence reports said we'd find the most enemy soldiers. That was our job; find the enemy and ruin his day. We went looking for a fight every day.

At this point, I was the commander of a "C" model Huey gunship, the most sophisticated and effective close-combat weapon the Army had in Vietnam. I was also a fire team leader. Gunships always flew in twos or threes, and one of the ships, the one flown by the most experienced or highest-ranking pilot, was designated the fire team leader.

By my eighth month in country, I found myself the most experienced gunship pilot in my platoon as well as the acting platoon leader. The pilots who were senior to me had been killed in action, had been wounded and sent home, or had finished their tours and rotated back to The World. So not only was I in charge of my helicopter and crew, I also supervised six other aircraft, twelve pilots, twenty crew chiefs and gunners, maintenance guys, and the armament crews.

I had all that firepower at my fingertips, and I was just twenty-one-years old.

We'd had a tough mission. We'd lost one full crew when its slick crashed in an LZ and four other ships were badly shot up. We couldn't get enough ships in the air for a full mission the next day, so I was ordered to take two gunships to Nha Be on the Saigon River and give air support to some Navy guys on patrol boats. They had reported an enemy buildup in the area, but I didn't expect a whole lot of trouble. I told Rose to get the clerk ready for his mission.

The next morning when I arrived at the flight line, the clerk had his flight helmet on while Rose gave him a crash course on the M-60 machine gun. I asked Rose about the helmet. He said it was a disguise so no one would recognize the clerk. Rose thought of everything.

All first timers are nervous on a combat mission, and the clerk was no exception. Hell, some guys never got used to being fired at or firing at live human beings. We found out later the clerk had serious second thoughts once he realized he was flying with us. Rose, Elton, and I had developed quite a reputation in the unit for finding trouble even when there wasn't any. We always found a way to kick some ass. That's what we were there for, and we were very good at it.

The mission went smoothly. The Navy PBR (Patrol Boat, River) engaged some VC in a sampan, and the clerk got to fire a whole box of ammo. He also almost fell out when I banked sharply left, but Rose had him well strapped in. We secretly awarded him a confirmed kill. He couldn't stop talking about it, and I was afraid he was going to blab it all over the company area and get us all in trouble. I told him if anyone found out we'd taken him along, I would take him up one more time and not strap him in. This time when I banked left, his ass would go flying. He didn't think I was kidding. Rose thought that was funny and reported that the young specialist was very discreet from then on.

Another good thing that happens when you work with the Navy is the food. They always took a break in the middle of the day, even in the middle of a mission, to eat. That was OK with my crew and me, since we were used to C rations. Sometimes they were even hot, but not usually.

We landed at Nha Be, refueled, and went to the mess hall. Not a tent, but a real mess hall on the Saigon River in South Vietnam.

The place was decorated, clean, and bright. The Vietnamese girls working there looked beautiful in their traditional *ao dai* dresses. We washed up before lunch, which was something we usually didn't feel compelled to do and rarely had the opportunity. Here, it seemed like the thing to do.

One look at the spread, and I thought I was back home on Thanksgiving. This was just a regular weekday meal for them. They had turkey, ham, roast beef, real potatoes, vegetables, real cooked bread, and desserts—we hadn't eaten like this since leaving home. We thanked them and went back to work. One problem, nobody felt much like fighting a war after a meal like that. I just wanted to take a nap. Needless to say, my copilot flew the rest of the day while I recovered.

The next week, I had a blank copy of the "Authorization of Award" paperwork I needed to get my rifle home. We were halfway there. I also made a note to fly with the Navy if I was still around next Thanksgiving.

Going home. I didn't think about it much. Most of the guys kept a short-timer calendar with them. They marked off each day spent in country and could tell you exactly how many days they had left before DEROS. Vietnam was the first US military conflict that had a specific time limit for troops in the combat zone. Everyone there knew that the tour of duty was one year. Twelve months. 365 days. If you survived the tour, if you lived through the experience, you went back to The World.

The World is the place you left when you went to Vietnam. The World is what you dreamed about every day you were in country. The girl or girls you left behind, your car, your friends, your family, real food, all your great memories were all back in The World. We didn't think about the reality that, like Thomas Wolfe said, you can't go home again. You aren't the same, and neither are the people you left behind. Things change. Times change. You change. Home changes. You can't go back to something that isn't there anymore. And when you do get back into The World, people are not going to understand what you went through, and most of the time they won't even try.

Combat, even though it was around us every day, was far removed from the reality waiting for us in The World. There is nothing to compare to it in normal life and normal society. You just can't explain it to someone who never experienced it. You learned real fast not to try. It was a waste of time. They weren't interested.

I couldn't explain my emotions to anyone, even to myself. All I knew was I was not ready to go home, not yet.

As my time got closer to my one-year mark, I continued to schedule myself to fly. Most short-timers enjoyed the down time at the end of their tour and were happy about going home. The Army unofficially but routinely started letting short-timers hang around base camps in their last days in country. What a waste to get killed or wounded when you are so close to the end of your tour.

I kept thinking, *what am I going to do? Where will that adrenalin rush I need come from? What will replace the thrill of combat? What is out there for me?*

That's when I first realized that my thrill-seeking attitude, my addiction to risk, had a solid hold on me, and I wasn't sure how to deal with it.

The commanding officer I'd had for six months left one month before my DEROS. His normal rotation came up, and he was ready to go home. I was happy for him. The new commanding officer was just that, a new commander with his first command who was not broken in yet.

I told him I wanted to extend my tour. He looked at me like I was crazy, as did everyone else I mentioned this to. Since experience is something all new commanders rely on, he took a good look at my record and reluctantly approved my request. This type of request could be handled at the company level but still was reviewed up the chain of command. That would take time, and I needed time to figure out my next move.

Eventually it was time to go home. The commanding officer called me into his office after a mission and told me my time was up. He had requested new DEROS orders for me, and I was going home. I had been in country for fifteen months, much longer than anyone else, and longer than was deemed healthy. He said my efforts and expertise would always be remembered and appreciated, but enough is enough. It was time for me to cool down and get out of the combat zone.

I didn't argue. I knew what he meant. I liked this too much. Besides, Rose had just left, Elton was gone, and there was no one left to help keep me alive. My odds were changing. The boss immediately took me off the flight schedule, and I just hung around for a few days waiting for my orders to arrive. He did ask where I wanted to go for my next duty station. He said he would try to get me wherever I wanted because I deserved my first choice. I told him I wanted a flight school, maybe Hunter Army Airfield near Savannah, Georgia. He came through for me. I got the orders to report to Hunter after a three-week leave.

Now I had to concentrate on getting home my SKS.

I had the proper forms. Now I just had to fill them out carefully and figure out which ARVN officer would sign them. I decided on the deputy commander of the III Corps. He was a one-star general, and I had worked with his men a few times. Besides, his name was General Cao Van Thu—that would be easy to sign and read. I filled out all the particulars in black ink—the Army loves black ink—and his signature was in red. I thought that would be a nice touch. The only possible downside was if my scam didn't work, they would confiscate the weapon and give some other guy a chance to get it home. No harm, no foul.

I went to the PX and bought a leather rifle bag. It made the whole scheme look official, and the fact I was not trying to hide the weapon made it believable, or so I hoped. I mean, who in his right mind would try something as outrageous as smuggling an enemy weapon through military security and customs? Besides, I was a decorated hero and had the ribbons on my chest to prove it.

My first challenge was getting the rifle off my own base. After I'd said all my good-byes to everyone and took a last look around, I was ready to go home. The executive officer was flying to Long Binh, and I hitched a ride with him.

He took one look at the bag on my shoulder and said, "What do you plan to do with that?"

I told him I was taking it home.

"Where did you get it? he asked.

"General Cao Van Thu from III Corps awarded it to me."

He smiled and said, "Good luck!"

I hoped the rest of my trip was going to be that easy.

I arrived at the 91st Processing Station and started the paperwork to leave Vietnam. I wore my newly purchased khakis and with my officer bars, flight wings, and chest of ribbons. I felt good and looked even better.

My Freedom Bird, the plane to take me back to the States, would take off the next morning at 8:00 a.m. I went to the officers' club for dinner and a few drinks and met a bunch of new recruits just arriving in country. Once they found out I was leaving, they were all over me with questions and concerns. It was July 1969, and the war was alive and well and still going strong. I decided not to tell any blood and guts stories and just told them to be real careful, keep their mouths shut in the beginning, and latch on to the guys with the most experience. Listen, learn, and be patient. They were anxious to hear more, especially about my medals, but I had a big day to look forward to and retired early. I had to be my sharpest to pull off this next mission.

After a quick breakfast, I reported to the checkout area for final inspection before boarding a bus to the airport in Saigon.

The first MP in line was a sergeant. He looked at my paperwork—then at the bag on my shoulder.

"Sir, what's in the bag?"

"A Chicom rifle," I said.

"Sir, are you aware that no weapons of any kind are allowed to leave this country?"

"Yes, sergeant, I am aware of that directive. Are you aware of the war souvenir award act?"

"No, sir, I never heard of any such thing," he said.

I opened my chest pocket, right under my medals, and pulled out my paperwork.

"Sergeant, this weapon was awarded to me by General Cao Van Thu, deputy commander of III Corps in recognition of my outstanding service to his country," I said in my most official Army officer voice. "He honored me in a full-company ceremony at the III Corps headquarters at Xuan Loc. Here are my orders, signed by General Thu.

"Now you can waste my time and go and get your superior officer to look over my orders and delay all the guys in line behind me and possibly delay the flight because I'm not moving. I'm also not giving up this award that was given to me. Or you can appreciate what General Thu has done for our morale and let us all go home, your choice."

For a speech that was not rehearsed, it sounded pretty good, I thought, especially the part about the company ceremony. I just thought that would be a nice touch.

The MP grilling me was a staff sergeant. A sergeant first-class walked over, having heard the whole story, took my orders, looked them over, and handed them back to me. He saluted and said, "Sir, have a good flight home."

"Thank you, sergeant, I'll do just that," I replied.

I returned his salute and headed for the bus. The ride took twenty-five minutes. A bunch of the guys in line behind me asked if my story was true. Mainly they wanted to see the SKS. I was getting a rush.

The next challenge was the MPs guarding the Saigon airport and the gate to the Freedom Bird. Another staff sergeant stopped me and started in with the same questions. He said he couldn't understand how I had gotten that far with my rifle. I whipped out my orders and proceeded with my explanation. Halfway through my story, a fellow warrant officer MP walked over, looked at my orders, and said, "General Cao Van Thu—I believe I've heard of him. He was educated at NYU, wasn't he?"

"I'm not sure about that, but anyone from NYU is a friend of mine," I said.

He looked me straight in the eyes. I don't know if he really believed my fanciful story or if he just thought it was such a funny thing to do that he wasn't going to stop me.

"Have a good flight, mister, and be careful with that if you get it to the States," he said.

I boarded the plane, and, even though it was still early morning, I was tired. This transfer of war souvenirs was exhausting work.

The flight to Travis Air Force Base by way of Guam was uneventful. The flight home was a controlled party, unlike the flight to Vietnam. The airlines had gotten smart and added male attendants to the formerly all-female stewardess crew. It was all harmless fun, and watching all these guys—about 250 of them celebrating the fact they were still alive and that they had survived Vietnam in 1968 and 1969, two years that became the peak of the war, was a refreshing sight. I was a bit subdued. I wanted to celebrate, but I was busy thinking about my next move after I got home. I also was concerned about what would happen to my SKS when I went through customs at Travis.

We landed safely and went through more out-processing. As expected, I received strange looks as I walked around with a rifle on my shoulder. I felt a sinking feeling in my gut when I got to the front of the line where the US Customs agents waited. I'd come this far; surely I could get past this roadblock. I decided to play it cool and not get upset and just calmly explain my orders and the fact that I was escorted out of Vietnam by an entourage of Vietnamese military.

The ranking agent said, "Is that a working weapon on your shoulder?"

"Yes, it is a war souvenir," as I handed him my orders.

"Is that the Silver Star on your chest?" he asked.

"Yes, sir, it certainly is."

"Is that the Vietnamese Cross of Gallantry?"

"Yes, sir, it is."

"Are you planning to fly somewhere in the States?" he asked.

"Yes, sir, I'm going home to New Jersey," I replied.

"I don't know what the airline is going to say, but you are welcome back in the USA. Thank you for your service."

It worked like a dream.

It was 11:00 a.m. California time, and there was a bus ready to take us to San Francisco Airport. I started to board the bus when yet another MP asked where I thought I was going with the rifle bag. I immediately went into a torrent of words.

"Damn it, sergeant, I don't mean to come down on you, but I've been traveling for three days to get here and at every stop somebody has been busting my balls about this souvenir," I said, holding nothing back. "Here are my orders awarding this to me by General Cao Thu. Now you can—"

He had no idea what he was looking at but realized how upset I was. So while I was still in mid-tirade, he just stepped back and saluted. I returned his salute and boarded the bus—a prison bus with bars and screens on the window and doors. I would have preferred a limo. As we pulled out of the base onto the main highway, I got my first look at the United States in 1969.

Protesters were lined up waiting for us with signs, banners, and angry faces. "Killers," "Baby Killers," "Murderers," Rapists," the signs said, and then they threw things at the bus—rotten garbage, bags of urine, and who knows what else. So that was the reason for the bars and screens. We were all confused and had no idea what their problem was. We had been sheltered and spared the truth about what was going on in our country. Hell, I expected them to thank me or at least recognize the fact that I fought for our country.

Welcome home, soldier.

I thought this was an isolated case and didn't spend too much time thinking about it. We arrived at San Francisco International and got out at the departing flight area. I carried my duffle bag on one arm and the SKS on the other. There was a small group of us in uniform, and the people gave us a wide birth.

I walked up to the American Airlines counter and made eye contact with a beautiful round-eyed girl who was glad to help me get on a flight to New Jersey. She said, "I don't know what you are carrying, but I'm sure you can't take it on the plane. You'll have to check it."

After all I'd been through I didn't want to let it out of my sight, so I put up a mild objection. But I wound up checking my SKS anyway.

The flight across the country was uneventful. There were a few movies, a few meals, and then we landed. I had called my girl from San Francisco and asked her to pick me up. I walked off the plane in Newark and kissed the ground. I got some weird looks, but I was getting used to them. I looked in the crowd and there she was, my girl. What a sight. I finally realized how much I missed her and how good it was to be home. Suzanne's eyes were filled with tears, but this time they were tears of happiness. We were going to have a great homecoming! And my SKS was waiting for me at baggage claim.

My three weeks' leave was spent visiting relatives, seeing friends, and eating good food—as much of it as possible. I tried to sleep late but had trouble falling asleep and staying asleep. I kept hearing incoming rounds and machine-gun fire in the background. This coming home business would not be an easy task.

Suzanne and I talked about the future and marriage. I decided to get to Savannah to see how things would work out for us from there. I just wasn't ready to make a decision. She didn't like that. She was ready to get married now. We were both twenty-two, but I felt closer to thirty.

I wanted to talk about my experiences with friends and family, but I got the distinct impression no one wanted to hear. When I first walked into my mother's house, after hugs and kisses, she asked me to shut off the living room lamp. I did.

"I turned that light on the day you left for Vietnam," she said. "I knew that as long as the light was on, you would be safe and would come home. You are the only one who can turn it off."

That bulb had burned for fifteen months non-stop while I was in Vietnam, and it burned out three weeks after I got home. Maybe it did have something to do with me getting home safely. Or maybe it was just my mother's prayers.

That was about all the Vietnam talk my mother wanted. She changed the subject when I brought something up, so I got the message. Suzanne was better. She asked a few questions about things I mentioned in my letters but did not want to hear any serious details. My high school friends who went to college or stayed home were still kids. Some of them protested the war, but for the most part, they were oblivious to what was going on over there and didn't care. I never had a serious discussion about the war with any of them, ever.

One of my special missions after I got home was getting with Donny and spending the ten dollar bill he'd ripped in half when I left for Vietnam a *long* time ago. I'd looked at that bill several times while I was away and couldn't wait to put the two halves back together again. It had helped me keep things in perspective. That night with Donny was a real celebration, no girls, just two childhood friends who took different paths and came back together like nothing had happened, even though we both knew nothing would ever be the same again.

After three weeks, I headed for Georgia. I had saved most of the money I earned in Vietnam, so I had a wad of cash on hand. I went down to the Buick dealer and picked out a brand new 1969 Buick Skylark, gold with a black vinyl top. It was a two-door, eight-cylinder beauty with custom interior and loaded with extras.

I was anxious to get to my next station. I knew there would be a lot of Vietnam veterans there, and I wanted to see if they were feeling the same things and thinking the same thoughts that kept running through my head. Mainly, I didn't understand why I was so bored and couldn't wait to get back in the air.

Chapter 13

In the 1970s, Vietnam veteran helicopter pilots dominated the helicopter industry. There weren't any better-trained or better-qualified pilots in the world.

When I returned home from Vietnam, I still had two years left on my service commitment. I thought at that time I wanted to be an airline pilot. They were prestigious and made a lot of money.

A would-be airline pilot had to have lots of fixed wing flight hours and a lot of instrument flight hours. I had neither. What I did have was a neighbor in New Jersey, a good friend of the family, who was a vice president for Eastern Airlines. I couldn't wait for the normal application process, especially with my lack of those qualifications, so while I was home on leave, I called my neighbor and arranged for a private meeting to find out what I needed to do to fly the big jets.

The meeting was to be at his office at Kennedy Airport. I had never been there before. A young man about my age greeted me at the Eastern Airlines headquarters and escorted me to my neighbor's office in the vice presidents' building. This was cool. My neighbor introduced me to the vice president of marketing, the chief pilot for Eastern, and two other employees.

They were all ex-military and supportive of our troops in Vietnam, which was unusual in 1969. They explained what I should do with my remaining two years in the service to better qualify me for a flying job with Eastern. My association with my neighbor had gotten me this fantastic interview, but it would not get me a job.

The only downside of the meeting—and it was a big one—was that Eastern flew three pilots in the cockpit. The junior man was the flight engineer who wouldn't touch the controls until the more senior pilots retired or left. Hell, most of these guys were WWII or Vietnam pilots and still young. Besides, there were plenty of Air Force and Navy pilots looking to land the same job I wanted. And they all had the experience I lacked. I had more combat experience than any of them, I had confronted more of the enemy, I had more confirmed kills, and I had lived through more crashes, but that was not what Eastern was looking for.

I left Kennedy Airport that day a little depressed, but I never looked back, and I never regretted it. It just wasn't my destiny. My neighbor moved out of the area, and I never spoke to him again.

My next two years in the military were spent as an instructor at Hunter Army Airfield near Savannah. At first, I was teaching students in flight school, but that was way too boring. There was simply no challenge to it. My next assignment was teaching pilots just back from Vietnam to get their instrument rating. Not bad. I would be assigned an aircraft, a military gas card, three students, and three weeks to get them through the course and the check ride.

One week we flew from 6:00 a.m. to noon, and the next week noon to 6:00 p.m. The rest of the time was free time. I took the students anywhere I wanted as long as they passed the exam after three weeks. Since they were all Vietnam vets and knew how to fly visually, this was a piece of cake. We told war stories, traded tactics, and had lunch in a different city every day. I knew the material and was able to teach it successfully. I became a good instructor.

I also took the instrument examiner course that qualified me to give check rides. They were final grade tests to students going through flight school and experienced pilots getting their instrument tickets.

One particular day I was told to give a few check rides to a class of RLOs (real live officers, not warrants like me). That was always fun because the pilot in command of an aircraft outranked all the other on-board pilots, passengers, or students. They might outrank me on the ground, but in my helicopter, I was lord and master.

My first ride of the morning was with two captains going through flight school. One was armor, and one was infantry. One of their names rang a bell with me, and I thought to myself, *there is a God, and the world really is round.*

The captain's name was Blackthorne.

Check rides can be intimidating, so I made small talk to ease their tension. We were told to keep the students calm and relaxed before a check ride. They both had served a tour in Vietnam in the rear area, not in combat, and now wanted to add flight wings to their credentials. I was particularly interested in what Blackthorne did before Vietnam. He was company commander of a basic training unit at Fort Polk in 1967.

Well, well, well. How nice. This check ride was going to be fun, at least for me, and this captain was going to sweat bullets before I got through with him.

Fortunately, he was a decent pilot. That was not the point, however. He had locked my heels when I was a private in basic training and made me sweat for no reason. It was my duty and responsibility to return the favor.

During the check ride, I put him through the wringer. I wanted to see what he was made of—if he could handle the stress. I've seen too many good pilots and good soldiers that got freaked out when thrown into all out combat. When we finished flying and got back to the classroom, I started asking him questions I knew he couldn't answer. At that point he knew he was in trouble.

I said, "Captain, aren't you prepared for this exam? Do you take your flying lightly? Would you rather be a pilot or an infantryman?"

He was sweating and started to stutter. I wanted to take this further, but I started to feel sorry for him. And he did, finally, do the right thing and let me finish basic training on time so he was going to get a passing grade.

I asked him if he remembered a young recruit back in basic training at Fort Polk who came down with a bad case of poison oak, and he had to decide whether to recycle him or not. He said he vaguely remembered that incident and asked if I knew that recruit. I told him I was that recruit. He got a scared look on his face and just sat there with nothing to say.

After a long moment of silence, I got back to the flying and the check ride. I told him he had passed the ride, and he had handled himself well. My parting remark as I handed him his check slip was, "Captain, the world is round and what goes around, comes around." I never saw Captain Blackthorne again.

Since my gunship experience was extensive, I also traveled around to different helicopter assault companies to teach tactics and strategies. It was interesting and rewarding. The number of aircraft I was qualified to fly and the number of weapons systems I was familiar with, along with my instrument and instrument examiner certificate, made my résumé in the Army quite impressive.

I didn't realize until much later what a difference the two years I spent as an instructor made in my "cool down" period. Most vets finished their tour in Vietnam and went straight from the military to civilian life, especially the draftees.

The grunts—the foot soldiers, the guys on the ground every day, the guys doing the shooting, getting shot at, killing, and watching their friends being killed—could be in a fire fight in Vietnam on Tuesday and be home on Saturday. There was no debriefing, no "cool down" time, no anything. Just go back home and act like nothing happened, soldier. Forget everything you did and saw for the last year of your life.

Bullshit. That ain't gonna happen. These poor guys had real problems. They had nobody to talk to because civilians didn't want to hear what they had to say. So they kept it bottled up inside, only to have it explode later.

My situation was better, but it still didn't solve all my own problems, particularly my obsession with thrills and my addiction to excitement.

Chapter 14

I got an aviation job when I got out of the Army, but it wasn't flying jets from coast to coast. Instead, I became the company pilot for Columbus Sand and Stone, a construction company in the Northeast. The company owned a five-seat Jet Ranger helicopter and a six-seat Piper Aztec airplane. For four years I did everything the manual said those aircraft can do and a few things the manual said they couldn't do. The guys who write these manuals don't really put the aircraft through their paces and reach for the maximums like I did.

If the book said maximum altitude for safe flight was 12,000 feet, I'd take her to 15,000 feet.

If the book said the maximum safe airspeed was 150 knots, I tried for 170 knots.

If the book said I could fly three hours with seventy-three gallons of fuel, I pushed it a few miles and a few minutes more.

I decided long ago that it was not my destiny to die flying a mission, so I had nothing to lose. Taking chances like this gave me the adrenalin rush I needed.

One Saturday morning I was pissed off about having to fly at the last minute. It was just a routine mission that involved flying people all over Manhattan, from the east side to the west side, and back again. I should have refueled at the 60th Street heliport, but I didn't want to shut down and spend the twenty minutes to refuel. I was in a hurry to get back home for nothing really special.

I headed back to Rockland County, northwest of the city, knowing it would be a stretch with the fuel I had left. The whole way I looked for a place to set her down if the engine ran out of fuel and quit. I made it back to Spring Valley and shut down to refuel and park.

The manual said the Jet Ranger held seventy-five gallons of fuel. Two of those seventy-five gallons were in the bottom of the tank, the fuel pump, and fuel lines—and were not useable. That left seventy-three gallons of useable fuel, and that was what the maintenance crew put in my Jet Ranger that day—seventy-three gallons.

I had used every drop of fuel available. *How stupid*, I thought to myself. *How would I ever have explained that screw-up?* That was pushing my destiny, even for me. I gave the kid on the refuel truck twenty bucks not to spread it around that I had basically landed out of fuel. I swore I'd never do something like that again. But, of course, I did.

Our company worked on the World Trade Center in downtown Manhattan. We built a helipad right next to the Hudson River on the site of one of our Redi-Mix concrete plants. I flew big shots into that site every week. I flew the architects, the engineers, the head of the Metropolitan Transit Authority, the head of the Port Authority, the mayor, the governor, my bosses, and anyone else they told me to fly. I got quite an education talking to these people. The architect explained how the building was designed to implode in a dire emergency situation. The buildings, being a quarter mile high, just could not fall over; they were too big. At that time I could not imagine what he was talking about. What kind of dire emergency could possibly have that kind of impact on this superb structure, all concrete and steel. The buildings were designed to withstand anything nature threw at them. The designers did not plan on the situation that wasn't controlled by nature, however. I was in a small way involved with the building and success of that project. It was a real symbol of United States technology and capitalism in its truest form. I wouldn't appreciate anything that screwed around with my favorite project.

Generoso Palubo was a skinny little kid of eighteen with no family in this country when he arrived from Italy in the early 1900s.

What he did have was a great worth ethic that led to him becoming the owner of Columbus Sand and Stone.

Back in Italy, his father had taught him about concrete and how to build buildings. He taught him how hard work would always reward him. They were close, and he took it very hard when his father was killed in a construction accident when Generoso was seventeen. They used to talk about coming to America and getting jobs in the booming construction industry they'd heard so much about. After his father's death, Generoso told his mother he wanted to live out his father's dream and go to America. He kissed his mother good-bye, got a spot on a Greek freighter, and off he went.

Generoso Palumbo might have been skinny, but he was healthy, strong, and had a good head for business. So after he made it off Ellis Island, he headed into New York City. He knew what he could do and had a burning desire to learn more. He'd grown up with a feeling that he was destined for greatness.

Generoso settled into the growing Italian community in lower Manhattan, since they were the only people he could communicate with. Many of them were in the construction trades, working hard as masons, bricklayers, carpenters, or laborers. He was a great example of the Italian family tradition and strong bond of loyalty that I came to respect and admire.

There were other Italians in New York early in the twentieth century. They had not come to work hard and succeed; rather they came to America looking for the easy life. Let somebody else do all the hard work. The newcomers—many of them from Sicily—preyed on the fears, ignorance, and inexperience of other Sicilian immigrants to this new world. These were the Italians that became known as La Costa Nostra, organized crime, the Mob, the Mafia.

Generoso was a fast learner and landed a job with another Italian who had a small construction company. The company had a reputation for doing good work. The company had important clients and a nice flow of business and profits.

Lower Manhattan was off and running, and so was Generoso. He realized early on that one of the keys to his future success was the ability to communicate with his customers and meet their needs.

He wanted to do this on their level and not like some uneducated Italian immigrant. His first goal was to quickly learn to speak English without an accent. Living in Little Italy made that difficult until he met a young American girl about his own age who agreed to teach him English in return for work she and her widowed mother needed at their house.

So it began. Generoso spoke his native Italian only to other Italians. He made it a point to speak and listen to people who spoke English with no foreign accent.

His boss had made a lot of money and had become part of the *nouveau riche* class emerging during this period. He became deeply involved with drinking, women, and betting the ponies. He soon found himself behind on his debts and losing favor with some of his bigger clients. The handwriting was on the wall. The company that had been so successful and well respected was in danger of going under.

Generoso knew the business was essentially sound, but it had to be managed better. With his English ability and his honest and sincere approach to the business, Generoso was already dealing with the customers and estimating for the jobs. One of the company's good customers agreed to help him buy the business and take the next step to his future.

The next few years in the construction business and the booming New York economy led Generoso to believe that while the building business was great, supplying the materials for the construction industry was even better. That's when he started what would become the largest Redi-Mix concrete company in the Northeast.

The ingredients in concrete are sand, gravel, cement, and water. Generoso needed his own supply of these commodities to service his growing concrete plants. He bought sand mining plants in Upstate New York and out on Long Island. He bought gravel pits wherever he could find them. He built a cement plant in upstate New York. The concrete business boomed, and he needed a way to deliver all these commodities to his different locations, so he bought a fleet of tugboats. All the Redi-Mix plants were built near water so the tugs could service them.

Years later, helicopter landing pads were built on most of the sites. By the 1970s, Columbus Sand and Stone had over a thousand vehicles—everything from mixers, dump trucks, cement trucks, and compressors to flat beds, tow trucks, and cars for some of his more than five thousand employees. There was a beautiful headquarters building on Broadway in New York City, three limousines, one helicopter, one airplane, and me.

Columbus supplied the materials for any construction job of any size in New York, New Jersey, Connecticut, and parts of Pennsylvania. While I was there we were doing the Long Island Expressway, the Southern State Parkway, the George Washington Bridge extension, the Westside Highway, Yankee Stadium, Shea Stadium, expansion projects at LaGuardia, JFK and Newark airports, and the Twin Towers of the World Trade Center, the tallest, most modern, best-designed, and best-built high-rise buildings in the world. Flying to all the different company sites in and around New York and the surrounding area, I became a walking map of New York and New Jersey. I could fly anywhere you wanted to go with my eyes closed.

So what does the pilot for a construction company do with himself when he's not flying important people around? On one typical day, one of the tugboats in our fleet on the Hudson River broke down and needed a fuel pump. The tug was pulling ten scows filled with sand and stone. If this load were delayed, it would cost the company thousands. I just happened to be at one of the plant locations and overheard the conversation. I asked where the new pump had to come from and how big and how heavy it was. I told them to get the pump to a place I could pick it up, and I would get it to the tug within an hour.

They got the pump to another one of our plants that had a heliport, loaded it on the helicopter, and off I went. Finding the broken down tug and its load was no trouble since I knew the Hudson River like the palm of my hand by this point. Landing or getting the pump down to the tug was a different problem, one I hadn't figured out yet, but as usual, the how was not the problem, accomplishing the mission was the goal.

I had no communication directly with the tug so I had to pass messages to the crew by calling the company dispatcher. They knew I was coming, so the six-man crew was all on deck waving. The back of the tug was flat enough but didn't give me enough room to set down with the blades turning. I decided to land on one of the scows filled with sand. If I could do that, all the crew had to do was get the pump from the scow to the tug. I landed on the scow with no problem—it was big enough. I just had to wait for two crewmembers to use the lifeboat to paddle over to the scow and get the pump.

It took two hours from the time I heard about the problem until they had the pump on the tug. They had the old pump out when I got there, so it only took two more hours to install the new one. From what I heard, we saved about two days, and that's a lot of money for a company that size. Needless to say, everyone was appreciative of my efforts.

I became good friends with the company president Fortunado Palumbo, Generoso's son, during my four years with Columbus. He treated me well and always wanted to fly with me in the front. Both our aircraft were dual controls, so Fortunado wanted to learn how to at least land each aircraft in case something happened to the pilot. A lot of my pilot friends were flying for corporations, and they told me stories about them being treated like glorified chauffeurs. I never felt that way. Everyone I flew treated me with respect and honor.

Most of the workers in the plants were first- or second-generation Italian. Most of them spoke little English or broken English. I hadn't spoken much Italian since growing up in New Jersey, so I was a bit rusty.

Every time I landed at one of our locations to drop off people, I waited for them to finish their business and then take them to their next destination. Some of the executives took me with them to their meetings so I could learn about the business. At one point my goal was to stay in this business after I got tired of flying. The president, his brother, and a few other executives thought I could be an asset to the company and were willing to groom me for the future. One of the places they liked to do business and eat was Patsy's Italian restaurant on 56th in the city. It happened to be one of Frank Sinatra's favorites also.

As luck would have it, Patsy's family, the Palumbo family, and the Sinatra family all came from the same region in Italy. The Italians shared strong family bonds. I got to know Patsy and learned to eat great Italian food and meet interesting people. Patsy loved to take pictures of all the celebs that came to eat there. The walls soon filled up with photos of celebrities and dignitaries from around the world.

I flew with the vice president of maintenance quite a bit. Donto Pascarelli went to all the locations to make sure the preventive maintenance programs he put in place were being accomplished. There was so much equipment to keep track off, it was mind-boggling.

The main truck repair facility was in Astoria; the main tugboat and scow dock and repair shop was on Hempstead Harbor at Port Washington out on Long Island. The machine shops were in Astoria and Long Island. On any given day there were thirty to forty pieces of critical equipment in the shop for repair. The maintenance people worked three shifts around the clock to make sure things were ready for next day's mission. It reminded me of Vietnam and how the maintenance crew worked all night and slept during the day to make sure we had enough aircraft to meet the mission. Back there, the crew fixed bullet holes, flushed engines, and fixed guns. Here the crew was busy fixing transmissions, clutches, and tires—dozens of tires every day.

At this point in the 1970s the unions were alive and well and strong. They practically controlled the construction industry, and their power later helped to destroy it, too. Local 228 of the Teamsters Union controlled drivers of every kind of truck in New York City. They could make life miserable for a boss and an owner. It became unbearably difficult just to fire someone. The drivers were from all over the world, not just Italy, so the work ethic and loyalty the company was used to was evaporating. The drivers constantly broke equipment through carelessness. It became a huge problem.

I got a call to take Donto Pascarelli from Upstate New York to Manhattan to check out a report that one of our fully loaded concrete mixers had fallen into a hole. I landed at the 30th Street heliport on the Hudson River and took a cab to the accident site. The truck was in a hole all right, a huge hole dug by the telephone company so workers could repair underground lines. The truck had fallen in backward, and the hole was so deep you could not see the truck from the street. The truck was fifty-five feet long, so the hole must have been sixty feet deep.

The driver had parked the truck up the street on an incline and gotten out to get coffee while the truck was running and the mixer was turning. The truck rolled backward down the hill, across the street, and into the hole. It was the middle of the day. People were walking all around, cars were on the street, and the telephone crew that was working in the hole had just come up for their coffee break. The truck sideswiped two parked cars but nothing else. It was a miracle fifteen people didn't get killed.

The truck was a total loss. The concrete inside had hardened. A crane was called in to lift out the truck. It was so heavy that the crane broke cables on the first two attempts. A crew finally had to go down in the hole with cutting torches and cut the truck into pieces to get it out. It took two days of working around the clock. The telephone company put in a claim for lost time and damages and so did the city for extra security and barricades around the work area. The damage to the cars, along with paying company employees involved with the recovery effort, amounted to a hefty sum of money. Yet the driver that caused this fiasco somehow walked away clean. He was not fired or even suspended. He was only reprimanded and put back to work in another truck. So went the union and work in New York City. This event stuck with me. It was a perfect example of justice gone wrong, or the lack of justice. I had a small sampling of justice when I worked for my cousin after college. In Vietnam, all the justice I needed was in my right hand, the hand that controlled the mini guns, the rockets, and the radio to my crew. I made a mental note: someday I might be in a position to make a difference on justice. I came to realize there were many kinds of justice. The kind that the courts dealt out or tried to deal out was only one aspect of justice in the world. There were many others.

Chapter 15

From the time I was a kid, I had been fond of Italians, with their close family ties and traditions. I was born in Boston, but we moved to North Jersey when I was eight years old. The first person I met on my new street was Dominick Santori. His family had moved from Harlem the year before. His parents were first-generation Italian Americans, so that made him and his sister second generation. This meant nothing to me at age eight, but it became important later. Dominick, or "Donny Boy" as his family called him, was a year older than me. We hit it off right away, although I don't know why because we had nothing in common.

He came from New York City at a time when East Harlem was an Italian neighborhood. Now it is known as Spanish Harlem. I came from Massachusetts. Donny Boy was a street kid. Both his parents worked in the film industry, so he and his sister, who was two years older, were home alone every day after school. He had already been in a few fistfights in his nine years, while I had never seen one. He was tough, but, according to him, I was a Melvin. I had no idea what that was, so he felt it his duty to teach me.

"You don't know how to spit", he said. "You don't know any curse words, you can't fight you don't even know that girls are different than boys, and you probably still believe in Santa Claus." Well, he was right about most of those things. I had started to have doubts about Santa, but since my mother didn't work, she watched over me like a mother hen. She was appalled when Donny Boy became my best friend. I guess my mother was a Melvin, too.

On weekends, his mother cooked—always Italian, always delicious. His grandmothers were a lot of fun when they came over. Both of them spoke broken English, and they were my first experience with accents. The way they spoke was funny—it made me laugh. They spoke Italian to the rest of the family to find out what was so funny and why was I laughing. His family was fun and close, so I spent a lot of time at his house whenever possible.

His ancestors came from Sicily. His mother made pizza a lot. My first taste of pizza was at Donny's house—homemade pizza with thick crust, square pieces, and a lot of sauce. I loved it. Later on as a teenager, I ordered a piece of homemade pizza at a pizza parlor for the first time.

The guy looked at me funny and said, "What do you mean homemade?"

I pointed to the square, thick crust pizza and said, "That one, that's homemade."

"You mean Sicilian, that's Sicilian pizza," he said.

Donny Boy's father, Dominick Sr., was in the union at the film plant. He became an officer of the union, so things were always tense at his house when there were elections or negotiations at work. That's when I had to stay away. I lived across the street, and during those times I watched the cars coming and going into his driveway, and his mother made a lot of food to feed these people. I had no idea what that meant, but it became clear later on. When I asked, "Donny, what does your father do?"

He just shrugged, "My dad works for the union and helps some people get what they need." This different lifestyle made me curious.

I liked the sound of them speaking Italian, so I tried to pick up as many words as possible, and over the years I picked up quite a lot. One of his grandmothers thought it was neat that I wanted to speak Italian, so she tried to help me when she was around. Donny Boy wasn't as interested. He understood a lot but couldn't speak much.

I especially loved the traditions they followed. Every holiday was a big deal to them. They were Catholic, while I was Lutheran. My four grandparents came from four different backgrounds: Holland, Norway, Germany, and Hungary. My ancestors started coming to the United States in the 1800s, so I didn't have any real roots, ethnic background, or traditions.

I wanted to be Italian.

Kids in our neighborhood could name the make and model and year of every car on the road. We had contests to see who could name them first. We went from the late 1940s to the current year, and I was good at it.

That's the way it was with people, too. Growing up in North Jersey in the 1950s and 1960s, we became aware of where people came from. We heard their last names, then their first, listened to them speak, and could tell where they were from. Paramus was quite a melting pot of Italians, Poles, Jews, Germans, Scandinavians, and a few Dutch. I went through twelve years of public school and never had a black kid in my class or school. We were never prejudiced, and we never discriminated. We were just aware of the differences.

I knew all the ugly nicknames, too, like *Guinea*, *Wop*, *Kike*, *Spic*, *Polack*, *Wetback*, *Gook*, *Jew Boy*, and *Jap*. I also learned quickly when and where to use those names and when not to use them.

Me, I was a mutt with no roots. Somewhere about four generations ago, a great, great, great grandmother on my mother's side married an Italian named Santino. That became very important to me later in life when I decided to become Italian and use his name.

Fortunado, the middle son, went to work for his father at Columbus Sand and Stone the day after he graduated from college. Before his father died in 1967, Fortunado was already president of the company. In 1967 he became chief executive officer and chairman of the board. The company went public in the early 1960s, but the family maintained the controlling interest. By the time I went to work for them in 1972, they were doing $75 million a year in sales. I developed a good relationship with the boss, and he took me under his wing and made a point to explain things to me. I was not just a helicopter chauffer: I was part of his team and I liked it.

Chapter 16

I had achieved my goal of becoming a pilot. I had fought in a war and come home alive and in one piece. And I had been awarded the Silver Star, my country's third highest award for valor. Now I had a good job as a corporate pilot. I felt good about myself.

Now I had a new goal. I wanted to own a bar and restaurant.

I had casually started looking for a place when Fortunado told me the news about the company. He and his brothers had decided to sell their interest in the company to a group of New York investors. During one of my flights with Fortunado after the news came out, Fortunado said, "Daniel, what do you want to do? I don't think these new people are interested in running Columbus like we did. I think they are interested in our valuable real estate and selling off the different divisions for profit. I can ask around for you and see if any of my associates need a valuable team member with your talents."

"I appreciate your being honest with me, boss, I've been thinking about getting out of flying for a while and doing something else. I've always wanted to own a bar."

"I've sensed you've been a little restless." Fortunado said, "You know I had plans for you in the company after you got tired of flying. I think you can go places. I really appreciate your loyalty and eye for respect."

"Thank you, boss. You have taught me a lot and I will never forget it."

"Will you need any help in your next venture? I do know a few people."

"Mr. Palumbo, one of my goals in life is to be as respected as you are."

"Thank you, Daniel. I want to stay in touch with you."

"Thank you, boss, so do I."

After that conversation, I stepped up my looking. New York City was the hot spot for the bar and restaurant business. The bar business is tough anywhere, but it is especially challenging in New York City. It is almost prohibitively expensive, besides being quite a daily drive me for me. I lived in New Jersey close to Ramapo Airport where we kept the company aircraft.

The Alcohol Beverage Control board controlled the bar business in New Jersey through liquor licenses. Each town set its own rules and fees. It could be an expensive proposition because the state was not issuing any new licenses, which meant you had to buy an existing license from someone who wanted to get out of the business.

Rockland County, New York, was different; the county issued new licenses if you were qualified. No criminal records were allowed, and you could not be associated with any undesirables. You also had to prove you were financially sound. The process was not difficult, but since it was a government agency, it was not a quick process.

My service record was an asset, and my most recent employment didn't hurt, either. I mentioned to Fortunado as I was leaving that I planned to buy a bar in Rockland County. He wished me luck and asked if he could help, but I said no, I would try it myself.

I picked out a run-down saloon with an existing license. I thought I could fix the place up and make it successful. The application process went fairly smoothly. The lawyer I hired to help me with the process said it was a fast approval. I didn't ask for any help this time, but maybe I got some anyway. That whole destiny thing, you know?

Once I bought the place, I started some minor renovations with plans for more later. I enjoyed working with my hands, so, along with local help, I did a lot of the work myself. After the old owners moved out, and the place was closed down, the locals were curious. They wanted to know what the new deal was going to be.

Spring Valley, New York, is just across the border from New Jersey. The drinking age in New Jersey was twenty-one, but in New York it was eighteen. I was twenty-seven years old and decided I wanted to cater to a young crowd by creating a place with good drinks and live entertainment. The bar was big enough to hold 125 to150 people standing or dancing or about eighty-five if they were sitting at tables. I named the place Squatters. I don't know where I got that—it just came to me.

It took a few weeks to get the place ready, so in the meantime I went around to the other bars in the area and introduced myself as the new owner. Most everyone welcomed me to the area. I was not competing with their type of business. Most of the questions I got were along the lines of "Why would you want that type of business and all the headaches that come with it?" I wasn't real sure what they meant since I still went to bars and had fun.

But since the beginning of time, a lot of young men who start drinking have a problem handling booze. I never drank that much, but I knew a bunch that did. Once you mix alcohol and testosterone and throw in a female or two, you can wind up with an explosive concoction. Things often get physical, and I mean *physical*. Young men love to fight. Squatters had plenty of beer and liquor, loud music, crazy dancing, wild women and crowds, plenty of crowds, so right from the beginning my place became a breeding ground for trouble.

The possibility of breaking up fights, or getting in a few myself, didn't bother me. I had been able to take care of myself for a long time.

My high school years were good. I was a tough kid after Donny Boy finished with me. He tried his best to convert me from being a Melvin to being a tough kid with respect. Respect in the Italian tradition is a big word. By the middle of my sophomore year, I was starting on the defensive line on the varsity football team. My junior and senior year, I was starting right defensive end. I loved defense, and I loved hitting, tackling, and sacking quarterbacks. Football suited me.

I was also on the wrestling team. My senior year, I was captain of the wrestling team. I received two letters in wrestling and three in football. I thought I was good at defending myself and protecting the people around me from danger. When I got mugged in Newark as a nineteen-year-old, I was quite upset and swore I never would let that happen again.

During basic training in the army, we had that short course in hand-to-hand combat, but I never used it in Vietnam. I always had the fear of being shot down and taken prisoner. The stories we heard and are still hearing about POWs are horrible. I don't know how I would have survived that ordeal.

I decided to learn more about self-defense and looked into the different forms of martial arts. Martial arts had the combination of mental and physical training I needed and wanted. And, frankly, martial arts went well with my addiction to thrills.

Karate caught my attention, and the Korean method of Tae Kwon Do seemed the best. I found a school close to home. The training center or *dojo* was big enough to hold twenty to twenty-five students per class, yet intimate enough to encourage personal attention. The instructor, or *sensei*, was a Korean with a sixth-degree black belt. He was not as small as most Koreans, and he didn't speak much English. He taught by showing and by example. He was also gruff and harsh. A few of the students didn't like his method of teaching and quit early.

I was there to learn how to fight and defend myself and learn self-control. I rallied to his approach, and we hit it off well. We never became friends, but we had a mutual respect, and I knew he could teach me what I came to learn.

My schedule at Columbus was erratic. I was on standby to fly when they needed me, which wound up being almost every day. That fit in well with my karate classes since the school had no set schedule, either. While I was still working at Columbus before I bought the bar, I was able to fit in many classes at the gym. The *sensei* kept track of each student's progress and taught them accordingly. I liked that. As long as there were at least two students at the same level it worked out great.

Considering that some weeks I went three times and sometimes I wouldn't go for three weeks, I felt I learned well because I practiced hard. The workouts were good, and once the *sensei* found out how serious I was, he pushed me harder. In the first fourteen months, even with my uncertain schedule, I went through all the color belts and earned my black belt. The *sensei* never gave me a word of praise, but I could tell he was proud of my progress, my speed, and his own teaching ability. He and I sparred, and he used me in a lot of his demonstrations.

The more I learned and the better I became, the more my self-control grew. The excitement came from the knowledge that I would be superior in most any circumstance or physical encounter, but I was still looking for more. I wanted the peace and solace I heard came with the martial arts. I was not at peace.

After a few more months at this *dojo*, I decided this *sensei* had brought me as far as he could, and it was time to move on. I wanted to find a style that would teach me a different discipline. We practiced at only half-speed in Tae Kwon Do, and I wanted more.

In 1972, David Carradine starred in a television show called *Kung Fu*. It was about a Shaolin monastery in China that taught young men to be monks. The teaching consisted of years of physical training in a special martial arts method the monks had developed. It followed the movements of wild animals and their natural predatory tactics. The monks also learned how to find peace in the universe and within themselves. Their spiritual learning was just as important as the physical aspects. I watched the show whenever possible, and I liked the new method and philosophy. It seemed to me so much more advanced than Tae Kwon Do. After I finished with my first *sensei*, I started my search for a school in Kung Fu.

Other than the popular TV show, the Shaolin monks and Kung Fu were a well-kept secret. The Chinese had great respect for the Shaolin monks but did not know very much about them. I searched high and low for a school or an instructor that knew the method.

I found a few schools that offered classes, but they were just playing off the popularity of the show and were not teaching the real Shaolin system. I finally found a school in central Jersey about an hour away. This school had one instructor: a Chinese man who had either been at a monastery for a while or had studied under one of the retired monks—I never found out for sure. He was the closest to the real thing and had to do. I did a bunch of reading and studying on my own and working out at various gyms around the area to develop my Kung Fu skills.

◆

When I decided to leave the flying business, I was concerned about my addiction to excitement. Would I find enough to keep me happy in the bar business? I had no idea.

If the youngsters who came to Squatters wanted to get rowdy and fight, so be it. They just had to realize who they were dealing with. I like nothing better than a full-blown melee on a nice evening. My bouncers and I went right in the middle to break up fights, and along the way we kicked ass and took names. Then we threw out the trash, and I mean threw it out. It didn't take long for the word to get out: don't mess with the owner at Squatters.

Everyone told me it would take a year or more to get established, but within six months we started to attract a number of regulars and make money. The boys from Jersey, where the legal drinking age was twenty-one, loved to come to my place. One Wednesday night a group from New Jersey came in with the intention of showing the New York boys who was tougher. Before too long a fight broke out and the glasses started flying.

I had only one bartender working that night, so it was up to us to break it up. Normally, that would not have been a problem, but this crowd was big, and they came to cause trouble. Rob, a married guy in his thirties who was one of my new regulars, was sitting at the bar with a friend when things broke out. He asked if I could use a hand. Without thinking, I said, "Sure, if you don't mind."

I had no concerns about my safety because I could take care of myself. The bartender had been through this before, too. I did not know Rob or his capabilities in a situation like this and, sure enough, he ended up on the bottom of a pileup. Chairs and glasses flew all around, but we almost had it broken up when Rob yelled out in pain.

At this point everyone but Rob was back up on their feet. But one of the little prick troublemakers was trying to hide a knife under his shirt. I was furious. I didn't mind fights as long as there were no weapons.

He stood about six feet tall and weighed about 190 pounds. He looked to be about nineteen or twenty years old and obviously had had too much to drink. I didn't know how badly Rob was hurt, but I knew this little prick had something to do with it.

"What the fuck are you doing with that knife in my place?" I asked, ready to kick his ass.

"Who the fuck are you, and why should I care?" he said.

"You little shit, I should take that knife away from you and—"

Before I could tell him where I was going to put his knife, he broke from the crowd and lunged at me with his knife in his hand. I blocked the thrust, grabbed the knife arm, and knocked it to the floor. I had his right arm in my grasp with my back to him. Then with my left elbow I hit him square in the side of his head. While he was going down, I twisted his hand and broke his thumb. He was on the ground moaning and holding his hand.

I stood there, glaring at the crowd, and said calmly, "Who else wants to try something stupid like that?"

One brave idiot reached for a chair to throw. I took a step toward him and said, "Don't even think about it."

The rest took a step back. I stood over the prick on the ground and said, "Don't ever let me catch you in my place ever again. In fact, don't let me ever catch you in New York. Now get out of here." His friends picked him up, and they all left. Then I told all the rest of the people in the bar to leave also—the bar was closed.

I went over to check on Rob. He was sitting on a chair bleeding from his back. He was pale. The knife had caught him in his side right above his waist. I wanted to call an ambulance, but he said, no, his friend would take him to the hospital. He didn't want me to get in trouble. The ABC and local police severely frown on violence in bars, especially when weapons are involved. That was the easiest way to lose your license or get it suspended. I appreciated Rob's concern. He wound up in the hospital for a few days and recovered nicely, just a scar, but he was out of work for a week just before Christmas.

As luck would have it, Rob's father-in-law was connected.

There are many definitions of connected or "involved with the mob." There are the "wannabes," the guys who "know a guy" who is involved. Then there are associates, the guys who do some work for the mob. They are not in the inner circle, but they have access. Then there are the members, the made guys, the real mobsters. Rob's father-in-law was somewhere between a wannabe and an associate, but he had access, and that was important.

The father-in-law paid me a visit and introduced himself as Paul Teranova and started his story. He played the role well, nicely dressed in a black suit, dark glasses, and a deep voice. His claim was since Rob was just sitting there minding his own business when I asked him for help with the troublemakers, I had some responsibility. It happened in my place, Rob was in the hospital, and he never said a word to the cops about what happened.

"So, what do you intend to do about helping his family?" he asked.

I was taken a bit off guard. I never expected this turn of events. I told him I would think it over and get back to him.

"Where can I reach you?" I asked him.

He looked at me with a crooked smile and said, "I'll be back in three days."

This was not my first encounter with this element of society. I had experience with the Mafia as a kid working for my cousin in New Jersey, but that from a distance. I also had quite a few encounters with the organization when I was with Columbus Sand, but this was my first personal encounter, and I knew it needed my attention. I was in new territory, and I needed friends not enemies. I had to do something.

It just so happened another of my new regulars, Louie Vellucci, was sitting at the bar and heard the whole conversation. He was not there the night of the melee, but had heard about it and knew Rob. He called me over to the side and said he might be able to help since I was probably a bit confused.

"My cousin Antonio is also connected, with a different family, and could offer some help if you want it," he said.

"Sure, Louie, I'd like to meet your cousin," I told him.

The next day Antonio walked into my place and into my life. I didn't know it then, but it was the beginning of a relationship that I never dreamed of.

Antonio was right out of a novel. He wore a black leather jacket and black pants. He had black hair, a deep voice, deep-set eyes, and a mild manner. He was probably two or three years older than I was. My first impression was that he was a formidable individual, and I did not especially want to piss him off.

We spent a few minutes on small talk and checking each other out before he started asking me about the night in question with Rob. I never imagined a little insignificant altercation would cause so much attention.

We were both cautious about saying too much or revealing too much, just enough to get the point across. He acknowledged the fact that it happened in my place, Rob was involved, he did get hurt, and he was a stand-up guy by not saying anything to the cops. Since Rob did lose some work, and it was near Christmas, it was my responsibility to make restitution to his family. I never mentioned the fact that Rob volunteered his help; at this point it seemed irrelevant.

"I understand you take care of yourself quite well in these bar fights," he said.

"I guess so—it's something I learned in the service," I said.

"You were in the service? Where? Vietnam?" he asked.

"I was a helicopter pilot," I said. "How about you—did you serve?"

"Oh, I served all right," he said with what looked like a smile, but probably wasn't. "I was a guest of the state for some months, so that kept me out of the service."

I would learn more about that later. For now, I listened to his solution to this problem.

"This guy Teranova has a reputation for making a big deal out of small deals," Antonio said. "He does have some connections, and this is a family situation. You're new in this area, and you seem like a stand-up guy, so there is no sense in rocking the boat and creating any bad blood with these people."

"How much should I offer them?" I asked.

"Before we talk about money, I would like to touch base with him and let him and his people know that you are with me," he said.

To be "with somebody" meant you had a connection and you were somewhere between a "wannabe" and an associate. At this point I had no intentions of being "with somebody." I just wanted this situation to go away. I certainly was no expert, but I never thought you could be "with somebody" after one meeting!

"Aren't you sticking your neck out by doing that?" I asked.

"Yes, but I have a gut feeling about you," he said. "I know we just met, but I have a good feeling. Besides, my cousin Louie seems to like you and says you're a good guy to have on your side. He said you helped him out one night. I'm just returning the favor."

I was confused. This all sounded exciting, and I liked Antonio right away, but I didn't want to commit to anything or be obligated to anyone.

Antonio immediately read my concern.

"Don't worry. This is just a small favor," he said. "Maybe someday you'll be able to return it."

Not since my days on the battlefield with Rose could anyone read my thoughts and my feelings that quickly. This guy, Antonio, I wanted to get to know him better. I said, "OK, make the contact on my behalf and let me know what I need to do."

We talked a bit more, small talk about the business and the county and the people around there. Then he left, telling me not to worry about this situation; he would take care of it.

The day before, I had been concerned about this situation. I could handle just about any problem put in front of me, but this was new. It had to be handled correctly so it would stop there. But when Antonio left, my concerns left with him. I knew he would take care of it.

The next day I was anxious to talk to Louie to learn more about his family. Louie was young and had a direct bloodline to being connected, but he was not involved. He was a nice kid, and he liked to talk. I asked him a bunch of questions about his family, and he answered them all. I learned that Antonio's uncle on his mother's side was an important man in the county. Louie was a distant cousin and with no direct blood ties to the uncle. Since he was so willing to talk, I knew right away he did not know too much about their business. One of the first rules you learn is never talk to strangers.

Antonio met with Rob and his father-in-law, and they came up with an agreeable solution. I would help out with the medical bills, Rob would be more careful about who he helped in a situation like this, and Teranova would stay out of my place, at least as an adversary. That would be the end of it.

When Antonio came back to tell me the results and what my obligation would be, I just listened at first.

"Well what do you have to say?" he asked.

"Do I have a choice?" I said.

"Sure you have a choice. You could do nothing and deal with them yourself," he said.

"I don't mean to seem ungrateful, but this is my first sit down," I said.

"This is a good deal. I stuck my neck out for you—don't let me down," he said.

"I'm just busting your chops," I laughed. "Of course I won't let you down. I appreciate your help."

So it was. I went to Rob's house with a get-well card and some cash. We had a toast to his quick recovery, and I left.

Antonio came in to my place a few times after that, and we talked a lot. On a few of his visits small fights broke out, and I had to deal with them. Antonio just sat and watched.

"Does this happen often?" he asked.

"Not every night. It goes in spurts, depending on the moon and how the crowd is mixed," I said. "I pretty much know who the troublemakers are and keep them under control. I don't mind as long as there are no weapons, and it doesn't get too wild. It keeps me in shape."

"Yeah, I heard about how you handled the guy with the knife," he said. "Did he ever come back for more?"

"No, I made the message quite plain," I said. "I don't think he'll be back."

"Are you still training?"

"I'm not taking any lessons right now, but I make sure I stay in shape."

"Tell me about the war—what was it like?"

Most people were not interested in hearing about Vietnam, so I never talked about it. Antonio wanted to know about combat and how I dealt with the feelings. He was a good listener, and for some reason I felt comfortable talking to him and sharing those feelings. We talked for hours. Every time he came in he wanted to hear more. It felt good talking to him and sharing the feelings I'd never shared with anyone.

He was also interested in flying and the fact I flew helicopters and airplanes. He wanted to go flying with me sometime. He also liked the stories about flying for Columbus and the Palumbos. He knew about the Palumbos and their reputation in the business and the city.

He was slow at first talking about himself and his family. I expected that. When I asked him specific questions, he hesitated and then gave me partial answers. I was just as interested in his life and background as he was in mine. We hit it off well and started quite a friendship. I realized I could rely on him if need be, and he felt the same way. In Vietnam my crew and I spoke about who we wanted on a combat mission and who we didn't. The person made a big difference on the success of the mission, and we knew it. In a short time, I knew Antonio was a guy I would definitely take on a mission.

Chapter 17

My bar business was going well. There was quite a bit of building going on in the area, so I decided to open for lunch to cater to the construction crowd. Good food would not be enough. I needed an attraction. I needed a good-looking young girl behind the bar serving those hungry guys.

At night when the young crowd came in to drink and listen to the music and raise hell, there was a never-ending supply of great looking young girls. I interviewed a bunch without them ever knowing it was an interview. I felt like a kid with a sweet tooth working in a candy store.

The night she walked in I knew she was the one. Twenty-two years old, pretty face, a great figure, and outgoing. Her name was V, and she worked at a bar in New Jersey, so she was already trained. She lived in New York and wanted to work closer to home.

She worked out great. Once the word got out she was there and the food was good, too, we had a crowd. The lunch business was good and got better. I soon had to hire Cheryl, Samantha, and Heather.

V had a healthy sexual appetite and shared her weekend episodes with the customers. They hung on her every word, and she blushed and continued. I made it clear to V that whatever she did after work was her own business, but under no circumstances was she to have any contact with any of my customers at my bar. She told me most of her stories were not real. She just got a kick out of telling them. I told her she was playing with fire and to be real careful.

A few of the lunch crowd got rowdy and horny from time to time, and I had to calm them down. I did it right in the bar and not gently at all. I wanted everyone to know this was all look and no touch. The word spread fast how serious I was and how bad manners would be dealt with. Once the crowd got established and the food got better, the stories slowed down, and the testosterone relaxed.

Antonio and I met at a bar owned by one of his friends. We had a few drinks, just relaxing and talking, and I decided it was a good time to ask more questions.

"Antonio, I understand that your uncle is an important man in these parts," I said. "Tell me about him."

"What have you heard?"

"Just that he's a man to respect and who has some very good connections."

"My uncle, Uncle Joe, short for Giuseppe, is my mother's brother," he said. "My father died when I was young, and Uncle Joe helped raise me. I have no brothers or sisters. Why are you interested in my family?"

"When I first moved to Jersey, I met an Italian kid," I said. "We grew up together; he was my best friend. His father worked in the city with unions in the film business. I think he was connected, and as a kid I was very curious.

"My cousin owns a construction company in Jersey. I worked for him for a while and learned some of the ropes and met some people. After Vietnam, as you know, I worked for Columbus and met some very interesting people from different families. I've always been treated like a stand-up guy, and I like to learn all I can."

"I know all about your previous jobs and your associations with certain people," he said. "And you do have a reputation of being a stand-up guy. We've checked you out."

When he said that, it did not surprise me. Uncle Joe was a careful man, and the questions Antonio was asking me, I found out, had a purpose.

"My uncle is the boss of this area," he said. "He works from North Jersey to Albany, Yonkers, and Westchester County up to Poughkeepsie. That includes the Westchester Premier Theater. He's with the old Gambino family. His oldest son, who was my cousin, was killed in a dispute. My next cousin is his Number Two."

"How involved are you?" I asked.

"I won't go into too much detail right now," he said. "Let's just leave it that I am involved, and I do certain things."

My head spun with questions. I'd heard more than I expected and almost wondered why he'd told me so much. I found out soon enough.

"I've told Uncle Joe about you, and some day he would like to meet you and hear some war stories," he said.

"I would look forward to that," I replied.

Chapter 18

During one of our conversations about flying and aircraft, Antonio asked me about the markings on aircraft, the numbers, and what they meant. I told him each aircraft had its own unique registration number for identification.

"We use part of that number when we call an airport or air traffic controller so they can keep track of us," I said. He listened closely, and I could tell he locked that information away for future reference.

Antonio asked if we could go flying the next Sunday. It didn't matter to me what day, but he wanted to show me something. I said sure, Sunday was not a busy flying day, and I was sure we could get an aircraft. He wanted a helicopter.

There are 365 days in a year, and in northern New Jersey less than half of them are beautiful flying days. The rest are rainy, snowy, cloudy, hazy, or foggy. That Sunday turned out to be absolutely beautiful with clear skies and unlimited visibility.

Antonio asked me to fly north from the Ramapo Airport toward Newburgh, New York. He said he wanted to show me some land near the Catskill Mountains. At first I thought he was going to show me property he wanted to buy. That would have been strange because he didn't seem like a man who would want to be tied down to property. He concentrated on the ground and told me to follow Route 17 north for a while and then follow other roads as they wound north and west toward Ellenville. I flew about at 1,000 feet.

About thirty-five minutes north of Spring Valley, he asked me to fly higher. Then he pointed out a house on a beautiful plot of land. The area was not heavily populated. In fact, I saw very few houses. He pointed out landmarks and the valley that went through this property to the base of the mountains. It was more like a gorge than a valley, deep and narrow with steep sides. He pointed out the boundaries and said the farm was about five hundred acres. There was a herd of Black Angus cattle, deer, turkeys, quail, and fox. He said he hunted this property many times.

We circled the property a few times, and then he asked me to follow the valley back south for a few miles. Once we were out of view of the property, he asked me to drop down into the valley and fly back north again toward the property and that house. He was specific about his requests, and I asked him why.

"I want you to land in the backyard of that house I showed you, but I don't want anyone to see us coming," he said.

"Do you know who lives in that house, and are they expecting a helicopter to land in their backyard?" I asked.

"It's my uncle's house, and he is expecting us for Sunday dinner," Antonio said. "He just doesn't want anyone to know we are coming."

My mind raced. *What on earth was this all about? Why all the secrecy?*

"I'll explain it all when we get on the ground," he said. "Let's see what you can do."

Now I was in my element, and I had a challenge. I dropped the pitch and raced to the ground at 1,500 feet per minute. There was a small river at the bottom of the valley, so I leveled off twenty feet above the water. Antonio held onto his seat for dear life, but I could tell he loved it. That kind of descent feels like an elevator in a free fall.

Just like I've done many times before, the rotor blades on this Jet Ranger were lower than the trees on the banks of the river. We were going about one hundred knots following every bend in the river. I recognized a cut in the wall of the valley and popped up right in the backyard of the house no more than fifteen feet above the ground.

"Pull up right next to the house, and turn it off," he said.

I pulled up next to the stone wall that circled the back of the house and shut her down. Once the blades stopped turning, Antonio looked at me with a huge smile.

"That was fantastic!" he said. "Now I know why this kind of flying is so addicting. You handle this thing like you were made for each other!"

"OK, what's the story? Why are we here?" I asked.

"I told you, my uncle invited us for dinner. He wants to meet you," he said.

"Why all the secrecy and the hidden approach?" I asked.

"The FBI keeps close tabs on my uncle," Antonio said. "They've never been able to prove anything much, but they love to bust his chops and keep track of all the comings and goings. Most of the time they don't watch on Sundays. He just didn't want to take any chances and let anyone know we were here or how we got here."

The FBI relaxed its surveillance on Sundays? What a joke. Just like in Vietnam. When I arrived in Saigon in 1968, 525,000 Americans were in country. In the heat of battle, the brass called a truce on Thanksgiving, Christmas, and New Year's Day—just so we could have a peaceful dinner. I always thought that was funny, like saying, "Stop the world, I want to get off."

The VC and the North Vietnamese Army picked their Tet lunar new year for their truce, except in 1968 when they broke that truce and attacked every city and compound they could reach.

We got out of the Ranger, I tied down the blades, and we walked through the gate in the stone wall toward the house.

Two large fellows were standing near the back door. Antonio walked up and embraced each one, kissing their cheeks. He introduced me, but my mind was still in a whirl, so all I heard were Italian names. They took a step toward me and Antonio said, "No, no, he's fine," which apparently meant no frisking. They were both packing large weapons, just barely concealed.

They opened the door for us, and we walked into this huge room with a fireplace. The whole back wall was a window looking at the mountains. The house was three stories high in the back and two in the front. It was magnificent.

We walked over to the bar where an average-size fellow waited for our drink order. The bar was stocked as well as my bar at Squatters. I asked for a VO and club soda with a twist. It was one o'clock on a Sunday afternoon, and I needed a drink.

Five minutes later a man walked down the stairs toward us. He was in his fifties or sixties with grayish hair. He was distinguished and unassuming. He and Antonio embraced, kissed cheeks, and turned to me.

"Uncle Joe, this is Daniel Santino."

I extended my hand, and he took it.

"Daniel, I've heard so much about you," Joe said. "I am very happy to finally meet you. Thank you for accepting my invitation."

He dropped my hand, grabbed my face in his hands, and kissed my cheek.

"I feel like I already know you, and I hate formality," he said.

Embracing and kissing in this society are the ultimate in respect. It shows fondness, love, respect, loyalty, and sometimes farewell. Occasionally someone gets embraced just before he is sent to his final resting place.

The three of us sat near the fire and started talking. It was a beautiful sunny day but still winter. Antonio told him about the flight in and the low-level approach from the valley. He talked about our trips to the city and under the bridges and all the different landings. He liked seeing Riker's Island (the prison) from a different angle.

Joe listened intently and said he would like to try it sometime. He never did fly with me, however. His only interest was in my flying ability, not going for a ride as a passenger. His addiction was not thrills, but power.

The conversation remained light. Even though I needed more, I had to refuse his offer to freshen my drink because I still had to fly home. I don't drink and fly.

After a while a woman came down the stairs to tell us dinner was ready. She was Marie, Joe's attractive wife. She had a beautiful smile. The years had been kind to her. She looked like a loving lady. Joe said we were in for a treat because his wife was the best cook in New York and had prepared a special meal for us. Marie blushed a bit and said it was just Sunday dinner and hoped we were all hungry. I was looking forward to this.

We went upstairs to the huge dining room. The table sat at least twelve people, with upholstered chairs, candelabras, and a huge crystal chandelier overhead.

Joe said, "The dining room is too formal for today. We would be more comfortable in here since it is just the three of us."

Joe's wife said she had already eaten with her daughter and grandchildren, and she'd let the men talk. This was a common arrangement except on special holidays and family occasions in the dining room.

We went into a room off the kitchen with a round table that seated six. Windows surrounded it. Each part of this house was more magnificent than the one before. I wanted to ask for a tour, but I knew that was not appropriate.

The meal started with a huge antipasto. As soon as I started eating I wished I had not eaten for the last week so I could fill up on what was coming. The antipasto had everything I love, including homemade bread. I had a sip of Chianti.

The second course was spaghetti with meatballs and sausage in a thick red sauce made with pork. I wanted to eat all I could hold, but Antonio reminded me there was plenty more to come.

The third course was homemade lemon ice and small pear pieces to get our palates ready for what came next: veal piccata, roasted potatoes, and white asparagus. I had a sip of Joe's homemade red table wine.

For dessert we had homemade cannolis with espresso and anisette.

They all complimented me on what a great appetite I had and wondered how I managed to stay in such good shape. I told them how many times I would have to go to the gym after this meal and how I needed a wheelchair to move to the next room. I thanked Marie and complimented her cooking so many times I finally had to stop. How could anyone eat like this and not gain weight? I was proud of the good shape I was in. My training and workouts kept me lean. I was 175 pounds with no fat.

We went into a den on the other side of the house with another fireplace and bar, a large TV, and game tables. Joe offered more to drink, but I refused again. With all the liquor that was around and offered, I noticed that Joe and Antonio drank very little. They sipped each offering but never finished a glass. I learned later that drinking and getting drunk were weapons that could be used against people, but the smart ones never lost control under any circumstances.

Joe was behind the bar and asked if I liked anisette. I said, yes, very much, with espresso or on the rocks.

"Did you ever try it with Coke?" Joe asked.

"No, I can't imagine that combination," I said. "I've never heard of it."

"Yes, it's a bit unusual," Joe said. "But there is a reason. Sometimes signals can be sent very discreetly and in unusual ways. Lock that away in your memory for future use."

I had no idea what he was talking about. We sat around the fire. I'd noticed there were fires burning in every fireplace in every room we'd been in, but I never saw anyone tending to them.

"Daniel, my nephew has told me a lot about you, and I am intrigued about all your experiences at your young age," Joe said. "I'm a man with many resources, and I am in need of many solutions to complex situations. Antonio has told me that you've asked questions about him and his family, including me. What do you know so far?"

"All I know is what Antonio has told me and what I've heard on the street," I said. The street has and always will be a good source of information if you know where and when to look and listen.

"I know you are a very important man in these parts," I said. "I know you are a man who has earned and demands respect and a man who lives by his word and his code."

"Well said, Daniel," he said. "You have very good insight and, I imagine, very good instincts. Do you know any specifics about our family?"

"No, not really."

"Let me tell you some specifics about you," he said. "You are a highly decorated combat veteran. You saved many lives in Vietnam and took many, also. I know of your cousin in New Jersey, Mike

Pagliotti. This was many years ago before he got involved with politics. We had…mutual acquaintances. He's a good man, runs a good, clean business, and is well respected. In my business we don't get involved in politics. It doesn't suit our style, and only occasionally does it become important."

"I also know that you asked for help to get into the service. I think that was very admirable and unique for a kid as young as you. It says a lot about your character and the man you are growing into. Having a politician that you know is always helpful.

"I also know of Fortunado Palumbo. We have never met, but we have mutual acquaintances. I understand he is a very hard man to please, and you served him well when you worked for Columbus."

The look on my face was total confusion.

"How do you know all this and why?" I asked.

"Don't take this the wrong way, Daniel," he said. "I make it my business to know as much as I can about the people I work with. And I would like to work with you."

I looked at Antonio, then Joe, then back to Antonio.

"What kind of work are you referring to?"

"Your flying ability for one, Joe said. "Occasionally, I have a need to move people or cargo around quickly and discreetly. Your knowledge of martial arts is also very impressive. Your *sensei* said you are one of the best students he has ever seen, and he was sorry to see you go."

I couldn't believe what I was hearing. Did Joe know how I pee, too?

"I also know that the war has made you very unsettled and angry," Joe said. "The unsettled part I can understand. You haven't found your place yet. But the anger? Do you know what you are angry at?"

"Yes…no…I'm not sure," blurted out. "I just get visions, like ghosts from the past that need me to do things."

"I understand," he said. "I think we can funnel some of that anger and put it to good use doing things that will make you feel better."

"I'm not sure what you mean or exactly what you're talking about, but I am a good listener," I said.

"I think you have already seen that our justice system, the legal system, is not perfect. Some things get fouled up that really shouldn't.

Sometimes it's because people are corrupt. Sometimes it's because the system is just broken.

"You must be thinking, how can this guy talk to me about people being corrupt? Well, you're right—we don't do everything above the law, and we don't always follow its rules. Sometimes we break the law, but that's what we do. We never took an oath to abide by the law and follow all the rules. We took an oath to each other, to protect our families at all costs, and never hurt the people who do not deserve to be hurt.

"Some people take an oath to abide by the law—to protect it and live by it. Then they become corrupt and break the very same laws they swore to protect and uphold. Those are the ones we are against, the ones who hurt the innocent and protect the guilty. We take care of our own.

"Does any of this make any sense to you?"

"Yes, Joe, I think so," I said. "But up until now I've been in charge of my own justice and my own destiny."

"Yes, you have, and you've been doing a good job of it," he said. "But now it is time to expand—use your unique talents to help others obtain justice and accountability."

My mind swam with confused thoughts. I had problems with who this was and what he was saying. He was a mob boss, but he was talking like a preacher or a politician. Then he reverted to what he really was: a Godfather.

"Occasionally, I would like to come to you, Daniel, with a problem that needs to be solved," he said. "A problem where your talents can be utilized."

"Can you give me an idea of one of these problems?"

"Not right now," he said. "For now I want you to know that information is a valuable tool. The right amount of information can help you immensely, but too much information can be harmful. We will only give you enough information to complete your mission, no more."

"Mission" that was a word I hadn't heard in a while. I liked missions. I liked accomplishing missions. I liked the camaraderie of being on a mission with people I trust.

God, I miss Rose and Elton!

We spoke a bit more, mostly small talk until it was time to leave. It was 4:30 by then, and I didn't like flying in the dark. I left the farm the same way I came, down the valley and low level. No one saw us come or go.

We didn't talk much on the ride back. Antonio knew I had questions and concerns. When we landed at the heliport in Ramapo, Antonio helped put the Ranger back in the hangar and tie it down.

"You heard a lot today," he said. "I hope you don't feel I blindsided you by the way it all happened. I wanted you to be relaxed when you met Joe for the first time."

"I appreciate your concern, but a little advance notice would have kept my heart from skipping a few beats."

"Let's not talk any more tonight," he said. "Just think about all you heard, and we'll talk in a few days."

That was fine with me; I had a lot of thinking to do. It looked like my life was about to make another major change.

No matter what Joe said about justice and family, the reality was, if I accepted his offer, I would be working for organized crime. The Mob. La Cosa Nostra.

The Mafia.

Chapter 19

The Mafia had long been part of Italian heritage, especially on the island of Sicily. Peasants, who banded together to get justice from rich and powerful landowners and from the corrupt government, first organized it in the nineteenth century.

It all started honorably and for a good cause. As is human nature, some of the groups used their new power for profit. They started to deal in contraband, the black market, extortion, and fear of reprisal, hence the birth of La Cosa Nostra.

Italians immigrated to America by the thousands in the late 1800s and early 1900s. They sent back reports that this was truly a land of opportunity. The young country offered plenty to those who wanted to take advantage of it. Most of them came to work hard and earn the dream.

Others came to achieve the American dream without working hard.

Since the Italian family tradition was so strong and deeply embedded in the culture, it was easy to establish loyalty among the people. One of the strong Sicilian leaders to emerge from the immigrant community was Charles "Lucky" Luciano.

Lucky Luciano became one of the more famous New York mob bosses. He came to America in 1906 and quickly established himself as a man to be reckoned with. Luciano, who learned his trade in Sicily, had many loyal followers in his gang and became very powerful. In 1931, on the "Night of Sicilian Vespers," he eliminated all his competition and became the boss of bosses in New York and looked to expand his power and influence.

The government finally put a legal case together and put him in prison. New York District Attorney Thomas Dewey trumped up a charge of habitual solicitation of prostitution, and a jury convicted Luciano. He was sentenced to thirty to fifty years.

After WWII broke out, the Allies were looking for all the information they could find out about Sicily and Italy for the pending invasion. Through intermediaries, Luciano offered his help in exchange for leniency. He still had many contacts and useful information on Italy.

A secret deal was struck. Luciano provided the names and locations of Italian patriots. He also, through his control of the longshoremen's union, offered his help with security at the Brooklyn Navy Yard during the build up of World War II shipbuilding. He was allowed to run his vast empire of organized crime from his prison cell.

The Allies invaded Sicily in 1943 and freed Italy from the Fascist regime of Mussolini and the rule of Nazi Germany. The Allies emptied the jails and prisons, thinking the inmates were enemies of Mussolini and Hitler. Some of those released prisoners were put in positions of power. Since many of them were in prison because they were members of La Cosa Nostra, it was like putting the fox in charge of the henhouse. Things could not have been better for the Mob. Members became the mayors and police chiefs in many cities across Italy. Their lives, thanks to the United States military, had been made much easier. Justice became easier.

To me, this all seemed romantic and, yes, thrilling. In 1969, Mario Puzo published *The Godfather*. By 1972, it became a movie blockbuster, one of the most successful film franchises of all time. It was the first real look behind the scenes of organized crime. For all its killings and robberies and illegal activities, it was also intriguing and romantic.

Having Italian blood was a prerequisite for entrance into that all-but-closed society, and being Sicilian was even more acceptable to the inner circle. As a teenager working for my cousin, I saw a little of that society and how it worked. I actually thought it worked well. I liked it. Bending the rules was never a problem for me. I believed the end did justify the means. Working my way through college and getting into the service the way I did also suited me. I knew how things really worked, and it wasn't always the way the rules said. Learning how to treat people with respect and how to earn the respect of others are valuable skills in organized crime and in life.

My parents named me Daniel Theodore Govertsen. Since my four grandparents and my eight great grandparents were all from different countries, I had no ethnic roots. My experiences with Donny Boy and his family had shown me what ethnic heritage and family could mean. I admired the Italian family structure, their traditions, and their history.

Once I spent more time with Italians and learned the language, I realized there was a lot in a name. That might be superficial, but it is real. I wanted to be a part of something, but a part of what?

I wanted to be Italian, so I filled out the paperwork to legally change my name to Daniel T. Santino. I had researched the Santino name and learned it was a family name of a great-grandmother on my mother's side. It suited me well.

I was about to be asked to make a decision as to which path my life was going to take. So far I liked what I heard, I liked the people I was meeting, and I like the accountability these people demanded. I don't like to see the little guy getting hurt, and I don't like fat cats getting away with everything.

I decided to wait to see what I would be asked to do.

Hell, I could always just say no.

Chapter 20

It had been two weeks since our trip to the farm when Antonio came into the bar again. It was a slow Monday night, and I was working by myself. He sat at the bar and, with no greeting, asked for an anisette and Coke.

I looked at him funny, knowing he didn't drink, and asked, "Really?"

He nodded his head yes. I made the drink and put it in front of him. He raised the glass to me and took a sip. There was no one else within earshot.

"This is the way it will work," he said. "Someone will come to the bar and order this drink. When they do, you will know they have a message. It will be a short message, maybe brief instructions or directions. The messenger will have no knowledge of anything but the message. It will always be different people. Are you ready?"

I made up my mind the second before I said, "What do I do?"

"Your first task requires some flying," Antonio said, smiling. "You will take a helicopter to a certain location, pick up four people, and take them to a different location. Make sure no one knows what you are doing and make sure the aircraft cannot be traced.

"Be here Wednesday at lunch for more, OK?"

"OK," I said. And I meant it. I was OK. I was ready to do whatever came next. My heart was beating like a drum. I liked the feeling. I was getting pumped!

I knew from our previous talks that the identity of the aircraft would have to be disguised. That meant I could only use aircraft that did not have company names on them. I couldn't very well paint over the numbers on someone else's aircraft, so I did the next best thing. I had a sign maker make four different magnetic, flexible panels just as big as the numbers on the side and tail of a Jet Ranger helicopter or fixed wing airplane. The new numbers on the signs meant nothing. That part was ready. All I needed to know now was where I was going so I could figure how long it would take and how much fuel I would need.

Ramapo Airport in Spring Valley, New York, was an unlikely spot for a heliport or any significant aircraft presence, but it was the base for BEC AIR Helicopters. John Beckman, the B in the name, was once a vice president of Bell Helicopters in Fort Worth and one of the best-known helicopter men in the industry. He knew everything about Bell products from maintenance to flight safety to maximum utility. Since New York City was only a twenty minute flight away and the demand for helicopters was growing by the day, Ramapo was a great location. The C in BEC was Vinnie Castelano, a Vietnam veteran and a front man with a smooth personality. The E was, well, I don't know who the E was. Anyway, many of the New York-based companies that owned helicopters kept them at Ramapo Airport. There was quite a variety.

One of the companies was Wall Street Helicopters. A group of high-powered Wall Street owners bought a helicopter to take them back and forth from their homes in Long Island to the city. They hired a pilot, naturally a Vietnam veteran. His job every morning was to fly to different locations on Long Island, pick up the people, and fly to the Wall Street heliport in Manhattan where a limo took them to their offices. In the evening he flew them from Wall Street back to Long Island. During the middle of the day, he was on call but could do anything he wanted. Too boring for me, but he loved it. Occasionally I asked him to rent his ship. We agreed on a price, and I'm pretty sure he kept the money. His name was Tom Strickland, and I needed his aircraft for this mission.

He flew a Jet Ranger just like Columbus had. There was no name and no distinguishing markings, just the FAA-required numbers on the side and the tail boom.

Wednesday came, and I was working the kitchen for lunch, and V was on the bar. It was a normal crowd, nothing special. I kept looking at the crowd for someone new. After the lunch rush was over, I was cleaning up when V said a guy at the bar wanted to buy me a drink. He ordered an anisette and Coke. I made one for him and poured myself a VO. He took one big sip, reached in his pocket, pulled out a folded twenty-dollar bill, put it on the bar, and then got up and left. Inside the twenty was a piece of paper. I handed the twenty to V and took my drink back into my office.

All this cloak and dagger was new and exciting, just like in the movies. But was it really necessary? I'd have to wait and see.

I opened the folded piece of paper. It had a group of numbers arranged in a four-by-four grid. The words said, "A cabin on the west side of the valley 5 mi S. of the farm 7 am Sat." The numbers were map coordinates. I recognized that, and the cabin, who knows?

It was only Wednesday, and I had to wait for Saturday. I guess I was supposed to use the time to get ready. I drove to the airport that evening to wait for Tom to get back from taking the executives home to Long Island. He arrived about 6:30, and I asked him for his helicopter on Saturday. He said he had no plans to fly that day, so I was good to go. He never asked where I was going or what I was doing. I always had something in mind to tell him, but I never needed to.

I had a feeling Antonio would not be around for a few days, so I had to keep busy. I hate waiting.

I went to the gym on Thursday and Friday and worked out hard for several hours. I worked the bar Friday night. We had a new band I was trying out, and they brought a bunch of new kids from New Jersey. The night was going smoothly till about 2:00 a.m. The band had stopped playing at 1:30, and by 2:00 a.m. only the serious drinkers and the stone drunks were left. Bar closing time in New York was 4:00 a.m. Don't ask me why, but serious drinkers always stayed until the very end.

A group of the new kids and some of the regulars got loud, and I knew what was coming. I could have stopped it right then and kicked them all out, but I was uptight and needed a distraction to take the edge off. Sure enough, within five minutes a fight broke out. Nothing unusual, just kids having fun. I waited a bit to see if it would end by itself, but they started throwing chairs and glasses, so I got in the middle. Two bouncers were on duty, so I gave the word to move in, and we started to throw the kids out the door one at a time. Some of them were a bit stubborn and needed special persuading, so it took a little longer. I got careless and took an elbow in the side of my head. I saw stars for a second, and then finished off the last of the troublemakers. I was going to have a nice lump where I got hit.

We all pitched in and cleaned up the big stuff and left the rest for the cleaning service that came in at 8:00 a.m. I took the whole crew, Heather, the two bouncers, and the bartender, out for coffee at the diner on Route 59. It was 5:00 a.m. I was wide awake and ready to go.

It was still dark when I drove to the airport. I had already plotted the course on my map, so I knew I had to leave at 6:15 a.m. to get to the valley by seven o'clock. I had been in that valley on one other occasion and knew about where this cabin should be. The only problem from what I could remember was that the walls of the valley were steep, and the top was tree lined. *We'll see.*

I wheeled Tom's Jet Ranger out of the hangar and put my new numbers on top of the originals. No one was around at that hour on Saturday morning to see my handiwork. I checked the fuel and did the preflight inspection. Everything was cool; I climbed into the right seat, cranked the engine, and took off for the valley. The sun was just coming up, and it was going to be a beautiful day—a good day to start something new. If I only knew what it was.

I got to the valley right on schedule and headed for the spot I'd plotted. Sure enough, right at the spot on the map, there was a cut out in the side of the gorge and a flat piece of ground with a cabin that no one would find unless they were looking hard for it. As I got closer, I saw people on the ground. One signaled a flashlight in my direction. This must be the place. Who else would be expecting a helicopter at 7:00 a.m.?

I landed in the yard in front of the house. There wasn't much room, just enough for the blades to clear the trees and hover to a stop. One of the guys moved his finger across his neck to signal me to shut it down. I waited for the blades to stop and got out. There were two guys, no introductions, no handshake, just business. They motioned me to the cabin. Inside were a man, a woman, and two children about eight and ten.

"This is Frank and his wife and family," one of the men said. "This is their luggage. How much can you fit on board?" The Jet Ranger is not known for its large cargo capacity.

"We can take some of the smaller pieces, but the big ones will not fit," I said. "How far are we going?"

I glanced at the woman, and I saw pain in her face about leaving her stuff behind. I had no idea what was going on, but I could tell by the looks on their faces that they were taking a long trip or going someplace new for a while. *Why me? Why the secrecy—why don't they take a cab? Later, I'll find out later,* I kept telling myself. This did not seem to be the time or place for curiosity and I had my orders, that's all I needed.

One of the guys motioned me outside. He handed me a paper with map coordinates.

"There is a small landing strip right alongside the road, Route 214 near Norwich, Connecticut," he said. "It's on the Mohegan Indian Reservation. Some Indians will meet you there. They'll be in a white pickup. They'll ask you if this is the package going to Memphis. If they don't mention that, get the hell out of there and come back here."

I took the information and walked back out to the ship. I got out my flight charts and road maps. I always carried road maps for the surrounding states. I found the spot on the flight chart and plotted it on the road map. The landing strip they mentioned was not on either map. I figured it was about 150 miles from where I was and would take a little over an hour.

The woman and the two kids got in the back, and I helped strap them in. I had already put whatever luggage would fit on board. She asked if she could hold some of the other items. The two kids were small and didn't weigh much, so any luggage in the cabin not strapped down would only be a problem in a forced landing. I wasn't planning one of those on this flight, so I put a few more pieces on the floor in the cabin and let her hold one piece on her lap. Frank, who looked like he was in his forties and seemed a bit nervous, got in the front next to me.

The guys on the ground backed away from the aircraft, and I cranked it up.

I had almost a full tank of fuel and a heavy payload. I couldn't clear the trees on a normal takeoff so I hovered over to the edge of the cliff looking down on the valley. I took one final look at the gauges and turned to the woman in the back and told her not to get nervous because I was going to make a diving takeoff. I looked at Frank and said, "Don't worry—what I'm going to do is planned."

I faced the open valley below, and there was no wind to contend with, so I just eased off the cliff and dove into the valley to get translational lift. This is quite a scary maneuver for anyone not familiar with flying, and I heard the little girl in the back crying. I soon leveled off and climbed to altitude. It was a nice day, and my passengers relaxed once I got stabilized.

I wanted to fly as invisibly as possible so naturally there was no flight plan. And I wanted to avoid radar, so I had my transponder off and planned to stay out of the control zone of airports. I flew south of Danbury, north of Bridgeport and New Haven, and directly toward Norwich.

I stayed south of Norwich and crossed the river by Montville until I saw Route 214 where it crossed Route 117. I flew five hundred feet above the ground and saw what might have been a grass strip at one time, but now it was overgrown and surrounded by trees. It was quite isolated and hidden. I circled the field, noting a white pickup along with an old black Cadillac. I landed near the pickup. I was where I could see both vehicles and in a position to get the hell out of there if I needed to. I didn't know who my passengers were or what they did or where they were going, but for now they were in my care, and my mission was to deliver them safely.

I decided to stay in the helicopter to wait for the men on the ground to come to me. That way I had better control of the situation. One of the men, a nicely dressed man in his fifties with long white hair, got out of the pickup and walked toward me. I cut the throttle to idle and opened my door to speak to him.

He came up to the door, extended his hand, and said, "Welcome. My name is Little Boy. Is this the package going to Memphis?"

I was relieved at that question and the fact that the others had stayed in their cars until now.

Frank started to open his door, and I told him to wait until I shut the engine down. After the blades stopped turning, I got out and went to the back to help the family out. The woman seemed relieved this flight was over and her feet were back on the ground, but her day was not yet over. A man and a woman got out of the vehicles and came over. The two women greeted and introduced the children, got what bags they could carry, and went to the black Caddy. The men got the other bags and put them in the trunk. As soon as they were all loaded, Little Boy waved to me, and off they went. This was one strange mission.

I climbed back in the Jet Ranger and took off. I was light on fuel and planned to stop in Waterbury to refuel at the small airport there, I knew it had jet fuel. I put in fifty gallons, paid cash, and taxied to the end of the runway. I stopped and got out to remove the signs over the numbers, put them in my bag, and headed for Spring Valley. I landed at the heliport, filled out the flight log showing that I had flown to Bethlehem, Pennsylvania, and back. Then I drove home.

The old rush was there again, and I enjoyed the feeling. I had accomplished my mission and felt good about it. I was drained, but I needed to workout, so I went to the gym.

About a week after the delivery mission, Antonio came into the bar just before dinnertime. He handed me an envelope.

"This is for the ship rental and your time," he said. "I hear everything went well."

"It did go well, no glitches," I said. "Now I'm ready to hear what it was all about." Heather was working the bar, so we took a table in the corner of the dining room.

"Are you sure you want to know?"

"Yes."

He looked around, lit up a cigarette, and said, "Get us a drink."

Frangelico on the rocks for him and a VO for me.

"Are you familiar with the witness protection program?" he asked. I nodded, and he went on. "Well, this is the reverse of that. Or you might call it our version of witness protection. I won't give you any names, but the guy you flew was an FBI agent. That was his family with him. He got into some gambling problems years ago and started working for us to pay off his debt. He's been handing us information about the bureau's movements and its knowledge about certain people and activities.

"We took a liking to him, and he was very useful, has been for years. The feds finally found out it was he who was tipping us off and were ready to bust him and bust him hard. They wanted to make an example of him for other agents in case they had any ideas about working for us. We knew we had to either let the FBI have him, get rid of him ourselves, or take him away to safety. The decision was made to relocate him and his family and provide them a new identity.

"The FBI was waiting for the right time to catch him with us, so we set up a phony drop off. The cabin where you picked him up is on a road with only one way in and one way out. The feds were watching the road, waiting for him to come back.

"You did a good job. No one heard you or saw you come in or out. No one on the road knew anything. As far as the feds are concerned, the entire family vanished into thin air. The Indians over in Connecticut are our friends. They took the family to safety some place we will never know. This was a good deal. You helped to save a family's lives."

I could live with that story. I believed it, and I felt good after hearing it. There was no mention of the missing agent in any news reports, no mention of any phantom flights anywhere, and we never heard about the family again. The Indians in Connecticut received federal recognition a few years later and built the largest casino complex in the United States. It's good to have friends in the right places.

I looked in the envelope when I got home that evening. It was filled with one hundred dollar bills. After I took out what I owed Tom for the helicopter rental, there was still enough left to equal what I made in the bar in three weeks. The bar was going well, and I was spending less time there and making more money than ever. I was happy with these arrangements and yet…I was looking for more. Not more money, maybe, but excitement. Working for the Mob was a kick. I liked it.

Chapter 21

Two weeks later, Antonio came to the gym where I was working out. I don't remember telling him where it was, but the people he works with can apparently find out anything they want to know. I asked him if he wanted to workout. He just smiled and lit up a cigarette. He was naturally in shape. Maybe he couldn't run too far, but he never needed to. He invited me to dinner the next evening at a pub in New City called the Sopwith Camel. I told him about a new invention called a telephone. It works well, I said, and saves time and money. He smiled and said he would look into it.

The next evening I went to the pub. I took a few minutes to look around the parking lot for anything unusual. I wondered if I was getting paranoid or just more cautious. There wasn't anyone sitting in any parked cars, so I went in. I saw Antonio sitting at the bar. I hesitated until he motioned me over. We had a drink and made small talk for a while.

He looked over my shoulder and pointed out two women sitting at a table eating. They looked to be in their thirties. Just ordinary women, I thought. He also nodded toward the back corner of the pub where a man and woman sat. It was Joe, Antonio's uncle. I assumed the woman with him was a friend because it was obviously not his wife.

The woman with Joe spoke to the other two women. Then one of them got up and went back to Joe's table. I had no idea what was going on. But I had already learned that I would be told what I needed to know when I needed to know it. So Antonio and I just kept talking and drinking.

Finally, Joe's friend came over to Antonio and me, and he introduced her. Her name was Concetta, and she was beautiful. She asked me to join Joe at his table. She didn't invite both of us, just me. I walked with her to the table and greeted Joe. He seemed happy to see me again and thanked me. He introduced me as "Dominick." The woman's name, he said, was Mrs. Summerfield. Whatever. I knew something was up.

I sat down, and Joe started telling me about a court case involving Mrs. Summerfield's son. She started to cry, saying her son was a good boy and did not deserve the treatment he was getting. This whole thing had been a nightmare, she said, and she wanted justice. I had no idea what she was talking about or why Joe wanted me to hear her story.

Joe finished talking and thanked Mrs. Summerfield for telling him the story. She thanked him and went back to her table with her friend. I noticed the crowd around us. No one seemed interested in us or in anything we were doing. When Mrs. Summerfield was gone, Concetta asked to be excused, and I was alone with Joe.

"Daniel, how have you been?" he asked. "I wanted to personally thank you for the mission you flew for us and to make sure the envelope was OK."

"Now Daniel, I would like you to help us take care of a little problem involving Mrs. Summerfield's son. Antonio will fill you in on the details. I just wanted you to meet her so you would know what kind of situation this was."

At this point I didn't even know it was a situation. I just nodded and smiled. I figured I'd find out what I needed to know soon enough.

Joe got up when Concetta came back, so I did, too. He kissed my cheek and commented on how good I looked. "The world must be treating you well," he said. "It's good to see you. Until next time, my friend." And they left.

I walked back to the bar where Antonio was waiting. He just smiled and took a drag off his cigarette.

"How about dinner?" he asked.

"I thought that was why you invited me here," I said.

"Yes, but not to eat here. There's a good steak house in Jersey called Stegeman's. Why don't you follow me?"

We drove about twenty-five minutes south to the steak house and had dinner. We always headed for the darkest corner of a restaurant. My first choice was always to sit with my back to the wall. He felt the same way so most of the time we ended up sitting next to each other.

The story about Mrs. Summerfield and her son Eric took up the whole dinner of steaks, baked potato, sautéed mushrooms, salad, wine, and dessert. Erik was a teenager and gay. That made him different from the other kids in his school, so he was not accepted.

He didn't care about being part of the group. All he wanted was to be left alone. But a group of kids decided they didn't want to leave him alone, so they beat him up. There were at least three boys and one girl involved with the beating, and it was so bad that Erik was going to have permanent damage.

First there had to be a criminal trial to prove their guilt. Then there would be a civil trial to get monetary help for Erik's treatment. The kids involved were from prominent families in the county, and their parents got together and hired a famous attorney from New York City.

Getting simple revenge on the kids for beating Erik was no problem. That was easy. And getting to the defense attorney was no problem either, but it wouldn't help Erik. The problem was that hate crimes were not a legal issue in the state yet, and it looked like someone had gotten to the district attorney and maybe the judge. They both seemed a lot more interested in protecting the thugs than the innocent and badly injured victim.

That's where I came in. A message needed to be sent to the D.A. "reminding" him that his job was to protect the innocent, not the guilty.

"What kind of message did you have in mind?" I asked Antonio.

"Pain, something involving pain," he said. "The D.A. is an avid golfer and jogger. If some of his favorite things are taken away that will be a good start. This is different than flying, can you handle it?"

"You must have a lot of people that could do this job—why me?" I asked.

"We cannot have any involvement with these individuals," he said. "They are also pursuing cases against some of our people. We don't want there to be any misunderstanding about the message we're sending. This is about an innocent kid, not us. And we want this done cleanly. They don't deserve to die. They just need to learn a lesson."

"I saw a mother in pain over her son," I said, remembering that mother's sobs. "I'll take care of it. All I need to know is when and where."

"Someone else will give you that; this is as far as I go," he said. "You understand?"

"Yes, I'm beginning to understand a lot," I said.

This mission was very different from the last one I had performed for Uncle Joe and his associates. Getting a judge and a district attorney to see the light and do the right thing would put me in a whole new category. I wasn't just flying a helicopter. I was now muscle for the Mob. I thought about it a long time and then decided, yes, I'll do this. Mafia involvement or not, it was the right thing to do. Somebody had to stand up for that kid, and I was just the guy to do it. Besides, it paid really well.

Antonio came into my bar less and less after that. We still saw each other a lot but in different places. I saw Uncle Joe a few times, but never in the same place, and I never went back to his farmhouse again.

I read in the paper about Erik's case, and with what I already knew about it, it didn't sound too good for justice. The names of the district attorney and the defense lawyers were also in the paper, so it would be easy to find them when the time came.

The time came a few days later when a guy I'd never seen before came into the bar and ordered — you guessed it — an anisette and Coke. He took a few sips, laid a twenty bill on the bar, and left.

I picked up the money, took out the folded paper, and handed the bill to V. Back in my office I read the note: "Jogs every weekday 6:30 a.m. Jasper Street. Pearl River."

That's all I needed to know, the where. The rest, the how, was up to me.

From the beginning of my high school wrestling and especially during hand-to-hand combat training in the service, I learned that the proper use of a weapon could be very important. It could be an external weapon like a gun or a knife or internally like superior strength and knowledge over your opponent. Once I became adept in using my hands and feet in martial arts, I started studying the weapons the masters used years ago. Their weapons were effective against opponents who were armed like they were, but these days you're more likely to face an adversary who's armed with a gun or a knife. The swords, lances, or throwing stars used by the martial arts masters were not all that much good against a nine millimeter semi-automatic pistol.

A knife is a close-quarters weapon. You have to touch your opponent to hurt him. A gun, on the other hand, is a distance weapon. Fortunately, most of the gun-slinging opponents you're likely to meet on the street these days are inexperienced. They tend to want to get close to their opponents, and that's when the gun loses the advantage of distance.

I wanted a weapon I could use without causing attention or suspicion. I had enjoyed learning to use nunchucks. They are two small wooden shafts held together by a chain. Nunchucks can be used at a short distance or to jab within close quarters. They can be effective against any opponent, even one with a gun if he is close enough. Speed was critical, and so was hitting the right spot. If you hit a hand holding a gun the right way, that hand would never hold a gun again—or a knife.

The problem was, they were weapons, and they looked like weapons. Any law enforcement officer who saw them would be wary and would likely confiscate them. The weapons were not easy to carry or conceal. I needed to modify traditional nunchucks to make them look less threatening and obvious.

I cut a plain-wood broom handle with about a three-quarter-inch diameter into two eighteen-inch pieces. I wrapped tape around one end for a good grip, and I had my weapon of choice. I kept a pair under the seat of my car, one in the trunk, one under my bed, one in the garage, one behind the bar, and one in my office. The police could look at them and think nothing of it. I even carried them in my bag on an airplane in the 1970s and 1980s. I was ready for anything.

My weapon decided on, my next job was to scout out the target to get my bearings. I was vaguely familiar with Pearl River and found

Jasper Street easy enough. It was in an upscale neighborhood with nice homes and yards. It was quiet looking and within walking distance of a small group of office buildings. According to the news, the case was going to court any day, so I had to move fast.

The first day I drove a borrowed car and arrived on the street at 6:30 a.m., just as the sun was coming up. Houses lined one side of the street while the other side had a mix of houses and vacant lots, and it had a sidewalk. A man came out of a house, did stretching exercises, and started to jog down the sidewalk. This had to be the target: male, forty-ish, a bit over six feet tall and weighing 200-plus pounds. He looked to be in good shape, so I didn't want to have to chase him down the street. Whatever I did, it had to be fast and discreet.

The next morning I put on my jogging outfit along with a long, blonde wig from Halloween. This was the 1970s, and guys were wearing their hair long, so the wig fit right in. It was still cool at this time of the morning, so I wore sweatpants, a hooded sweatshirt, and a pair of thin-rimmed aviator glasses. I started from his opposite direction, as if I were coming from a different neighborhood. I saw him jogging toward me, and as we got closer he slowed a bit. As I passed him at a good pace, I said hello and kept going without looking back. We were in front of a house when we met, so I had to adjust my timing for tomorrow. My plan was to meet him in front of an empty lot.

The next morning I drove another borrowed car and parked it at one of the nearby office buildings. I checked my watch and headed for Jasper Street. As I turned the corner I saw him heading toward me. I had to plan it right so we passed at the vacant lot. He did not slow down when he saw me coming toward him. I moved over to make sure he was on the street side. We were almost next to each other when he started to say good morning. By that time I was already pulling my nunchucks from my left sleeve. I swung around behind him as he passed and hit him squarely on his right elbow with a smashing blow. I felt the bone break. He yelled out in pain and started to fall. I got closer and swung once more at his left knee. The look on his face was total bewilderment. I leaned over him and said, "Erik Summerfield."

I ran across the empty lot to the next street over. The sun was up, but the streets were empty. I took off the wig and glasses along with the sweatshirt and walked briskly to the car. I drove away slowly in the opposite direction from Jasper. There was a good chance that man would not be playing golf or tennis for a long time to come. I returned the car and went home.

I had a strange feeling after that encounter. It was the first time I'd had any kind of physical encounter with someone who was not acting aggressively or threatening me. I had to remember the reason for what I'd done. I had to think of Erik, helplessly lying in a hospital. I was still getting a rush, but it was different this time. Not bad, my conscience didn't bother me. It just felt different from combat or flying. The media reported that the district attorney had been in an accident, but there was no mention of Erik or of a blonde assailant. I suppose the DA's office didn't want a public investigation or a public inquiry into the D.A.'s handling of the case.

The trial was delayed two days to give the authorities time to appoint a new prosecutor. The new assistant district attorney immediately asked the judge for a delay to give him time to review the case. His request was denied. He then requested a change of venue because all the publicity had made it more difficult to get an unbiased jury. The press had been all over the story, and the rich kids from the town's most prominent families had come off looking much better than a little homosexual boy nobody liked. Not granting the delay or change of venue told me all I needed to know. It was obvious the judge had been compromised and justice would not be found in his courtroom. Jury selection was scheduled for one week later.

The judge's name was in the paper every day, so his address was easy enough to find. I just had to wait for my instructions, and I knew they would come.

The next day a woman came to the bar dressed in business attire. She saw me walk around the bar and asked if I was the owner. She was attractive, and I thought maybe she wanted to play. She asked if she could buy me a drink. Naturally I got excited and said yes. She asked for an anisette and Coke. I sat down at the bar next to her, and Heather handed us our drinks. She raised her glass, said "Here's to your success," took two big sips of her drink, and then went into her purse. She put a twenty-dollar bill on the bar. And then, just like the other messengers, she was gone. No one in the bar paid us any attention. I picked up the bill, removed the note, and went into my office. If anyone was watching my place, or me, they would have seen nothing.

The note read, "The fat man has a mistress. Thursday night. Blue house on Castor Street. Haverstraw. No one else."

Well, well, well. So the judge was married and had three kids and a girlfriend—not very honorable for His Honor. I also learned that his lavish lifestyle did not coincide with his judge's pay. The extra income came from someplace, not his family. I guess he was just cooperating with the wrong people.

The seventies, like the sixties, was an angry time in America. The kids listened to radical music. If you listened to it long enough, you couldn't help but come away with a bad attitude. The times were antiwar and anti-government. The problem was that the anger, the protests, the marches, and the shouting weren't focused in the right direction. The Kent State tragedy is an example of just how out of touch with reality our military, government, and academic leaders really were. Giving live ammunition to a scared National Guardsman who had never been in combat, who had never been properly trained, and who was being led by people just as inexperienced and scared as he was, was a recipe for disaster. Allowing radical protestors to get right into the face of that heavily armed and terrified kid was a travesty. But the only people punished were the scared soldiers who should never have been there.

I was no exception to the angry mood of America. I could function well on a daily basis, but I still needed an outlet for my rage and discontent. The criminal justice system and our elected officials were right on the top of my list of things to be pissed off about. I couldn't believe some of the things I heard and read about injustice, payoffs, and corruption.

My problem with all this stuff was just what Joe said at his farm. Some people swore to uphold the law and do the right thing by people. Then they turned around and screwed the people who elected them and counted on them for justice and fair play. I learned that this judge not only sold out Erik, he also sold out other young kids who got stiffer penalties than they deserved while real crooks got off with nothing.

Shit like that made me sick. So I decided to make him sick.

The note from the girl gave me the time and place. "No one else" meant I was to stay away from the mistress and any other associates who might be there. Otherwise, the *how* was up to me. I went to Haverstraw two days before the judge was going to visit his little cookie. I found the street and the only blue house. It was a poorer neighborhood than the district attorney lived in but accommodating for my purposes. There were no streetlights, and the blue house was in a cul-de-sac, so no cars would be driving by. Since I didn't have His Honor's time schedule, I would just have to wait. It was summer, so it got dark after 8:30 p.m. I figured he would go after dark. He got there at 9:15 and stayed less than an hour. What a stud, huh?

I waited behind the bushes next to his car for him to come out. A perfect setup. I had on a dark wig this time and different glasses and had both nunchucks stuck in my belt. I was glad his honey didn't walk him to the door. In fact, he went out the back door and then came around the house. He walked to his car and put the key into the door. I walked up behind him and watched while he fumbled with the keys. He never heard me.

"Are you the judge?" I said.

He spun around startled and dropped the keys. "What? Who are you?" he stammered.

I said it again: "Are you the judge?"

"Who wants to know?" he asked, turning into Mister Tough Guy.

I picked up his keys just to throw him off balance. I handed them back and asked very softly, "Are you the judge?"

He stood about six feet tall, weighed at least 250 pounds, most of it fat. He was out of shape, he was breathing hard, his face was red, and his breath stunk of liquor.

"Yes, goddammit, I am a judge and who the fuck are you?" he said, feeling full of himself. He was used to having people tremble when he spoke.

"I have a message for you," I said, softly.

"I don't know you," he growled. He started to get loud, and I didn't want any spectators, so I slapped him so hard his head snapped back. He attempted to lunge at me, but I parried his lunge and in one move took my nunchucks from my belt, and hit him in his left knee. No matter how big or tough they are, hit them in the knees, and they go down. He fell to the ground grabbing his leg and moaning.

I looked at this big lump on the ground. How pompous he was when he had his robes on, rendering deceitful decisions that affected people's lives. Later I would find out just how many innocent people were given harsh sentences and how many crooks went free.

I started jumping up and down on his fat stomach. He gasped for air and puked all over himself. He started to cry and begged me to stop. He just lay there in his puke. I leaned over him and said, "Erik Summerfield. Do the right thing."

He was in no position to get up fast or yell out, so I just walked away.

A few days later I met Antonio for lunch in Ramapo on Route 59. "How have you been?" he asked. "You've done us another good service and we thank you." He handed me an envelope.

"Can you fill me in on some details?" I asked.

"The judge is out of commission for a while," Antonio said. "He's taking a leave of absence from the bench, and the speculation around the courthouse is running wild. He hasn't seen anyone and hasn't left his house since that night." The depth and amount of information that Antonio and his people were able to get never ceased to amaze me. He was a walking news station.

"What about some of his other indiscretions?" I asked. "What about the other people he screwed?"

"Just suffice it to say he was a bad egg and should have been retired a while ago," he said. "I have a strong feeling that a bunch of his past decisions are going to be reviewed and hopefully some of them reversed. You sent a strong message, and we don't expect him to come back for a while. As far as Erik's case goes, there is a new district attorney and a new judge handling it. He'll get his justice now."

"I noticed the newspapers are taking a new angle on the punks who beat him up," I said.

"Isn't it funny how things work out?" he asked, smiling. I liked this kind of justice. It was working for me.

Chapter 22

"Anything new on the horizon?" I asked

"Are you anxious already to do something else?" Antonio replied between puffs on his cigarette.

"Just wondering."

"When you study the martial arts are there many different weapons and things to use?" he asked.

I didn't know what he was getting at, so I just said, "Yes, there are many, why?"

"Variety is good," he said. "Variety keeps people guessing and throws watchers off balance."

"I understand," I said. And I did. Changing routines and methods kept the watchers, as Antonio called them, from figuring out patterns and kept them from being able to predict what will happen next.

"Believe it or not, even with Uncle Joe's reputation, some people who know him still think they can take advantage," Antonio said. "It's not too often, but still it happens."

"I find that hard to believe."

"I understand things at your bar have quieted down, not as many fights and rowdy crowds as there were."

"How the hell do you know that?"

"My cousin, it seems like he lives at your place. Did you know that your shuffleboard game is one of the hottest gambling sites in the county?"

"I knew there was gambling but not that much."

"My cousin made a grand last week playing shuffleboard. We'll have to teach you how to get your cut, so we can get our cut," he said. Then he smiled and took a long drag off his smoke. "I guess you have developed a reputation for not taking any shit, and it's working."

"I guess."

"There's also a little chatter about you being with us. That will keep some bad elements out of your hair. We just have to be careful about you getting too close to us. We don't want any suspicion on you at all. *Tu capi?*" You understand?

"*Si, capisco.*" Yes, I understand.

"There's a money manager, a Jewish guy who's been hustling people, using a Ponzi scheme," he said. "There's a local investigative reporter looking into him, so maybe you'll read about it. But it looks like nothing will come of that because he's got too many friends in high places. What he does have is a young nephew he likes a lot. The kid's a loser, a drunk and a degenerate gambler. The guy also always travels with an armed bodyguard."

"It sounds vaguely familiar—what's the catch? Did he take some of Joe's money?" I asked, joking.

"Somebody like that needs to be humiliated," Antonio said. He was not joking. His voice was as cold as his steel-gray eyes. "He needs to be embarrassed in front of people and knocked down a few pegs. The courts are not capable of dealing with people with power, money and connections. It's a shame."

"Do I hear a mission in the making?" I asked.

"Do you want anything else?" he asked. "I have another meeting."

Sometimes he just ignored my questions like he never heard them. He just was not ready or willing to comment right then. When it was time, I'd find out. If nothing else, I was learning patience.

"Occasionally, it's a good idea to have another person around for crowd control and another set of eyes, you follow?" he said.

"I like to work alone."

"I know, but sometimes more hands can make things easier."

The way Antonio talked and gave subtle hints was effective. He could never be accused of saying anything because most of the time he didn't really say anything. When it came to business, he was smooth, cautious, and smart.

"By the way, so you hear it from me, Uncle Joe is having a big party to celebrate his sixtieth birthday," he said. "You will not be getting an invitation. I hope you understand. The Feds will probably be very interested in the guests, and we don't want you on any list."

"I understand."

"Goodbye for now. I'll keep in touch," he said. "Stay healthy. You might need a vacation."

He left. I stayed in the bar and ordered another drink. This conversation was confusing. He mentioned a guy, a Jewish guy, who had a drunk for a nephew and traveled with an armed bodyguard. The guy was a moneyman who was screwing people with a Ponzi scheme. I can't believe somebody who knew Joe even a little would think about screwing him. He must have a death wish if he really took some of Joe's money.

I didn't know too much about Jews. When I studied World War II in school and learned about the Germans and the Holocaust, someone told me that the reason the Germans and others wanted to get rid of the Jews was because they were afraid of them. They were afraid of their business ability and their ability to handle finances. The Aryans didn't want any competition. In the 1970s in towns like Monsey in Rockland County, there were plenty of Hasidic Jews. They walked around on Saturdays in long black coats, black hats, and long beards. The women, covered head to foot, walked behind the men. I heard they controlled the diamond district in New York and worked on Wall Street.

I tried to find out more about the guy on my own, just in case he became a target. His name was Marvin Mendelbaum. With a name like that his parents must have really loved him. He was a financial planner with a house in New City, an apartment in New York, and offices in Nanuet and New York. He was well known and traveled in big-time circles. I can't imagine a guy like that being a scam artist. He had plenty of money, but greed is a powerful vice. It makes people do strange things. The bottom line: if they are going to screw people, they need to be held accountable.

My bar was doing well. The girls were bringing in a nice crowd, and I kept adding things to the menu as people requested them. The bands at night were keeping the kids coming, and they were drinking. Boy, were they drinking.

I was able to take more time off because of Bob Rossi, who was dating my sister. He'd lost his job at a telecommunications company and came to work for me tending bar until he found something else. Bob was Italian. Both his parents and grandparents were from Sicily. Bob stood six feet, four inches tall, and weighed 250 pounds. He was huge. He had a dark Sicilian complexion and a smooth, calm way about him. His size alone made it easy for him to quell most explosive situations. His very presence demanded respect.

We became great friends. He liked working at the bar and working nights. He and my sister were getting serious, and I wanted to look after them both. In return, he looked after my interests when I wasn't there. The customers liked him, and he liked being around the girls. He never strayed and always respected my sister and me.

He knew Antonio, and they talked when Antonio came in. But he never asked me questions, and I never told him anything about my association with Antonio and his family. I knew he talked to Louie, Antonio's cousin, but in reality, Louie didn't know that much. We respected each other's privacy, and I didn't want anything getting back to my sister. I just knew that when he was in charge things were OK, and I never worried.

A guy came into the bar about a week after my lunch with Antonio. I was working since it was Bob's night off. The guy looked scruffy, not the usual messenger type. He ordered an anisette and Coke, raised his glass to me, and mumbled a few words. Then he ordered a beer to go, put down a twenty-dollar bill, and left. I put the twenty in my pocket and started to close up the bar. It was 2:45 a.m.

Usually I would go to the diner to chill out from a busy night, but I was tired, just worn out. I was anxious to read the note folded inside the twenty, but I waited till I got home. I poured myself a VO and sat down to read the note. It was longer than most.

"Poker game. Friday. Starts 10 p.m. 5–9 players. Guards heavy. 114 Montvale Apartments, Chestnut Ridge Road by Garden State

Parkway Exit. Meet Enrico. Code *Capisce ingles.* Marvin only. Get the money back."

This was going to be a challenge. I had to get into an apartment where there was a high stakes, invitation-only poker game. There would be five to nine people there, and at least one of them would carry a gun. I had to disarm the armed guard without hurting him or any of the other players, publicly embarrass Marvin, and leave without anyone seeing me go. Oh, yeah, I also had to take their money.

No nunchucks on this trip. Enrico would be watching my back while I was dealing with Marvin. I had to brush up on my Italian.

I found the guy's office in Nanuet and went into the coffee shop across the street. I sat by the window and waited. After three cups of coffee and a muffin, I saw three guys coming out of the office. They fit the descriptions I'd been given. One was definitely the guard, a large fellow with broad shoulders who looked to be in good shape. He would be a challenge. Marvin was in his fifties, about five-foot ten-inches and 225 pounds with white hair and nice clothes. The third guy was in his twenties with shoulder-length blonde hair, average height and weight. He must have been the nephew. If he was, I had just found my in. I followed them into the parking garage and got close enough to hear them speak. Marvin had a deep voice, the kid sounded like a kid, and the guard walked behind them saying nothing.

From there I went to Montvale to check out the apartment. The complex was upscale. Each unit had a garage and a closed-in garden area in the back. Some of them were two stories high, but number 114 was only one story. All the entrance doors had peepholes and windows on one side.

Friday came, and I decided to show up about midnight, hoping all the players would be there by then. The last exit off the Garden State Parkway in New Jersey was in Montvale. There was a rest stop near the exit and a service road that let you get on and off the parkway without paying a toll. I chose to park there. No one would notice anything special about any car in the lot. I had to walk about a mile to the complex. The walk gave me a few more minutes to go over my plan.

I stayed in the shadows until I got near the apartment. I was looking for any movement that would tell me where Enrico would be. I moved around the bushes like a cat until I heard a light cough; shame on Enrico if he had been the target. I came up behind him being careful not to startle him too much. I knew he was packing, but I knew nothing about him and didn't want any surprises.

I softly said, "Enrico." He turned and started for his piece. I quickly said, "*Capisce ingles.*"

He relaxed a bit and said, "*Si, capiscso.*"

"Do you have a pistol?" I asked him in Italian.

"*Si.*"

"May I see it?"

"*Si.*"

With that he pulled a nine-millimeter pistol with a silencer out of his belt, showed it to me, but did not offer it.

I wanted to know what I was dealing with, and I didn't want any shooting.

"I will get us in the apartment and disarm the guard," I said. "You keep the guard down and make sure all the other people stay calm and quiet. *Capisce?*"

"*Si.*"

I opened my shirt and pulled out my blonde wig and dark glasses. The wig was shorter than the nephew's hair but should work in a pinch. I knew that if I could get in the door acting like the nephew, I had only a few seconds to quiet the guard and get control of the room.

"Are you ready?"

"*Si.*"

We walked to the door. I stood sideways in front of the peephole, and Enrico crouched on the side with no window. Since the bodyguard would probably be at the door, I had to get to him before he had a chance to draw his weapon. I hoped there were no other weapons in the room. The best way to take the guard out was to hit his throat. I could silence him quickly with a blow to the throat and bring him to his knees. A blow too hard could break his windpipe and kill him, too soft would do nothing. I had to be careful.

I knocked on the door and heard steps coming.

"Who is it?"

Since I didn't know the kid's name, I mumbled, "I want to see my uncle, I need to see my uncle now."

Someone looked out the peephole. I brushed the hair away from my face and looked down. Words were exchanged inside, and I heard the door chain being opened.

"Your uncle is busy now. He will talk to you—" the guy who opened the door started to say. He didn't get it all out before I shoved the door open and went for him. It wasn't the bodyguard I'd seen earlier with Mendelbaum and the blonde kid. That guy stood three feet away, and I knew he would be drawing his gun any second. I couldn't wait. I lunged at the guard and hit him squarely in his throat. He had his gun halfway out, and I hit him again on the side of the neck. The gun fell to the floor, and he went to his knees. I hit him again on the back of the neck, and he went flat to the floor, out cold.

I turned and went for the guy at the door and saw that Enrico had his gun out, and the doorman had his hands up. The poker players sat at a round table with their mouths open, looking stunned. Enrico walked the door guy over to the table and sat him down. He held his gun in his big right hand. Every player at the table felt like the gun was aimed between their eyes. And if Enrico was as good as he looked, it might as well have been.

"Do any of you have any weapons?" I asked. No answer. So I walked behind each one and frisked them from the waist up. One of the players was an attractive woman in her thirties. I frisked her, too. She didn't seem to mind, and neither did I. About that time I heard the guard stirring, so I tied him up and gagged him to keep him quiet.

Two young women were sitting on the couch. "Is there anyone else here?" I asked them. "You won't get hurt if you tell me the truth."

"No this is all of us," one of them, a cheap-looking brunette who looked terrified, said.

"Why are you girls here? Who are you with?" I asked her.

"We're waiting here with Marvin," she said, glancing nervously at the poker table.

Marvin had had enough. I figured the best way to get to him was through his women. Even a scared man will fight for a woman, even if she is paid by the hour.

Marvin stood up. "Who the hell do you think you are? Do you know who I am?" he shouted.

"Sit down, Marvin. I will tell you who we are in a minute," I said, calmly.

"You little shit—I will have you castrated for this," he blustered.

"That's an idea I didn't think of, Marvin" I said, then smiled. "Maybe that's what we'll do—cut off your little nuts and feed them to you."

Marvin knocked over his chair and came toward me. That was a gutsy move with Enrico holding a gun and all. I had to hand it to the guy. He was brave. Stupid, certainly, but brave.

"Marvin, don't think about it. Sit down," I said in a soft voice.

He stood there frozen and opened his mouth to speak. I slapped him full speed right in his fat face. There is something about a slap. A fist punch can knock you down and out. A slap, on the other hand, just hurts. It's humiliating to get slapped. Girls slap. Kids slap. It's like getting spanked.

He looked startled at first and then a wave of anger washed over his face. So I slapped him again with my other hand. Now he had two large welts on his face and was turning red. But he sat down like a good little boy.

"Everyone put your hands on the table and stay seated," I said, still cold and calm. "We'll be out of your hair in a while.

"Marvin, you come over here. You've been naughty, haven't you? You've been stealing people's money and getting away with it."

"I don't know what you are talking about," he said.

"Don't even think about denying it, Marvin," I said. "You're guilty, and you're going to be punished. Now take down your pants and get on your knees."

"Go to hell, you little prick," he said, trying to sound tough.

I slapped him again on each side of his face. Then I slammed my fist into his soft gut. And while he was on the way down, I hit him in the back of his head. But old Marvin wouldn't stay down. He was halfway to his feet when I reminded him, "Your pants?"

He unbuckled his belt and dropped his pants to his knees.

"Get on your hands and knees," I told him.

I reached behind me and took out the two paddles I'd stuck in my belt. You know the kind, the ones that come with a ball on a string, and that Marilyn Monroe made famous in *The Misfits* with Clark Gable. If you are going to spank someone you need a paddle, and I wanted two in case one broke.

I started to paddle on his ass at full speed. He fell to the ground and started to cry, "No more, no more." It was humiliating, sure, but it also hurt like hell.

"Stand up, you piece of shit, and show your friends what a waste of a man you are," I ordered. Marvin got up, and I whacked him a few more times, just for fun.

He was standing there in his shorts and shirt, totally humiliated.

"One last thing, Marvin. Drop your shorts."

"No, no please."

"Drop them, Marvin. I want everyone to see what a needle dick you really are."

Even though they were scared and bewildered, I heard chuckles from the poker players. Even the girls on the couch were smirking. When a guy is in that kind of pain and embarrassment, his dick shrivels up like a prune. He stood there in the middle of the room red-faced trying to cover himself. I slapped each of his arms with the paddles.

"No, no Marvin, let everyone see what a real man you are, you are a thief," I said. Tears rolled down his cheeks, and he was dying of embarrassment. The girls on the couch were giggling now, and the crowd at the table just stared. I made him turn around to show them the huge welts on his bright-red ass cheeks.

I pulled Marvin over to the side and whispered in his ear: "You have three days to give back all of Joe's money. If you don't, this will happen to you every week, wherever you are and whatever you're doing. You have no place to hide because we will find you."

I turned to the crowd, "Marvin is finished in this town. Make sure you tell everyone you know what happened here tonight or the same might happen to you."

Enrico was by the door with one foot on the bodyguard. He gave him a tap on the head with his nine millimeter for good measure, and we left. We walked out of the complex without saying a word. When we got to the street, I turned to him.

"*Ciao, Enrico, and grazie,*" I said.

"*Ciao, amico,*" he said.

I took off the wig and the glasses and put the paddles back in my belt. I didn't think we'd be followed, so I just walked to my car and drove home. I couldn't sleep, so I poured a VO and watched a movie I'd taped. I felt good about what I'd done. It was different than the thrill of flying in combat, but this guy deserved what he got. I was anxious to see how successful it was going to be. Any guy with a big ego like Marvin's had to be totally humiliated and embarrassed about an episode like that. But if he didn't pay up, more drastic measures would have to be taken. I wanted that job, too. That guy really pissed me off.

Yes, I was working for the Mafia, and, yes, some people might think that was wrong. And maybe it was a rationalization to keep my conscience from bothering me, but the way I looked at it, I was hurting the bad guys. And that was a good and honorable thing to do. In many ways, I was still doing what I'd done in Vietnam.

I was still a soldier, just in a different suit.

Chapter 23

It had been ten days since the card game, and I was dying to hear the results. I had only an emergency contact for Antonio, and this was not an emergency. Then Louie came to the bar and told me to meet Antonio at the Camel in New City at 10:00 p.m.

I walked in at ten. The bar was crowded, and a band was playing. I ordered a drink and looked around. Antonio was at a corner table with a few girls and guys. Whenever I saw him out with girls, they all looked like models or movie stars, absolutely gorgeous. He motioned me over and made a feeble attempt at introductions. Then he ordered another round of drinks for everyone but himself.

With my bad hearing from all the turbine engines and loud machine guns right next to my ears, I hoped he wasn't planning on talking at the bar. The band was loud, and I was lost. I had a few dances with the girls and got two phone numbers for another day. I was enjoying the girls but couldn't hear a word they were saying. After thirty minutes or so, Antonio motioned me toward the door. We went out into the parking lot, and the quiet was welcome. Antonio walked to his car, a new white Lincoln, and said, "Let's go for a ride."

"How have you been?" he said as he pulled out of the lot. "What's new?"

"Cut the shit, Antonio, you know I'm anxious to hear about Marvin."

He smiled, lit a cigarette, and headed for the Palisades Parkway. After making a few turns, going slow, and speeding up to make sure we weren't followed—he was always very cautious—we headed north on the Parkway.

"You had quite a night with that asshole Marvin, I hear. Enrico couldn't stop talking about it. He said he never saw anything like it. He had no idea what the guy had done but figured he could never show his face in public again. Enrico is used to a different kind of persuasion, the kind that uses pain and breaks bones, so he was amused."

"Well, did it work?"

"I guess so," Antonio said. "Joe got all his money back and more. Marvin started liquidating his accounts and was "encouraged" to sell a bunch of the toys he had accumulated with other people's money. I expect he is going to give back a lot of what he took. The people who were there that night, supposedly his friends, are spreading the word about him all over town. People are treating him like he has the plague, and he has no choice but to move away. Now he is under investigation by the feds and will probably go to jail. You did good, Daniel, real good. You have quite an imagination—we like that."

"Thanks," I said. "I'm glad you get a kick out of my methods, and I'm glad they worked."

"How would you like a little vacation, a little thank you gift along with the usual?"

"Sure, what do you have in mind?"

He reached down and handed me an envelope.

"Here are plane tickets to Vegas," he said. "A room is reserved for you at the Aladdin Hotel right on the Strip, and all your expenses are paid. As you will see, the name on everything is Paul Servino. Just go and relax and have some fun. You deserve it."

"Will this be all vacation or do you have any surprises in mind?" I asked.

He smiled and looked over at me. "As you will see in that envelope, you might have to use your talents and maybe go for a joy ride."

We talked about the Yankees and the upcoming season for the Giants, and then we were back at the Camel and my car.

Back at my house I opened the envelope, and once again I was surprised. There was a wad of cash and plane tickets in the name of Paul Servino.

What on earth was in store for me next? But there was no time to think about that. I had to make a few calls and pack. My flight was at 11:00 a.m. the next day out of Newark.

Chapter 24

I drove to Newark Airport the next morning and parked in the long-term lot. The flight to Las Vegas was smooth with no problem. I got to the baggage claim area, and there was a guy holding a sign for Paul Servino. It took me a second to remember that was me. The guy greeted me and told me he was from the hotel. He took my bag and showed me to his limo. This kind of first-class, VIP travel was getting addictive, but then I had enough things I was already addicted to.

We pulled up to the Aladdin Hotel and Casino on the famous Las Vegas Strip. The bellboy opened the limo door and led me straight to the front desk. The chauffeur brought in my bag and told the clerk, "This is Mr. Servino." I held out a tip, but he said it was all taken care of and wouldn't take my money. Wow, I thought. I assumed everyone in Las Vegas took tips.

The desk clerk welcomed me to Las Vegas, asked me if it was my first time, and handed me my keys and a package. I started to say something, but he said I was already registered, and everything was taken care of. I thanked him and followed the bellman with my bag to the elevator. My room was on the tenth floor, not the penthouse level, but a special access key was needed to get onto the floor. The room was large and beautiful with a great view of the Strip and a huge bathroom with all the things I needed. The bar had a full bottle of VO, four glasses, club soda, and lemon twists. They knew I was coming.

I poured a VO, lay back on the bed, and opened the package. I was surprised once again. There was driver's license in the name of Philip Sanders with my personal information and some address in Alabama. There was also a commercial pilot's license with all my ratings: single-engine land, multi-engine land, helicopter, instrument helicopter, and airplane, along with an FCC radio license, a medical certificate, a credit card, and maps of the surrounding area. The package had everything I needed to rent a plane. There were no other instructions. I figured I'd wait to see if someone ordered an anisette and Coke.

It was still morning in Las Vegas, and I was jacked up and happy to be there. I changed clothes and went down to the casino. The room was not full due to the time of day, so I went over to one of the blackjack tables. A well-dressed and distinguished man greeted me and asked if I was Paul Servino. He introduced himself as the casino manager and offered his full service for anything in the casino. I had no idea what that meant, but I learned quickly.

He told the pit boss standing there that I would start off with $500. He looked at me and asked if that was enough to start. I just nodded yes and sat down. He instructed the pit boss to see that I received whatever I needed.

There were a few people at the table, and I was a bit embarrassed by all the attention. I didn't know what to make of it. I was just an airplane driver and bar owner from Jersey, and here I was, being treated like a celebrity. But this was the 1970s, and Vegas was still wide open and privately owned. The corporations had not moved in yet, and personal attention was still the specialty of the house.

The bar waitress asked for my order. She was gorgeous. In fact, there was nothing here but beautiful girls dressed in cute and skimpy costumes. It was still morning, so I asked for a cup of coffee. If this was the way the days started around here, I wouldn't make it to nightfall if I started drinking too early.

I played a few hands, lost most of them, and got ready to move on when the dealer shift changed. The new dealer was a beautiful girl. I am such a sucker for beautiful females, especially redheads, and this one was great. There is no way they could know my weakness for redheads, so this had to be just a coincidence. *What the hell,* I decided. *Let's stay and play a few more hands.*

Her name was Blair, and she changed my luck. I went from $250 down to $300 up during her shift. When she changed tables a half hour later, I decided to quit for a while. The casino manager asked if everything was OK. I said yes, just taking a break, and commented on how beautiful I found the sights. He smiled and handed me a card.

"Call this number and request whatever you want," he said, mysteriously.

I thanked him again and went to the restaurant for lunch. After I ate, the waitress asked if I wanted to sign the check. I was starting to feel guilty and said no I would pay. I was still paying with the money I'd won at blackjack, but I felt better about it.

At this point I knew very little about Vegas. I did know that the Aladdin was constantly in the news as to who really owned it. At one point it was the group from Detroit, then the group from St. Louis took over, and then multiple individuals from California and Nevada. All I knew was that someone from New York must have called and made my arrangements. Whoever it was had made them well. The Aladdin had a golf course out back, which drew a lot of golfers, but not enough gamblers. It was the first casino to offer a million-dollar prize on a slot machine, and it always had top entertainment. Frankie Valli was there that week, and I wanted to see him. I was enjoying myself, but there was no word yet on any mission for the family.

I walked outside into the Las Vegas sunlight and got hit with a blast of hot air. It took me back to Vietnam. That was nothing new. I thought about Vietnam a lot in those days and always wondered what my life would have been like if Kennedy hadn't been assassinated and I had never gone to Southeast Asia. It only took a second for me to go from the Las Vegas Strip to the Mekong Delta to Dallas, Texas, and back again. I guess that's what they meant about flashbacks. Your memories come and go at the speed of a flash bulb.

I walked down the strip toward the Desert Inn, the Sahara, the Dunes, and the Sands. I remembered hearing that The Rat Pack hung out in the Copa Lounge at the Sands when they were in town. Tony Bennett was playing the Sands that week, and I wanted to see him, too. I didn't know how long I would be staying in Vegas, but so far I was being treated like royalty, and I liked it. I liked it a lot.

I went back to my room and thought about calling the number the casino manager had given me. But I was a little tired from the flight and knew I had to get some rest if I was going to keep up with Las Vegas.

After a good nap, I showered and decided to have some fun, so I dialed the number.

"This is Gino," a voice said.

"Gino, this is Paul Servino," I said. "I'm at the Aladdin and I was told—"

"Yes, Mr. Servino," he said, cutting me off. "I was expecting your call. I'll be at your room in fifteen minutes."

I never told him what room I was in, but I guessed he knew. Sure enough, exactly fifteen minutes later there was a soft knock on my room door. I opened it to find a smiling, friendly looking man.

"Mr. Servino, I am Gino," he said.

There was no reason to doubt him, and no one knew I was here, so I let him in.

"How can we be of service to you?" he asked, still smiling.

I still wasn't exactly sure who "we" was, but I decided to go for it and see what happened.

"Gino, I would like some company for the evening," I said. "A young, beautiful redhead. In fact, there was a blackjack dealer this morning who caught my eye." I suddenly realized I sounded like I was ordering a nice steak or a bottle of wine.

"I'm sorry, sir, but the casino does not allow employees to date guests," he said. "But I do know another young lady who might also catch your eye."

What the hell, I thought. *Don't be an idiot. Go for it.*

"That sounds nice," I said. "I would like to meet her in the lounge. When can she be there?"

"I understand, sir. The young lady will meet you in about one hour. Would you like dinner and show reservations also?"

"Probably, but that will depend on the young lady," I said. I didn't plan to spend my evening with a dog or a cheap hooker. It was my first time as a VIP in Las Vegas, and while everything had gone beautifully up to now, calling room service for a woman was new to me.

"I understand, sir. I'll make the reservations, and you can decide later," Gino said. "Would you like to see Frankie Valli?"

"Yes, that would be great," I said. "And we'll have dinner here in the hotel tonight."

He nodded, and he hesitated for just a moment.

Are these arrangements OK?" I asked

"Yes, perfectly," he said. "I just thought you would be older."

I had no idea what he meant by that strange comment. Had he heard something about me? *Oh well, we'll see how good he is at being a pimp,* I said to myself. I didn't particularly want to think about it, but if he was arranging an escort for me, I knew money would be changing hands somewhere. The girl, no matter how pretty and charming she might be, was obviously being paid for her time and talent. But I was young, well rested, and ready to party. I poured myself a VO and headed to the casino.

The crowd was building, and things were heating up. I walked past a roulette wheel and stopped to watch. I put $20 on number eight and watched number seven come up. I put another $20 on twenty-seven, my favorite number, and number thirty-one came up. It was obviously not my night for roulette, so I moved on to the craps table. I started to play, but my heart wasn't in it. I was horny and anxious to see a beautiful redhead sitting next to me.

I walked around a bit more. The pit boss came over and said hello. He asked if I was enjoying myself and offered me a table. I said no thanks, and walked to the lounge. I ordered a VO and club soda with a twist and sat down. I was talking with the guy next to me when someone tapped me on the shoulder and said, "Are you Paul?"

I turned around and nearly fell off the stool. "Yes, I'm Paul," I managed to get out, trying hard not to sound like some high school kid meeting the head cheerleader.

"My name is Amber," she said. "I'm glad to meet you."

Thank you, Gino.

She was a doll. She looked to be a few years younger than me, and she was absolutely gorgeous with a stunning figure that was dressed to kill. And that hair. Beautiful red hair. I couldn't wait to see if it was real, if you know what I mean.

"What will you have to drink?" I asked.

"What are you drinking?"

"VO."

"I'll have a glass of champagne, please," she said.

The bartender heard her request and poured the drink. I had to smile. I was thinking about the bar girls in Vietnam who ordered Saigon Tea. The GIs paid for champagne, and the girls got sparkling water. Tonight, though, who cares? I wasn't paying for it.

After a little small talk, I mentioned I had dinner and show reservations. She leaned over to my ear, put her hand on my leg, and said, "Let's hold off on dinner for a while. Let's go back to your room and get acquainted."

She was intoxicating. I put a twenty on the bar and headed for the elevator.

Back in my room she poured me a drink, unbuttoned my shirt, and told me to lie on the bed and get comfortable. I took off my shoes and laid back. She walked over to the stereo and turned on some sexy music. She had done this before. She danced over to the middle of the room and stripped to the music. I thought I had been around and knew what girls looked like and how they were different from me, but this girl was writing a new book.

"I hear you like redheads, real redheads," she said. "I won't disappoint you."

There is a God, and He is shining down on me tonight, I thought to myself. *I don't know why, but He is. Thank you, God.*

She stripped down to her underwear, garter belt, and all the rest. It took her a long time, or maybe it was fast, I can't remember. By the time she crawled next to me in the bed I was way beyond ready.

All she said was, "Slow down, we have plenty of time." I can't say how long I spent between her legs but the fact that she was a real redhead and a beautiful one just kept me going and going. That young girl knew more about pleasing me than I did. She was fantastic and worth...well I don't know how much she was worth because no one ever told me how much she cost. And I did not care.

They say a stiff dick has no conscience. My mind and my conscience were complete blanks. There was just Amber.

We never made it to dinner or to Frankie Valli's show. Oh well, maybe tomorrow. I'm just glad I took a nap and had only a few drinks. My goal was to have this night last for days!

Sometime later the sun came up and I realized I was hungry. Amber said she should go, but I said, "First a shower, then some breakfast, and then we'll see."

She smiled and blushed and said, "OK." A hooker who blushes. Gotta love her.

I ordered a huge room service breakfast for two and told the employees to open the door and bring it inside if I was in the shower. Off we went to the large and luxurious bathroom. She was hesitant to get all wet with none of her beauty supplies handy, but I was persuasive. I thought I heard the room service come in, but my hunger was directed elsewhere. Even in the shower she showed me things I never knew before. This Vegas place is quite a learning experience. I recommend it highly.

We got out of the shower exhausted and hungry. We put on the rich, plush robes the hotel provided and sat down at the table to eat. She was as hungry as I was. After breakfast she dressed as best she could, put her hair in a ponytail, and commented on how much trouble she was having just walking. That was OK with me.

I talked about getting together the next night, and she said I'd have to go through Gino to make the arrangements. I understood and would definitely give him a call. She smiled, said she hoped so, kissed me softly, and left.

What a night. I'd lost track of time and didn't really care. They say there are not a lot of clocks in Las Vegas. I can see why. It is where, if you are lucky, the party never ends. And I was Mister Lucky.

Chapter 25

I decided to get dressed and look around Vegas some more. I also wanted to see how well I could walk. Even if I had to limp a little, what the hell, it was worth it for the memories.

There was a knock at the door. "Who is it?" I yelled, trying to get my shirt buttoned, my pants zipped, and my shoes on.

"Well, come and see," said a voice I recognized right away. Had to be Antonio.

"Antonio, what a surprise," I said, although it really wasn't. Somehow I figured he would be part of this plan, not that I knew what it was.

"So how is Vegas? It sounds like you're having a good time," he said. I guess I should have known that all my movements here had been closely watched. That was OK. At least for now.

"This is some town," I said. "I've been treated like royalty."

"We appreciate what you have done for us, and we want you to know that," he said. "Besides, the flying weather out here is beautiful."

"When will the flying start?" I asked.

As usual, he just ignored that question and went on to talk about Vegas and a little history about the different families involved. Things had worked out well, he said, except for problems with a few individuals on the Nevada Gaming Commission.

"Some people just get too greedy and try to use their position to rob and extort others," he said. "There is so much money to go around out here that it's a shame some people are never satisfied."

That sounded to me like a minor problem. But since he was talking to me about it, maybe it wasn't that minor.

He asked if I wanted to play golf, but I reminded him I didn't play. It didn't matter to him. He said he wanted to hit a few balls, so we went out back to the golf course. The staff greeted him warmly and by name in the pro shop, except they called him Jack instead of Antonio. I didn't say anything, but he could tell I was curious. No big deal, he said; most of his people went by other names out here. We went to the driving range and hit a bucket of balls. Or at least he hit the balls. I swung a club a few times and hit Nevada dirt.

"Since you didn't get to see Frankie Valli last night, how about tonight?" he said. "We'll do dinner at the club and get some girls for company and then see the show."

How could I resist?

He had to meet a few people first and would meet me about 8:30 in the casino. I needed to workout, so I asked him about the health club. He showed me where it was and started to leave.

"By the way, the girl I was with last night, Amber? She'll do just fine for tonight," I said, smiling.

"Somehow I knew that," he said. "I'll take care of it. See you later."

I had no idea how he knew about Amber, but he always seemed to know everything about everybody. I was just glad we were on the same side. I would not have liked to go up against him or his people.

I found my way to the health club and went to the desk. Another attractive young girl greeted me. She was a hard body who spent some time in the gym herself. I gave her my room number and asked about workout clothes. She picked up the phone while I looked around in the shop. I never gave her my name, but when she hung up the phone, she came over, greeted me by name, and said I should pick whatever I needed, and she'd have it delivered to the locker room.

I asked her if she had worked out today. She said no, her shift didn't end till 9:00 p.m. The way things were going I was tempted to call the desk and see if I could have her shift changed so we could work out together, but I thought that would be pushing my luck. She called over a young man and asked him to show me the locker room and facilities. He showed me the locker room and the steam room, sauna, massage room, and gym. By the time he was done, another young man brought me a complete set of workout clothes.

I worked out hard on the machines and free weights and spent time on the body bag. I took a shower and went into the steam room. There were people all around, but it never got crowded. The attendant brought us cool drinks, and then I decided to have a massage. I was going to be ready for a good long night of fun and pleasure. I hadn't done this whole spa deal in a long time, and it brought back good memories. Back in Vietnam, we were able to take one week of R&R, rest and relaxation. I chose to go to Hong Kong for six days. I met up with a beautiful, blonde round-eyed girl from Illinois. She had just been hired by TWA and was taking an around-the-world tour waiting for her placement. We got massages together and spent a little time in the steam room. Later we found a romantic little spot and had serious and memorable fun.

I went back to my room after my workout. I fixed myself a drink and put on a silk sport coat, linen pants, and a sport shirt. I felt good.

I had no trouble finding Antonio when I got to the casino. He was at a craps table with two beautiful girls by his side. One was a tall blonde and the other was Amber. They all stopped playing to give me a big hello. Amber threw her arms around my neck and gave me a big kiss. I was ready to scrap the show once again but decided to stay. The pit crew all knew Antonio by name and treated him with respect. We stayed at the table for a while and let the girls throw the dice. Beautiful girls dressed to kill are a big attraction at a craps table, especially when they're winning. And these girls were quite an attraction.

After a few winning rounds, Antonio said he was ready to eat so we headed out. The pit boss was disappointed. The crowd that had been two deep around the table drifted away when we left. Antonio flipped him a hundred dollar chip and said we'd be back later.

We went into the club for the dinner show. Frankie Valli would be coming on at ten, the maître d' said as he gave Antonio a big greeting. He personally showed us to a table right up front, seated the girls, and started to pour the champagne already chilling on the table. Amber looked at me with her big green eyes and started some small talk about what we all did all day. I don't really care for champagne, so I asked the waiter for a VO. For a few seconds I just sat there, looking around the room and the company and marveling at my good fortune. Antonio and I ordered steak and both the girls had lobster.

The music started at 9:30, and Frankie Valli came on right at ten. He started out doing some songs from his days with the Four Seasons. Then he went into some of the ones he and Bob Gaudio had written together. The show was fantastic, and Amber let me know she was anxious for later. It was turning out to be a great night on the town.

During the show I thought I saw Frankie look at Antonio a few times and wink, but I couldn't be sure. He acknowledged there were a few friends in the audience from back home—he's from Jersey, too— but he never mentioned Antonio by name. I found out later that Antonio and his guys never wanted any public attention.

After the show I was antsy and ready to leave, but Antonio asked the girls if they wanted Frankie's autograph. Naturally they squealed and said yes. Antonio asked the maître d' to ask Frankie if he would we be good enough to give the girls an autograph. They took off for the powder room, and Antonio took me to a lone table in the casino lounge.

"I know you're ready to go back to your room, but remember, we have a breakfast meeting at eight a.m. tomorrow," he said.

"Eight a.m.? Aw, man, have a heart," I said. "I need at least two hours' sleep!"

"OK, make it nine, but no later. We have some work to do," he said. "I put a gym bag in your room. Make sure you bring it with you in the morning."

We stood up, and he kissed my cheek just as the girls were walking up. We all said good night, and Antonio and Crystal walked away. I asked Amber if she wanted another drink. She just smiled, took my hand, and started walking to the elevators.

Antonio never drank much, and these girls didn't drink much, either. They had a mission, too. I had to remember that.

Back in my room Amber started to mix me a drink—there was always fresh ice in my room—but I told her no. She asked me if I wanted her to dance again like last night or just get in bed. I still had the memories of last night embedded in my brain, and I couldn't resist. "I want you to dance, but not too slowly," I said. "We only have about six hours."

We made the most of the time. I'm not sure what time Amber left because I had fallen asleep. As hard as I tried to stay awake and savor every minute with her, she had worn me out. If I was going to last out there in the desert, I was going to have to lay off the VO. But what a night!

The phone rang at 8:15 a.m. with a wake-up call. I took a long, cold shower, put on some clothes, picked up the gym bag, and looked inside. There was a blonde wig, shoulder-length like mine, but good quality and expensive. There were a pair of aviator sunglasses, a University of Alabama shirt, and a set of tail numbers for a Jet Ranger, just like the ones I'd had made, and a map of the local area. I guess I had my flying mission. My blood started to rise, and I started to get the warm feeling. I was ready.

Chapter 26

Antonio was already in the restaurant, drinking coffee and smoking, when I arrived.

"You know those things will kill you," I said, nodding at the pack of smokes on the table.

"Yeah, and so will tall blondes with extra long legs and insatiable appetites," he said.

I ordered decaf coffee and a muffin. "So, what's the mission?" I asked while the waitress was bringing my breakfast.

"Are you wide awake, or are you still dreaming about redheads and fairytales?" he asked, grinning.

"Give me a few days to stop dreaming, but I'm ready to go," I said.

"First, I want you to get away from here," he said. "Go down the block someplace, change your identification, and go to the North Las Vegas Airport and do whatever you need to do to secure a helicopter for rental."

"Wait a minute, hold on, what kind of a helicopter operation is at the airport?" I asked. "Normally they don't let just anyone off the street come in and rent a machine by themselves."

He took a sip of coffee, put out his cigarette, and said, "I understand the place is run by Vietnam veterans. Do whatever you need to do—just make the arrangements."

"OK, when will I be actually renting it?"

"Either tomorrow or the next day. I can't tell you right now."

"OK, what's the mission?"

"A few of the casinos let helicopters land on their property," he said. "Find out which ones do and of those, which one is the least visible. You will be landing there, picking up two people, and taking them to another location. That's it."

"That's it?"

"That's it," he said. "Then you'll take the 'copter back to the airport and get yourself back to The Strip. Make sure you're invisible, and no one can trace your steps."

"That's a tall order since I don't know a soul out here," I said.

"If it was easy, we wouldn't need you to do it. Make it happen," he said. We were usually very cordial but today he seemed annoyed.

I finished my coffee and got up to leave.

"By the way, Tony Bennett is at the Sands tonight," Antonio said. "I've got a table for us."

"Good deal—I'll see you later."

I walked out of the hotel and headed along the Strip to find some place to change my identity. There were trucks and television cameras all over the place. A crew was filming episodes of the TV show *Las Vegas* at the Aladdin. I thought I saw Robert Urich, the star of the show, but I had things to do, so I couldn't stop and play tourist.

I walked down to Caesars. Sugar Ray Leonard was in town working out and thought I could catch a glimpse. I'd watched him fight his way to a gold medal in the Olympics and became a fan. There was plenty of activity around the front, so I walked in and found a men's room right off the lobby. I walked into a stall and opened the bag. I put on the wig and UA shirt and waited a few minutes before I left the stall. I went over to the sink, adjusted the wig, and put on the glasses. Hell, I looked so good I didn't recognize myself. I left the hotel and went to the street for a cab. A bellman asked, "Cab, son?" Son? I guess I looked young. After I got into the cab and was out of earshot of the bellman, I told the cabbie to take me to the North Las Vegas Airport. I said it in my best slightly Southern accent.

The cabbie talked about Vegas and all it had to offer. I was only interested in the helicopters at the north airport. There were three airports in the area. McCarran was the largest and the main commercial field. Henderson, to the south, had an airport to take care of most of the executive aircraft traffic, and the North Las Vegas field, where the helicopters were supposed to be.

When we arrived at the field, I asked the driver if he knew where the helicopter operator was located. He did, and I told him to take me there. He asked if I was going for a sightseeing ride and started to talk more. I thanked him for his help, paid the fare, and got out. He asked if I wanted him to come back and get me. I said no, thank you. I made a note of the cab company and the number.

I walked up to the reception desk and asked the girl, "Is the chief pilot busy, I would like to speak to him.

"May I help you with something?" she asked with authority.

"I would like to see the chief, what is his name?" I asked with a big soft smile and a slight southern accent.

"His name is Buck Novak" as she dialed his extension.

I sat in the waiting area looking out the window to the flight line.

"I see you have a few Jet Rangers and a few Bell Thirteens." I said to the pretty girl, "do you have others" not needing an answer. I saw all I came for.

Buck Novak looked like he'd walked right out of the Wild West and into the waiting room. He was about six feet tall, wore cowboy boots, and a ten-gallon hat. He introduced himself and asked how he could help.

I told him I was Philip Sanders. I was here from Alabama, and I was checking out the area for business associates who wanted to do a little sightseeing and have a look-see at land they were interested in. He said that was what they did best and asked how many passengers would be going. I told him these were important associates and wanted to remain anonymous. He said OK—that's no problem. I told him I was a licensed pilot, and I wanted to rent a Jet Ranger and fly it myself. He took off his hat and sat back in his big chair. He was a few years older than me, tan and rustic looking. I wanted to bring up flying in Vietnam, but I wanted to know where and when he'd been there so I could make my story real and make sure we did not cross any paths.

"I understand you flew in Vietnam, Buck. Where were you?" I asked.

"I flew one tour in I Corps in 1966 and a second tour in the Delta in 1970," he said.

"What did you fly, and how's your leg?" I asked. I had noticed his slight limp when we walked to his office.

"I flew 'Slicks' in sixty-six and 'Loaches' in seventy," he said, using army slang for unarmed transport Hueys and light-observation helicopters. "My second tour was cut short after seven months when I caught a round through my thigh. It wasn't a million-dollar wound because I still have this damn limp, and it ended my flying career in the army.

"Who told you I was there?" he wanted to know, eyeing me suspiciously.

"When I asked around about flying, I was told there was only one place worth going to and that was with you," I said. I figured blowing a little smoke wouldn't hurt.

He didn't ask if I flew, just what I flew, and where. I didn't want any conflict and running into anyone he might have known, so I borrowed the career of one of my classmates.

"I flew 'Slicks' with B Troop, 227th Aviation Regiment in the 1st Cavalry Division out of Camp Evans in 1968," I said. "I got out in 1971 and flew Rangers out of Louisiana for the oil companies."

We stood up, shook hands, and welcomed each other home.

He told me they didn't rent their aircraft to pilots they didn't know or who didn't fly with them regularly. I told him this job was important to me and suggested that he give me a check ride if that would satisfy him that I knew what I was doing.

"I'll pay whatever rate you want or even over the normal rate if that will help," I said. "I really need to get these guys in the air soon."

"What aircraft do you want?" he asked.

"One of your Rangers," I told him. "And if you've got the time now, let's go flying."

He stood up and walked to the door. He stood there for moment thinking. Then he turned back to me, smiled and said, "Let's go flying."

He told the lady at the desk that we were going up in the Ranger and would be back in about an hour.

We walked out to the pad where the Ranger was parked. He said there were dual controls and asked which side I wanted. I told him it didn't matter, but I'd take the right side. There is a big difference in the two sides when you're flying. Some people had trouble adjusting, but I flew so much from both sides, I was comfortable on either.

Before we got on board or even did any preflight, I opened my bag and took out my flight gloves. He looked at me funny.

I said, "Old habits die hard." In Vietnam we would never think of flying without gloves, but civilian flying is different. The real reason for the gloves was simple: I didn't want my fingerprints anywhere near this aircraft or this mission.

We finished the preflight inspection, and I checked the logbook for any recent entries. I made sure I did everything by the book so he would feel comfortable with me. We both got in and fastened our seat harnesses. He said, "OK, do you want to start?"

"I'll do the checklist and watch you the first time," I said. We put on our headsets, and I pulled out the checklist. I knew the list by heart and could do it in my sleep, but today was by the book, so I read off each item and waited till he completed it. The Ranger started right up and purred like a kitten. Jet Rangers have Lycoming turbine engines with a high-pitched whine. Being around them long enough without the proper ear protection will ruin your high-frequency hearing. Mine was already going fast.

Buck turned on the radios and tuned to the tower frequency. He told me he would hover to the takeoff spot and then hand her over to me. He showed me the route from his pad to the departure spot and showed me landmarks to be aware of. He put the Ranger on the tarmac, I read off the pre-takeoff list, and he said, "You got it."

I said, "I got it," and took the controls. It had been a few weeks since I'd flown, but it felt good. I picked it up to a hover and did a 360-degree turn to check the controls and check the area. I turned 90 degrees left and then 90 degrees right and then said I was ready.

He said, "The radio call is to North Tower and we're Five-Four Whiskey. Make the call and go."

I pushed the radio button: "North Tower, this is copter Five-Four Whiskey, ready for takeoff."

"Roger, Five-Four Whiskey, you are cleared for takeoff," the air traffic controller responded. There were no other aircrafts in the pattern. I took one more look at the gauges and pulled pitch, and we started to climb out. Buck said to keep the east heading and climb to a thousand feet. As we cleared the airport, there was plenty of desert to the west. When I leveled off at one thousand feet I could barely see the skyline of Las Vegas.

He told me the Grand Canyon was due east, the city was south, and McCarran airport was further south. I told him I would be taking my people to the canyon, but today I wanted to concentrate on the local area and the airport control areas. He said, "OK, let me show you. I got it."

"You got it," I said, following procedure by the book. He took the controls and showed me the boundaries of the North Airport and McCarran and the executive strip near Henderson.

We were still east of the city, and he said, "OK, show me what you've got."

I put my hands on the controls and said, "I got it."

"You got it," he said.

I asked him if I could go to 1,500 feet here. He looked to the west and said we better stay under 1,200.

I climbed to 1,200 and started to do an acceleration-deceleration maneuver. This was a maneuver we learned in flight school that demanded total command of all the controls in the helicopter. Very few students ever mastered it in flight school. It took a lot of concentration and experience to get it right. I started at 1,200 feet on a heading of 090 degrees at 100 knots. I slowed down to 60 knots and then accelerated to 120 knots, staying on the course 090 and 1,200 feet all the time. Usually you were allowed a variance of ten degrees right or left and one hundred feet up or down. I varied maybe one degree and five feet. It felt good.

Buck looked over and said, "Not bad; you obviously have some time in this model."

I just nodded.

I asked him to fly over the city and show me where there were safe spots to land on the Strip. He showed me the pad at the Aladdin, a construction site behind the Stardust and a spot behind the Desert Inn. The construction site behind the Stardust had an area roped off. He said that the contractor from California had a chopper and landed there sometimes, but it was private.

We headed back to the North Airport. He told me to land near where we took off. I called the tower, got clearance to land, and headed for the ground. As I was hovering to the pad, I stopped and said, "Hovering autorotation?"

He sat up straight and said, "Whoa, what for?"

I said, "Just for kicks."

He hesitantly said OK and put his hands near the controls. Hovering autorotation is another maneuver that takes real command of the aircraft. I settled at five feet above the ground and cut the engine to idle. The aircraft sat for a split second and then started to fall to the ground. I slowly pulled the pitch, and we touched the ground as smooth as a baby's ass. He just smiled and said, "OK, you know how to fly. Just take us back to the house."

I parked in the same spot we'd left from and used the checklist to shut her down. He made the entries in the logbook. We got out and headed for the hangar.

Once inside he introduced me to the lady at the desk and asked me for my papers so he could make copies for his files. I gave him my pilot's license, driver's license, medical certificate, and FCC radio license. He looked them over and gave them to the lady to copy.

"When is your flight?" he asked. I told him it was either tomorrow or the next day, my associates were not in town yet. He said tomorrow is partly open but he has some flights for the next day that he could juggle if he had to. We walked back to his office.

"I have one more request," I said. "My associates prefer to pay cash for everything they do."

He said that was a bit unusual. I could tell he was curious, but he didn't ask any more. He said OK, and figured a price per hour. It was a bit steep, but I agreed. We said goodbye, and he walked into the shop.

I asked the lady at the desk for a phone book. I looked up cabs, making sure I did not pick out the same one I came in. I asked the lady to call for me and gave her the number. I was still using my southern accent and had to concentrate. I grabbed a soda from the machine and waited outside in the heat—no more talking. The cab was there in twenty-five minutes. I told the cabbie to take me to the Westward Ho.

The cabbie asked if I'd had a good flight. He thought I had taken a sightseeing flight since I was obviously was not from around here. I said yes, it was a good flight and asked him to put on the radio. He dropped me off at the hotel. I paid him and added a normal-size tip, nothing to remember me by, and headed for the men's room. I found a stall, took off the wig, glasses, and shirt, and then waited a few minutes until the crowd changed. I fixed myself in the mirror and went out a side door. I walked next door to the Stardust to check out the landing pad behind it. It looked like they were doing demo work on the Vegas World and the Royal Inn. It was 2:00 p.m. on a weekday, and there was no activity around this site. It would suit us just fine.

I walked back to the Aladdin. It was still hot, and I needed a drink. When I got to the hotel they greeted me, and as I was walking past the front desk, the clerk handed me an envelope. I went to my room, took off my clothes, made a drink, and stretched out on the bed. The note was from Antonio.

"Hope things went well," he'd written. "We'll meet in the lounge at eight, dinner, then the show at the Copa Lounge in the Sands. No girls tonight, get some rest."

I was thinking about working out, but decided to rest instead. I also thought about calling Amber since we were going to be stag tonight, but I didn't. She certainly was on my mind. What a beauty.

I went down to the men's shop and decided to get a new outfit. I still had some winnings left, and I hadn't spent any money yet. I walked into the shop and, sure enough, there was a gorgeous brunette standing behind the counter. It was the middle of the afternoon, and no one else was in the store. I gotta hand it to these Vegas people—they really know how to find the most beautiful women. The Beach

Boys sang about California girls and girls from all over. They need to do another song just about Las Vegas.

This girl, Illona, put together a nice outfit for me: jacket, pants, silk shirt, and socks to match. She asked if I wanted to charge it to my room, and I said no. I never gave her my room number or my name. I was starting to get a bit antsy about my up-coming mission and where it would take me.

Chapter 27

At eight sharp I went to the casino to look for Antonio. He was at the bar talking to a few guys. I hesitated until he waved before I went over. He introduced us everyone, just first names. We had one round of drinks, and then they left. He never said who they were, and I didn't ask.

"How did things go today? Any hitches?" he asked.

"No problem, everything is set," I said. "I just need a little notice to arrange for the aircraft."

"I'll know tonight," he said. "It will be tomorrow or the next day, no later. OK? How much money will you need for the helicopter?"

"I figure a grand should do it, depending on how long the flight will be."

"Figure on two hours, no more. I'll fill you in later," he said. "Have you ever seen Tony Bennett?"

"I saw him a few years ago at the Copa in the city, great show," I said.

"The show he does here is better," he said. "We're going to meet a few guys and have some fun. For tonight you are Paul Servino from Jersey. No talk about flying at all, got it?"

"Roger," I answered, using flying lingo. He just looked at me and smiled.

We walked outside and got into a limo. The driver greeted us and drove away. I started to say something about the mission, and Antonio held his finger to his lips. No talk. The limo pulled up in front of a small restaurant a few blocks off the Strip, Italian no less. Antonio said we were having dinner there then going to the eleven o'clock show. The owner greeted us fondly and showed us to a table in the corner. He recommended a few of his house specials and left. The place was small, seating about seventy-five people, and was half full. We ordered drinks and dinner. I had veal saltimbocca. Antonio had veal piccata. We both had gelato and espresso for dessert.

We talked mostly about Vegas and how things were beginning to change. During dinner a few people came over to our table to say hello, but he never introduced me. It wasn't impolite; it just wasn't important they knew my name.

Antonio paid the bill and tipped everyone in the restaurant. I told the owner how much I enjoyed the meal and was looking forward to coming back. Back in the limo, Antonio told me he had to go there and pay his respects to Paulo, the owner. He and Uncle Joe go way back, Antonio said. Their families were together in the Old Country.

"When we get to the Sands, I'm going to talk to some guy from the gaming commission," he said. "When I do, I don't want him to meet you or get a good look at you, so make yourself invisible."

When we got to the Sands, it was like old-home week. People from all over came up to say hello to Antonio. Some were greeted with embraces and some just casually. Some he introduced to me, and some he didn't. If I thought I was treated well so far in Vegas, it was nothing to how he was treated and greeted.

We walked around the casino and made a few throws at a craps table. I put a bet on the pass line. Antonio looked at me and said, "Here he comes." I just turned and walked away. After I got far enough away, I turned to see who it was I needed to avoid. He was average looking, about forty to forty-five, six feet tall with a horrible polyester leisure suit, and white patent leather shoes. The fashion police should have arrested him.

Antonio walked away with the guy. They went off to the side and talked for about ten minutes. The conversation did not look friendly.

Antonio came over to where I was standing. "Did you get a good look at him?" he asked. I nodded, and he said, "Let's go have some fun."

We walked into the Copa. The club boss greeted us fondly and showed us to a table on the second row from the stage. The table was set for five. We ordered drinks, and since I could sense this was definitely a working evening, I slowed down and ordered a club soda.

If the rumors I'd heard were true, the Rat Pack frequented the club when they were in town. Sometimes they'd go on stage with the performers, whoever they were, and clown around. As far as I knew, none of them were performing that week, but the way things were going, who knew what would happen?

Just before eleven, the other three guests arrived. We all stood and shook hands. One of them, Bruno, embraced Antonio. We all made small talk, and they spoke a bit about the current sports bets they were making and winning. Tony Bennett came on, and the show was great. He had two girls in red evening gowns as backup singers. They were tall and gorgeous and could really sing. At one point Tony said hello to the friends he saw in the audience and made a special wave toward our table. If all these people out here knew and respected Antonio like this, I couldn't imagine what it would be like when Uncle Joe was there. They must fall all over themselves. At one point I asked Antonio how often his uncle came out here. He said not that often—it's too hot for him. I couldn't tell if he was referring to the weather.

After the show, our waiter brought us another round of drinks. Compliments of the cast, he said. Antonio whispered to the waiter, "Please tell Mr. Bennett I will catch him next trip."

Two of the guests got up to leave. They paid the bill and said good-bye. Antonio held my arm and said we'd stay a few more minutes. We sat back down. Bruno sat next to me.

Antonio told me Bruno would be a passenger on the flight, and there would be two others.

"What spot near the Strip did you find to land?" Antonio asked.

"Behind the Stardust, there's a construction site with a makeshift helipad," I said. "It's not controlled."

Bruno looked at Antonio and said, "That's perfect. I'll have them there at noon tomorrow."

Antonio looked at me, "Will that work?"

I said, "That's short notice. Can you make it 2:00 p.m. to be safe?"

Bruno looked frustrated, "I might get them to go to 1:00 p.m. but no later."

I looked at Antonio. "I'll make it work," I said.

"Good, it's set—tomorrow at 1:00 p.m." Antonio said.

We all got up to leave. Bruno said goodbye and said he'd see me tomorrow.

Antonio walked around and handed out a few more tips and thanked the staff. "Thank you Frankie, we had a good time as always." The club boss whispered something to Antonio and they shook hands. No intimate embrace in this setting.

"Do you want to gamble any more tonight?" Antonio asked when we were out of earshot of the staff.

"No, I would like to know a bit more of the mission if you care to share any of the details," I said, sarcastically.

We walked over to the bar and sat at a table. A waitress came right over, and I asked her to give us a few minutes. Antonio took a paper out of his jacket pocket.

"These are map coordinates of a spot where you're going to land. You will pick up your passengers at that place you told Bruno. Get in and out real fast, and make sure no one recognizes you. From there, fly out toward the canyon and then to this spot. Some Indians will be there to meet you. The three guys will get out, and you will leave unless Bruno wants you to wait. Make sure you are gone no more than two hours total.

"Be as invisible as possible, and make sure Paul Servino and Daniel Santino are nowhere to be found. When you get done, return the aircraft, and get back to the hotel."

This was the first time I had ever gotten specific instructions from Antonio firsthand. This must have been a big deal, but I wouldn't know the specifics for a long time, if ever. I had enough information to get the job done. Antonio motioned for the waitress to come back; we did not order anything but he gave her ten bucks anyway. That is just the way they were, I had to watch everything and pay attention.

We left the Sands and went back to the Aladdin. It was about 2:00 a.m., and the place was jumping. Antonio said something to the pit boss. We walked over to a craps table. The pit boss talked to the box man, and the box man put three five hundred-dollar chips in front of me. Antonio said, "Play with $200 to $300 of it, and then take the rest to the cage and cash in. That is for the chopper." He said goodnight and left.

I played a few rounds, lost two hundred bucks, and called it quits. I cashed in at the cage and went to my room. I set a wake up call for 8:00 a.m. and went to bed. I was tired and excited and tried to force myself to sleep. I had plenty to do tomorrow. It's a good thing I have an imagination because I needed one to figure out this mission.

Chapter 28

At 8:00 a.m. the phone rang, but I was already awake, I never get into a deep sleep, just habit. I threw on some clothes and went down to the lobby to the pay phone area. I called Buck Novak and asked him to reserve the Ranger for noon.

He said, "Hold on," and went to check the schedule. He came back and said, "How about 10:00 a.m. or 1:00 p.m.?"

I said, "Buck, I really need it at noon. Can you make it work?"

He left again and came back and said, "OK, noon it is. How long will you need it?"

"About three hours." I said.

"See you when you get here."

When I got back upstairs, there was coffee and a muffin in my room. Not bad. I showered and dressed casually. I checked my bag for all the things I needed: wig, glasses, gloves, aircraft numbers, map, money, all my papers, and the University of Alabama shirt. I took out the map and plotted the coordinates Antonio had given me. It was a desolate spot west of Nellis Air Force Base, north of the canyon. What on earth? I started to get the feeling someone would not be coming back from this trip.

I double-checked everything and left my room. I walked quickly through the hotel and tried to avoid everyone. The television crew was there again, so people were busy. This time I walked to the Marina Hotel. I found the men's room, and put on my outfit. I did not put on the University of Alabama shirt this time. I left the hotel through the side door and walked to the street. I headed north on the Strip and hailed a cab. I told the cabbie to take me to the North Las Vegas Airport and sat back to think. I tried to plan the timing so as not to be early or late and still have time for anything unforeseen that might come up. A helicopter can be a touchy piece of equipment, and I knew nothing about the maintenance at this place. It was about a twenty-minute flight from the airport to the Strip avoiding McCarran and any controlled airspace.

I checked in with Buck Novak, and we signed the rental agreement. He walked me to the pad and said everything was ready to go with a full load of fuel. Full fuel meant about two and a half hours of flight time. I was not going to take any big chances on this flight. I handed Buck two hundred dollars, and he said we would settle up when I got back. I said this was just for making the schedule work out.

As he was walking away he turned and asked, "I just have to ask, what's with the long hair?"

"I guess it's just left over from my hippie days and living in the South," I said in my best Rhett Butler drawl.

I preflighted the aircraft and cranked it up at about 12:30 p.m. I called the tower and took off to the east. I headed toward the open desert about ten miles from the airport. Once I spotted an open area, I landed and got out to change the numbers. Luckily, this Ranger had the exact same numbering locations and no other writing or names. The new numbers on, I headed for Vegas.

The sky was clear but hazy and hot as usual. I stayed below a thousand feet because I did not want to talk to McCarran's air traffic controllers. The transponder was off, and I tried to stay below radar. I tuned to McCarran's frequency to be aware of other air traffic in the area. I went down to under 500 feet and followed the Strip to the Stardust. There were two cars near the pad and three guys standing nearby. I landed quickly, cut the engine down to idle, locked down the controls, and got out. I opened the back door for the two guys and the front door for Bruno. I wanted to make sure the doors were closed and latched. I'd had problems before with doors that opened in flight.

I nodded to Bruno, and he nodded back. I got back to full rpm and pulled pitch, and we lifted off. I was on the ground for less than four minutes.

The two guys in back were dressed in polyester leisure suits and wore name-tags. I showed Bruno the map and pointed to the spot I had circled. He nodded his head and said we will be met there. I headed to the east as fast as she would go. Bruno leaned over and asked me to head toward the canyon and act like a tour guide. Tour guide! I had no idea where the fuck I was or what I was doing. Bruno kept looking at his watch. I asked him if we were on a schedule, and he said we had to meet our people at 2:15 p.m. If we were on a time schedule, I had to keep track of where we were and how long it would take to get to the landing zone.

The desert out there was big and empty. It all looked the same except for a few roads. I knew I had to stay south and east of Nellis Air Force Base and well away from their airspace. I told Bruno it was time to head for the landing zone. He turned to talk to the guys in the back, and they seemed confused.

Bruno told me they were going to look at some property to buy. I stayed east of Nellis and headed north toward Apex and Highway 93. I crossed 93 north of Apex and headed west. There was nothing but barren desert for miles. I didn't think this would be a good area to buy land, but I wasn't in real estate. I came up on the landing zone and started to circle. I saw a small truck all alone next to a dirt road that went nowhere. I circled to the right so I could see and looked at Bruno.

"Is that the spot?"

"That's it."

I started to descend, and the two guys started to quiz Bruno. They wanted to know why we were landing in such a god-forsaken place. I got the impression that was not the spot they had planned on. Bruno told them to hold on—it was just a quick stop. Bruno said to land next to the truck.

It was an old pickup with multiple colors and multiple dents. Three guys were standing near it, two large and one small. All had long hair, big hats, boots, and vests. Two of the guys had hunting rifles, and the small one had a shotgun. I could tell as I was flying into this spot that there was nothing out here to hunt. Nothing could live out here very long, so these three guys were not looking for any wild game.

I landed, and Bruno said, "Stay put—wait for me." He got out, left his door open, and opened the back door. The two guys in the back objected and said they weren't getting out here. The three Indians—at least they looked like Indians to me and that's what Antonio had called them—came over to the chopper with their guns raised and motioned the two guys out.

They didn't move. The smaller Indian hit the first guy in the gut with the butt of his shotgun. Then he grabbed his jacket and pulled him to the ground. I leaned over and closed the front door. The second guy in the back got out on his own. The Indians frisked them and headed them to the pickup.

One of the suits pulled out his wallet and looked like he was showing some sort of badge. One of the big guys hit his arm with a rifle and the wallet fell on the ground. The other big guy picked up the wallet, and the two of them put the suits in the back of the pickup while the shotgun guy covered them. Then the big guys got in back with the suits while the little Indian with the shotgun drove. Bruno had his pistol out, too.

Bruno got back in the left side of the helicopter and said let's get out of here. I rolled throttle, pulled pitch, and started to climb. The pickup made dust rolling north.

The last time I delivered people to some Indians I had a feeling the situation was going to have a good ending. I didn't feel that way this time; these two guys were going to become invisible.

Bruno said to head back to that road we'd crossed. I guessed he meant 93. We crossed at about Apex, but there wasn't much there. He said to follow the dirt road east to a farmhouse about six miles away. He spotted the house and recognized it. There was a long dirt drive leading to the house and a new model Pontiac parked halfway between the house and the road with a guy sitting behind the wheel. He said to land by the car.

Once on the ground he said, "Thanks for the ride—you're done."

He closed and latched the door this time and got into the car. They drove away, and I got out and took off the fake numbers. My fuel was getting low, so I stayed north of Nellis and landed at the airport. I parked at the pad I left from and shut down the aircraft. I filled out the logbook: two passengers from North Airport to Grand Canyon and back, two hours and fifteen minutes flight time. I scribbled a signature no one could read and got out. I packed up all my gear and checked inside the aircraft to make sure no one, especially the two guys in back, had left anything, and I wiped down all the surfaces anyone could have touched.

The same lady greeted me in the office and asked about my flight. I was anxious to get out of there, but I didn't want to act like it. I asked her to call me a cab. I needed to get out of that wig and that hayseed accent. Buck came out of his office and greeted me. He wanted to chit-chat, but I needed to go, so I asked for the bill to settle up, and we went into his office. I told him I used almost a full tank of fuel and two hours and fifteen minutes of flight time. Without really looking at the bill, I handed him ten one hundred dollar bills. He glanced at the bills and put them in his drawer. I grabbed a soda from the machine and said I had to meet my people in an hour so I'd better get going. We shook hands and nodded to each other.

I didn't know what he thought, but he was cool, and I felt I could trust him, at least up to a point. Helicopter pilots who flew in Vietnam had a common bond, and you knew your back was covered.

Chapter 29

The cab took me to the Desert Inn. The traffic was light, so we got there fast. I went to the men's room and took off my costume. I was hot and needed a shower and a drink and maybe some Amber. I hoped Antonio had no plans for the night. I wanted to chill and get laid.

I also wanted to get a drink, but I would wait. I checked to make sure I had everything with me and went out the side door. The walk to the Aladdin was good. I needed to stretch. This mission was different; I had a different feeling about it from the others. Maybe it was because I really didn't know anything about it. Who were these guys, and what did they do? Maybe I would find out. Or maybe not.

I walked into the lobby. The television crews were gone, and I walked up to the bar. I ordered a drink and, out of nowhere, Antonio came over.

"How did it go?" he asked.

"Very smooth as far as I know," I said. "Have you heard from Bruno?"

"Yes, but we'll talk later," he said. "You have a flight to catch."

"A flight? Where am I going?"

"You need to get out of Vegas," he said. "You're going home."

"Well, hell, I have plans for tonight, and they don't include you," I said. I was getting really pissed. It had been a stressful day, and I wanted to kick back with Amber, a steak, and a bottle of VO.

"Maybe next time," he said, not smiling at all at my cranky complaining. "Your bags are packed, and there's a cab outside waiting."

OK, so much for Amber, the steak, and the VO. Shit. But like it or not, I knew these plans were for my safety and continued good health. So I did what he said.

"When can I know about this mission?" I asked.

"When I get back to New York we'll get together," he said. "But not for a while. Stay invisible. Is all your flight stuff in this bag?"

"Yes."

"Give me all your papers for Philip Sanders."

I handed him the whole wallet and my bag.

He handed me my tickets and the wallet from my room with Paul Servino's name on the identification. Nothing like privacy when you're on a mission, huh? We stood up, embraced, and I headed for the door.

He said, "I'll see you when I see you," and walked away.

The doorman opened the door and showed me to the cab. My carry-on bag was in the back seat, and the doorman said my bags were in the trunk. I handed him a tip and got in. I never told the cabbie where to go. He already knew.

This is not what I had in mind. I came here in a limo, and I'm leaving in a cab? What the fuck is up with that?

Once in the airport, I went right to check-in and handed the girl my ticket. She might have been beautiful like most Vegas girls, but I wasn't paying attention. I had ninety minutes before my flight. I didn't want another drink—I wanted Amber, goddamn it—but I went to the bar anyway and ordered one.

I was just staring into space when a small brunette came over and asked me for a light. I looked at her and took some matches off the bar to light her cigarette. She asked if I was just getting into town. I said, no, I was just leaving. She asked if I would be coming back. I said yes and she handed me her card. The working girls in Vegas are very up front. She smiled and left.

Chapter 30

Unfortunately, my plane was on time. I was actually hoping it would be canceled, but I had my instructions, and Amber would just have to wait until my next trip. There would definitely be a next trip. I was sure of that. I liked Las Vegas. I liked how I was treated there. Las Vegas could become habit forming.

The flight was easy. I landed at Newark and tried to stay in the shadows as I went to the long-term parking lot to get my car. The drive home up the New Jersey Turnpike was as forgettable as the flight. My mind was still in Las Vegas, and my thoughts were about fun, pleasure, and, yes, at least a little bit about the two guys who went for that long ride in the desert. One of these days I would find out their fate, but at that point I really didn't care.

I got back to my apartment, poured a drink, and started to go through the mail. Nothing of much interest. I thought about calling Bob at the bar but decided to just hit the sack and get back to life tomorrow.

Sleep came hard. I lay awake thinking about all the things that had happened over the past year and where things seemed to be heading in the future. I started feeling more unsettled. I felt like I had unfinished business, and it was weighing heavily on my soul. I needed to decide what I was going to do with the rest of my life, and more and more it felt like mob life wasn't it.

The next day I called my bar manager, Bob, and he sounded surprised to hear from me. I asked him to come in a little early so he could bring me up to date. I drove to the bar just before lunch, and V greeted me with a big hug and smiles. She told me how well things were going at Squatters and how she and Bob had hired a new girl to work nights. She was excited and animated about it, but I wasn't really listening.

Lunch that day got busy, so I went into the kitchen to help out. I liked being back on the line for a change, and it felt good to be this kind of busy again. Bob came in about two, and we went into the back office. He showed me all the receipts since I'd been gone, and it was clear that business was picking up. One of our competitors up the road got shut down for a few weeks for a liquor license violation, and those customers were coming to Squatters.

"We had to weed some of them out," Bob said. "They had a pretty rough crowd over there, but for the most part things are working out, and business is good."

The last month's receipts were good, and I told Bob to give the staff a little extra and keep the rest of the profit for himself. He started to object, but I cut him short. He thanked me and said he enjoyed what he was doing and appreciated my trust in him. My sister and he were getting along well, but she wished he were home more. This bar life is addictive and not healthy for a lasting romantic relationship. I told him that after a few years he might want to get a real job, but right now I needed him and appreciated all he did.

Bob asked me about my trip and seemed anxious to know all about it but never pushed for more than I told him. I gave him some bullshit story about being in Dallas and what a great city it was and how great it was to see some old army buddies and do a little flying. He just smiled. I felt close to Bob and was proud to have him as a friend and brother-in-law, but I knew I had to keep my other life at arm's distance from him and my sister. There were things I wanted to tell them—they were my family—but they just wouldn't come out.

I got back into a routine of working out in the morning and going to the bar later in the day. Some days I went in to help with lunch; others days I worked the night shift and stayed until closing.

Bob and the crew had changed the menu a bit and changed some of the music at night to accommodate the crowds. They were doing a great job running the place without me. I liked hanging around and trying to be helpful, even if they didn't need me, but my mind was far away from Squatters.

It was almost three weeks after I got back from Las Vegas before I got a message from Antonio to meet him at a new place on Route 59 in Nyack. I walked in at 10:00 p.m. and didn't see a soul I knew. Being a bar owner gave you a lot of exposure and introduced you to a lot of people, so not seeing anyone you knew at a local bar was odd.

Antonio walked in a few minutes after me, and we headed for a booth in the back all alone. We ordered drinks and made small talk before he started his update on my trip.

"The heat was on the whole town for a while after they realized those two guys were missing," he said.

"Who were they, and what were they involved with?" I asked.

"They were both Nevada Gaming Commission agents," he said. "They were working on full-disclosure issues. The Nevada powers that be are convinced the stated owners of some of the casinos are not the real owners, but they're having trouble proving it. They've created a special task force to investigate the casinos in question, and these two guys were part of that task force."

"Were they supposed to be undercover?" I asked.

"Some of them tried to be, but they did a poor job of it," he said. "These two guys and a few others were using their positions to shake down casino owners and extort money from them. If that wasn't enough, they were also rigging slot machines to pay out jackpots to people working with them."

"It never ceases to amaze me how people know—or think they know—who they're dealing with and still try to take advantage of them," I said. "Didn't they read *The Godfather*?"

"Yeah, can you imagine?" Antonio said. "Anyway, the gaming commission was aware of what they were doing and was getting ready to bust them. They'd been under surveillance for a long time."

"Oh, great, you mean people knew they went for a joyride in a helicopter?" I sputtered.

"Don't jump the gun," he said. "I'll get to your part. These guys were bad news, and the system was breaking down."

"What are you talking about 'the system'?" I asked. "I thought we were dealing with two guys who were trying to rip you off!"

Antonio looked at me with cold eyes.

"We never want you to be emotionally involved with these jobs," he said, quietly. "Just do your work and move on—it works better that way."

"Look, I know it works better that way, but I want to know what we're dealing with here," I said. "What system are you talking about?"

"The gaming commission in Las Vegas has a mind of its own, and it does as it pleases," Antonio said. "The commissioners write their own rules as they go along. They have two levels, insiders and outsiders. The insiders are relatives, friends, friends of friends, and assorted scumbags and assholes. The outsiders are all the other people. When an insider gets caught being too crooked or aggressive, they get slapped around and transferred to another area. Meanwhile, the honest outsiders try to do the right thing, but they usually get overruled.

"So, as you've seen with some of your other missions for us, we don't wait for the justice system to fix our problems. We fix them ourselves. The fact that these two guys were trying to rip us off would normally not have been a big deal. The fact that they disappeared right in front of the feds' eyes, let everyone involved know we are serious and to cut the shit. The message was strong and permanent."

"Is it really permanent or just this issue?" I wondered aloud.

"It's permanent until it happens again," he said, shrugging his shoulders. "Then we deal with it again, like always."

"So, tell me about the flight," I asked. "How'd we get away with that? Or did we?"

"They were being watched and were about to be brought in," Antonio said. "But that day, their tail somehow 'lost' them on the Strip and didn't know we had taken them for a ride. Imagine that.

"The feds got involved and looked all over. They brought in dozens of people to question and uncovered some big issues within the commission. Naturally, they had some anonymous help with that," he said, smiling.

"Anyway, they found their way to the airport and found out about this one mysterious helicopter rental and looked into it. All the paperwork was in order, but they couldn't find the pilot or any passengers to question. They labeled it suspicious, but finally had to drop it when it came to a big dead end. There were no prints, no witnesses, no radar, nothing. They'll probably keep the file open for years, but no one knows anything."

Later I got the full story of our little adventure in the desert. The Gaming Commission assigned two special agents to find the missing men. One was a guy named Hernandez. He'd been born in Mexico but came to the United States several years before. He had worked for the Gaming Commission for ten years. The other one was Barefoot, a Native American put on the commission to meet a quota, but it turned out that Barefoot was a good agent. He took his job seriously and performed well. Once the FBI got wind of the situation, it wanted to send in its own agents, but the Commission asked the FBI to hold off until their investigation ran into trouble.

At first Hernandez and Barefoot thought the two missing agents had run away, figuring they were about to be busted, but they left no trace, and these two guys were not the sharpest tacks in the box. The Commission knew they were dirty and was just waiting to get enough evidence to nail them to the wall. Their intention, though, was to do it quietly. They did not want to make an issue of any rogue agents working for the state. They did not want to make an example of them.

That might have satisfied the commission, but it would not have sent the message the Mafia families back east wanted to send. The families wanted everyone to know how they feel about being ripped off and just how much they would not stand for it. The two guys disappearing would send that message.

Antonio said that Hernandez and Barefoot took up the search. They interviewed the team following the agents, but still couldn't figure out how they had lost them. The car they were driving showed up at the airport, but there was no proof they flew anywhere. They went to all three airports in Las Vegas and talked to everyone they could. They talked to Buck Novak, and he went over the logs for the days before and after the disappearance with them. When the two investigators noticed our flight, he told them a fellow Vietnam veteran rented a helicopter to take some real estate folks out to look at property. He never mentioned that the day before, the vet had asked to see downtown and any spots to land. Helicopter pilots have a bond that is not written or described—it just exists.

"That flight went east toward the canyon," Buck said.

The agents asked how he knew the flight went east. A flight plan? Radar?

"No, there was no flight plan required, and there was no radar," he said.

"Did any of the other airports have them under their control?" Barefoot asked.

"No, they were not required to report to anyone," Buck said.

"So you really don't know which direction they went or where they went," Hernandez said.

"I know they went to the canyon because I saw them head in that direction, the log book says they went there, and the pilot told me he went there," Buck told them, crossing his arms and leaning back in his chair.

"What information do you have on this pilot, and how well do you know him?" Hernandez demanded to know.

Antonio told me Buck gave the investigators copies of the pilot's papers, and they left. Buck never heard from them again and figured he would never see that pilot again, either.

Thanks, Buck.

The bar was getting crowded by this time, and the jukebox started to interfere with my hearing what Antonio was saying. I suggested we go outside to finish our talk. Once outside we walked over to his Lincoln. He lit up another cigarette and asked if I'd heard enough.

"I guess my efforts to be invisible worked out OK," I said.

"You did good," he said. "At first, I wasn't sure about you—all I had was a gut feeling. Now I know my feeling was right. You're a natural for this work. I consider you a great asset to our organization and a good friend. It's too bad you're not all Italian."

I stared off into the stars. I liked what I was hearing from him, but I didn't have a great feeling. I liked the idea of this rough justice.

It was the only way you could be sure the guilty people got what they deserved, but something was chewing on my gut.

"What's wrong? You seem very distant all of a sudden. Are you OK?" he asked.

"Yeah, I'm fine," I said. "I appreciate your trust in me and your friendship. I feel the same way. You're the guy I'd want on a mission with me. I just guess I'm a little tired."

"I would suggest some time off in Las Vegas with a certain girl, but I think you need to stay out of Nevada for a while," he said.

"How about meeting that certain girl in Miami or Chicago or L.A.?"

He smiled a big smile and said, "You did get bitten, didn't you?"

"No, not really," I said. "OK, maybe just a little." If I'd been a kid, I would probably have been blushing.

"Hold off on the time off for a while," Antonio said. "We need you for a small job this week."

He always said "we" and not "I." He was a true member of the organization.

"There is nothing illegal about this, but we need your knowledge of the city from the air and the different places a helicopter can land," he said. "Go to the 60th Street Heliport, pick up three guys, and show them Brooklyn, Queens, Harlem, and Manhattan from the air and point out where they can land. They'll tell you more when you see them."

"What's going on?" I said. "What's the job really about?"

"That's not important right now. Just show them what they want to see, and we'll work out the rest later," he said.

"When do I do this?"

"The day after tomorrow. What's a good time of day?"

"Actually, the middle of the day is the best for traffic," I told him. "The airports are real busy earlier and later in the day."

"OK, meet them at 11:00 a.m.," he said. "You'll be picking up Cicero and his two buddies."

"Cicero?" It was all I could do not to laugh.

"Yeah, any problems with Cicero?" he asked. He wasn't laughing.

"No, I love Cicero," I said. "I just never met a Cicero."

"Well, you'll meet one on Tuesday." With that we embraced. He kissed my cheek, got in his car, and took off. This mission was going to be a piece of cake. No big deal.

Chapter 31

I woke up the next day, worked out at the gym, and went to the airport to reserve a chopper for the next day. I talked for a while with the guys there, something I hadn't had time to do in months. They told me how busy things were and how it looked like it was going to stay busy for a while. Tony, the owner, even asked me if I wanted to come back to flying regularly or at least part time for him. He needed another experienced pilot he could count on for special missions with special clients. Tony and I always had a good relationship, even though I never actually worked for him. I told him I was too busy to take on more missions.

All the pilots who worked for Tony were Vietnam veterans, and I enjoyed talking and joking with them. Helicopters were getting larger, the maintenance crews were working two shifts and Tony and his partners just leased two more Bell Long Rangers. The skies around Manhattan and the three airports were busier than ever, and everyone in the air had to be more alert than ever. Vietnam experience came in real handy when things got crowded up there.

I worked at the bar that night and tried to get back in touch with the customers. The crowds were changing, or maybe it was just me. Either way, I was becoming less in tune with them. They seemed so young. I used to work behind the bar and be able to judge the mood of the crowd and be instantly ready for any disturbance. Now I felt disconnected. That night I was in no mood for any aggressive behavior, so I went out from behind the bar and into the crowd to just mingle and listen. I used to know a lot of the people who came in, but that night I recognized very few. I'd been away a lot, and it showed.

After we closed up Squatters that night, we all went to the diner and had a good time drinking coffee and telling stories like old times. I realized then how much I missed my old life. Being there with people I liked seemed simple and familiar. It was a lot different from the world I'd been in lately.

The next morning I got up, showered, and went out for breakfast at the little coffee shop in Mahwah. It was 10:00 a.m. when I got to the airport, and the place was hopping. Small planes were taking off and landing on the runway, and choppers were buzzing around doing maintenance run-ups or customer pickups. I went into the office, signed some papers, got my tail number, and headed for the flight line. I was flying 66H, an aircraft I had flown many times before. I did a brief preflight check. I had so much confidence in the maintenance crew at Ramapo I let my guard down and relaxed, which was very out of character for me.

I radioed flight operations and then took off to the south and headed for the city. It was a beautiful fall day, unlimited visibility, and practically no wind. I climbed to 1,500 feet and sat back to enjoy the flight. After seeing those fixed wing on the runway, it reminded me I hadn't flown an airplane in months. I needed to do that to keep my license current.

I dropped down to 1,000 feet and started down the Harlem River. I saw the Yankees getting ready for a play-off game at the stadium, but everything else was just a beautiful fall day. I called the tower at LaGuardia to tell them what I was doing, and then I called in to the 60th Street Heliport. I dropped down to go under the 59th Street Bridge and landed at the heliport. There were two other Jet Rangers on the ground, so I landed on the third pad. I turned around to face the East River and get ready for my next takeoff.

I radioed to the operations trailer and asked if there were three packages waiting for a tour of the city. Jake, the guy in the trailer, said hold on. I looked up and two guys were walking out of the trailer toward me. They were escorted by one of the heliport crew. The last thing anyone wanted was some guy stumbling into the tail rotor. It would remove his head in a second.

The attendant opened the front door for one of them and opened a back door for the other. The one in the front said in a strong Italian accent that he was Cicero and his companion was Alfonso. I asked what happened to the third passenger. He said the third guy didn't like flying.

Cicero took out a map of the city and told me he wanted to fly over Brooklyn, Queens, and Long Island to see where we could land. He mentioned that the passengers could be male or female and the landing sites needed to be private places, not airports or heliports. I already had a good idea what he was implying, but I just rolled on the throttle and called 60th Street to tell Jake I was leaving. I brought the chopper to a hover, checked all directions, and took off south down the East River heading toward Kennedy Airport.

We flew down the river into the harbor area. I gave them a thrill and went under the Verrazano Bridge and headed east along the coast. Once we got closer, I called Kennedy and told them I was low level on the coast headed toward Cedarhurst. Kennedy advised me of the traffic in the area and cleared me through.

Columbus Sand and Stone, the outfit I used to work for, had a plant in Cedarhurst with a small helipad, so I checked to see if it was still there. We stayed at 300 feet and flew right over the plant. The pad was still there, but it looked like it hadn't been used much lately. I pointed it out, and Cicero turned to talk to Alfonso, and they jabbered in Italian. I picked out a few words here and there and got the gist of what they were saying. They seemed delighted and waved me on.

Next we flew to College Point, right next to La Guardia and another old plant I knew about. It was still there and available for something even though I didn't know what for. I pointed out all the airports and public places, but they weren't really interested. We flew all around Long Island then back up the North Shore and across the sound to the Bronx. I showed them quite a few places that we could land and helped Cicero mark them on his map as we were flying.

I told them time was up. I needed fuel, and I headed back to 60th Street. I called the trailer and requested fuel. After I shut down, we just sat in the ship and waited for the fuel truck to finish.

Cicero said he'd heard I was in Vietnam and asked if I shot any guns. He'd heard that helicopters over there had guns on them. I said yes, that was my job. I flew heavily armed gunships. He wanted to hear more about that. I told him maybe another time.

When we were all fueled, I cranked up, did my preflight checks, and took off to the north. I went under the 59th Street Bridge, and they got a big kick out of that again. There is some thrill about flying under a bridge, I guess. I'd done it so many times that it was no big deal anymore. We flew over the Upper East Side and looked at all the jammed-up traffic.

Looking down at the gridlock, Cicero said, "Don't you wish sometimes you could just open fire on those stupid people and stop all that dumb traffic?"

What a ridiculous thing to say. Where on earth did this guy come from? Open fire and shoot innocent people? What for?

After touring around the Bronx and part of Westchester, I headed back south and landed at the 60th Street Heliport without calling anybody. What this guy had said really upset me.

Cicero wanted to talk more and thank me, but I just had to just shut down and try to relax.

It all came back in a whirlwind as I sat alone in the helicopter. I hadn't thought about that day in years. I had hoped I would never think of it again, but there it was, staring me right in the face.

The sounds, the smells, the fear, the stench. Vietnam.

Chapter 32

Combat missions in Vietnam never became routine, but we got used to the fact that on most flight days we were going to shoot at some people we didn't know, and they would most likely shoot back at us. Some days it was hard-core troops from the North Vietnamese Army. Some days it was hard-core Viet Cong guerillas, and some days it was ordinary village peasants brainwashed into hating the Americans in their country.

That particular day in April of 1969 started out no differently than a hundred other days. We were flying support for the 9th South Vietnamese (ARVN) regiment in IV Corps near Can Tho. The ARVN ground troops had encountered minor resistance in their assault, and my gunship team stayed around long enough to neutralize the resistance and secure the area.

We went back to the staging area and waited around for a while to see if the 9th was going to be pulled out and sent back to its base camp or stay in the area for the night. The executive officer, the second in command of our unit, was in the command and control helicopter that day overseeing the mission. At about 4:00 p.m. the exec released the slicks to go back to our base camp and call it a day. He told me to take my two-ship fire team and go back, too.

For the most part the day had been uneventful. We had not fired much ammo, so we were restless and ready to do something besides fly around in big circles. Whenever the opportunity arose, I would let Rose, my crew chief, soul mate, and the guy who has saved my life more than once, get in the copilot seat of the cockpit for some "stick time." I wanted him to be familiar enough with the aircraft to at least get it on the ground in one piece if something should happen to the copilot or me. The copilot usually bitched about being sent to sit in the back of the bird, but I didn't care. It was my helicopter. I was in charge.

My wingman that day was a first lieutenant who had just been selected to be an aircraft commander. He still had plenty to learn, but we were shorthanded, and I didn't have a lot of time left in country to teach him the tricks of the trade. In army slang, I was "short."

I decided to break away from the slicks and look for fun. They were flying at 2,500 feet, and that altitude always gave me a nosebleed. I broke away from the flight and headed for the coast. I told my wingman to follow behind and stay close. We came up on a village that had a Viet Cong flag flying on top of a hooch, and I decided to get it for another souvenir. I radioed my wingman and told him what I was going to do, but before I could make my cowboy move, I got a radio call from Badger Five, our executive officer in charge of this mission.

"Badger Two-Seven, this is Five. What is your location, over?"

Holy shit, he knew I was out of formation and was going to bust me sure as hell.

"Five, this is Badger Two-Seven. I am low level behind the slicks," I said. I figured he couldn't see me, and I'd have time to get back in formation.

"Two-Seven, this is Five. Can you see me? I'm at 3,000 feet and seven to ten klicks west of the slicks."

"Five, this is Two-Seven. Negative, I don't have you in sight."

I immediately turned west and headed in his direction like a bat out of hell not having any idea what he wanted.

"Two-Seven, this is Five. I want you to get over here right away. We've spotted a company-size element of North Vietnamese troops lounging around in a field just waiting for you to roll in on them."

"Roger, Five. Give me the coordinates, and we'll take care of them," I radioed back. It looked like we might get some real action after all.

He gave me the coordinates, and it turns out I was about seven minutes from that location. My wingman was on the same frequency, so there was no need to relay anything to him. I told Rose and the copilot to switch positions and get ready for rock and roll.

"Badger Two-Seven, do you have my location yet?" the exec asked.

Rose, back in his crew chief seat, keyed his mike and said he had the command and control chopper in sight three klicks to the west and higher than we were.

"Roger, Five. I have you in sight."

"Roger, Two-Seven, I have you in sight, too. Stay at tree-top level, and I'll guide you to the target. I can't drop smoke because I don't want to let them know you're coming."

"Roger, Five. Are they still in the same location?"

"Roger, Two-Seven. They're just hanging out down there."

That seemed strange. A unit of North Vietnamese regulars this far south and just waiting to be dealt with? This day may be worthwhile after all.

I told my crew to recheck all the guns and told my wingman to follow my lead, but not too close. A low-level gun run like this didn't leave much time over the target and not much room for error.

"Two-Seven, turn right to 180 degrees. They are two klicks in front of you."

I brought my rocket sight down and told the copilot to hold off on the mini-guns until I could put at least four rockets into the middle of their formation.

I could see their location, but something still didn't make sense. I didn't understand why they were still there. Two gunships make a lot of noise, and they had to have heard us coming.

I rolled in and got off four rockets, dead center. Then I heard Rose and Elton working out on their machine guns and the copilot firing the mini-guns.

That's when I saw what we had done.

It was like a punch to my gut.

As soon as I broke right I started yelling into the radio, "CEASE FIRE, CEASE FIRE!" But my wingman was already on target and firing into the crowd below us.

Rose could see the ugly truth, too. He keyed his mike and said in a sick voice, "Sir, can you believe what we just did?"

My mind was a whirl of confusion, and I was pissed. This kind of mistake was inexcusable!

"Five, this is Badger Two-Seven. What the fuck is going on? They're friendlies! They're South Vietnamese troops, not NVA! What did you do, sir?"

"Two-Seven, are you sure? My counterpart up here swears none of his people are in this area, and they can't be friendlies." South Vietnamese officers often flew with American officers precisely to keep this kind of tragedy from happening.

"Bullshit, Five. You get down here and take a closer look. We just rolled in on a friendly position." I didn't say "sir" that time, and I didn't think about my language—I was pissed!

I radioed my wingman to stay clear of the area and stay behind me. The troops on the ground were confused, angry, and starting to fire at us. Who could blame them?

I asked Rose, "What do you think the body count is?"

"A bunch," he said. He sounded as upset as I was.

I tried to orbit the area and assess the damage. The ground troops were running in all directions, waving their arms and weapons at us.

"Five, this is Two-Seven. Call for medevac now! There are bodies all over the place."

"Roger, Two-Seven, this is Five. We've already called for air evacuation. You head back to base. There's nothing else you can do here."

"Roger, Five, I'm leaving the area."

I called my wingman: "One-Three, this is Two-Seven. Are you OK?"

"Roger, Two-Seven. We're OK. Just a bit dazed and confused."

"Roger, One-Three. Follow me back to the base and don't say a word to anyone until we talk."

"Roger, Two-Seven. We'll talk." He sounded as shaken as I was.

The conversation in my ship on the flight home was short and to the point. I told my crew that I was the aircraft commander, and the decision to fire was mine. They had just followed orders. I also told them I would take care of the situation, and they had nothing to worry about. I would take care of the executive officer that sent us in there with guns blazing to kill friendly troops.

But I really didn't know what "take care of the exec" meant. There were plenty of friendly fire accidents in Vietnam, just like there were in every other military conflict in history. But this one was different. This one involved my crew and me. Up until now, after all this time in combat, I had been careful to protect our guys on the ground and my guys in the air. This fiasco upset me terribly. I knew exactly how it happened: somebody fucked up, and now people were dead. I had no problem sending the bad guys to their final resting place. I did it many times, but this…this was heartbreaking, sickening, and a waste of human life.

The flight line was empty except for the maintenance crews when we landed. I called the two crews together and told them I would do all the talking about this incident. I told them to answer any questions they were asked by investigators. Don't lie, but don't offer any excuses or information not specifically asked for. This was my responsibility. After all, I gave the order to fire after I identified the target. That was it, pure and simple. I told them to get some sleep, and we'd talk the next day.

I went to our makeshift officer's club, a tent off to the side of the company area, and ordered a shot and a beer. The other guys from the unit were sitting around, bullshitting, and telling war stories as usual. I decided not to say anything to anybody until after I talked to the executive officer, so I waited. Over an hour went by when a private came up and said the exec wanted to see me in his office.

He tried to explain what happened with him and his South Vietnamese counterpart. He said there was confusion about whether ground troops were supposed to be in that area. Then he tried to ask me why I didn't identify the troops as friendlies before my gun run.

I looked at him in pure disgust. He was a major, and I was just a lowly chief warrant officer, but that didn't stop me from saying what was on my mind: "Don't even try to go there, sir. You called me to the area of operations. You gave me the coordinates. You told me to stay low so I could not see the target until I was on top of them. I had no time to see they were friendlies until it was too late, sir."

"All right, Two-Seven," he said. "You're right. I gave the order, you did what you were told, and that was it. There most likely will be an investigation, and you'll be called to testify. We'll talk more later. You're dismissed."

I saluted and left. I went back to my bunk and tried to sleep.

What a fucked up day.

Chapter 33

The clear and painful memories brought back by Cicero's stupid comment about shooting innocent people had been tough to deal with, even after all those years. What we did to those South Vietnamese troops would be with me forever. But I finally got my emotions in check well enough to safely fly back to the airport after dropping Cicero off at the 60th Street Heliport. I hoped I'd never see that bastard again.

The flight back to where I kept the chopper was uneventful. But it did give me a chance to think about my future. It didn't take long to get a clear vision of what I wanted—and needed—to do. I parked the helicopter in the usual place at the airport and headed straight to my apartment. I had things to do.

My mind whirled with all the details I had to consider and the arrangements I needed to make. I had trouble sleeping, so I just stayed up and made my lists of things to do.

The next morning I called my attorney and told him I needed to see him right away. His secretary said he was busy, but I pushed hard for a few minutes of his time. She finally put him on the line. It didn't take long for him to understand my need for things to happen in a hurry.

It took me two hours to detail all the paperwork I needed him to take care of, things like a power of attorney, deeds of trust for my property, a will, and a few other things he suggested. He knew I planned on being away for a while and wanted to cover all the bases.

I then got on the phone to Louisiana. I'd kept in touch with Kurt Rose over the years, but not nearly as often as I should have. We were close in Vietnam—we saved each other's asses more than once during our time there—and that sort of thing creates a bond that time and distance can't break. The years since had been strange for both of us, but I knew the bond would still be there. It was just too strong for anything to happen to it. Combat vets understand, even if civilians don't.

Kurt's life since the war had been tough. He'd gone through two wives and had a couple of kids he didn't get to see very often. He got shot in the leg in a hunting accident. Hell of a thing. A year in Vietnam with all the combat we saw, all the crazy shit we pulled off, two Purple Hearts for combat wounds—no permanent damage, thankfully—and he gets shot hunting in Louisiana. Life isn't fair sometimes.

I called and asked him how things were going. Then I told him about the trip I was planning, a little bit about why I was going, and told him I needed him to go with me.

He hesitated for only a second. Then he said to let him know when and where to meet me, and he'd be there. I told him to pack for a long stay. He said there was nothing keeping him in Louisiana, so let's roll. It had been a long time since we'd served together in Vietnam, but he was still the same Kurt Rose I'd known, up for anything.

I thought about calling my door gunner, Elton, too. But he was married with a few kids and a wife and living a normal life on the west coast. He wouldn't be able to go even if he wanted to, so I decided not to tempt him.

Then it was time to talk to Antonio. I'd never really asked him for anything, but I knew he was always there for me. Now I needed him, so I called his number and left a message with—surprise, surprise—a female. I told her it was important and for her to get word to Antonio. I had no doubt she would.

About an hour later, I was in my office at the restaurant when I got a call from Antonio. He wanted to know how soon I wanted to meet and where. I told him it wasn't life or death, but some time that day at the bar would be good. He said he was in New York City, but he'd be there as soon as he could. I'd tried to sound relaxed, but he could tell it was important.

I worked in the office for a while. Bob was taking care of everything, so I messed around, pretending to work while I waited for Antonio to show up. He did, sooner than I expected. We took a booth in the back. This time it was he instead of me who wanted to know what was going on.

"Antonio, you know I've been restless and unsettled for a long time now," I said. "I think I've finally figured out why."

He smiled. "I think your next mission and then some time in Nevada will help you a lot," he said. I just smiled back because I knew he was just busting my chops about Amber.

I pressed on. "I need you to get me two passports," I said, "one for me and one for my old crew chief. They need to be from Holland or Norway or some place neutral. I've got some unfinished business to attend to, and I can't have the authorities thinking I'm an American."

He looked at me funny.

"I'm going back to Vietnam," I said.

Chapter 34

President Richard Nixon signed the Paris peace accords with North Vietnam in January 1973. On March 29, 1973, the last American combat troops left the country. That date, many years later, would become "Vietnam Veterans Recognition Day."

By April 1975 the South Vietnamese government collapsed, the last Americans fled from the roof of the embassy in Saigon, and the communists from North Vietnam took over. Vietnam was united once again—this time under communist rule.

From 1963 to 1973, over 3,000,000 United States troops served in Vietnam. Over 58,000 were killed, and over 300,000 were wounded. And then one day the American government said we were through, and everybody just left. That was hard for a lot of us to swallow.

Once the country was under communist rule, the United States severed all relations with Vietnam, and the country became off limits to all American citizens. No visas, no travel, no nothing having to do with Vietnam.

"I guess you've thought this thing through, and you know what you're doing," Antonio said.

"This is what I need to do," I said.

"I'm not going to ask you why," he said. "But how long do you think you'll be gone?"

"I really have no idea. I just know I have to go and go now."

"OK, I think I understand," he said. "I don't want to see you go, but what makes you think we can get government-issued passports?"

"You and your people are wizards, and I wouldn't be surprised if you got them signed by the president," I said, laughing.

He smiled, took a drag on his cigarette, and asked how much time he had for this outrageous request.

"By the end of the week would be good, no big rush."

"Yeah, right," he said. "I'll see what I can do. Do you have passport pictures or do I need to get them, too?"

"I'll get you the pictures," I said.

Antonio was quiet for a long time. It was obvious he had something important to say, and he wanted to get it right.

Finally, he spoke. "I just want you to know that when you do come back, we'll be here, and we'll be ready to continue doing business with you. Our system of justice is taking on a different tone. We've partnered up with some international heavy hitters and even some federal government types."

"That sounds interesting," I said. "But for now I've got to go."

"I know. I just wanted you to know your special talents are still needed." He stayed a little while longer making small talk, and we decided to hold off on any friendly toasts until the next time we met, whenever that might be.

I thought about taking time and having him arrange a get-together with Amber, but as usual I decided to get on with the mission at hand. I thought about seeing Suzanne, but then why open up old wounds? Hopefully, she was on her way to a new life—my loss. The thoughts of a nice, quiet life settling down with her and getting a job entered my mind, but I knew it was not for now. I just wasn't ready. I did go to the airport in Ramapo and told the guys I was leaving for a while and thanked everybody for their help and support.

I called Kurt Rose to make sure he was sending his passport picture, and I went to get mine. I thought about wearing a wig but decided to stay with short hair.

The next day I met Bob at the diner and told him my plans to be away and asked if he would be willing to step in and take over everything I had. We talked a long time about the reasons for what I was doing and what the journey really meant to me. I told him I was giving him full power of attorney for all my dealings, the legal ones at least, and full power to do with the bar as he pleased. My only other option was to close it up and walk away. I had put together a staff of excellent workers, the crowds we drew became controllable, and the place was a success. It was making a good living for quite a few people.

Bob wanted to know about the profit and what he should do with my share while I was gone. I told him to keep it and have a good life with my sister. My two nephews, Peter and Paul, were growing up nicely, and everyone needs a little help from time to time. We decided to keep my apartment. He could use it when he needed to, and what stuff I had could stay there.

He left and went to the bar. I left and went to the gym. I had a deep feeling of loneliness, and I realized my life was pretty empty right then. I needed to clarify a few things and set some records straight.

I needed to start with the SKS rifle I'd brought home from Vietnam. I guess you could call it a souvenir of the Vietnam War, but to me it was more, a lot more. It came to represent the lives I had taken, especially when I looked at the diary I'd found in the rifle stock. I couldn't read a word of it, but the handwriting touched me. A real soldier, a guy like me, who had wanted to survive the war, too, had carried this weapon and had written in this diary. In some strange way, that made us brothers.

I'd shown the rifle to a few people since coming home and told them the story about how I got it, but I never got the diary translated. At first I didn't care what it said. But years later, after Vietnam had fallen and my life had taken such a twisted turn, I started to think about it.

What if the soldier who carried that rifle and wrote in that diary and died that day had just gotten word that his first child had been born? What if he had just gotten word that his parents had been killed? The "what ifs" could go on forever. I wasn't sure if I wanted to know the answers, so I never got it translated. His family never got to know what happened to him. He just disappeared one day.

He was missing in action, just like the American soldiers who didn't come home. I knew I needed to find his family and let them know that although he had died in combat, perhaps because of me, he had died honorably and bravely for his cause. I had no idea what I was going to do, or how I was going to do it, but I was determined to try.

For the next few days, I worked out at the gym and at the bar waiting for Antonio to come through with the passports. I never doubted his ability to do the impossible. If I did come back, I'd like to get more involved with him and his people and see just how far his influence reached.

It had been a little more than a week since I had given Antonio the two passport photos when one of his guys came into the bar and said Antonio wanted me to meet him at Stegeman's Steak House that evening at nine. He still never used the phone. I put on my silk outfit from Las Vegas and went to the restaurant. He was there ahead of me.

"How are you?" he asked.

"Good, thanks," I said. "Are you alone tonight?"

"I thought about bringing some entertainment for us, but since this is sort of a 'see you later' dinner, I'm alone," he said.

We'd met at Stegeman's a few times, and it had great food and good memories. We ordered our usual, and then he showed me the passports. They were from Holland with Dutch sounding names and looked as real as can be.

I told him my plans about flying to London then on to Vietnam. I told him a little about the SKS rifle and the bloody fiasco in the Delta in the spring of 1969. Not a lot of detail—those I kept to myself—but just enough so he'd understand.

He said he'd never been in any of those situations, but he could see how they would weigh heavily on a soldier's mind.

"You seem to have no problem serving justice in any way necessary—is it just our kind of justice?" Antonio asked.

That was easy for me: "I have no problem at all taking care of the bad guys in whatever way is necessary. It's the other guys I have a problem with. Like Cicero.

"The other day you mentioned something about a new approach you were going after. Was that just bullshit to get me curious, or are you really taking a different route?"

"We have a new agenda in the works," he said. "The world is getting smaller, and we are going after bigger deals."

"What else can you—"

"That's it for now, my friend," he said. "We'll talk more when you get back. I do have one question for you, though. It sounds like you're trying to make peace with yourself. If you do find what you are looking for, how will it affect your life and your ability to carry out... well, you know."

"I know what you are thinking," I said, looking around to see if anyone could hear us. "If I become a nice guy and start being a good citizen, will I still be of any use to you? Is that it?"

He looked at me and smiled his all-knowing smile.

"We'll just have to wait until I get back," I said. It was all I could say because I didn't know myself.

We finished dinner and had espresso. Antonio raised his glass and toasted to my safe journey and quick return. We left the restaurant; I went back to Mahwah and called Rose. I told him to make his plans and meet me in New Jersey.

I'd never been so ready to do something in my life.

Chapter 35

I met Rose at Newark Airport a few days later, and we caught a flight to London. I had gotten a tape narrated by a Dutch guy speaking English, just in case I needed an accent. My recent experiences with Antonio and his people made me aware and cautious. I needed to cover all bases and always watch my back. It was illegal, sure, but it was no big deal to travel to a communist country as an American citizen.

Traveling around the country without speaking any of the language and still managing to find somebody whose name or whereabouts I didn't know was a big deal, however. I had no picture or description to give to people, even if I could find someone who would or could help me.

Being history buffs, Rose and I spent a few days looking around London and checking out a few World War II sites. We talked a lot about my ideas for this trip and how we were going to go about it. He reminded me of that bad day in 1969 and the hearing we later went to in Saigon. I had forgotten about that, or maybe I had just put it out of my mind.

We'd been called to the hearing at the United States Army-Vietnam headquarters in Saigon by a panel of officers looking into friendly fire accidents and other acts that were brought to the attention of the Vietnamese government and a civilian action committee. A year after our incident, Lieutenant Calley and Captain Medina were called to a similar hearing about the My Lai massacre.

Rose reminded me how I had briefed the crew about what happened that day, as if they could have forgotten, and how I said I would try to do all the talking and take the heat. Our executive officer had already given his statement on a previous day. I had no idea what he'd said or how he explained it.

I was called into the hearing along with the commander of my wing ship, just the two of us to start with. We were sworn in, and I was questioned for a while. I gave short answers, not vague, just short. After the questions they asked me to summarize the incident. After they finished with me they just asked my wingman if everything I said was how he remembered it and whether he had anything to add. He did not. We left the hearing and went to downtown Saigon to look around and have a few drinks. That was a real treat for us. We never had that kind of luxury in the jungle where we lived.

After a few hours, we flew back to our unit, and I never heard another word about the incident or the hearings. The panel never called the rest of the crew to testify. I guess they believed my version and how I presented it. We were left to live with it as best we could.

Kurt and I flew from London to Hong Kong. We spent two days there. We had no idea what to expect once we got to Vietnam. We'd heard all the stories about the repatriation camps around the south. The camps were designed to re-educate the South Vietnamese and get them tuned into the communist way of doing things. Seems like the communists were doing all the things westerners thought they would do if they took over.

They confiscated all the land and all the businesses. They didn't actually take possession of them—they just took all the owners' rights away and let the public know they were now working strictly for the people, the government, The People's Republic of Vietnam. The "attendees" or the "guests" of these re-education camps were the civilians that had anything to do with the Americans as well as veterans of the South Vietnamese military. The time spent at the camps depended on what rank they were and how involved they were with us.

During the 1970s and 1980s thousands of South Vietnamese rebelled against the communists, this time without guns. They did it by just leaving the country. They still did not want to be communist, even if they had lost the war. They became known as the "boat people." Many died trying to escape, and many of those who made it came to the United States.

Some of the other stories we heard were about the American prisoners of war and missing in action. They had not all returned or been accounted for. It looked like we had abandoned 2,500 Americans to their fate. The stories we'd heard from former POWs were hard to listen to. The torture and inhumane treatment they endured were unbelievable. It made me angry, and it was going to be hard to accomplish what I came over here to do without being extremely prejudiced. But I had to try.

We took a flight from Hong Kong to Saigon, now named Ho Chi Minh City, and went through customs with only a little scrutiny. I spoke with my new Dutch accent, and we presented ourselves as writers, looking to tell the true story of the People's Republic of Vietnam.

What a crock!

My first mission was to get an interpreter we could trust and who could help with navigating the country and the communist rules. If they found out we were American, we would be in trouble, especially if they found out what we were trying to do. Finding the families of killed soldiers was not going to be easy.

The money I was able to save from the bar and my side job with the Mafia was quite impressive. Funding this trip would be no problem. Just figuring out how to carry cash and keep it safe was the problem. In London I found a gold dealer and stocked up on gold coins, the worldwide universal currency. I also found out that the United States greenback was still in high demand in Vietnam, but only on the black market.

We spent time in Saigon to feel out the city and the mood of the country. Things seemed tense and on the wild side. The communist soldiers were all over the city, strutting around, and trying to control everything. The citizens were meek and subdued and not talkative, at least during the day. At night the whole scene changed, even the soldiers. The nightlife was what I could deal with, what I was familiar with, and what I was looking for. Rose was having a ball with the girls. They were everywhere and willing and reasonably priced. I was never a big fan of Vietnamese girls, so I concentrated on finding our guide.

I started to take notes and pretended to be a writer, just in case we were questioned about our purpose in this far-away country.

In 1978 the first Vietnam movie came out: *The Deer Hunter,* starring Meryl Streep, Christopher Walken, and Robert De Niro. At the end, De Niro went back to Vietnam to find his friend as Saigon was falling. The place was in chaos and out of control. This was ten years later, not nearly that bad, but it was still not a comfortable place to be. The scenes from that hard-to-watch movie kept flashing in my memory.

Rose met a girl who spoke good English and seemed OK to talk to. We told her we wanted to go down south toward Vinh Long and My Tho. She said she was from a small village outside of Vinh Long and would be happy to guide us. Her name was Tuong Ti Mai Thu, and she was about nineteen years old. We decided to call her Mai. She spoke Vietnamese, French, and some English, was very cute, and headed for big trouble if she stayed in Saigon much longer under the present circumstances. She took a liking to Rose, and that suited our situation just fine.

She helped us get on the buses heading south and helped us get more accustomed to the local economy. Every time we saw a soldier, she would shy away and avoid him. That was OK with me. I just wanted to know if she had any history with them. At first I thought maybe she was just looking for a free ride and some extras. After a few days with her, I knew Mai was just a young girl with no direction and a good heart.

We got to Vinh Long and found that it was a much milder version of Saigon. The people seemed to be settling into their new way of communist life and trying to survive under the rules they never knew before.

Mai introduced us to a few people she knew and found us cheap rooms to stay in. She had no idea what we were really doing there, so she said we were writers.

She stayed close to Rose and started to loosen up as the days went by. Her English got a little better, too. Everyone in this country was on alert. One night, as we were checking out the bars in the underground area—she seemed to know what places to see and which ones to stay away from—she mentioned her uncle. I think he was her uncle, but her explanations were sometimes vague and confusing. She called him Lam Van Tien. He lived on a small island in the Long Ho district in Vinh Long province. She said we needed to meet him and maybe he could help us.

My radar immediately went up, and I wondered what my crew chief had told her. When we got back to our rooms that night, I asked Rose what he'd said.

He told me he really liked this girl and trusted her. I was thinking he needed to spend some time with Antonio and his people and see where trust and faith really got you. He had told her we were looking for some families of Viet Cong and South Vietnamese soldiers. He reminded her that we were writers, and talking to these people would help our story. At one point I could tell he was being hesitant and holding back relating their conversations.

"OK, Badger, tell me the whole story, what's going on with this girl?" I asked him, using our old call sign.

"I like her," he said. "I think she can help us, and I know her uncle can really help us."

"I know you like her, but that should have nothing to do with the mission," I said. "I need to know why we're here and how her uncle can really help us?"

"Don't get excited or go off the deep end when I tell you what she said," Kurt said.

"Just tell me what's going on."

"Her uncle was a Viet Cong captain, and his area of operation was from Vinh Long south."

"Holy shit," I blurted. "This girl wants us to hook up with a Viet Cong captain so he can help us? You want us to go along with this?

This guy could have been shooting at us and us at him. What are you, nuts?"

"See, I knew you were going to go ballistic. Just hear her out—meet the guy as if you are a Dutch writer, and then we'll see if he can help," he said, trying to calm me down.

We talked more about our mission here and what we expected to accomplish. After hearing his explanation and thinking how hard it was going to be to navigate the language, the communists, and the people we were looking for, I agreed maybe it would be a good idea—if we could trust him.

Two days later, we left the city of Vinh Long and headed for an island in the Long Ho district to the south. Since Mai was not real familiar with this area, she hired a guide to take us. The only means of travel in this remote area of South Vietnam in the 1980s was the sampan.

Rose and I had attacked sampans just like these on a regular basis in 1968 and 1969. We took two on this trip. Old women we'd called "Mama-sans" were rowing and steering. There were no motors. One boat had Rose, Mai, and some supplies. I was in the other one with the guide and more supplies. Mai suggested we bring gifts in the form of supplies to her uncle as a gesture of good faith and necessity. Vietnam was still a poor country, and the mere basics of food and clothing were appreciated.

After the communists took over in 1975, they rounded up all the South Vietnamese soldiers and US allies and retrained them in the camps. The ones who finally got out of the camps were treated like fourth-rate citizens. No medical help, even for the disabled, no financial help, no job help, and the people were told to ignore them.

Another group on the bottom of the heap was the Amerasian children, the offspring of American soldiers and Vietnamese women. The communists detested these children, especially the ones with dark skin, and tried to run them off into the jungle. The World Catholic Organization tried its best to help the kids and set up orphanages around the country. The communists reluctantly allowed them to exist. Still, poverty abounded. With the communists taking over everything, the boat people leaving by the thousands, the workers rebelling by not working, and China and Russia demanding repayment of the debt from the war, the country was a mess.

Here we were, Rose and I, riding in sampans on the same canals and waterways we had patrolled during the war looking for the enemy. Now we were on our way to the home of an enemy to ask him for his help. What an eerie feeling. Every time I saw a Vietnamese male on the bank of the canal, I reached for my weapon and had to remember where I was and why. That boat ride will be forever engrained in my mind.

The guide took us to an island and let us off. The whole trip I was thinking how vulnerable we were and how anyone could have knocked us off, stolen our stuff, and no one would have known or cared. We unloaded our supplies, I paid the mama-sans and the guide, and off they went.

We stood on the dock, the three of us and just listened to the quiet. No planes, no motors, no telephones, no nothing. We heard the fish in the water and the birds in the air. Mai had tried to send a message to her uncle that we were coming, but who knows if he ever got it. We picked up some gear and started walking down a trail. Halfway down, we met up with a young man. Rose and I immediately went on alert and got ready. Mai started talking to him, and he smiled.

Mai looked at us and said, "Why are you so jumpy? No one is going to hurt you here—this is my family."

That took the edge off for a minute, but the situation we were in was one I would never have imagined in two lifetimes.

The young man took us to the main house. There were quite a few structures in the area, all stick-built with thatched roofs and open air. Everything looked neat and orderly but primitive. People started coming out into the clearing and speaking in Vietnamese. They all seemed to know Mai, and that relieved some of our tension.

A man came out of the house and stood quietly to the side. He was about my age, had a little potbelly, and wore the typical Vietnamese pajama-style pants and shirt. This time they were blue, not the black that designated the Viet Cong years ago. I watched him, his manners, and the frown on his face, not knowing what to expect next. Mai finally saw him and ran up to him for a big hug and kiss. His frown changed to a big smile and a happy tone of voice. She introduced us to them all. There were cousins and aunts and her uncle, Lam Van Tien.

He welcomed us with open arms and, through Mai, thanked us for coming to his home and showed us to a dining area where we sat in the shade. There was a fan on the ceiling, and I heard the faint hum of a generator in the background. Mai showed us to the restrooms, a small group of outhouse-type structures with running water, no pressure, and toilets with dugouts and a shower. We washed up and went back to the dining area. Lam's wife, some nieces, and some other women served us food and drink. Getting used to the menu in this country was an ongoing experience. I had not recognized one thing on my plate since we left Hong Kong almost three weeks before.

After we finished the meal, one of the girls showed us to our room. It was a structure with a raised wooden floor. All the floors were raised three to four feet above the ground. Since everything in this part of the country was at sea level, I was not sure if the raised floors were for flooding or animals. There were six bunks in this room; each had mosquito nets and a small dresser. We were not sure what this place was or what it was used for. Mai made no mention of it.

Rose and I felt relaxed for the moment and decided to take a nap. The trip getting here had been quite an experience.

A young woman dressed in a beautiful and traditional Vietnamese *ao dai* dress woke us and said dinner would be in one hour. We showered and changed and looked around the island. Considering where we were and the circumstances, this was a very peaceful place.

"Two-Seven, I like this place," Rose said, using my old call sign. Old habits die hard, and as far as Rose was concerned, I was still the aircraft commander, and he was the crew chief. It worked OK that way.

"You're right. This is so different than I ever imagined it could be," I said. "Let's see what the Viet Cong captain has in store for us."

We went to dinner in the dining area. There was a table that could seat twenty and another table for eight. We sat at the small table with Lam, his wife, Mai, and two teenage girls, nieces, I guess. The food was good, the presentation was surprising, and the conversation flowed as fast as Mai could translate. After dinner Lam, Rose, Mai, and I went to an outdoor seating area where we were served rice moonshine and rice crackers. I'd bought Cuban cigars in Hong Kong and offered them around. Lam seemed excited and thanked us again for the gifts and supplies we brought.

The conversation was light and cautious. But it didn't take long for me to realize I wanted to get to know this man, this former enemy, to ask him for his help. After a few drinks he stood up and opened his shirt. Mai tried to stop him, but he wanted her to tell us his story. He showed us his huge scar from the middle of his chest to his navel. He also had one on his arm from his shoulder to his bicep. He was a captain in the National Liberation Front Army—known as the Viet Cong—and during the Tet Offensive of 1968, he was shot by the Americans and almost died due to lack of medical help.

Rose and I looked at each other and prayed he was not shot by a helicopter since his operational area was also our area. I asked how he was shot, and he said it was in a ground fight just west of there.

We were relieved.

As far as I knew, he still thought we were Dutch and knew nothing about the war. He did not let on to anything else. He went on to say he did not blame the Americans. He just wanted his country free from war and free from those who want to control him.

For the next few days we were his guests, and all of us tried to get to know each other. I tried hard to learn as much of the language as I could. Vietnamese, like most Asian languages, is hard for westerners to learn. The intonation of your voice, the inflection of the sounds, all have different meanings. You can say one word in six different tones, and it has six different meanings. I wished I could communicate better with Lam or that Mai was older and more aware of what I needed.

We found out that the communist government did take care of the military and the guerilla veterans like Lam. They received small pensions and reasonable terms buying land. Since the government owned it all, it could set any price it wanted.

Lam bought this island deep in the south for a small amount of money in exchange for living here and starting a business. Lam thought this was far enough away from the central government that it would leave him alone. So far it had. He had started out being a Nationalist working to end the corruption in Saigon in the early

1960s. He wound up being swept into the party and becoming a Viet Cong captain before he knew what happened. His wife was also a party member and worked in Saigon as an intelligence agent.

The land was bought by Lam to be a retreat of sorts, a place where ex-soldiers and ex-enemies could relax and heal and get back to the task of living. As time went on the government relaxed its tight hold on the people and let this type of place exist.

One day, Lam, Mai, and I walked down a trail to the water. He sensed my frustration with our language barrier. He turned to Mai and asked her to leave us alone for a while. She hesitated slightly and walked off. She went looking for Rose, I expect.

We sat by the water, just the two of us, a Viet Cong captain wounded by the Americans in his own country and a helicopter gunship pilot who would have shot him if the opportunity had arisen. He looked at me and said, "Why are you really here?"

Needless to say, I was quite surprised. He spoke perfect English.

He went on to tell me he was a good student and had been chosen to go to a Catholic-run school in My Tho where he learned French and English. His knowledge of our language made him useful to the Viet Cong, and they recruited him aggressively. He did not like the war, but he saw the devastation of the B-52 attacks, what napalm and the helicopter gunships were doing to his country, and he became angry at the attackers. After the fighting was all over, he decided he wanted to do some good for his country, which he loved, and help his people.

He and his wife, who also spoke some English, had been listening to Rose and me speaking, and they had been deciding what to do with us. He knew we were American from the beginning, but was not sure yet if we were soldiers. Since I was in his home and more or less at his mercy, I started to tell him of our mission here and why we came back to his country. We sat there for hours, still feeling each other out and getting better acquainted. We decided to speak English only when we were alone. He told me he was enjoying listening to me learn his language and wanted me to continue.

We went back and washed up for dinner. This man and his family were traditional. They all had strong family values and made a point of it. They had two children, and his wife was home schooling them.

He mentioned that in two days a group of ten people were coming to the retreat and asked if we would mind sharing our hooch with them. We said of course not, not knowing who they were or why they were coming. There were sleeping quarters for about twenty people on the compound.

Rose and I pitched in and started helping with the chores. There were a lot of them. Since this was a tropical zone the trees and bushes grew fast. The trails had to be trimmed constantly along with the laundry and cooking. I enjoyed cooking, so Lam's wife got a kick out of showing me her kitchen and letting me help prepare the meals. The place was full of guests for the next two weeks. They were paying guests who came for various reasons or to just relax. There were some meetings and classes of some type, but we were not invited to attend.

Lam said he saw me working out once and wondered how long I had been practicing martial arts. I told him it had been many years with many different instructors. He said he tried to learn martial arts but never could catch on.

"I have a very good friend in the next village. I would like for you to meet him," he said. "He has spent his whole life dedicated to the workings of the body and the mind."

"I would very much like to meet him," I said.

Rose, Lam, and I went down to the river to chat. I enjoyed the peace of where we were and the company, but it was time to fulfill the mission. Rose and I decided that this guy, Lam, this ex-Viet Cong was the one to help us if anyone could.

I told him the story of the SKS rifle and the diary and my dilemma of what to do. Rose then started to tell him of that day in the Delta when we fired on the friendlies. He listened intently, and at times I thought he felt our pain. He asked when that was and where. We told him as best we could, and he went silent. He said he had heard about that day from the wife of one of the dead soldiers.

"War is not a way to solve anything," he said. "It just destroys people, the dead and the living. Too much pain. I need to think about what you want to do. For now we will just be."

For the next week, Rose and I got involved with the running of the retreat. There was plenty to do, and we both felt a sense of accomplishment in helping.

One night after another great meal with entertainment, Lam brought in some friends and relatives to play instruments for the guests. There was a one-string guitar, a *dan bau*. The young girls danced, and the world seemed at peace, even in this communist country that we used to be at war with. Lam asked me if I had any more Cuban cigars, which I gladly passed around. He told us that he had enjoyed getting to know us, his former enemy, and that it had been a strange sequence of events that led us to this place. He asked if he could see the diary from my SKS. He looked at it and told us the war was over and that bringing up old wounds for families would serve no purpose.

Life in Vietnam was going on, he said, and most of the people wanted to put that terrible time behind them and go on living. They have already buried the dead and put them to rest. He would read the diary and decide later what to do with it.

"Do you want to know what it said?" he asked me.

"No, I don't think I do," I said.

"Do you want to know what I decide to do with it?"

"You are an honorable man. I am convinced you will do the right thing, whatever it is, and I do not need to know."

We finished our cigars and our drinks and headed off to bed.

On the walk back to our room, Rose was silent for a while then said, "Two-Seven, I feel good about what Lam said. I'm putting these issues to rest."

"I know what you mean. I feel fifty pounds lighter," I said. "I never realized just how heavy these memories were. I think I'll sleep very well tonight."

"Me, too."

The next day Lam and his wife invited us to stay on their island to help out with the retreat. Lam said it would be a good way to help his people and settle some of our frustrations. This man was full of insight, and I wanted to get to know him better and learn from him and learn more about his mysterious friend in the next village.

So that was it. Rose and I, two warriors who had done our best to kill as many of these people as possible, decided to stay in this country halfway around the world and put our past to rest. It was time to get on with the job of healing, living, and helping.

Vietnam was a good place to start.

THE END

Epilogue

Kurt Rose and I ended up staying in Vietnam for almost three years. Mai's uncle, Lam Van Tien, the former Viet Cong captain, had graciously opened his home and life to two former enemies. His generosity gave us the peace, time, and space we needed to finally shed the dark memories that had weighed heavily on our souls for so many years. Captain Tien became a friend neither of us would ever forget.

Captain Tien's friend, Tran Giap, lived in a nearby village. He'd dedicated himself to a quest for the meaning of life and total discipline of the body. He became my mentor as well as a great friend. I learned things about myself, my body, and the universe I never dreamed existed.

But all things end, and after these years, Kurt and I left the jungle and came home. After checking in on my apartment, I stopped by the bar to see how Bob and the others were doing. While we were talking, a man came in and sat down at the bar. He said "Are you Daniel?". I replied yes. He asked. for an anisette and Coke.

Editor

Dennis Rogers served more than eight years in the military, much of that time as a counter-intelligence agent. He later spent thirty-five years as a newspaper columnist and editorial writer. He and his wife HollyAnn wander the country full-time in a motor home.

DAVID SAMUELS

PRESENTS

THE MOB NEVER SLEEPS

Coming soon in paperback

Turn the page for a preview of

THE MOB NEVER SLEEPS........

PRELUDE

Once again Daniel returns from Southeast Asia to be greeted by a new set of circumstances. His flight home was anything but ordinary. Once he boarded the flight from Paris to JFK his radar went on alert. A few of the passengers were........ just different. Daniel spent the last three years training and learning under one of the world's foremost martial arts experts. But it was much more than just martial arts, he was taught about human behavior and psychology He learned what makes up the human psyche and all the functions of the human body. *'If you know how a body is put together, you can better understand how to neutralize the different parts'* Three of the passengers on this flight were on a mission to either hijack this plane or crash it into the Atlantic with no survivors.

Daniel was alone in his suspicion of these men and would be alone if it came to any physical response to this dilemma. His only weapon was the training he had and the ability to be one of the most lethal human beings in the world. He was right, the terrorists killed one stewardess, one passenger, and one of the cockpit crew before anyone could respond.

Daniel was able to neutralize the three and help the Captain of the plane land safely in Portugal. He then disappeared into the crowd and continued his return to the US. The Press, the different countries and the State Dept. all wanted to know who this individual was that helped divert a major disaster. The militant group that sent the three to complete their mission also wanted to know who this was and how could these specially trained Jihad soldiers have failed so miserably. No one knew and no one came forward to claim the title.

Once back in the states he resumed his association with Antonio, the underboss of one of the biggest NY crime families. He was told that the 'Family' was now working with a government agency, far above any government agency known to the public. This agency had the responsibility to protect the constitution and certain powers at all costs and sacrifices. The agency was headed up by Ely Drake, a formidable man with unlimited assets and resources. In Daniel's first meeting with Drake he was told: 'there are certain individuals in this country and in the world that think they are above the law of the land and feel that their power, wealth and position make them untouchable. It is our job to make sure they understand there is no place to hide from the power and force we can inflict on anyone anywhere. This is where you come in Daniel, with your cool demeanor and physical abilities; we will want you to deliver some of these messages.'

This new association opens up a whole new chapter of intrigue and manipulation in the worlds of politics, gambling, government and wealth (and the mob.)

Be sure to find out what happens when:

THE MOB NEVER SLEEPS.

Author

David Samuels served as a helicopter pilot during the Vietnam conflict and was awarded the Silver Star for gallantry in action. He stayed in aviation for many years after the service. David now resides in North Carolina with his wife Elizabeth.